Contemporary Asian Cinema

Asian Cinema series

Edited by Anne Ciecko, University of Massachusetts-Amherst

Asia, the world's largest and most populous continent, is also the world's largest film producer. Film theory and criticism reinforces Hollywood and European cinema as the dominant and exemplary paradigm, relegating Asian cinemas to the margins. The *Asian Cinema* series aims to re-position Asian cinema at the center of film studies and will cover national, regional and pan-Asian cinema as well as the global, transnational, and diasporic flows of cinematic production, distribution, and reception.

ISSN 1744-8719

Forthcoming in the *Asian Cinema* series

Bollywood Babylon: Interviews with Shyam Benegal
edited by William van der Heide

Contemporary Asian Cinema

Popular Culture in a Global Frame

Edited by

ANNE TERESKA CIECKO

Oxford • New York

English edition
First published in 2006 by
Berg
Editorial offices:
First Floor, Angel Court, 81 St Clements Street, Oxford OX4 1AW, UK
175 Fifth Avenue, New York, NY 10010, USA

© Anne Tereska Ciecko 2006

Berg is the imprint of Oxford International Publishers Ltd.

Library of Congress Cataloging-in-Publication Data
Contemporary Asian cinema : popular culture in a global
frame / edited by Anne Tereska Ciecko.—English ed.
    p. cm.
    Includes bibliographical references and index.
    ISBN-13: 978-1-84520-237-8 (pbk.)
    ISBN-10: 1-84520-237-6 (pbk.)
    ISBN-13: 978-1-84520-236-1 (hardback)
    ISBN-10: 1-84520-236-8 (hardback)
    1. Motion pictures—Asia. I. Ciecko, Anne Tereska.
    PN1993.5.A75C655 2006
    791.43095—dc22   2005037133

British Library Cataloguing-in-Publication Data
A catalogue record for this book is available from the British Library.

ISBN-13 978 1 84520 236 1 (Cloth)
         978 1 84520 237 8 (Paper)

ISBN-10 1 84520 236 8 (Cloth)
         1 84520 237 6 (Paper)

Typeset by Avocet Typeset, Chilton, Aylesbury, Bucks
Printed in the United Kingdom by Biddles Ltd, King's Lynn.

www.bergpublishers.com

Contents

Introduction to Popular Asian Cinema

In terms of sheer volume, Asia is by the far the most prolific producer of cinematic fictions; and increasingly, Asian movies have captured audiences' attention all around the world. This book examines the most universally popular (and commodified) form of the medium, the narrative feature film, as well as the processes, institutions, policies, and discourses that impact the ways these films are made, seen, and interpreted in particular national, regional, transnational, and global contexts.

Contemporary Asian Cinema: Popular Culture in a Global Frame provides an overview of contemporary trends in Asian cinema – with an emphasis on popular films in a global age. This book examines Asian film through critical lenses that combine cinema studies and cultural theory. Seventeen scholars and critics of Asian cinema and media, each focusing on a specific country or territory, describe and discuss recent developments, film texts, and contexts. While this volume focuses principally on contemporary Asian cinema, the contributing authors also situate these manifestations of the popular historically within film industries and cultures. In this book you will find chapters on cinema in the Philippines, Vietnam, Thailand, Singapore, Malaysia, Indonesia, Sri Lanka, Bangladesh, India, Mainland China, Taiwan, Hong Kong, South Korea, and Japan; but you are also invited to consider the ways contemporary film production, exhibition, distribution, and reception crosses borders "within" and "outside" Asia.

Shall We ...?

Let's begin the conversation with a few examples from the movies. Cinematic reflexive narrative moments where characters actually see themselves on the screen can offer an insight into the ways films function culturally – or at least the ways movies imagine they do. Witness Ah Hock, Sameer, and Pooja at the cinema:

In the 1998 film *Forever Fever* set in late 1970s Singapore, supermarket clerk Hock is persuaded by buddies to check out a re-release of the 1972 Hong Kong film starring Bruce Lee called *Fist of Fury* (*Jing wu men*, released in the United States as *The Chinese Connection*). Instead, to their chagrin, they are greeted at the Majestic Theater by a poster advertising an unknown flick, *Forever Fever*. Hock thinks it is probably a boring "hospital movie." When he finds out it's a dance film, he first dismisses it, but then, suddenly, Hock is awakened to the magic of the screen image, captivated by a charismatic American on a disco dance floor in a white polyester suit. Drifting hypnotically further into the movie, Hock actually sees himself on the screen strutting down the street to the beat. "Stayin' Alive!" he frantically mutters when he is rudely awakened in his bed in a cold sweat from his cinema-fueled dream by the cruel morning alarm. Hock is late for work at the supermarket, but before he faces the manager's stern gaze, he uncrumples a flyer he's tossed in his trash announcing a disco dance contest. Enticed by the cash prize (enough for the motorbike he covets) and inspired by the fancy moves he's seen on the screen, Hock has a new mission: to learn how to dance.

And in the 2001 Bollywood hit *Dil Chahta Hai* (*The Heart Wants*), three former college-mates in Mumbai find their way into twentysomething adulthood and try to keep their friendship alive. The notoriously susceptible-to-love Sameer, recently humiliated by a jealous girlfriend and ripped off by a sexy European scam artist while on vacation in Goa, is faced with a new challenge: his matrimonial-minded parents arrange an introduction to the daughter of a friend, to the dismay of both the young people. At first resistant to his parents' old-fashioned plan, Sameer is shocked to discover his attraction to the gorgeous Pooja and is disappointed to learn that she has a boyfriend. Sameer cultivates a friendship (*dosti*) and in a "serious" moment on a park bench finally admits to her that he's falling in love (*pyaar*) with her, although she laughs it off. Nevertheless, in the next scene, the two seal the transitional moment in their fledgling relationship with a movie date. The fictional film-within-the-film is called *Wo Ladki Hai Kahan* (*Where is the Girl?*); and as the two settle in to enjoy the show they are shocked to see characters on the screen that look exactly like themselves in elaborate dance numbers, vignettes, and outfits that affectionately parody popular Hindi movies styles – retro to more recent. As the voices of the onscreen mountain-top lovers echo across a canyon, Sameer and Pooja turn to each other, mouthing the refrain of the song. Pooja: "Where is the girl?" Sameer: That girl is here." As they slowly rise, looking deeply in each other's eyes, haloed by back-lighting from the movie projection, all the smiling members of the theater audience around them spontaneously erupt into movements that mimic the delirious screen choreography and reinforce the couple's romantic revelation made at the movies.

Although these film-viewing moments are part of screen fictions rather than purported documentary "realities," the stories they tell represent and comment on aspects of Asian cultures and societies. *Forever Fever*'s Hock is a Chinese Singaporean (the ethnic majority), living in the postcolonial society of the Southeast Asian city-state. Hock and his friends speak a lively mixed form of English – Singlish – sprinkled with Chinese words and local Malay expressions. (The version of the film distributed in the US was initially dubbed over;

although the original dialogue was finally retained, snatches of Hokkien Chinese go untranslated without subtitles.) Hock finally successfully synthesizes his own form of disco dancing that combines kung fu moves (à la his hero Bruce Lee) with "American-style" disco (taught by an Indian teacher in the local dance studio). Sameer and Pooja likewise inhabit a world – in their case a very upper-middle-class, urban, cosmopolitan, consumer-oriented one – that is somehow both modern and traditional. The film expresses their romance at/through the movies by allowing them to see their reflections in popular Hindi cinema as a prologue for their "updated" story. Thus, the characters in *Dil Chahta Hai* find pop culture-mediated ways to express Indian identity in a rapidly transforming global society.

Such changes are also evident in the forms these film narratives take and the different ways they are packaged for domestic and international audiences. The transactions of production, exhibition, distribution, and reception remind us that films as cultural texts are subject to a variety of social, economic, and political processes. Contemporary Asian feature films, as commodities, are often boundary-crossers. *Forever Fever*, the first Singaporean film to have commercial release in North America, was re-titled *That's the Way I Like It* by the company that bought the distribution rights, Miramax.[1] The new title was determined to be more palatable to US audiences, and the film captured the interest of the company in the first place (its only acquisition at the Cannes Film Festival that year) because of its perceived "universal" appeal. (Reportedly the movie even had another working title *Don't Call Me John Travolta*, which was scrapped because of potential legal issues.) For its part, *Dil Chahta Hai* found eager young audiences in India but also in the diasporic community of (especially well-to-do) "Non-Resident Indians" or NRIs around the globe. A number of the film's stars even took the show on the road as part of a live global traveling meta-entertainment showcase where the performers lip-synced, danced, and acted out scenes and choreographed song sequences from the film. The hit soundtrack also circulated worldwide.

Within the "diegesis" (a film-studies term referring to the narrative world of the film), Hock "projects" himself onto his cinematic dream-screen, and Pooja and Sameer recognize their own potential story in the frolicking Bollywood screen figures. Film viewers are thus also reminded of the power of the movies in manufacturing, mimicking, and fueling fantasies. Both films also raise questions about the relationship between Asian films and other cultural products competing and circulating within the global marketplace. During the mid-1970s (the time period in which *Forever Fever* is set) the local film industry in Singapore was dormant; Southeast Asia (including Singapore) was, and still is, a major market for Hong Kong films. Hock's favorite screen hero is an Asian role model, Hong Kong (and global) star Bruce Lee; he can even get a Bruce fix on television – albeit interrupted by local commercials. "Disco" as an imported, appropriated, and hybridized cultural fad expressed through trendy dance moves, media (radio, records, movies – *Forever Fever*, the movie-within-the-movie, is a "knock off" rather than the real thing), and fashion (hairstyle, clothing, accessories) is given nostalgic treatment in the film. *Dil Chahta Hai* in turn represents an example of an increasingly globalized hyper-hip, slick, youth-oriented contemporary Bollywood cinema. The film is conspicuously teeming with consumer products and uniquely-mixed songs that add even more ingredients to the *masala* (spice combination) – the term for the generic hybridity that popular Hindi films are famous for. (For example, "Wo Ladki Hai Kahan," the musical number picturized as snippets from Bollywood through the decades, has Celtic-flavored instrumentation and a step-dance beat.)

Mapping Asia and Asian Cinema Studies

Asia as a geographical concept is amazingly expansive. It can be mapped over forty different countries and a variety of dependencies, islands, and territories; it encompasses more than half of the world's population – with China and India the world's most populous nations. (Indonesia – the world's largest archipelago with the world's largest Muslim population, Pakistan, Bangladesh, Japan, the Philippines, and Vietnam are also in the top fifteen.) The locations of contemporary Asia on the world map today still bear connections to centuries of cartographic, political, and cultural representations of land masses and seas, civilizations and human geographies. The term "Asia," although its exact etymological origins are in dispute, was used throughout history to define a place and people from the perspective of Europe, providing "a backdrop or coherent and culturally distinct 'other' against which a diverse and fragmented Europe could define itself."[2] The Latin-derived term "Orient" referred in directional relation ("Near East" or "Far East") to the "Occident" or the "West." As argued by postcolonial critics – most notably Edward Said – "Orientalism" uses a Eurocentric logic to construct Asia in relation to the West, to assert imperialist power through representation.[3]

Asia is extremely culturally diverse in terms of languages, religions, political systems, and cultural practices; therefore the suggestion of monolithic culture and homogeneity is extremely fraught. Nevertheless, "Asian" has been used – to different ends – to convey shared cultural attributes or experience, geographical origins, and/or race.

As an identificatory category in the United States, the federal government census bureau's racial category of "Asian" refers to people with origins in the "Far East," "Southeast Asia," and the "Indian Subcontinent." In the cultural politics of the United Kingdom and in Anglophone Africa, largely because of particular legacies of colonialism, the term "Asian" refers mainly to people from South Asia. ("Black British" has included people of Asian descent.[4]) In the twentieth century and onward, English-language use of "Asian" has also served a politicized function in coalition-building of minority and marginalized peoples in dominantly white societies, and a celebration of multiple identities. Exclusionary hegemonic discourses also exist within Asian national and cultural contexts, marking and marginalizing those perceived as minorities and foreigners – including "other" Asians.

As a concept, "Asia" becomes especially arbitrary when we consider the rise of international co-productions and the dispersion of Asian-produced and Asian-themed films, Asian audiences, and filmmaking talent around the globe. There is no one Asian cinema, although there are contemporary pan-Asian modes of production and finance schemes, as well as distribution and marketing initiatives that encourage Asian transnational and regional consolidations in the face of globalization.

Some of the theoretical implications of the "global" for Asian cinema studies are discussed briefly in the following chapter on "Theorizing Asian Cinema(s)," but the charged concept of "globalization" also needs to be noted here. Globalization (and its impact) has been defined in innumerable complex and contradictory ways, but a few of the concatenated strands of its most familiar definitions and perceived effects include the following: the exchange, flows, and migrations of goods, ideas, and people across borders; development and expansion of communication and information technologies and media (and the emergence of global networks); time-space compression; and world-wide market expansion and economic integration driven by free (i.e., deregulated) trade and foreign investment.

Does globalization mean that Asia continues to be subject to ongoing "cultural imperialism" of imposed Western lifestyle, values, products – and Hollywood box-office domination? To quote Michael Hardt and Antonio Negri on the ideology of the world market, "The global politics of difference established by the world markets is defined not by free play and equality, but by the imposition of new hierarchies, or really by a constant process of hierarchization."[5] In the late twentieth century and into the new millennium, major US studios increasingly have become part of multinational media entertainment conglomerates and linked to foreign funding. Overseas grosses of films in Asian markets provide a major source of revenue, a crucial way to recoup any domestic losses. Hollywood and European companies use Asian locations and talent. English-language film production in Asia is on the rise, and firms have launched "American-style" multiplexes throughout Asia. North American and European (and, increasingly, Canadian and Australian) investors co-finance "Asian" films. Hollywood is constantly scouting Asian product to purchase remake rights. As the authors of this volume reveal, Asian film industries have reacted in ambivalent ways to globalization and the (inter)dependence it presumably engenders.

Shekhar Kapur, an Indian filmmaker who has worked as director and producer on art and commercial films in India and abroad, has predicted for the current millennium, for the near future, an inevitable seismic shift toward an Asian-centric global media culture.[6] It is clearly time to redraw the map of world cinema and put Asia in the center, and this urgency fuels the passionate pedagogical and scholarly goals of this book.

There are many inherent challenges in articulating what is Asian cinema – or Asian cinemas plural. Because of the enormity of Asia and the topic of Asian cinema, the geographical remit of this book project is necessarily subject to limits; *Contemporary Asian Cinema* primarily encompasses the countries and regions of East, Southeast, and South Asia. As such regional and national geo-industrial mappings are essential to the discursive functions of institutions such as film-industry trade newspapers, international film festivals, corporate structures, and trade policies, this representation dialogically engages with the ways Asian cinema circulates in the global image market. The country coverage within this book is also selective, based upon volume of annual film production, established history, and current perceived viability of local industries. Further, it should be noted that the category of "Asian Cinema" might well include parts of the Middle East and Southwest Asia, Central/Inner Asia, the former Soviet Republics in Transcaucasia, Turkey, Australasia, and the Asian diasporas.[7] Most of these areas are beyond the scope of this current book, although considerations of national border-crossings and diaspora inflect almost all of the chapters.

Concepts of the "Pacific Rim" and "Asia Pacific" cinema and film markets offer regional composites related to socioeconomic processes and patterns of migration. As Shirley Geok-lin Lim and Wimal Dissanayake explain, "The Asia Pacific region is a vast territory encompassing Japan, the newly industrialized states of East Asia and China, the Southeast Asian countries, Australia, New Zealand, the South Sea islands, and the Pacific coast of North America."[8] But the region cannot be viewed as a geographical given; it "has to be understood in terms of colonialism, postcolonialism, multinational capitalism, globalization, the complex and multifaceted interplay between the Asia Pacific and the Euro-American Pacific, and their diverse and intersecting discursive productions."[9] Western Academic institutions are still largely oriented towards regional area studies – as in the case of "Asian studies." In the United States, area studies emerged as a post-World War II and Cold War phenomenon as a means to regulate and maintain knowledge and power. More recently, discourse of regionality, ethnicity, and globality has given birth to interdisciplinary and comparative interdisciplines such as Asian Pacific American Studies and inter-Asian cultural studies[10]. Discursively bridging multiple Asian identities is another desirable goal of this book.[11]

There is no homogenous Asian monoculture. As Asian films become more prominent in the "West," they pose challenges to Western-centric hegemonic models of global film culture. It is not uncommon to see rhetoric of Asian "invasion" used in Western media to describe the influx and impact of Asian films. As Minh-Ha T. Pham has noted, this construction bears a complicated relationship to paranoid discourse, dating back centuries earlier, of a homogenous race and continent of menacing hordes.[12] Scholars such as Robert Stam and Ella Shohat have proposed an "unthinking" of Eurocentrism and a "rethinking" of Cultural Studies as *"multiCultural* Studies since all national cultures, especially in the age of globalized mass-media, are inevitably touched and altered by the cultures of close or distant neighbors."[13] *Contemporary Asian Cinema* can be constructively used as a catalyst for conversations about Asian cine-cultural diversity.

As Asian cinemas enter the global image market with increasing frequency, they are challenged by recontextualization and the effacement of a mass cultural phenomenon: the popular film. In the schizophrenic world of global capitalism, Asian films develop multiple identities and audiences. As they are often exhibited and distributed outside Asia as "foreign" films or "auteur" cinema, movies that register domestically as "popular" can become labeled "art house" fare or genre-driven "cult" films. Within local markets, "art" and "popular" cinema are also not always mutually exclusive categories. The authors in this volume take up such issues, investigating and unpacking what constitutes popular and commercial cinema. (For example, Emilie Yueh-yu Yeh discusses the ways international art-house recognition has fed what she refers to as the domestic crisis of the "invisibility" of Taiwanese popular cinema.)

The privileged status of particular Asian cinemas within "world cinema" is connected to geopolitics, as well as perceived cultural currency. Asian cinema has indeed been impacted by the Western gaze, and its selective canonization illustrates a variety of cross-cultural issues. Postwar Japanese and post-Independence Indian art films were the first to garner major critical attention in the West. As film scholar Donald Richie has noted, the celebrated Japanese film *Rashomon* (1950) was not primarily made for export or with Western viewers in mind (and had also not been especially well-liked by prominent Japanese critics.)[14] Indian filmmaker Satyajit Ray's humanist Bengali cinema likewise won him attention and sealed his reputation as a world cinema auteur, with awards at major international film festivals. Influenced by Italian neo-realism and French poetic realism, Ray's *Pather Panchali* (1955) became a box office success in Bengal – after its international festival recognition. A more recent Western "discovery" is represented by the case of the so-called Chinese Fifth Generation films made starting in the mid-1980s by the first generation of filmmakers to graduate from the Beijing Film Academy after it reopened at the end of the Cultural Revolution. Subject to state censorship but celebrated by film festivals in the West and in the international arthouse, these films stirred up academic debates about Chinese cinema's exhibitionistic "self-Orientalizing."[15]

On the other hand, the domestic box-office successes of popular contemporary Asian cinema speak to resurgences of national pride, economic recovery, and the revitalization of national film industries. For example, in the wake of the Asian economic crisis in the late 1990s, South Korea, Thailand, and the Philippines all produced films that broke the domestic box-office record previously held by Hollywood's *Titanic* (1997).[16] Film narratives with local resonance, revamped genres, homegrown stars, intensified use of special effects, perceived enhancement of production quality, crafty financing, cultural policies such as screen quotas and tax breaks, and savvy marketing strategies are just some of the factors that have contributed to renewed and refreshed production activity and local audience interest in domestically-produced Asian films.

In mapping the terrain of this volume on Asian cinema, the authors of *Contemporary Asian Cinema: Popular Culture in a Global Frame* have all conducted Asian research within and outside Asia, and are located in a variety of institutional vectors in relation to Asian cinema. They are situated in Australia, Bangladesh, Canada, Hong Kong, the United States, the United Kingdom, the Philippines, and Thailand. Three of the chapters are collaboratively researched and co-authored by teams of academic film scholars and/or professional film critics. In addition to teaching at the university level, the authors have also curated festivals and other public screenings of Asian films. Several have also been active in film production. The idea for this book was born out of a need for an updated English-language resource for teachers, students, scholars, and aficionados of Asian cinema – especially those interested in screening across, and making connections between, Asian cinemas.

Making Asian Movies Available

As Asian cinemas have in recent years seen a surge in creative activity and international exposure, student interest has likewise grown. More and more universities, globally, are offering courses in international films and Asian cinema. This is a critical time to expand, diversify, and deepen academic film studies curricula.

Film historians, theorists, and critics generally have been instrumental in the processes of recognizing the cultural value of Asian films. In US academic studies of the Asian Pacific region, the East-West Center in Hawaii, originally established in 1960 by the US Congress to support scholarly research and strengthen dialogue and cooperation between the US and Asia Pacific, produced the influential *East-West Film Journal* (1986–1994). Periodicals such as the US-based *Asian Cinema* and India-based *Cinemaya: the Asian Film Quarterly* publish English-language scholarship on Asian cinema. Organizations such as the Asian Cinema Studies Society (which produces *Asian Cinema* journal), the Asian Pacific Media Center, and NETPAC (the Network for the Promotion of Asian and Pacific Cinema, for which *Cinemaya* is the official journal and the Asian Pacific Media Center is the US headquarters) have been intensively involved with the promotion of Asian cinema.

There are growing numbers of influential Asian and Asian diaspora film festivals, dedicated symposia, and industry expos (such as Hong Kong International Film and Television Market and Pusan Promotional Plan) that function as showcases and marketplaces. Asian-cinema specialist Julian Stringer, employing anthropological discourse, calls such events "interzones" or sites of cultural exchange.[17] Festival programmers are important "shapers" of Asian cinema – as are fans, and even pirates. International festivals that showcase Asian and Asian Pacific films are flourishing in metropoles such as Busan, Hong Kong, Manila, Tokyo, Singapore, Taipei, Tokyo, various Indian cities, Honolulu, Vancouver, Toronto, San Francisco, New York, Sydney and elsewhere. However, access to Asian films outside Asia via corporate and independent distribution remains a perennial challenge. As San Francisco-based journalist G. Allen Johnson has astutely noted recently, Asian films in the United States are often "remade, held hostage, or released with little fanfare."[18] The comparative dearth of Asian films on Western theatrical screens, despite the volume and range of films produced in Asia annually, reflects an uneven world. While Asian films are clearly perceived as potentially lucrative commodities, their introduction to Western audiences has been frequently botched by dubbing practices, weak marketing, limited releases, and stockpiling and hoarding of titles to which rights have been bought. There is a dire need for timely intervention.

In an ideal international image arena, all the films mentioned in this book would be available affordably to viewers worldwide via products that helps to sustain Asian film production. However, because of market inequitability and asymmetrical flows, readers of this book may unfortunately never have the opportunity to watch some of the popular films discussed throughout. Scholars, students, and fans of Asian cinema need to continue to address this curatorial imperative. *Contemporary Asian Cinema* encourages you the reader/viewer to discover and experience as many of these films (and related popular culture texts) as possible, to engage with them actively and critically, to participate in dialogues.

ACKNOWLEDGEMENTS

This book is deeply indebted to the work of pioneering researchers on Asian cinema. There are many, but I'd like to personally acknowledge a few here. John Lent's book *The Asian Film Industry* and the journal he edits, *Asian Cinema*, remain important landmarks in English-language scholarship. In many ways, *The Asian Film Industry* provided a model for this book, as both volumes' chapters combine industrial and cultural profiles with case studies. The period from the publication of Lent's book up to the present has also been marked by extraordinary cultural, social, economic, and technological developments that have profoundly impacted film industries and film culture. In an era of proliferating digital production and diversified material formats, "Asian cinema" now means digital video productions as well as films shot on 16mm and 35mm celluloid, videotape, VCDs, DVDs, and movies on television and the Internet. It includes films that have been translated, subtitled, re-titled, edited, and recontextualized in so many different ways. (It should be noted that throughout *Contemporary Asian Cinema: Popular Culture in a Global Frame*, standardized romanizations and English translations are provided whenever possible.)

Another influential and prolific scholar in the field of Asian cinema studies, Wimal Dissanayake, has also made numerous contributions that innovatively think across Asian cinemas. Dissanayake has been instrumental in creating a new map for international cinema studies that does not relegate Asian cinema to a marginal position. He has also elegantly infused his contribution to this volume, a chapter on Sri Lankan cinema, with his insightful perspectives on Asian cinema and critical theory. I thank him and all the authors in this book for their participation.

A final acknowledgement: I am profoundly grateful for my experiences a decade ago as a longtime volunteer and the first curatorial intern in the Department of Film and Video (now, sadly, defunct) at the Carnegie Museum of Art in Pittsburgh, guided by the visionary curatorial leadership of Bill Judson. There I had the opportunity to do broad and intensive research for the Asian cinema files to develop film series – and to see so many Asian and international films that I would have never had the opportunity to view otherwise. It was truly foundational to my formation as a scholar, teacher, curator, and cinephile/fan. As a film professor who teaches, researches, and curates Asian and Asian diaspora cinema, I am also appreciative of the interdisciplinary collegial dialogue and support at the University of Massachusetts-Amherst: the Department of Communication, the College of Social and Behavioral Science, the Interdepartmental Program in Film Studies, the International Programs Office, the International Scholars Program, Asian and Asian American Studies, and the Asian Arts and Culture Program.

I look forward to reading and discussing this book with my students – "real" characters that continue to inspire my love for "reel" fictions.

Contemporary Asian Cinema: Popular Culture in a Global Frame launches Berg Publisher's new series of books on Asia Cinema. This project addresses the explosive growth of academic interest in Asian cinema and culture, by creating innovative texts that serve the needs of students and course instructors. The "Asian Cinema" series promises to become a forum for exciting new English-language scholarship for an international readership. These books will emphasize the diversity and plurality of Asian cinema(s) – as well as historical, geopolitical, and cultural connections.

CHAPTER 1

Theorizing Asian Cinema(s)

Anne T. Ciecko

As illustrated in the introduction to this book, the characters of Hock in *Forever Fever* and Sameer and Pooja in *Dil Chahta Hai* represent moments and positions of spectatorial identification with the screen image. Identification occurs within and across individual and collective subjectivities – and within and across racial, ethnic, gender, class, and sexual identities.

The very idea of what constitutes an "Asian" film is a flexible construction, subject to perspectives of such elements as target audience, content and themes, historical and material conditions of production, and identity of film-makers and screen talent. For the purposes of this book, contemporary Asian films are defined as narrative features produced within the territory, by film-makers who identify as Asian, for primarily Asian national (but increasingly pan-Asian, diasporic, and global "cross-over") audiences.

As Robert Stam has noted in his account of the evolution of film theory, proto-cinematic or pre-cinematic cultural forms and aesthetic philosophies pre-date the birth of cinema.[1] The history of cinema has often been presented as a narrative of Western invention. However, throughout Asia, cultural phenomena that originate centuries before the movies have cinematic qualities. For example, shadow puppet theater has localized forms throughout Asia. The Malay compound term for cinema, *panggung wayang*, fuses words that connote the film theater and audience and the shadow puppet legacy.[2] Similarly, the Chinese name for cinema, *kan dianying*, translates to "electric shadows." Contemporary Asian cinema continues to build upon traditional forms even as it engages with global popular culture. Scholars K. Moti Gokulsing and Wimal Dissanayake have demonstrated, for instance, how classical epics, theatrical forms from different historical periods and regional/ethnic contexts, Hollywood and MTV have influenced contemporary Indian cinema's narrative structures, audiovisual styles, and modes of performance.[3]

Because cinema is itself a hybrid, interartistic, multilayered, audiovisual phenomenon, scholars of Asian film are concerned with the ways it relates to other cultural texts. Dissanayake discusses intertextuality as the cultural interplay with "tradition, cultural memory, and indigenous modes of symbolic representation."[4] As Asian films enter the global public sphere and are circulated to international viewers, they are often mediated with another layer of textuality: subtitles or dubbed voiceovers. "Asian" cinema is polyglot. The dialogues in the movies mentioned in this book are in Tagalog/Filipino, Vietnamese, Thai, Chinese (various dialects including Hokkien, Cantonese, Mandarin, Taiwanese), Malay (official "national" languages of Bahasa Melayu and Bahasa Indonesia), Sinhalese, Bengali, Hindi, Urdu, Tamil, Korean, Japanese, English, and hybrid vernaculars. They employ a variety of regional slang and accents that signify the origins of their characters (or the actors that play them). Many contemporary Asian film characters speak more than one language – sometimes in the same sentence.

Accounting for audiences who might speak and hear English differently, "accented" English-language dialogue in Asian films may also be translated into its own language via subtitles, and subtitles may vary when Asian films are distributed in different Anglophone markets.

As movie narratives are conventionally not an exclusively visual sensory experience, contemporary Asian cinema includes sound in the form of music, spoken dialogue, and effects. It is therefore useful to attend to the ways cinema appeals to the senses more holistically, and intertextuality allows for the multiplicity of interpretive possibilities and meaning-making by different audiences.

Texts and Contexts

Is there such a thing as "film language"? Some approaches to film theory highlight elemental structural, technical, or formal aspects of cinema as a medium. Theorist of the signifying practice or "semiology" of film Christian Metz conceptualized cinema as a textual system, using as his main model the fiction film.[5] Cinema can be described as a communicative phenomenon through the use of linguistic metaphor – in particular the notion that the medium of film possesses its own vocabulary, grammar, or idioms. Within popular culture studies drawing from the structural semiotic science of linguistic codes and cultural signs, textuality deals with the production of cultural meaning.

One of the key figures in what might be called classical formalist film theory and revolutionary film practice was deeply influenced by "Asian" cultural forms. Soviet filmmaker/theorist Sergei Eisenstein, writing in the 1920s, was fascinated by what he perceived to be pictorial and ideogrammatic aspects of Japanese and Chinese language, imagistic poetics, and fragmented gestural theater acting of Kabuki theater.[6] This cross-cultural appropriation and interpretation of Asian representational practices (coupled with many other discourses – most significantly, dialectical Marxism) assisted him in developing in theory and practice a concept of "montage": editing as a revolutionary cinematic technique to engage the spectator and transform reality. In turn, Eisenstein's own hybridized contributions to cinema in theory and practice have had an international impact – as did Soviet "social realist" aesthetics. According to Hu Ke, the development of film theory in China has its roots in Soviet film theory which was positioned in opposition to Western theory.[7] As an example of cross-cultural cinematic affinities, Indian director/producer/star Raj Kapoor's film *Awaara* (*The Tramp*, 1951) found enthusiastic audiences in the Soviet Union who experienced it as both familiar and fresh, identifying a recognizable social(ist) message and other pleasures in the narrative, visuals, and music. Comparable examples of the contemporary popularity of Asian films such as Hong Kong martial arts films and Hindi musicals can be found all over the globe, across identities. For example, Bollywood films are popular in Africa, in places where there are large concentrations of diasporic Indians (e.g. East Africa), but also, as anthropologist Brian Larkin has shown, among Hausa-speaking Muslims in northern Nigeria, in a country that is experiencing its own explosion in popular video-film production (aka "Nollywood").[8]

Aspects of international narrative feature films can also be identified via formal analysis of story patterns, generic codes and conventions, cinematography, editing, sound, and *mise-en-scène* (including costume, lighting, setting, props).[9] The study of cinematic style enables a synthesis of the component parts that have been broken down and examined, but it is also important to attend to cultural coding of these formal strategies and to contextual issues. In my examples from *Forever Fever* and *Dil Chahta Hai*, such analysis can demonstrate the ways realities are blurred and the characters are "sutured"[10] into the narratives. The screen image of Hock as Tony Manero/John Travolta is established as a culmination of a progression of subjective point of view and reaction shots as Hock watches in the movie theater, and in his own dreams. In *Dil Chata Hai*, visual images and sound are also intricately connected to confound the ability to discern where reality begins and ends. As Pooja and Sameer look at each other in a meaningful, epiphanic way, there is a cutaway to the movie screen with an intertitle bearing the simple words, "The Beginning ..."

Polysemy matters to popular-culture studies because it grants agency to the film viewer/consumer, allowing for alternative reading "against the grain" – as in the previous example of the ambiguous image of working-class Singaporean Hock dressed up Travolta-style and his appropriative use of the "Hollywood" film to achieve his own fantasy goals. In turn, the film *Forever Fever* can be viewed as a celebration of a resistant form of Singaporean identity that refashions and twists imported or imposed culture into its own creative vernacular. (This is an especially critical point when the State has been so active in regulating the way pop culture "speaks," as Jan Uhde and Yvonne Ng Uhde illustrate in their chapter on contemporary cinema in Singapore.) And the Hindi movie *Dil Chahta Hai* can be used to support a dominant narrative of nationalism perpetuated by contemporary Indian cinema. Within the context of their movie date, Sameer and Pooja form an "interpretive community"[11] that "reads" the film as the answer to their own narrative quest: "Where is the girl?" *Dil Chahta Hai* thus reminds its extra-diegetic audience within and outside geographical India that these modern young people don't have to look far to find love, or images of Indian-ness.

The Social Life of Asian Cinema: Starting a Dialogue ...

The trope of dialogism I employ here is closely related to the work of theorist Mikhail Bakhtin that addresses generative dimensions of social expression.[12] Dialogism can be used to describe multiple voices within (and outside) the cinematic text, as well as the interactions between films and their audiences. To offer a specific filmic example, the parodic and reflexive aspects of *Forever Fever* overtly imitate the Hollywood disco movie, but with a twist, as the Hollywood classic *Saturday Night Fever* is both re-made as the film-within-the-film, and recognizably referenced in the film narrative itself. As Hock combines elements of popular culture to become a disco-dancer-cum-martial-arts-performer, the comic film invites its viewers to potentially enjoy a heightened sense of awareness of cultural hybridity and its pleasures, or to critique the appropriations as derivative – or to do both.

The "popular" in relation to Asian cinema has multiple possible connotations.[13] We can think of "popular" Asian cinema in terms of mainstream audience appeal and consumer behaviors (the predominant meaning – although theatrical box office success can't be a sole factor here because of piracy, television, and home video.) Also, "popular" can refer to the over-determined nature of production and marketing strategies such as the use of winning generic formulas and favorite stars, and narrative accessibility. "Popular" is also sometimes a denigrated or inferior "other" to that which is deemed "high culture" or "art."

In a global economy driven largely by capitalism, cultural currency and commercial potential of films at the domestic and international levels is determined by a range of regulatory mechanisms. "Discourse," as interpreted by post-structural theorist Michael Foucault, refers to the social uses of language, and systems of thought, power, and knowledge; it also is related to the institutions and disciplines and mechanisms that control them – aesthetic, political, economic, and so on.[14] For example, contemporary cinemas can be linked to economic discourse of Asian crisis, including currency devaluation and debt, and subsequent recovery in the late 1990s.[15] Additionally, the religious and philosophical traditions historically dominant in Asia including Buddhism, Confucianism, Taoism, and Islam impact the ways cinematic meaning is made – as do discourses that may not be considered indigenously

"Asian," including Christianity and Capitalism. The Asian territories covered in this book have a wide range of governing sociopolitical structures and systems including constitutional monarchy, parliamentary and multi-party democracy, socialism, and communism. These elements all contribute to the contextual fabric of Asian cinema as cultural production and social experience. "Context," as communication scholar John Fiske explains, addresses the environment for an interaction or a communicative exchange, and larger circumstances and conditions – the "determining forces that constitute and regulate social activity."[16]

Questions of National, Transnational, Regional, and Global Asian Cinema

National cinema (and related concepts of national identity and nationalism) is relevant to the explorations of Asian cinemas throughout this book; therefore it is fitting to offer an extended discussion here. However, it is also necessary to provide a disclaimer and qualification as well. To quote media-policy scholar Albert Moran, "There is no such thing as a 'national cinema' if the phrase is used to designate a single, unitary object."[17] Arguably, none of the Asian cinemas represented in this book presents a cohesive, integrated, monolithic portrait of a nation; and indeed the very idea of the nation-state is unsettled in a contemporary global world. Regional and international co-productions are increasingly becoming the norm. What appears to be an exemplary national text, for example Vietnamese filmmaker Tran Anh Hung's *The Scent of Green Papaya* (1993), may be scarcely national at all in terms of finances and location. Although set in Vietnam and made by a Vietnamese-born filmmaker with a Vietnamese cast, the movie was filmed on soundstages in France where the filmmaker had lived for the past twenty years and was financed with mostly French funding. Film scholar Hamid Naficy calls such filmmaking "accented" cinema, and his concept suggests a commonality across exilic, diasporic, and postcolonial film production.[18] In the case of the Singaporean film *Forever Fever*, both director Glen Goei and the film's star Adrian Pang (Hock) had each been living abroad and working in the theater in Britain for years when they made this film together in Singapore – a homecoming of sorts.

The discursive function of the national thus remains significant for Asian cinema studies. The multiethnic, multilingual city-state of Singapore, for instance, has only been an independent nation since 1965. In cultural terms, it is still in the process of building a national identity and a national cinema. After celebrating fifty years of independent statehood in 1997, India declared film a national industry the following year, making film production officially eligible for bank financing. Investment in the national at the economic and emotional level is essential to the survival of domestic film industries and domestic film cultures. Nationalism is expressed in a variety of ways – from diffuse, "imagined" sense of community[19] (as in diasporic subjects or in the concept of queer nation), to constructed notions of national inclusion ("One nation, one people, one Singapore," as characters in another contemporary Singaporean film *Chicken Rice War* sing), to potentially or fundamentally exclusionary strains. It can be argued, for instance, that myriad religious and ideological discourses of Hinduism permeate "national" representations in contemporary Hindi cinema. Discourse of dominance also impacts the ways selected filmic texts metonymically represent national film production. Bollywood (a term synonymous with popular Hindi cinema from Mumbai) is recognized as the most dominant expression of Indian film production in the world, despite the fact that there are many regional cinemas within India. Additionally, the term Bollywood remains highly contested because of the implied comparison with or derivation of Hollywood.

Within Asian and international cinema studies, the value of the national continues to be interrogated. As a seminal writer on the national cinema question, Andrew Higson, has written, "The cinemas established in specific nation-states are rarely autonomous cultural industries and the film business has long operated on a regional, national and transnational basis."[20] Ultimately for Higson, the complicated nexus of production, exhibition, distribution, and reception means that cinema can be variously national, regional, transnational, and global. He argues that state policy is one level at which national cinema still retains meaning, "as governments continue to develop defensive strategies designed to protect and promote both the local cultural formation and the local economy."[21] In the case of contemporary Asian cinemas, Korea, Thailand, and the Philippines are all examples of countries that have all instituted cultural policies and established organizations that have essentially or directly functioned like a quota system, insuring local films get shown on domestic screens. Higson also points out a critical issue that has been widely overlooked in much of global cinema studies but has definite implications for Asian cinema production, local labor, and international investment: tourism and the promotion of a country as a tourist destination. To cite a few of my own examples, in the UK in 2001, the British Tourist Authority launched a movie map campaign that invites visitors to the many British locations where Bollywood films have been made; and at Hong Kong International Airport airport, visitors have recently been welcomed by a life-size cardboard cut-out Jackie Chan, Hong Kong native son turned biggest star in Asia turned global superstar. It can also be argued that the mobility of stars and film talent and movie locations across national boundaries contributes as well to the commodification of place. In Thailand (the only country in Southeast Asia never officially colonized by a Western power) the government has become active in promoting Thai locations for international films such as Hollywood's star-studded big-budget epic *Alexander* (2004), developing local film studios and new technologies, and supporting a national film festival.[22]

Virtually every facet of the classical definition of the nation-state can be challenged in an analysis of individual Asian countries and the films produced within these territories: notions of sovereignty, unity, territorial boundedness, political autonomy, and common cultural experiences. However, even if the concept of the nation-state is critically abandoned or declared dead, it still exists discursively as what we might call a "nation-function" (to adapt the concept of author-function theorized by Michel Foucault).[23] And because the national is a construct, it is particularly apropos to consider it in relation to a multisensory representational medium, cinema.

As Dissanayake has noted, the idea of national cinema also remains closely tied to narration and stories about the nation, to the human desire to tell/hear/see/experience these stories. Drawing from and building upon the work of David Harvey and Benedict Anderson (the latter a specialist in the study of Southeast Asia who coined the concept of "Imagined Communities"), Dissanayake points out that in contemporary society, cinema is the dominant, far-reaching medium of communication, appealing to both literate and illiterate populations.[24] It is striking that the films from South Korea, Thailand, and the Philippines that broke the local box-office record in the late 1990s fixate on familiar myths (as in the case of a Thai folk-ghost movie, a Philippine national hero biopic, and prospects for national "reunification" in a Korean espionage thriller). But there is no one way to experience the popular, or the national-popular (to loosely borrow a term employed by Italian Marxist Antonio Gramsci).[25] The filmmakers and marketers in each of these cases tuned into local tastes and desires at timely moments of the resurgence of publicly displayed nationalism.

Higson has suggested that it may be beneficial to strategically imagine ways in which concepts of national cinema might be used supportively in certain political circumstances to advocate and "usefully advance the struggle of a community for cultural, political and economic self-definition."[26] In addition to postcolonial and postimperialist situations, Asian cinemas have struggled to define their own inter-Asian bordered identities as in the cases of countries with entangled cultural histories, sovereignty issues, and political differences: e.g. Malaysia, Indonesia, and Singapore; North and South Korea; the "Chinas"; Bangladesh, Pakistan, and Sri Lanka in relation to India.

The partition of the Indian subcontinent along religious lines continues to have a profound impact on flows across borders. In Pakistan, the once prolific film industry of Lahore's "Lollywood" currently remains in a state of dire economic crisis with radically reduced annual production and domestic film attendance, although negotiations of trade restrictions between Pakistan and India – even possible collaborations – are ongoing.

In the post-1997 Handover era, to cite another example, it seems all the more significant to talk about a "Hong Kong" cinema (never officially a "national" cinema to begin with, although it could be discussed in such terms) as something at once connected to and separate from the concept of "Chinese" cinema. Scholar Jenny Kwok Wah Lau proposes a look at the "East Asian" societies of China, Hong Kong, Taiwan, South Korea, and Japan – linked by their shared histories, responses to Western modernity, and the circulation of cultural products and mass media in the region. She notes how since the 1990s scholarship on East Asian cinema and popular culture has been moving discursively in the direction of the "transnational."[27] The transnational trope can be employed, for instance, to conceptualize the complexities of contemporary Chinese cinema and geopolitics. Sometimes used as a synonym for films made in the People's Republic of China (PRC), Chinese cinema can also refer to films from Taiwan (Republic of China), the island once ceded to Japan that continues to negotiate issues of nationalism and self-determination in its relationship with the PRC, and films from Hong Kong (Special Administrative Region) the former British colony that was "returned" to the PRC in 1997. The idea of one unified (or re-unified) China is alternately a nostalgic and a contentious one, and this is a theme that continues to find its way into contemporary films.

Further, terms such as "Greater China" (widely used in economic discourses) and "Cultural China" (debated in Chinese cultural studies) suggest a Chinese culture or cultures that exist before or after nation-formations, and is/are deeply connected to contingent statehood and transnational relations. According to Tu Weiming, Cultural China is an emergent cultural space and global site of Chinese identities.[28] Singapore is thus, by this formulation, part of "China proper." By such logic is *Forever Fever*, then, a Chinese film? Isn't it important to assert a strategic nationalism and insist that it is (instead? also?) a "Singaporean" film?

Concepts such as the East Asian "Tiger" or "Little Dragon" economies have retained currency through the past decade and encourage groupings of Asian nations (and other entities) such as South Korea, Taiwan, Hong Kong, and Singapore based on industrialization and economic growth rates – movement from "third world" to "first world" status. However, the "opening" of the Chinese and Indian economies and the impact of the Asian economic crisis have made the limited collective trope even more dated. Indonesia, Malaysia, the Philippines, and Thailand have ascended into the discursive Tiger pantheon. The regional conceptual identity of "South East Asia" is further perpetuated by organizations and institutions such as the Association of South East Asian Nations founded in 1967 with the goals of promoting economic and political cooperation and stability in the region. Currently there are ten nations in the ASEAN collective (including countries covered in this volume – Malaysia, Philippines, Thailand, Singapore, Vietnam, and Indonesia). ASEAN has helped create a shared sense of regional identity in a variety of filmic ways: through film production for purposes of tourism, as categories for national film awards, and via regional archival initiatives – to cite a few examples. Economic initiatives such as APEC (Asia-Pacific Economic Co-operation, founded in Australia in 1989) and ADB (Asian Development Bank, founded in 1966 and based in Manila) have also worked toward increasing international and interregional trade and economic growth and development.

The assertion of such regional alliances can activate what Ackbar Abbas and John Nguyet Erni, in identifying speaking positions for international cultural studies, have called triumphalism.[29] The promotion of liberalization and democratization in the Asian millennium taps into discourse of a kind of post-national utopia. In film industry terms, Derek Elley, who covers the Asian scene for the influential trade paper *Variety*, has recently noted the loosening of restriction and political and economic barriers in East Asian countries (and new film collaborations), and a "we're all Asian, anyway" logic expressed by film executives.[30]

In his essay titled "Concepts of National Cinema," Stephen Crofts identifies a taxonomy of eight varieties of nation-state cinemas: United States cinema, Asian commercial successes, other entertainment cinemas, totalitarian cinemas, art cinemas, international co-productions, third cinemas, and sub-state cinemas. The category of Asian commercial successes addresses "large domestic and reliable export markets" and cinema that "outstrips Hollywood imports at the local box-office."[31] Crofts makes mention here of India, Hong Kong, and Japan specifically, but other Asian countries might be included in the list. South Korea is an extraordinary example of a nation that has cultivated its own film industry by building an infrastructure for support of local film production and consumption of local films. Asian cinemas can also variously fit into Croft's other categories, with popular Asian cinemas potentially described as "other entertainment cinemas" (i.e. ones that do not dominate local markets – he mentions "Bangladeshi imitations of Indian cinema"), international co-productions, and sub-state cinemas (which could include regional production in India, for instance).

Another ranked or layered list of world cinemas is that of the "first", "second", and "third" cinemas. In the late 1960s Argentinean filmmakers and theorists Fernando Solanas and Octavio Getino proposed the idea of "third cinema" as a way of articulating film's possibilities as a vehicle for social change.[32] Building upon this manifesto, Teshome Gabriel and others continued the dialogue, formulating critical theories. Such models counterposed the third (or sometimes "third world") cinema to first cinema represented by

Hollywood and to second cinema in the form of European art cinema. Gabriel identified three phases of Third World Films beginning with "the unqualified assimilation" (industrial and thematic identification or imitation of Hollywood), followed by "the remembrance phase" (local control of production, exhibition, and distribution; thematic and stylistic attempts to indigenize and nostalgically return to the past), and culminating in "the combative phase" (a by-the-people-for-the-people ideal similar to Third Cinema).[33] Aspects of assimilation and remembrance continue to be manifested in Asian film production; however, these phases aren't necessarily so discrete and evolutionary. Arguably, contemporary popular Asian cinema has the potential to imitate, indigenize, and subvert at the same time.

While these theoretical and practical considerations of cinema within a world system have had revolutionary impact, a "developmental" model of (third) world cinema cannot accurately characterize filmmaking from Asia that has proven to be economically viable, attracting mass audiences at the domestic level (and increasingly worldwide.) Admittedly, though, there is extreme unevenness among Asian film industries themselves that speaks to issues of economic growth, and their inability to participate equally in a "free market" or "liberalized" world economy. Dissanayake has argued the limits of using the "Third Cinema" model: the application to a new context (from Latin America to another part of the world) and the dangers of homogenizing non-Western cinema.[34] Susan Hayward has also pointed out that, "It is something of a paradox to think of Indian cinema as a Third World cinema" given the volume and diversity of annual production.[35] Further, it can be argued that Asian popular culture is imbricated with modernity and – as Asian film cultures are impacted by multinational capitalism – postmodernity as well.[36] Expanding his theory of postmodernism and the cultural logic of late capitalism, Marxist literary scholar Fredric Jameson introduced a concept of "national allegory" in relation to all Third World texts in the age of multinational capitalism. While the national allegory idea has undeniably impacted scholarly analyses of non-Western and postcolonial cultural texts (including cinema), it also sparked a lively interdisciplinary debate that continues to this day. Aijaz Ahmad, for instance, has critiqued the third world's paradigm and the homogenizing ideal of allegory.[37] Theorist and historian of postcolonialism Robert Young reminds us that the twentieth century was marked by anti-colonial struggles in Asia (as well as in Africa and the Caribbean) "in the course of which one third of the world's population succeeded in breaking away from the capitalist world system in the age of late imperialism."[38]

Global film/media studies encourages a critical engagement with borders and boundaries as well as alternative geographies, the interstitial and the intercultural, myths of cultural purity and authenticity, cognitive limits of binary logic, locations and dislocations. Arjun Appadurai, for example, proposes a framework for examining the disjunctures of global cultural flows through his concepts of "ethnoscapes," "mediascapes," "technoscapes," "financescapes," and "ideoscapes."[39] Appadurai's idea of "mediascapes" in particular has far-reaching implications for the study of world cinema, suggesting the profound interconnection of forms of media, including film, and the ways images are experienced and consumed by viewers around the world. Like Appadurai, John Tomlinson sees the multiplex as a "deterritorialized" cultural space, but "[w]here there is deterritorialization there is also reterritorialization" which reinserts elements of the local in the global.[40] We can find many examples of this interplay within "global/local" or "glocalized" contemporary Asian film culture(s).[41] In Thai multiplexes, film screenings are preceded by a newsreel of the king and the playing of the royal anthem. Concession patrons in a South Korean film theater might be just as likely to buy dried squid as they would popcorn as a movie snack.

Globalization has been associated with simultaneity, a sense of instant communication and shared experience. World cinema's close ties with media such as television and with other converging forms of mass communication, reflect cinema's own ongoing technological evolution. Contemporary Asian cinema's production, exhibition, distribution, and reception is linked to digital developments (such as production and editing equipment, as well as the Internet), cable and satellite television, and crossovers with other media and popular cultural forms such as pop music. Transnational (specifically here, inter-Asian) television broadcasting has been viewed as a means to consolidate Asian audiences by resisting globalization or Americanization of televisual product, as in the popularity of Asian-produced serial melodramas across other Asian national and linguistic boundaries. However, MTV Asia, originally launched by Hong Kong's satellite service Star-TV (bought by media mogul Rupert Murdoch in 1995), offers another paradigmatic example of a dominant global popular formula that has become localized.[42] Further demonstrating local/global convergences, contemporary films such as Singapore's *Chicken Rice War* (2000), Indonesia's *Ada Apa Dengan Cinta* (which broke the local box-office record in 2002), and Malaysia's *Spinning Gasing* (2000) all feature soundtracks, diegetically inscribed musical performances, and youth styles influenced by music television.

Because globalization is such an amorphous concept, it can unify or disaggregate "Asian cinemas," underscoring ideological and cultural similarities or differences. The idea of the public sphere as articulated by philosopher Jurgen Habermas (developed within Asian cultural studies as a zone of debate and public modernity) opens up possibilities for dynamic interchange.[43]

The Habermasian notion of the public sphere is connected to democratization, begging the question of whether there is such a thing as "Asian values," and if so, how they (these values) mesh with democracy. This is an exceedingly challenging question, one that has been discussed by scholars, grassroots organizers, civic leaders, government officials, and citizens in diverse Asian contexts. The impulse in this volume is to examine these matters on a case-by-case basis. It is important to note when cultural practitioners within and outside Asia such as film producers, directors and actors and other screen workers, teachers, curators, and audience members are silenced by censorship or restricted access or imposed authoritative "readings" (what the authors of the recent book *Global Hollywood* call "textual gatekeeping") – when they are made less active.[44]

The idea of "Global Hollywood" suggests a complex overlapping and interconnectedness between Hollywood (the dominant "Western" model) and the global. The possible implication for contemporary Asian cinema is that it is effaced, subsumed, or marginalized in such a structure. In their intricate analysis of the topic, Toby Miller, Nitin Govil, John McMurria, and Richard Maxwell demonstrate the ways contemporary cultural policies have restructured capitalism and the financial systems that impact the production, exhibition, distribution, and reception of films. A perpetual cycle of dominance and dependency is enacted as "US governments and businesses continue to assault other countries' attempts to assert rights to national self-determination onscreen via barriers to imports."[45] The controversial World Trade Organization (WTO) established in 1995 as a global entity which oversees trade between nations, is one such institution that promises to have long-lasting effects on the perceived "developed" and "developing" culture industries of Asia, as well as Asian participation in this global public sphere. Bangladesh, for instance, is at this time considered one of the "least developed countries" that are part of the WTO. As cited in *Global Hollywood*, two-thirds of the world's film screens are in China and India alone. Although the PRC still severely restricts imported Hollywood product, and Bollywood and other Indian films dominate the screens in India, both India and China are viewed as important theatrical markets for Hollywood. According to the rules under which China joined the World Trade Organization, foreign investors are permitted to hold up to 75 percent investment in movie theaters. Additionally, "treaty and equity co-productions intersect scales of political modernity (the super- and supranational), vertical industrial scales (production, promotion, distribution, and exhibition) and horizonal industrial scales (conglomeration and synergies)."[46] Asian countries and regions are considered top "piracy hotspots," and Hollywood's attempts to retain and legislate intellectual property rights and ownership have had the impact of monopolizing and maintaining dependency, limiting trade.[47]

It has also been suggested that globalization is a centuries-old phenomenon, not just a contemporary one. David Harvey, for instance, has criticized current globalization discourse for its historical myopia. Reasserting the social theory of Karl Marx, he contends that late twentieth-century capitalism, serving largely US class interests, has created uneven geographical development. Harvey sees East and Southeast Asia as having challenged this hegemony (the Gramscian term for state dominance) with economic gains and the building of regional alliances.[48] In business school-speak, "The New Asia" connotes both open market possibilities and resistance with the development of Asian multi-nationals that demonstrate synergetic "cross-border integration" and reveal the limits of Western reach, outsourcing efforts, and economic opportunism.[49] Asia no longer becomes "subsidiary" to a Western corporation when the multi-national originates from within.

The national cinema tag obfuscates internationalism both within and outside Asia. Exactly what part of the film experience is "domestic" and what part is "foreign"? Film financing might seem possible to parse out at first, but sources frequently overlap or become encrypted. Exactly how Asian, Chinese (Hong Kong, Taiwan, Mainland China), American independent or Hollywood is a movie like *Crouching Tiger Hidden Dragon* (2000) – the film currently holding the position as the top-grossing "foreign-language" film in US box-office history? The combined concepts of national cinema and the popular critically enhance the use-value (a Marxist term for the functions a commodity can serve) of specific Asian films – in this case, the promotion of "sustainable" Asian film industries and film culture within and across and outside Asian countries. And of course, whether or not it is an illusion, the recognition of a globally successful film as a "national" product can stir up national pride.

Asian Cinematic Spectacle

In the "archetypal" disco-drama *Saturday Night Fever*, John Travolta's Italian-American character Tony Manero actually has posters of Asian/global super-star Bruce Lee on his own Brooklyn bedroom wall. In a moment of cross-cultural confluence, Tony (and *Forever Fever*'s Hock in his own "mir-roring" scene) sees his image in relation to that of Bruce Lee as he flexes his muscles in front of the mirror and appropriatively grooms his own masculinity. I have suggested previously that "Hollywood" has been deeply influenced and endlessly fascinated by Asian cinema; with production, distribution, and mar-keting re-making contemporary Asian films in its own image (or in contradis-tinction to it.)

Some of the highest-profile contemporary Asian films released and remade by Hollywood include spectacular and "excessive" body-focused genres such as martial arts, horror, and action films. A genre can be defined as a filmic taxonomic category or label recognized by specific narrative con-ventions and iconographic elements (audiovisual motifs). In the business of contemporary world cinema, genres are used as marketing tools, as short-hand to address audience expectations and preconceptions. Genre films are also subject to comparative organizational strategies because they are defined in relation to and in opposition to other cultural texts. A label such as "foreign films" can function like an amorphous "other"-genre (defined against domestic or non-foreign films), as evidenced by shelving practices in videostores – sometimes with nation (default national cinemas) designations acting as sub-genres. Occasionally Asian films break away from such group-ings in compound niche/cult categories such as "Japanese anime" or "Hong Kong action." In the case of Jackie Chan (i.e. a "Jackie Chan film"), a video-store and multiplex staple, his successful crossover into Hollywood in the 1990s (after earlier aborted attempts) is an extraordinary case of a translated and repackaged "brand" of film genre and star performance, a particular combo of personality-driven, self-deprecating comedy and high-risk *vérité* physical stunts.

Culturally-rooted aesthetic formulations and popular perceptions of what constitutes the real in representation and performance (e.g. classical Western mimetic notions of "mirroring" reality) also impact cross-cultural reception, as in the conventional (albeit very stereotypical) judgment of what makes Bollywood stylistically "different" from Western cinema: exaggerated acting styles, the conventions of lip-syncing to playback and post-dubbing of sound dialogue (the latter changing as more films are being recorded live); artificial aspects of the *mise-en-scène*; and ruptures in linear narrative logic, especially in song and dance sequences.

Observing trends across contemporary cinemas, Asian cinema "reality" is often coded as such in serious "art" cinema (or in documentaries). However, as Augusta Lee Palmer and Panivong Norindr argue in this volume in their respective chapters on Mainland Chinese cinema and Vietnamese cinema (both cinemas developing from a strong ideological/aesthetic orientation toward realism and propaganda), commercial Asian cinema has found ways to incorporate documentary dimensions and journalistic discourses. The binaries and antinomies of "art" and the "popular," "reality" and "fantasy" – not to mention "East" and "West" and "Asia" and "Hollywood" – are challenged throughout cinematic narratives of modernity. The sensory and experiential aspects of modernity and the conceptual relationship between art cinema and popular cinema are further examined in this volume by Wimal Dissanayake in his Chapter 8 on cinema in Sri Lanka.

While resisting any fixed notions of inherently Asian film qualities, we can nevertheless identify repeated generic conventions and stylistic modes of expression within and across Asian national and transnational cinemas, including the pervasiveness of melodrama across genres of Asian cinema and other cultural forms.[50] Melodrama is not an exclusively cinematic phenomenon in local/global Asian popular culture – as evidenced by the enduring popularity of television serial dramas (soap operas) and sentimental pop music, and the proliferation of sensational tabloid media.

According to many film theorists, melodrama is not officially a film genre, but rather more of a "structure of feeling" (a term developed by Marxist cultural critic Raymond Williams) that permeates film narratives, impacts representational strategies, and regulates and unleashes displays of affect.[51] Melodrama is evident in the romantic comedy *Forever Fever* in the family dynamics that bubble over into crisis after Ah Hock's brother breaks taboos by revealing his transgendered identity, and stops being the "good son." Melodrama also is at the core of the Bollywood film *Dil Chahta Hai*'s star-crossed romance between introspective artist Siddarth and the divorced, alcoholic older woman Tara (a relationship his mother does not approve of), and in the filial loyalty and sense of *dharmic* duty that compels the film's third female love interest Shalini to almost marry a man she doesn't love. The extravagant or excessive song and dance numbers enable the characters to express as-yet-unspoken or repressed feelings.

Throughout the discussions of Asian films in this volume, melodrama becomes a way for contemporary Asian cinemas to engage dialogically with history and memory, and traditional values and gendered roles (especially the institution of the family and its surrogates), in a time of social, economic, and political change.

In his pioneering study of Asian film industries, John Lent identified some of the "commonalities" of escapist Asian popular films as follows: "sex [broadly inclusive of all types of erotic and/or titillating display], slapstick comedy, kung fu, melodramatic love, cute animals, and youth oriented types."[52] While the cute animals are relegated mainly to Asian animation or subgenres of children's films, the other aspects still apply to popular live-action films, although genres are increasingly hybridized. Fast-paced and spectacular action sequences, computer-generated special effects (as well as digital filmmaking more generally), and product placements characterize many commercially successful films throughout contemporary Asia. Appeal to younger target audiences is also a broad Asian trend, as is an interest in examining events of the past as a way of commenting on the present. Gangster motifs (crime syndicates such as yakuza and triads) find their way into everything from gritty urban dramas to caper comedies. Government censorship of filmic genres, specific subject matters, and representational strategies varies widely from country to country, and as Lent notes, standards have been unevenly applied to domestic and imported product. In terms of Asian film exports (within and outside the continent), profound cinematic generic cross-fertilization is evident in films with elements of action, horror, fantasy, romance, comedy, and melodrama.

Terms like "lunar new year movie" (*hesupian* in Mandarin) also serve as umbrella categories, as in the example of the Chinese-produced films released during this festive season. The economic reforms in the PRC have resulted in a crumbling of industrial monopoly and more opportunity to make films, but the domestic film market has, in turn, been threatened by the influx of an increasing number of Hollywood blockbusters. One way to fight Hollywood's market share on local turf is the creation of a Chinese blockbuster, as in the example of the commercially successful *hesupian* films of director Feng Xiaogang.[53]

The Cultural Value of Film Authors, Stars and Fans

Like genres, film "auteurs" and stars and even fans are constructed as critical, structural, and social categories. (We have already seen how they can collapse into genres as in the "Jackie Chan film.") The "auteur" refers to the film artist/ author, a term drawn from French criticism and film theory's *politique des auteurs* – specifically referring to the distinctive styles of certain gifted film directors.[54] The "auteur" or "author function" concept still has considerable currency, especially with regard to international art cinema, but it also is connected to directors of popular films and commercial film genres. However, given the director's status as a prominently "credited" (and celebrated) individual agency on the average feature film, and the most frequently identified filmmaker on the production team, it is critically important to continually remind ourselves that, while an individual director's name usually serves as a shorthand, commercial feature films are produced as the result of collective labor. This work includes the stamp of the film producer who helps to shape films and national industry profiles at many different levels, and contemporary Asian cinema indeed has its share of prominent moguls and producer personalities such as the legendary "Mother" Lily Monteverde, Executive Producer of Regal Films in the Philippines.

Likewise, as mentioned previously, audiences engage with films as cultural recipients and meaning-makers. Film-going is a social experience, which is why film audiences are of special interest to academic cultural studies. Throughout Asia, theatrical movie attendance has been impacted by rising ticket costs, but even if they are not always buying movie tickets, people are definitely watching films – on television, on the Internet, at home via VCDs, DVDs, and video. As Asian media outlets proliferate, fans have found their own ways to "own" (and act out and on) filmic texts through creation, dissemination, sharing, and textual poaching (to use Michel de Certeau's term as interpreted by media scholar Henry Jenkins).[55] The latter is a type of participatory fan culture that uses the text in ways other than those initially "intended." Fan websites, blogs, e-zines, and list-serves devoted to Asian cinema are seemingly ubiquitous in cyberspace. Asian and Asian-diaspora pop culture 'zines from a variety of perspectives are also influential in creating and building community within fan cultures and subcultures. Chatty Bollywood fan magazines written in English (and "Hinglish") are commonly available at Indian import groceries and specialty shops, as well as through online sources and subscriptions. Descriptive words for enthusiastic aficionados/consumers such as "fanboy" and the Japanese term "*otaku*" circulate cross-culturally and resonate with a variety of meanings depending upon the context, some of them congratulatory and some of them disparaging.

Film fans help perpetuate the cultural currency of stars as iconic screen images. The combined activities of industrial production, marketing and distribution, and fan culture produce a pantheon of stars that can represent ideas/ideals of national identity. However they are also frequently not exclusively bounded by media, nation, culture, and language. Hong Kong's Cantopop (Cantonese-dialect pop music) industry has produced hugely popular transnational film stars. Some recent Korean film and television drama stars, most notably Bae Young-joon, have found large and especially female audiences in Japan (where Bae is known as Yon-sama). Bollywood superstar Amitabh Bachchan won the BBC's (global) online poll as entertainer of the millennium.

Images of stars are used at a corporate level to sell movies and endorse other consumer products; but given their clout and popular appeal, many international stars are becoming entrepreneurs, film producers and directors, and politicians.[56] Like the United States, the Philippines had a former movie star as a president (the ousted Joseph Estrada). India's venerable Bachchan (aka "Big B") has been a movie star, game-show host, and a member of Parliament.

In terms of the construction of female screen beauty, globalized standards have influenced the look of movie stars (as in the example of Bollywood's light-skinned, model-slim beauty queens turned top screen heroines). However, there is no universally uniform standard for the looks of Asian onscreen talent. In regional cinemas in southern India, audiences have historically preferred their heroines to be darker-skinned and more voluptuous. Mixed-race stars (e.g. "Eurasian") are especially popular in Southeast Asia. As field research and studies of Asian film audiences have repeatedly shown, fans from different class backgrounds identify with stars, and star worship has been connected, sometimes ambiguously, with a variety of cultural discourses such as religion and ideology and race and gender. Stars serve complex "bridging" functions.

In countries and regions in which there are radical disparities between the lives and opportunities of the rich and the poor, stars provide fantasies of escape and hope. Yet many popular film narratives reinforce hegemonic messages about the ways men and women should behave within society, within a national context. Stars are sometimes positioned as "ambassadors" of national cinemas, and as maintainers of the status quo. However, as these figures and their films circulate within and across boundaries, their images accrue new sets of meanings.

The "Subject" of Asian Cinema

When watching Asian films, whom and what do you see? The interpretation of cinema relies on a series of transactions between the film viewer situated within a particular "subject position" (to borrow another Foucauldian concept), constitutive elements of individual and collective identity-formation and identification, perception and memory, filmic politics of representation, material culture, the imagined (or desired) audience for the film, and colliding realities.[57] States of consciousness and self-awareness are analogous to the cinematic experience, the projection and reflection and loss and recognition of ourselves and our own stories. We can identify as (dis)associatively with the movies as with the images of our dreams and fantasies, using them to shape our own identities as media consumers in a global society as Hock's vernacularized disco hero does in *Forever Fever*. We can, like Sameer and Pooja in *Dil Chahta Hai*, narcissistically see ourselves through our screen surrogates and the image-repertoire of popular cinema. In a fascinating short essay on cinema and subjectivity called "Leaving the Movie Theater," cultural critic and structural theorist/semiologist Roland Barthes described such an experience as being "glued" to the mirror.[58]

The mirror in question is the film screen, itself a meta-metaphor for the "mirror stage" identified by post-structural psychoanalytic theorist Jacques Lacan, building upon the earlier work of Freud.[59] For Lacan, the unconscious is structured like a language; and identification is connected to developmental paradigms that form and control our realities. The mirror stage is the child's first recognition (or mis-recognition) of its own reflected image. Barthes's film spectator is thus also compared to the historical subject glued to ideological discourse.

As they emerged in the 1970s and 1980s, Euro-American feminist film theories engaged in dialogue with psychoanalytic theory as well as political philosophy (especially Marxism as interpreted by Louis Althusser in his concepts of ideological state apparatuses adapted to theorize cinema) and semiotics.[60] Film feminism countered the ways classical Hollywood cinema positioned the spectator as an "ideal" subject – i.e. a white heterosexual male identifying with his onscreen surrogate who in turn desires the passive object, the female. In her ground-breaking essay "Visual Pleasure and Narrative Cinema," Laura Mulvey describes this as the male gaze, fueled by scopophilia (the obsessive desire to look) and masochism.[61] Accordingly, the woman on the screen poses a potentially castrating threat to masculinity that must be regulated. As feminist film theory has continued to evolve, indigenize, nationalize/internationalize, and globalize (influenced by critical race theory, queer theory, transnational gender studies, and postcolonial theory, among others), it has challenged classical paradigms of narrative cinema and spectatorship further – positing ways for the female subject to actively look rather than just be looked at, countering the privileges and epistemological limits of Western feminism.[62] In terms of the national cinema question, marginalized or "subaltern" subjects have traditionally been denied access to hegemonic representational power.[63] Therefore it is important to observe the representations, presence, and voices of gendered, raced, and classed subjects within Asian film texts and film culture.

What happens when Asian cinema as cultural commodity (re)produces images that the West expects and imposes on it; when it recognizes itself as the object of the Western gaze and represents accordingly; when it perpetuates stereotypes? Dialectical relationships of self and other are negotiated within Asian regional, national, and transnational film industries and markets. In the ever-shifting contemporary global mediascape, appropriation and imitation, the assertion of indigenous cultural expression, subversion and reinvention, and the creation of "new" forms all contribute to the production of multiple Asian cinematic identities.

Postcolonial theoretical approaches thus provide vocabulary for critiquing cultural texts and contexts (e.g. the impact of colonialism and cultural imperialism, Orientalism, and racism). They can also assist in conceptualizing paradigms of cinematic spectatorship and representational politics – the gaze, power, and representation in ambivalent, doubled, and interdependent relationships.[64] The study of international cinema and visual culture – including Asian cinemas – has benefited enormously from such interdisciplinary theories. One widely-used key concept in particular, the notion of "hybridity," is carefully unpacked and creatively applied in an analysis of cinema in the Philippines by José Capino in Chapter 2 of this volume.

Throughout this volume, the authors of the essays on cinema in the Philippines, Vietnam, Thailand, Singapore, Malaysia, Indonesia, Sri Lanka, Bangladesh, India, Mainland China, Taiwan, Hong Kong, South Korea, and Japan combine cultural and critical perspectives as they/we discuss contemporary popular Asian cinema's fictions and their functions.

CHAPTER 2

Philippines: Cinema and its Hybridity

(or "You're nothing but a second-rate trying hard copycat!")

José B. Capino

Contrary to what one might expect of a national cinema from the Third World, one of the most famous scenes in contemporary Philippine film is set not in the verdant rice paddies, the teeming slums, or the seedy girlie bars for which the country is justifiably well known, but in a posh record-launching party for a rising chanteuse. The scene isn't about white slavery, natural disasters or political unrest – but a catfight between a fading diva and the young upstart who covets her career and lusts after her ex-boyfriend. Following the neophyte singer's rendition of Stevie Wonder's "I Just Called to Say I Love You," the scorned diva fires back with memorable insults: "Those who insist that I have finally found my match must be nuts!" she snaps in Filipino. Then, in perfect English and with eyebrows arched to the maximum, she hisses: "You'll neeeeever make it. You're nothing but a second-rate, trying hard, copycat!" To punctuate her diva offensive, she douses her enemy with a goblet of cold water before hastily exiting the premises.

The irony of this scene in Emmanuel Borlaza's *Bituing Walang Ningning* (*Fading Star*, 1985) is that the diva's words may very well be directed toward the film's overall plot which, while credited to a serial graphic novel (the vernacular *komiks*) by Nerissa Cabral, is clearly "inspired" by the 1950 film *All About Eve*. Those who intentionally look for correspondences between the two films will notice uncanny resemblances beyond the story, from the sparkling dialogue to the antagonist's own version of Bette Davis's dagger eyes. Paradoxically, these elements that make the films seem so totally similar also render them most thoroughly different. The colorful dialogue is not only commonplace in Philippine melodrama but also characteristic of the vernacular *komiks*. Similarly, in the context of Philippine cinema, the eyes under arched brows do not primarily evoke an appropriation of Bette Davis's memorable acting turn but a signature cliché of performing female villainy in local tearjerkers. Quite significantly, whereas *All About Eve* is by and large a dark comedy, Borlaza's film is a musical drama, with its dueling song numbers suitably replacing the epigrammatic bickering of the Hollywood classic. Indeed, to local spectators, including those who saw *Eve*, *Bituing Walang Ningning* would seem so quintessentially Filipino.

These intriguing similarities and differences between a Filipino film from the late 1980s and a Hollywood picture from the early 1950s highlight the importance of the impact of foreign films and cultures on local cinemas. Because the survival of local films is premised upon fierce competition from foreign releases, their relationship must not only be one of radical difference but also of fundamental similarity. Moreover, lodged within this central paradox is an intricate array of combinations and permutations of sameness and difference on various registers, including those of genre, cultural references, and film style among others.

Strategically repressed in order to emphasize national specificity or to bolster the cultural sovereignty of "marginalized" or "peripheral" film traditions, this aspect of national cinema criticism and historiography seems to me both refreshingly pragmatic and particularly instructive in understanding how local cinemas function symbiotically in relation to the foreign films that share the nation's screens.[1] The aim here is to gain an understanding of Philippine national cinema that emerges from an explication of the myriad and dynamic strategies – cultural, industrial, aesthetic, economic – that fashion the specificity of Philippine cinema in local and global contexts.

In conceptualizing the interpenetration of practices, elements, and influences in Philippine cinema, hybridity seems to me a strikingly rich and supple framework.[2] The concept, used mostly in horticulture and animal husbandry, was also prevalent in colonial discourse, particularly in engendering fear and hatred of racial degeneration or degradation through interracial mixing ("miscegenation") or, more rarely, in evoking the beneficence of colonial occupation and social engineering ("creolization" by colonial education). It has since been reclaimed by literary scholars to characterize the heterogeneity of postcolonial cultures (e.g. cultural syncretism or amalgamation) or to describe the capacity of literary works or of language to contain a multitude of voices which could either complement or contest each other (e.g. Bakhtin's concept of the dialogic novel or Bhabha's notion of ambivalence in colonial discourse.)[3] Hybridity connotes an intrinsically uncontrolled, if not always unwieldy, mediation that both doubles and splits the combinatory elements and results in a distinct third object. The concept is also supple enough to embrace the differences between the effective assimilation of influences on one hand and the unstable juxtaposition of elements on the other, between wholesale piracy and creative – or even subversive – appropriation.

To better understand the concept of hybridity and how it illuminates Philippine cinema, let us take the case of the Filipino superhero Darna who, having been featured in at least twelve films since 1953, is arguably one of local cinema's most popular and representative figures. She sports an outfit that looks a lot like Wonder Woman's – a red bra or bustier with gold accents, gold bracelets that repel bullets, red boots, wings on her headdress – except, most notably, for a strip of loincloth that modestly drapes over her shiny skivvies. Like Wonder Woman, Darna has a human alter ego, though one that is more suited to her third-world origins: in contrast to her American counterpart's introverted middle-class Diana, Darna's alias Narda is a working-class cripple. Unlike Wonder Woman, who appeals only in fantastic adventure yarns, the Darna movies are decidedly multi-generic, supplementing the standard fantasy routine with horror (e.g. scary zombie chases, jousts with bloodsuckers), comedy (most notably when Darna goes on maternity leave and conscripts a middle-aged man to pinch for her), and social drama (e.g. almost every Darna film rehearsing a battle between the rich and the poor). Not only is Darna herself a hybrid figure, so also are many of her nemeses: the snake-maned Medusa knock-off named Valentina (whose turban and sleek dresses also recall Norma Desmond), the Hawk Woman, an evil female tree stump called Babaing Tuod, and a band of fashion models from outer space, among others. Finally, and quite ironically, many of the actors cast to play this quintessential Filipino superhero do not possess "native" Malay features but are instead, like many Filipino actors, racial hybrids.

Darna accentuates many aspects of Philippine cinema's hybridity that are either routinely derided by local critics for their colonialist predilections or, more normatively, taken for granted because they are so fully naturalized or deeply sedimented.[4] Both positions are, I think, untenable, especially in making sense of a film industry and culture that routinely produces films with English titles and Hollywood references and is thus positioned ambivalently in relation to Hollywood/dominant cinema on one hand, and to Filipino culture and aesthetics on the other. In the balance of this chapter, I will attempt to illuminate various aspects of contemporary Philippine cinema, in both its popular and artisanal modes, through a discussion of their hybrid configuration.

Hybridity I (Generic)

Hybridity is the key to understanding genres in contemporary Philippine cinema, for its generic staples are decidedly mixed: transgeneric or multi-generic. This preponderance of mixed genres evolved not only out of Filipino cultural hybridity but also as overcompensation for the ubiquity and strength of foreign films in the Philippine box office.[5] Consider, for instance, how the teen films of the 1980s battled foreign blockbusters such as the American "Brat Pack" films and sex comedies by packing a smorgasbord of genres, production numbers and set pieces into each film. Zombie chases, song-and-dance routines, melodramatic discoveries of illegitimacy or adoption, romantic interludes in soda fountains, bits of social drama about petty theft or with drug experimentation, comedic moments involving trickster housemaids or chauffeurs, fantasies of talking animals or native mythical figures reaching out to modern humans – these impossibly disparate elements could only be accommodated by using a multi-generic, hybrid form – a homegrown supergenre bred to face the Goliath of the Hollywood blockbuster. The picaresque 1980s teen film cycled relentlessly through genres as well as through contract players of varying degrees of popularity, in the process consolidating audiences for different film types and actors. Its expansive scope (and itinerant locations) evoked the vastness of national space while also celebrating the fecundity of Philippine cinema (and, by extension, the national imagination). The teen films of the last two decades, following changes in their Hollywood counterparts, feature fewer characters and more streamlined plots but remain, as ever, more hybrid and hyperbolic on different registers.

One may also use hybridity as a model for understanding the almost paradoxical co-existence of high melodrama with the hypermasculine fisticuffs and gunfights of the Filipino action film. Unlike the non-stop gunfire of Hollywood action films, the Filipino action film employs a greatly expanded melodramatic frame, frequently a biographical story or a fictive social drama, to surround its kinetic spectacles. Not only does melodrama – with its inevitable dénouement of redemption – rationalize the violence of action films to its "Christian" spectators (or more precisely, to self-righteous censors), it also creates a strong supplementary audience of female spectators who patronize its didactic and lachrymose pleasures. This mixed genre of the Filipino action film effectively creates a hybrid mode of spectatorship in which the logic and codes of action and melodrama are both fused and distinct, that carves its own niche and thus perpetuates its existence. Most recently, local action films have also upped the ante on sexual content, publicizing a lead actor's butt exposure and the leading lady's feelings of sexual violation during the shooting of a racy love scene.[6]

Generic hybridity may also be extended to an analysis of Filipino pornography. Like the action film, it employs a generic split in order to guarantee its legitimacy and wider appeal. In the case of the local porn flick, it is mostly comedy or melodrama that frame the sex scenes together, diffusing (while also heightening) the tension or titillation created by sexual displays with raunchy humor or with Catholic-inspired moralistic tales of fallen women and depraved men. Nested within this generic hybridity are several hybrid features, including the racial/national hybridity of female leads (a number of them are either Amerasians or Filipino-Americans, made suitable for baring by their "liberated" foreign upbringing or their desirable Caucasian features) and, as in the case of American porn, the hybridity of versions of each film (i.e., most films exist in more explicit versions which are shown illegally in the provinces or second-run theaters).

Hybridity II (Cultural)

But the hybridity of Philippine cinema is more than just a strategy for economic survival; it is also, in many ways, the result of the complex cultural practices that attend a postcolonial people's mode of existence. In the dizzying mix
of permutations, juxtapositions, and combinations that attend the hybridity of
Philippine cinema, one discerns the larger patterns of cultural negotiation that
operate within its system.

Consider, for instance, the cultural tactics of mimicry and appropriation at
work in contemporary Philippine film. The literary critic Homi Bhabha con-
ceptualizes mimicry as the often detrimental result of the colonizer's desire to
refashion the natives after his image through the institutions of colonial education and order. The natives' imitation of the colonizer gives the effect of a
distorted (and distorting) mirror, reflecting back to the colonizer an unflat-
tering and fractured image of himself.[7] A film such as Tony Y. Reyes's *Barbi:
Maid in the Philippines* (1989) draws our attention to the strategic and/or inci-
dental mockery generated by the gesture of imitation and to the dynamics of
its operation in Philippine cinema.[8]

Both the film's title and the way it is drawn in the poster are filched, with
impunity, from the popular Mattel doll. The film's premise – a straight guy
forced to pass for a woman in order to get a job – is lifted from the then-recent
Dustin Hoffman drag comedy, *Tootsie* (1982). But the film is nothing close to
a simple imitation of Hollywood. In fact, its wicked and fairly sophisticated
humor derives from its self-reflexive mimicry of Hollywood, from poking fun
at the practice of speaking the former colonizer's language, and from the liberating potential of playing American dress up.

The film's loose structure is strategic for an extended parodization of
Hollywood, the English language, and cultural impersonation. Its threadbare
plot follows the misadventures of a country bumpkin named Bartolome who
witnesses a fatal stabbing on his first day in the big city. He tries to aid the
victim by removing the weapon from the victim's chest but is instead charged
for the crime after being found with the knife. To flee persecution, he dresses
up as a woman, assumes the identity of Barbi Doll/Del Rosario and seeks a job
as a governess (a profession generally unheard of in the Philippines, save
perhaps for Julie Andrews's role in *The Sound of Music*). Barbi's job – his misadventures with the kids, their atrocious miseducation, his faux pas with
authority figures – and his cross-dressing create numerous opportunities for
stringing together a wide range of unrelated comedic episodes.

Much laughter is generated by the Filipino's incorrect and uncanny use of
the English language. Barbi's most fervent suitor, the Chaplinesque, few-
toothed security guard GI Joe (GI means "guard inside", as in stationed inside
the property), serves as the film's most reliable sources of malapropisms and

broken English. When he professes love, for instance, he does so in English: "Barbi, I loooove you." But when she replies, asking him to give her time, he replies eagerly by handing her his watch and saying in Filipino: "You want time? Here, you can have my time. You can have all the time you want!" In the same vein, one of the film's duo of heavies, named the Mario Brothers (after the Nintendo video game characters), reassures a prospective accomplice that their kidnap plot will be faultless: "Don't worry, attorney, you'll be happy after the kidnap. Don't worry, be happy."

Interestingly, some of the film's humor derives from moments in which the characters demonstrate their skill in using the language and acknowledge the same level of mastery from their audiences. Several times in the film, punnery is used adeptly. In one scene the pretty daughter of Bartolome's first boss introduces herself: "Don't call me Señorita Mercedes. Call me Mercy." Bartolome, aroused by the erotic pose struck by the boss's daughter, replies stammering: "Oh, God, have Mercy!" In one scene, Barbi, dismayed at the litany of duties being assigned by her employer, asks her rhetorically if the job description of a babysitter also included cleaning, cooking, and gardening. When her employer answers in the affirmative, Barbi, visibly irked, addresses the audience: "Tinanong ko pa kasi. [Why did I even ask?] Me and my big ..." He looks at his groin, but hesitates, and blurts out "Boobs!" instead.

The most dramatic (and comedic) proof of the characters' facility with the English language is shown in the film's musical production numbers in which they not only sing in English but expertly modify the lyrics of the songs to suit the situation. In one of these set pieces, the servants sing and dance a number, "I Enjoy Being a Maid," to the tune of a popular ditty from the Broadway musical and Hollywood film *Flower Drum Song*.

In Bhabha's concept of mimicry, even moments of seeming fidelity in the act of imitation are charged with the spirit of mockery. In *Barbi*, as Filipinos make fun of their inability to speak English properly, they also make fun of while having fun with the English language. The film's jokes assume the audience's mastery of the English language but they also denaturalize it, at times showing the absurdity of its usage. There is thus a gesture of celebration and mockery, of being both inside and outside the colonial language, evincing the kind of empowered in-betweenness or hybridity that Bhabha suggests. But the film's mimicry extends beyond the English language to Hollywood cinema itself: At the conclusion of one Hollywood-style musical production number set at a grocery, Barbi gratuitously imitates Marilyn Monroe's iconic skirt-blowing act in *The Seven Year Itch*, inviting the audience to laugh not only at his outrageous drag antics but also at his playful and uncanny impersonation of an American icon. So while *Barbi* uses English liberally and poaches shamelessly from Hollywood iconography, it also eschews uncritical and mechanical imitation, supplants the foreign originals, and reinforces a practice of Filipino spectatorship that engages the Filipino's unique configuration of cultural and cinematic references.

Appropriation, another common practice in Philippine culture and cinema, evokes the various strategies of taking possession and reallocation – wresting control, transformative absorption, the diversion of resources – usually involving unidirectional transactions between majority and minority cultures. Appropriation is much more complicated and confrontational than adaptation which, to use a hackneyed metaphor, evokes the transplantation of foreign elements into the receptive soil of native culture. Appropriation involves a gesture of violence: the forcible taking of a cultural object, the attendant process of subjugation and repurposing, and the object's resultant transformation (its radical incommensurability to the source).

To explain how a theory of appropriation may be evolved for Philippine cinema, let us take the case of *Dyesebel*, the iconographic Filipino mermaid since the 1950s with at least five films to her credit. Dyesebel's story is both radically similar to and different from Hans Christian Andersen's *The Little Mermaid*. Like Andersen's tale, the *Dyesebel* films, adapted from a graphic novel by Darna creator Mars Ravelo, are also about a mermaid who falls in love with a man and is later transformed by a sea hag into a human being. But quite unlike her Danish counterpart, Dyesebel is born to human parents. Since the sighting of a mermaid is traditionally interpreted in Filipino lore as a precipitant of bad luck, Dyesebel spends most of her youth in isolation, dwelling in her impoverished parents' seaside straw hut. In most film versions, she ends up as a side show attraction and, at some point after her temporary metamorphosis into a human being, figures in an ugly love triangle with her suitor's wannabe (in some versions, ex) girlfriend who eventually unmasks her literal hybridity (i.e., her "species climbing") in public. The rest of the tale, as well as the many details attending it, varies considerably from version to version. The remake from the late 1980s shows touches of the then recently shown Tom Hanks mermaid film *Splash* (1984), as when Dyesebel's suitor rescues her from a gigantic aquarium and carries her away in his arms. Some shots from the 1990s version – as when Dyesebel develops a crush for her man by seeing him up close in a dinghy – recall moments in Disney's animated feature, *The Little Mermaid* (1989). To be sure, the intertextual references to the American films are often encoded and decoded as citations, recognizing and building upon the Filipino spectators' fondness for their original sources. These appropriated "foreign" elements do not stick out, because they are not only governed by the *Dyesebel* supertext (i.e., the quintessential Filipino mermaid who has been around for ages) but are also blended into distinctly local elements. The story of the 1996 version, for instance, is underpinned by very timely Filipino concerns about the decimation of Dyesebel's world (i.e., Philippine marine life) through dynamite fishing and other unscrupulous practices. Even the snippets of English dialogue in the same version sound nothing but Filipino. Take, for example, the un-idiomatic dialogue accompanying the hissy fit thrown by Dyesebel's human nemesis when she confronts the mermaid and her man: "Come on, I know there's a saying that there are many fishes in the ocean [but] I didn't know that you'd catch the ultimate [fish]. Go ahead, you two hold hands and jump in the lake!"

So often and so differently has *Dyesebel* been retold and re-made that it is almost impossible to establish a comprehensive genealogy of influences upon it.[9] Equally important, the frequent rituals of reconstruction not only assert a claim to "lawful" appropriation – if not also of cannibalization – of Andersen's mermaid tale but also confer upon *Dyesebel* a patina and a title of national pos-session. The chain of referentiality that leads to the source has effectively been broken – eroded by time and its endless retelling. Moreover, within the context of Philippine cinema, *Dyesebel* successfully displaces both Anderson's tale and its American film adaptations, downgrading their status from the original and/or superior element to that of the peripheral, intertextual reference. Filipino audiences thus "read" Disney's *The Little Mermaid* and *Splash* in terms of the ever-popular *Dyesebel*, not the other way around. Moreover, when the American films were released, the Filipino mermaid continued to assert her preeminence by poaching from both of them with impunity and, by fol-lowing their releases with new remakes, further bolstered her box office appeal by mooching off the buzz generated by the foreign films. Appropriation is, therefore, in some ways even more subversive than mimicry or piracy because it inverts the traditional relationship of subservience between the typically foreign original and the native "copy." Proof positive is the fact that both *Dyesebel* and *Darna* have outlived and, in terms of cinematic outings, grossly outnumbered their foreign counterparts.

Appropriation is the most useful conceptual model in thinking about the sort of dispersed, anachronistic echoes of Hollywood and foreign cinemas that we find in such films as *Bituing Walang Ningning* (*Fading Star*) or in the plots and production numbers of teen films and musicals. These remnants and throwbacks remind us not only of the parallel history of foreign film con-sumption within national cinema formations but also of the industrial and aes-thetic ties between Philippine and foreign cinemas. Classical Hollywood Cinema remains an especially rich and significant source for appropriation because the moguls who revived the studio system in the late 1960s and 1970s were big fans of those films and had come of age in a postwar milieu deeply saturated with American popular culture.[10] The time lag that mediated these appropriations, to say nothing of the cross-cultural factors, engenders an attenuating effect that hastens their absorption into the vocabulary of Philippine cinema.

Art Cinema in the Philippines

Much of the scholarship on national cinemas, fueled by the dramatic but rare achievements of Italian Neo-realism, the French New Wave, and Japanese cinema, privileges art cinemas over the "debased" popular ones because of their assumed greater authenticity, enlightenment, or elevated quality.[11] Art films supposedly sustain the development of a uniquely national film language and engage in a more sophisticated and progressive expression of the nation's socio-political condition. While the latter is sometimes true – especially if one privileges both conscious and latent articulations – the former proposition is highly suspect, given that Filipino art films are highly derivative of European, American and, more recently, Asian art film models. Indeed, upon closer scrutiny, some of the nation's most valorized art films reveal obvious foreign debts. Ishmael Bernal's *Nunal sa Tubig* (*Speck in the Water*, 1976), a "naturalistic" (i.e., uneventful) observation of life and death in a small fishing village, is reminiscent of Luchino Visconti's *La Terra Trema* (1948). Laurice Guillen's *Salome* (1981), in which conflicting testimonies about a lover's killing reveal different perspectives on the film's titular murderess, boasts sumptuously photographed provincial locations but registers as an homage to Akira Kurosawa's *Rashomon* (1950). Gil Portes' *Munting Tinig* (*Small Voices*, 2003), the first Filipino art film to receive distribution from Sony Pictures Classics, looks as if it took its storyline about a children's choir in an impoverished school from a combination of Zhang Yimou's *Not One Less* (1999) and Stephen Herek's *Mr. Holland's Opus* (1995).

The dual address of art films – which are poised to speak to local audiences about their "true" condition but primarily in tropes and forms that are intelligible to and expected by international festival audiences (Rey Chow, borrowing from Mary Louise Pratt, calls this practice "autoethnography": postcolonial subjects "ethnographizing their own cultures" for others) – implants a hybridity of aesthetics and discourse at their core.[12] For instance, in the films of the late, much-missed Lino Brocka, one finds a complicated mix of gritty social realism and political activism co-existing with heightened melodrama which, in combination, read variably as metonym, allegory, and exposé. His landmark *Kapit sa Patalim: Bayan Ko* (*My Homeland: Gripping the Knife's Edge*, 1984), an action drama about a hard-up printing-press worker who robs his employers and takes them hostage, may be interpreted either as a macrocosm of Philippine life under Marcos, as a symbolic tale of the uphill battle against the Marcosian oligarchy, and as an indictment of the country's abysmal labor conditions. The filmmaker's allegiance to emotional excess – he made profitable melodramas on the side to sustain his art films – draws from a similar tendency in Italian neo-realism, effectively mounting a cogent critique of Marcosian Philippines that appeals to both foreign and local audiences while eschewing the distanced intellectual approach of the French New Wave or Latin America's progressive "Third Cinema."[13] Brocka's – and, by extension, Philippine art cinema's – typical predilection for the dense and often squalid visual field of Italian neo-realism may be interpreted as a negotiation between, on one hand, an attempt to inscribe Philippine social conditions into the cinematic *mise-en-scène* and, on the other, an accommodation of foreign art cinema's codes for rendering the Third World's impoverished, exoticized "other". Thus, in comparison to popular cinema, the hybridity of the art film, motivated as it is by an externally-oriented mendicantism, seems less progressive. Not only is the privileged audience of art cinema the international art-house audience (and the local cognoscenti weaned on foreign art films), it is also either foreign-funded or tailored to recoup its investment through its appeal to the international audience.

Consider Mel Chionglo's *Sibak: Midnight Dancers* (1994), one of the most successful art-house exports of Philippine cinema in the last decade. A follow-up to Lino Brocka's successful *Macho Dancer* (1988), Chionglo's film preserves Brocka's appealing combination of soft-core porn and social drama while considerably upping the ante on the incidence and centrality of sex.

The lone titular protagonist of *Macho Dancer* is multiplied in Chionglo's film to three stripper/prostitute brothers, each one representing a different physical type, personality, and sexual preferences. The film covers the brothers' exploits in and outside the bar, from their numerous stripping routines to their sexual transactions in the streets, making only the slightest effort to prop up the spectacular displays with functional plot points. Indeed, it is this logic of unraveling sexual plenitude – the successive and inexhaustible proffering of the fantasy of sexual availability – and not the theme of the brothers' eventual degeneration that truly structures the film.

The juxtaposition of sexual excess with material poverty intimates the film's ideal spectator: not the local gays who know better than to buy the film's insufferable clichés and who would only see the film's censored version anyway, but the foreign spectator who would derive maximum visibility and pleasure from the brown bodies on display and from the fantasy of their inexpensive accessibility. This explains why the film is nearly bereft of the conventional moralizing of local sex dramas. It is only at the very end of the film that the moral cost of the sibling callboys' sexual excesses is articulated. *Sibak*'s mercenary solicitation of the foreign spectator's lust paid dividends. Reportedly made because of a suggestion from an international festival programmer to cash in on the success of *Macho Dancer*, *Sibak*'s instant popularity among gay white men drew long, snaking lines at international and gay film festivals all over the world.[14] Like *Macho Dancer*, it paved the way for other art-house porn from the Philippines, including, most recently, *Burlesk King* (*Burlesque King*, 1999, also by Chionglo) which, along with the two other stripper films, were among the handful of American-released contemporary Filipino films on DVD by 2002.

The mendicantism of art films is further unmasked by the discourse of their publicity for international festivals. The censorship or banning of a film is worn as a badge of honor, almost always worded into the synopses of the festival programs. It functions to reassure the foreign art-house spectators that they are the privileged, enlightened, and critical audience of the films while simultaneously reifying the local audience's lack of access or "preparation" for the same work. In truth, producers of art-house films often knowingly shoot pictures that they know are incompatible with local exhibition standards in the hope that their film's artistic merits (or their loud appeals for freedom of expression) would warrant that rare special exemption from the local board of censors. Quite often, again as in the case of American pornography, two versions of the same film are generated, one for mass distribution (local audiences) and another for special audiences (the festival circuit).

The internationally oriented pandering of the art film becomes even clearer in cases of protest from local audiences or authority figures concerning the social or sexual representations of art films. Because the films are presumed to be tailored to the tastes of foreign spectators, some locals worry over the negative impressions they may generate or reinforce. Their response is often to strategically deny the accuracy of representations that are otherwise well accepted in the local context. While it is easy to fault local protesters for their repressive gestures, it is worth noting that the mendicant politics of art-house production overdetermine their response: if they say nothing, they consent to the reinforcement of stereotypes (some of them quite pernicious); if they say anything negative, they supply good copy for the film's success abroad.[15]

To be sure, many art films succeed in serving the best interests of the nation while catching the attention of foreign audiences. More often than not, art films evince an artistic and social vision that is more profound than garden-variety popular films. They are, however, no more authentically national, no purer, or no less hybrid than popular cinema.

What (then) is Philippine Cinema?

One might ask: While hybridity may be productive in understanding the configuration and sensibility of Philippine cinema as well as its position in relation to the local and global axes of culture, is it in and of itself a sufficient (or even desirable) sole descriptor of Philippine cinema?

The answer must be no. Hybridity characterizes many but not all aspects of Philippine cinema. Moreover, it presents a single and overdetermined perspective that does not always focus on the central qualities or issues within each film. Then and now one would be hard pressed to isolate or articulate what is uniquely national about Philippine cinema beyond its Filipino encoding – that is, its use of the national language, its evocation of Philippine culture and values, its employment of domestic locales, and the handiwork of Filipino artists and entertainment professionals, among others. Attempts have been made to define the "form" of Philippine cinema in terms of its similarities to traditional theatrical modes (e.g. vernacular melodramas, cloak-and-dagger plays) or to various forms of popular entertainment (e.g. the radio soap opera, the *komiks* or graphic novels), but the arguments they make about "national" specificity (e.g. that Filipino films share a high level of visual legibility with vernacular graphic novels or that they evince a staginess and a predilection for poetic dialogue that derives from Tagalog drama) speak of qualities that may also be found in early world cinema and classical Hollywood cinema.[16]

In truth, all national cinemas are hybrid. While they tell different stories that are staged in distinct, intricate worlds of their own, these films share a foundational narrative system that developed globally and that continues to change in the context of an international conversation (however unequal the participation and the terms may be). The acceptance of this universality does not occur under the banner of cultural imperialism, for the language of cinema is by no means proprietary to Hollywood. To embrace the hybridity of national cinemas is to adopt a perspective that is confident enough about the nation's cultural sovereignty to recognize contiguities where historiography traditionally sees divisions. To do so is also to reclaim the transnational formation of cinema from the global copyright of the American tradition while in some measure also resisting the romantic self-exoticizing tropes of national cinema. One might say that Philippine cinema's identity as national cinema emerges not from an essential national identity or from a uniquely national film language but from the specificity developed through the unique history and configuration of the local film culture's internal development and its responses to the global film culture and, indeed, to the transnational cultures that surround it.

Finally, thinking about Philippine cinema in terms of its many registers of hybridity may also be productive in understanding why the local film industry, though still one of the world's most prolific, is hitting a slump. From an average output of about 180 films in the 1970s and 140 films in the 1980s, local film production hit an alarming low of 89 pictures in 2001.[17] Various practical reasons are given, ranging from a weakened currency to a surge in video piracy, but more complex models are needed to account for such a dramatic change. In finding an answer, it might be productive to consider two aspects of hybridity. First, could it be that Filipino filmmakers are losing audiences to foreign films in part because they have failed to evolve a more dynamic relationship with them and with global culture – in other words, a complacency of sorts in tending to the strategic aspects of its hybridity? Given that hybridity engenders a symbiotic relationship to foreign cinemas and cultures, the balance between veering too close or too far away from the dominant cinema and global culture requires constant readjusting and, in a profound sense, re-imagination. It might be that the current crop of local films are too similar to Hollywood products and are thus doing long-term damage to the local audience base by eroding its own niche – or that a hybrid cinema's receptiveness to global culture is depleting the cultural differences upon which national cinemas thrive. A cursory survey of films from the last decade indicates, in my mind, a general lack of product differentiation between local and foreign offerings. Local films don't stand out because they are neither boldly different nor audaciously similar to foreign films; instead, a bland, unadventurous similarity prevails.

Yet another aspect of hybridity that may explain these changes is the industrial hybridity between Philippine film and television. With generally a single set of talents working for both industries – not to mention a common pool of financiers – television emerges not as a competition to national cinema but an extension of it. With support coming from advertising revenues from transnational capitalists and concessions for otherwise exorbitant above-the-line fees, Philippine television picks up the slack from the "ailing" film industry. Television projects are produced at a grossly accelerated pace, at a miniscule budgetary scale, and thus at a level of profitability that film productions simply cannot beat. Film actors, artisans, and technicians thus find themselves gainfully employed and quite a number of riskier film concepts are realized instead in made-for-TV movies called, appropriately enough, telesines. Rather than competition, the vibrant television industry serves, at least from the perspective of actors and technicians, as an additional venue for the redistribution of jobs and projects. The availability of stellar performers and projects on TV at practically no cost to the audience becomes an irresistible proposition to spectators.

For less fortunate Filipinos beaten and battered by the wages of transnational capital and the inequity of global commerce, Philippine cinema on television may just be the rational source and scale of entertainment.

CHAPTER 3

Vietnam: Chronicles of Old and New

Panivong Norindr

If *Gai Nhay* (*Bar Girls*), the 2003 blockbuster hit by director and co-scriptwriter Le Hoang, is a good barometer of the vitality of contemporary Vietnamese cinema, it also demonstrates that the Vietnamese film industry is undergoing a major and radical transformation. Le Hoang, Vu Ngoc Dang, and Phi Tien Son are members of a new wave of Vietnamese filmmakers who are reinvigorating the Vietnamese film industry with their films, *Gai Nhay* (*Bar Girls*), *Nhung Co Gai Chan Dai*) (*Long-Legged Girls*) and *Luoi Troi* (*Heaven's Net*), respectively. These young filmmakers are not only simply imitating Western ways of filming to insufflate new life to a struggling cinema, they are creating a viable commercial cinema eager to take on some of the most controversial topics in Vietnamese society, in a less moralistic and didactic fashion. The typical themes of war and its legacies and the struggle of poor people in the face of adversity, until now the mainstays of Vietnamese cinema, are being displaced by more entertaining if less edifying topics or reimagined to make them more compelling: nightclubs and the fashion industry are some of the new topoi of contemporary Vietnamese cinema. Sex and prostitution, drug abuse, HIV/AIDS, once only regarded as being unsuitable subject matters for the silver screen, unless they were part of a propaganda moral campaign, have now become appropriate subjects for contemporary Vietnamese cinema.

These radical changes in Vietnamese filmic practices have not occurred overnight. The transformation of the institutional film culture also needs to be examined in order to understand the reasons why film officials are gambling on these highly commercial films to save the embattled Vietnamese film industry. The impact of *doi moi*, or renovation policies, economic reforms introduced in 1986 at the Sixth Party Congress of the Vietnamese Communist Party, must be also be addressed for a more accurate assessment of the new filmic landscape in Vietnam. As the nation celebrated fifty years of filmmaking in 2003, the privileging of commercial cinema over auteur cinema must therefore be traced to both institutional and political changes as well as to some of these individuals' vision for a new cinema.

Let us begin with an assessment of the political and economic context that has brought on the gradual loosening of governmental control and led to the establishment of private studios in Vietnam. Until 2003, the Vietnamese government controlled all aspects of film production and distribution through its control of four major cinematic institutions, as follows.

First, the Cinema Department of the Ministry of Culture and Information (MCI) is the Institutional structure that grants film permits and authorization to film directors. It is also in charge of managing and allocating the funds budgeted by the Ministry of Culture and Information to film productions; and it is responsible for authorizing the distribution of Vietnamese films on both the domestic and foreign markets.

Second, FAFILM, a unit that reports directly to the Ministry of Culture and Information, is the exclusive exporter, importer, and distributor of Vietnamese and foreign films.

Third, the Institute of Cinematographic Art and Conservation, also under the patronage of the Ministry of Culture and Information, is in charge of collecting and archiving all films produced by Vietnamese film studios. It boasts a collection of about 80,000 reels.

Fourth, the Vietnam Cinema Association is the professional organization that brings together Vietnamese cinema's professionals around screenings, debates, and film festivals. It was founded by President Ho Chi Minh, who signed the Decree on Founding the National Agency of Cinema and Photography on 15 March 1953.[1]

Until very recently then, all film scripts needed to be submitted to the Vietnamese Board of Censorship for approval, a difficult process because, according to Richard Phillips, "Governmental officials still regarded film as a propaganda tool, rejecting script that attempted to critically examine social relations or mildly criticized the government." Months if not years would pass before an authorization could be granted. But many scripts were deemed "inappropriate" for a number of reasons or pretexts. Even if a script is approved, it still faces the often insurmountable question of financing. And there are many other technical obstacles to film completion.

Vietnamese filmmakers have to rely on poorly financed state studios that lack even some of the most rudimentary film equipment to shoot. In 2002, there were a total of twenty-six cinema studios in all of Vietnam, but currently only twelve are actively engaged in producing films.[2] All of them were subsidized by the Ministry of Culture and Information. Some of the most important ones are the Fiction Studio (400 films in forty years), the Documentary and Scientific Film Studio, the Animated Film Studio (Hanoi), and the Giai Phong Studio in Ho Chi Minh City. Until very recently, the majority of Vietnamese films were financed by the State. Because self-reliance is now being touted as the "official" modus operandi, it is only a matter of time when full-fledged privately held studios will no longer be required to work with state-sanctioned studios as co-producers.

Although this opening up trend bodes well for the future of Vietnamese cinema, the Vietnamese film industry is still facing incredible challenges. How can films produced with miniscule budget and filmed with antiquated equipment under these extremely difficult conditions achieve the same type of technical mastery that film viewers expect today? In spite of these material conditions, a few Vietnamese filmmakers have succeeded in producing truly remarkable films that have garnered critical accolades in international film festivals around the world. Viet Linh and Dang Nhat Minh are two filmmakers who have made memorable films that do not simply emulate the cinemas of old Cold War rivals, they have created a distinctive autochthonous Vietnamese cinema that has yet to find a large audience at home.

This type of auteur cinema has not found the domestic audience it deserves, in part because of the limited screening venues that welcome such unpopular art film "genre." These films do not attract movie-goers who prefer the special effects-laden Hollywood blockbusters and fast-paced Hong Kong action films imported and screened in Vietnamese movie theaters, or widely available on pirated videos and DVDs. This new generation of Vietnamese spectators, who have never experienced war, are turned off by didactic and poorly made state-sponsored Vietnamese films that hark back to the basic two themes of the war and the resilience of the people – peasants, the poor, etc. – who face hardship with dignity. Certainly, these types of propagandist movie no longer find a captive audience today, because these films are not very different from the cheaply made-for-TV series and movies that address the same war themes that can be seen on television for free.

In Vietnam, the weight of the omnipotent institutional cinematic apparatus has been, without a doubt, detrimental to filmic innovations and change. But before passing judgment too rapidly, it may be well advised to consider the extraordinary historical circumstances that have led the state to become the main patron of the filmic art in Vietnam and, over the years, to consolidate the film industry as a state monopoly. In addition, the importance of film history has yet to be taught seriously, not simply as part of the nation's Socialist propagandist agenda, but as an integral part of how the nation of Vietnam came to exist after its liberation from French colonialism, only to be divided after the fall of Dien Bien Phu in 1954 and finally reunified in 1975 after the Vietnamese victory over American imperialism. The stakes are indeed very high because historical and cultural memory is in danger of being forgotten or erased. Fortunately, the existence of a recent documentary film such as *Gao Rang (Grilled Rice)* by Claude Grunspan makes forgetting a much more difficult proposition, in part, because it identifies the origins of Vietnamese cinema as being in war documentaries shot by Vietnamese camera operators during the French Indochinese War (1945–1954). These men's testimonials shed light on an important, if heretofore neglected, cinematic history.

The history of Vietnamese cinema can, of course, be narrated from a number of perspectives or vantage points. The most common approach, widely adopted by both Vietnamese and Western critics, has been to provide a linear chronology of Vietnamese film production during the momentous events of Vietnamese history. In such a conception of Vietnamese film history, a close parallel between Vietnamese cinema and Vietnamese history is established, which also defines the four historical periods that shaped the history of the modern nation of Vietnam: cinema under the French colonization (until 1945), the revolutionary cinema during the decolonization and liberation struggle (1945–1954), the struggle for reunification (1954–1975), and cinema of the reconstruction (1975–today). The logic and transparent intelligibility in this type of typology certainly makes sense, especially when we know that the emergence of cinema coincided with the heyday of colonialism. It should therefore not come as a great surprise to learn that early cinema was unabashedly exploited by the French to promote colonialism in French Indochina and the rest of the French colonial empire.[3] At Ho Chi Minh's urging, the Vietnamese would adopt the same strategy and make effective use of cinema as a state propaganda apparatus. In her film, Grunspan tells a crucial chapter in Vietnamese film history by seeking out the testimonials of the surviving pioneers of Vietnamese cinema. Their accounts of the modest beginning of Vietnamese cinema during the French Indochinese war illuminates the desire of these men to fight, during the decolonization period, for their nation's autonomy. Eager to use some of the most advanced techniques of mechanical reproduction (photography) and cinema, or animated images (*hat bong*), they recorded historic pictures of the liberation struggle. They believed that they could further the cause of the resistance fighters by showing these moving images directly to the people of Vietnam, with the hope of enlisting them to the cause of freedom. Their work problematizes the effort and success of patriotic institutional propaganda, and sheds light, at the same time, on individual commitment and resourcefulness (perhaps too commonly recuperated by the Communist apparatus for the good of the collective) who labored under extreme material conditions.

Baptism By Fire or The Revolutionary Cinema, 1945–1954: The Struggle for Independence

Documentary war films contributed, in important if unacknowledged ways, to the creation of an incipient national Vietnamese cinema. During the French Indochinese War, these once anonymous camera operators, who had only a rudimentary knowledge of the formal language of cinema, trained on the job

– that is, they learned on the battlefield. Thanks to the documentary *Gao Rang* (*Grilled Rice*) the importance of the work of these camera operators is becoming better known in the West. Two figures, in particular, are presented as having played a crucial role in inaugurating Vietnamese revolutionary cinema: Mai Loc and Khuong Mê, from the city of Saigon.

Ho Chi Minh had proclaimed Vietnam's independence on 2 September 1945. But on the 23 September, the French reestablished their dominion over Indochina after the French army seized Saigon. Ho Chi Minh called upon all patriots to fight the French and resist, with whatever means available to them, urging them to leave cities to enter the maquis. Khuong Mê answered his call and fled the city to join the revolutionary ranks as a photographer, shooting battle scenes and scenes of everyday life from 1945 until 1947. Mai Loc, like Khong Mê, also began as a photographer. Both of these men understood very well the force of the animated image (*hat bong*) that made more of an impression on the rural population and the resistance fighters of the Mekong Delta than still photographs. In spite of their lack of experience, they persevered and revealed that they had filmed many battles, among them those of Moc Hoa and Tai Bac, for newsreel and propaganda films, developing them in a makeshift, clandestine laboratory.

In 1948, the very first camera used by Mr Mê arrived from France. Khuong Mê would go on to shoot the first "générique" (credits) in Vietnamese film history, a short film conceived to honor and recognize the contributions of the Vietnamese National Guard. As a member of the cinema crew of the 8th zone, he conceived of the image of a soldier holding a gun morphing into a soldier holding a camera. The image of the cameraman soldier is said to have been inspired by the French films he saw in Saigon when he was a young man. (Khuong Mê was the object of another, fascinating documentary, Samuel Aubin's 2003 film *La Chambre noire de Khuong Mê* [*Khuong Mê's Darkroom*].)

Like many of his peers, Ngoc Quynh enlisted at a very young age. He joined the People's Army cinematographic unit at sixteen. In 1954, he was drafted into the cinema crew in charge of following the historic battle of Dien Bien Phu. Because so little actual footage was shot or survived, the film *Dien Bien Phu* is but an reenactment of the famous battle that ended the French colonial presence in Southeast Asia.

During the Vietnam War, the filmmakers had better film equipment, and had learnt many tricks of the trade. Consequently, they were able to get much better actual footage that could be edited into a much more compelling film. Ngoc Quynh was now part of an 8-person crew. He and his colleagues were shooting one of the bloodiest battles of the war, Vinh Linh, on the seventeenth parallel, with four 35mm cameras, and one 16mm Bell & Howell camera. These men were now also better informed on the current operations so that they could plan their shots, and film many of the men who would not survive the battle, in the best possible light. Assembling these cameramen together would facilitate the capture of battle scenes and the bombing raids of the American aviation, at all times of the day and night. Even though 5,000 meters of film were lost during a bombardment, Ngoc Quynh succeeded in cobbling together a film that is considered a masterpiece of its genre, *The Vinh Linh Steel Rampart* (1970).

Lo Van Minh's experience during the Vietnam War earned him the reputation as being one of the best cameramen of the Anti-American war. He trained in Moscow at the National Institute for Cinema (VGIK), from 1972 until the fall of Saigon, and is today an Assistant Director of the National Hanoi Cinema School. The short footage he captured of the battle scene over Hanoi fails to reproduce both the intensity of the American air raid and the material difficulty in getting the shot. Another wartime filmmaker, Tran Van Thuy, works today in the Hanoi Documentary Studio. Between 1966 and 1969, he was a cameraman/reporter in the South of the seventeenth parallel.

Gao Rang (*Grilled Rice*) chronicles the history of Vietnamese documentary filmmakers during the French-Indochinese War and American Vietnam War, by highlighting not only the central role played by the documentary filmmakers in Vietnamese cinema history, but also by giving voice to the filmmakers who survived the bombings and the wars. The title of the film refers to the rice these soldiers/cameramen saved from their meager ration grilled and used as drying agent to keep their film stock from rotting and their camera from rusting.

These Vietnamese war reporters shared the life of embattled soldiers. They left for long period of time, to film under extreme conditions, with only a few minutes of film stock to capture the shelling and the close-range combat. Many of these filmmakers did not survive the wars. Many lost their lives during combat and their footage disappeared with them. It is therefore incumbent upon us to hear the voice of these filmmakers to supplement the loss of their images.

Vietnamese Cinema in Crisis?

The films of Vietnamese filmmakers showcased at international film festivals constitute a small fraction of the film production in Vietnam. They represent, arguably, some of the most original and innovative films Vietnam has to offer, and do not reflect the dire state of Vietnamese cinema as a whole. Films by such directors as Dang Nhat Minh or Viet Linh, one of the rare woman directors working today in Vietnam, fail to tell the story of the entire Vietnamese industry and the difficulties it has encountered on many fronts, from production to distribution, and even exhibition.

Since 1990, fewer people go to the movies. Some estimate the decline in audience attendance as high as 80 percent. Many factors have contributed to this dramatic plunge. The changing demography of Vietnam's population is an important, if unheralded, factor. More than half of the country's population is under the age of twenty-five, which means that most of them have never really experienced war directly, and have known (more or less) a nation at peace. Government-subsidized Vietnamese films were regarded as dealing mainly with war and nationalistic themes, providing a serious critique of society's mores and culture. These films are didactic and edifying movies but are seen as having very little entertainment value, which certainly did not appeal to the taste of young Vietnamese movie-goers.

Because Vietnam has been unable to meet their entertainment needs, they have found other means (if not always legal) to watch films that did, mainly action-film exports from Hong Kong.[4] The ubiquity of the video players in Vietnamese homes and availability of pirated videos cut into the movie industry business. Moreover, the average run for a domestic film lasts only a week (whereas foreign films like *Shakespeare in Love* played for weeks on end. As a ticket-booth attendant at Thang Tam, Hanoi's oldest movie theater, says, "People don't come to movie theaters to see Vietnamese productions. For that, they'd rather stay home.")

Today, pirated cassette videos are being replaced by bootleg video disks, as another important source of entertainment. In order to maximize production house revenues, the standard international film-industry practice is that films are first distributed to theaters, later released on video, and lastly, broadcast on television. But in Vietnam, this staggered release strategy is being short-circuited by the thriving black-market trade in pirated movies for which there are no estimates available, and the availability of films on DVDs shortly after (and even on the very day of) their release in theaters. The price of a movie ticket is also quite a deterrent. Many workers such as street vendors, whose daily income does not exceed 7,000 VND, could hardly afford the price of a movie ticket.[5]

The Development of the Film and Movie Theater Industries

In Vietnam more modern exhibition venues are being created in order to lure movie-goers back to the cinema, which saw a sharp decline, in the 1990s. Out of eighty cinemas the French Embassy study has surveyed, only twenty of them project 35mm films on a regular basis, with the rest specializing in video projection. Nationwide, there are only a handful still operating. In Ho Chi Minh City, the city's biggest film distributor Ho Chi Minh City Film found success in converting existing old movie theaters into modern "luxurious, modern entertainment facilities," which, according to the company's deputy director Nguyen Van Thi, improved the company's revenues in 2001 and 2002 by 30%. And in 2003, the company opened its newest cinema complex, one of the first multiplex screens in Vietnam. These co-ventures are much needed as the nation is strapped for hard currencies. Such pioneering developments provide only very limited scope for film distribution in theaters. But, as has been noted quite ominously by the US Department of Commerce, "Vietnam may be decades away from being a viable market for national film release."

It can be argued that with an increase in artistic freedom and liberties, a new generation of Vietnamese filmmakers seems to be rejecting the type of art and essay cinema of auteurs such as Dang Nhat Minh, and embracing a more commercial cinema that is catering to the sensibility of a young, more affluent urban audience whose members have, heretofore, kept away from domestic films that they find too didactic and deemed as having very little entertainment value.[6]

Several important factors have contributed to make Vietnamese commercial cinema more conspicuous/visible. The Vietnamese government seems to have loosened its grip. In 2000, Tran The Dan, Deputy General Director of the Vietnam Cinema Department of the Ministry of Culture and Information, declared the following: "At present, the Vietnamese movie industry has to learn how to rely on itself, in an open market economy. It has to build its own means of survival, without entirely depending on the state's grants. It is not a tool of propaganda anymore, but simply a means of entertainment. Yet, Vietnamese movies have to try to preserve Vietnam's cultural identity, its moral, familial and traditional values ..."[7]

New privately-funded film companies like the Thien Ngan Company have been allowed to raise private funds to produce films like the 2004 hit *Nhung Co Gai Chan Dai* (*Long-Legged Girls*). The authorities strongly believe that the future of Vietnam's film industry lies in the hands of young filmmakers who are committed to "make more entertaining and commercial movies [as] the best way to support the domestic film industry."[8] These young filmmakers have already won awards in new competitions such as the National Short Film Competition, an event designed to showcase and recognize emerging talent and identify promising new directors. The first-prize monetary award of VND 20 million ($1,300) may seem rather a minute amount in the West. Comparatively, a veteran filmmaker like Dang Nhat Minh's latest feature film, *The Season of Guavas*, was filmed for a mere $70,000, a budget that, of course, does not take into account the three-month post-production required to edit the film in a French studio. Similarly, the entire budget for Viet Linh's *Collective Flat*, in the words of the director, "was ridiculous. It wasn't even $200,000" which she compared to the $3 million for Toni Bui's *Three Seasons* (1999),[9] an American produced film shot in Vietnam, which was considered very low, for an American film. In an age of globalization, diasporic Vietnamese filmmakers and "postcolonial" Vietnamese cinema remain important cultural questions.

New Again: Vietnamese Cinema from 1986 to the Present Day

The conception of cinema as a propaganda tool is being challenged by a new generation of film directors who regard cinema as a popular form of mass entertainment. Their ambition is to rival the best that Asia has to offer and emulate the type of professionalism that has made Hong Kong, Taiwan, and more recently, Thai cinema, vibrant and at the same time very successful, domestically and beyond. They have embraced the ethos of Hollywood cinema that makes entertainment its central tenet, and have dramatically changed the look of contemporary Vietnamese cinema, its aesthetic. "Commercial cinema is a new type of motion picture in Viet Nam," said Vu Nugoc Dang, the director of the current blockbuster, *Nhung Co Gai Chan Dai* (*Long-Legged Girls*), "…I am a young director and must make the domestic film industry more professional."[10] In order to do so, he has fully embraced the so-called "commercialism" of the new Vietnamese cinema he is helping to create, by responding to his detractors that commercial cinema can also be an art.

Like many Vietnamese directors, Dang laments the fact that it is hard to find in Vietnam professionally trained technicians and film professionals. But Dang is ready to "assume total responsibility" for his films and is adamant about not shifting "blame to others" even if it means failure. To renew Vietnamese cinema, he has experimented with many new ways of filming and directing, emphasizing improvisational acting.

Another contemporary filmmaker Le Hoang's *Gay Nhay* (*Bar Girls*) broke all kinds of box office records and became the highest grossing film in Vietnamese film history, taking in more than a million dollars in the four months between its release in February 2003 and May. The success of *Gay Nhay* (*Bar Girls*) can be attributed to a number of critical factors. Its turn away from the didactic heavy-handedness of socialist realist films with its predictable concerns for a better society and its ambition to inculcate important life lessons to its audience coincided with the desire of young movie-goers to be entertained. They make up a large percentage of the Vietnamese population and have not experienced the ravages of war first hand, and merely want to be entertained.

Set in the nightclubs and slums of Ho Chi Minh City, *Bar Girls* focuses on the trials and tribulations of young and beautiful working girls, nightclub workers whose dream of improving their life leads to prostitution, heroin addiction, and incurable diseases like AIDS. The film's anti-drug message that followed the Communist Party's line against social evils appealed to censors who authorized its release to huge popular acclaim. The popular success of this film (and others of its type) may be attributed to themes that appeal to the concerns of its young viewers: the consequences of the debauched nightlife which may lead to drug addiction, sexually transmitted diseases like aids, and death. Although the film appears to adhere to the Communist Party's moral values, the sight of scantily clad women, dancing provocatively to make the men consume more liquor contributes to the visual pleasure experienced by the spectators. But it is quickly undermined by the underside, the less glamorous reality of night life, away from the atmosphere of the glitzy, discothèque scenes, filled with laser light and thumping music, where young Vietnamese men and women dance the night away. But one of the first dark scenes invades this perception. The brightly lit women's bathroom is a stark contrast to the artificial world of light and sound. In that unhygienic space, the working girls can be seen in their true light; they are taking a break, resting their tired bodies, smoking, playing cards, with debris littering the floor. Others are reapplying makeup. Fights erupt, and some of the girls get sick. A fresh kind of realism is thus achieved, one that owes as much to the type of acting required of this new breed of actors. The "bar girl" throws up in front the camera, and, exemplifying innovative ways of filming (at least in Vietnam), the camera has been placed in the toilet bowl. This chaotic atmosphere is made all the more frantic by the night club owner's eruption onto the scene, and his pushing the women out from the bathroom to force them to return to work. Although his actions have made the viewers identify him immediately as the film's villain, his blurred gender identity also singles him out for vilification as his mannerisms reveal effeminacy and questionable masculinity. Furthermore, as the film unfolds, the spectators discover that he is the one who provides many of these working girls with the heroin, in order to have complete control over them.

Of course, if there is a villain you must have a hero, in this case a heroine, in the figure of a young woman investigative reporter who wants to write a report of these bar girls' life. Naively she enters that world and even takes a snapshot of these women before she is forcefully removed from the premises by the bouncers. Undeterred, she returns completely transfigured. She goes undercover by wearing a slinky dress, heavy makeup, and sporting a new hairdo to blend into the crowd. Unfortunately, she is recognized by the bar girls as the journalist who had tried to interview them earlier, and they befriend her in order to teach her a lesson. After closing, they go on a wild ride of the city, and return to their dark slums, but not before severely beating the journalist, in a dark alley. The sight of the beaten journalist crawling on the pavement reinforces the type of realism that the filmmaker is trying to achieve, and the rest of the story is the journalist's attempt to find these women, not to turn them in to the police, but to tell their unadulterated story.

In a later scene, the three bar girls are seen cavorting on the beach, in a fancy seaside resort. Inside the hotel room, a man offers one of our heroines to pay for her sexual favors in US dollars. She takes them, only to use them to light her joint, as if to show that she can't be bought. But her drug addiction is too severe. She wanders the beach at night, to try to find the drug she needs for a fix, and stumbles upon a group of men who are willing sell it to her on the condition that she has sex with all three of them. In one of the most graphic scenes in Vietnamese film history, the men undress and violate her. She is found the next morning, passed out on the beach, by schoolgirls and their teacher who lend her a change of clothes. She reappears in a traditional, immaculate, white *ao sai* dress, in a beautiful lit shot. As she emerges from the tent where she changed, the virginal transformation seems complete as the camera follows her, cavorting with the children on the beach, in a scene perhaps too sentimental for Western viewers.

This innocence regained, however, is short-lived. When she returns to her hotel room, in an aggressive state of withdrawal, she needs a fix, shoots herself with heroin, and dies of an overdose, alone, a painful death captured on camera. Her death triggers another death when the club owner/pimp/drug dealer meets his death at the hands of her two girlfriends. The film ends as it began, at the hotel site where an international conference for the prevention of HIV/AIDS has been meeting. This time, it is not a high government official who is addressing convention members, but one of the bar girls who viewers thought had, in most likelihood, perished in an accident. She speaks before the assembled government officials, Western guests, journalists and cameramen, in order to tell her emblematic, personal story, so that the truth can be told. Of course, we are in the realm of filmic truth, but it certainly resonated with spectators fed up by unreliable official discourse. We are now in a better position to evaluate the popular success of *Bar Girls*, which transcends the mere visual inscription of sex scenes and drug-related deaths on screen. Its unsettling effect on the viewers can be traced to an old Vietnamese form of reportage that emerged in journalistic writings in the 1930s. The film's plot thematized the requirements of the genre perfectly since *Bar Girls* is also the story of the investigative journalist who goes undercover in order to write the most accurate account of the life of these working girls (the realism of the genre) by providing a first-hand account of their life with them. The vogue of the reportage (*phong su*), which, according to a critic, had been neglected during the Revolutionary period, has seen a resurgence in interest in recent years, which is interpreted "as a response to the rapid, if still spotty, urban change that has followed the 'renovation' of public policy that was first announced in December 1986"[11] which in effect means, "the integration with the world's capitalist economy."[12] The social and economic impact of this integration on the global economy is an important subtext of *Bar Girls*. In fact, the first few words heard on the soundtrack of the film are American English words, uttered by one of the bar girls who greets a group of Vietnamese men after she puts herself on display, dancing in a provocative fashion. It is also not an accident that in one of the panning shots in the discothèque, we can distinctly see Westerners dancing with Vietnamese women. The film seems to suggest that the attendant effects and deleterious consequences of the country's rapid opening to a market economy also encourage the type of sexual tourism readily made available to both Viet Kieu (Overseas Vietnamese) and American businessmen, now that the country has been opened to a market economy for almost two decades. Of course, the film never fully articulates nor does it develop this critique in a sustained fashion. It is at its most explicit when one of the bar girls burns the almighty dollar bills rather than surrendering herself sexually.

One of the most interesting aspects of this film is its representation of traditional Vietnamese femininity, which clashes with Western-dressed, high-heeled working girls who are performing their modern sexuality in the space of the night club. Outside this public space, they return to a more traditional domestic sphere, tending to the needs of infants or young children. More problematic, however, is the portrait of the club owner, as the villain in the film, as an effeminate and manipulative gay man who only wants to control and exploit the working girls for economic profit, oblivious to the tragic consequences of his actions. This film also blurs, in interesting ways, the fiction/documentary divide. It relies, at times, on hand-held camera work to capture in a documentary-like footage the vicissitudes of the life of these women. What led these women to work as bar girls? The viewers discover, little by little, the banality of their lives. Lured by the appeal of modern luxurious living, these beautiful single women yearn for social mobility to escape their impoverished condition as exploited women who provide for their young children and family.

Curiously then, we have traced a genealogy and found a certain coherence in the war reportage and didactic propaganda of the revolutionary period and the newest trends in Vietnamese commercial cinema. Fifty years may separate these two "genres," but they share the same goals of being able to document and chronicle, in a realistic fashion, the life and death of the people of Vietnam, by providing insights into the everyday practices of these men and women.

Onward

After having suffered, in the 1990s, a dramatic decrease in cinema attendance, contemporary Vietnamese cinema in this new millennium is making a comeback. This renewed interest in domestic production can be attributed to, as we have sketched out, many factors. An entire generation of Vietnamese has never known the hardships of war. It has been thirty years since the reunification of the country in 1975, and the historical memories of the French Indochinese

War and the American Vietnam War seem to be fading. Cinema as a state propaganda apparatus used to disseminate the ethos of a Socialist society no longer resonates with the desires of young audiences whose scopophilic pleasure is firmly entrenched in special effects-packed action films, and more technologically advanced films. This radical shift away from a socialist realism aesthetic that had defined the cinema of earlier generations can be attributed to market-driven, liberal economic policies introduced by *doi moi*. They have enabled the creation of privately owned production companies especially in Ho Chi Minh City, which privately funded these new commercial films, and contributed to accelerate the pace of change. The question is of course whether members of this new wave of Vietnamese filmmakers, who have been emboldened to imagine new ways of filming and who reject the socialist realism aesthetic of earlier generations, will continue to raise important questions about contemporary life in Vietnam. Not everyone is convinced. Auteurs and traditionalists regard commercial Vietnamese cinema as mere rubbish. We are, I would suggest, at a crucial juncture in Vietnamese cinema, where the sentimental, propagandist films of the pre-*doi moi* era, which never found a large and receptive audience among young Vietnamese movie-goers, is not only on the wane, but more importantly, being replaced by more commercial, popular, edgy films. One can only hope for the vitality of a new and pluralist Vietnamese film culture.

CHAPTER 4

Thailand: Revival in an Age of Globalization

Anchalee Chaiworaporn and Adam Knee

As mentioned in the first chapter of this book, Thailand (whose name means "Land of the Free") is uniquely positioned as the only nation in Southeast Asia never to be colonized by a Western power. However, the predominantly Buddhist country formerly called Siam has had a long history of complex cultural, economic, and military interactions with the West and its neighbors. In the face of globalization and in the wake of economic crisis and recovery, contemporary cinema in Thailand has emphasized aspects of Thai identity.

Setting the Scene

Although Thai filmmaking had a substantial lull in the mid-1990s, it has actually experienced a relative boom since 1997 (the year of the Asian economic crisis), with production picking up markedly over the course of a few years (from little more than two dozen features in 1997 to an estimated sixty in 2003) and Thai films generating significant interest at international film festivals. In a book on popular cinema it needs to be indicated that those Thai films receiving worldwide attention for their innovations are often not the ones achieving success with popular audiences back in Thailand; Thai audiences have often tended to stay away from some of the more formally challenging and/or socially engaged kinds of work represented on the festival circuit. And yet Thais have not been able to ignore the level of attention and acclaim some of these films have been receiving since 1997, a novel phenomenon that has indeed been helping generate popular local interest in the local product.[1]

To put the new "boom" into perspective, it should be noted that the current level of production is not near that of the 1970s and 1980s, when there would regularly be more than 100 features produced per year. This era of filmmaking was characterized, moreover, by a substantial number of "social problem" films from a number of politically engaged filmmakers, which particularly found an audience within an increasingly educated urban population and, in a handful of instances, attracted international attention. By the early 1990s, however, local production had begun to sink significantly (from 113 titles in 1990 to 64 in 1993) – in part owing to competition from video – and also to shift more toward teen-oriented projects in response to a number of major teen successes in the 1980s.[2]

The popularity of teen flicks continued to rise in the early 1990s when *Kling Wai Kon Phor Son Wai* (Somjing Srisuphab, 1990) broke all records for the Thai box-office in 1991. However, there was still room for other genres in both studio and independent production. The early 1990s independents were quite diverse, ranging from quality productions from well-established directors and producers (for example, director Cherd Songsri at Cherdchai Productions, director Prince Chatrichalerm Yukol with Phrommitr Productions, and producer Charin Nantanakorn of Nantanakorn Productions) to cheaply and quickly made B-grade works from more amateur directors, aimed directly for second-run theaters or provincial audiences. These latter works in fact comprised more than half of annual production and usually fell into the popular genres of horror, slapstick, drama, or action. In many instances, stories were taken from popular TV series and production rushed for completion in order to reach second-run theaters before the end of the series.

However, all kinds of production were disrupted by the launch of the first multiplexes in 1994, which occurred after the government bowed to pressure to reduce the film import tax regulation (imposed in 1976) from thirty Thai baht (US$1.20) to ten baht (US$ 0.40) for every meter of footage imported. These were so successful that by 2003, there were around 300 multiplexes in Bangkok alone. Hollywood blockbusters in particular benefited from this development, taking the majority of screens and total grosses. From 78 titles in distribution in 1991, their number rose to 223 in 1999. Thai films, on the other hand, as noted earlier began to dramatically drop from the level of 107 films at the start of the decade – eventually reaching as low as nine films in 1999.[3] B-grade productions were the first to be affected by the flood of Hollywood films: with an abundance of available titles, regional Thai distributors (those concentrating on provinces *outside* Bangkok) opted for Hollywood action films with better production values than those of the local product. Hong Kong movies likewise should have gained an advantage from the reduced import tax, but that industry was experiencing a dramatic decline in the early 1990s and hence was in no position to reap potential benefits.

Initially, some Thai movies also had a share of the pie, achieving unprecedented takings at the box office. Before 1994, only a few Thai titles could take in as much as US$1 million. Now, however, the releases of two record companies newly involved in film production – RS Promotion and Grammy Entertainment – surpassed this figure (RS's 1995 *Romantic Blue* with US$2 million and Grammy's film from the same year, *Sunset at Chaophraya*, with US $1.8 million). Both groups were already involved in media production and popular music, a fact which, not surprisingly, fostered a certain synergy among media products – in particular those aimed at teens. Singers were cast in movies and television series; actors released music albums. Many of the films were stylistically indebted to music video, and offered teen-oriented drama, comedy, or adventure plots.

Despite the precipitous rise in the number of screens in the mid-1990s, the production industry had become a virtual monopoly, with a handful of the more powerful companies having combined interests in (and thereby wielding considerable influence over) production, distribution, and exhibition. Under these conditions, independent production could not flourish. Veteran directors like Cherd Songsri and Bandit Ritthakol delayed their projects. At the same time, no fledging directors in Thailand were able to rise without making a deal with one of the established studios, and these studios were not particularly inclined to make such deals. Asia's sudden economic downturn in the middle of 1997 (of which Thailand's devaluation of the baht was the flash point) would have appeared to extinguish any hope of fresh energy infusing Thai film production. Ironically, however, it was precisely at this point that Thai cinema experienced the start of its new upswing.

1997: Film Culture Revives

In the early months of 1997, the industry was shaken up by the arrival of two unknown directors who had crossed over from work in television advertising, Penek Ratanaruang and Nonzee Nimitbutr. Penek startled the Thai film world when his directorial debut, the quirky contemporary drama *Fun Bar Karaoke*, premiered in Berlin – and he thus became an overnight success.[4] While *Fun Bar Karaoke* was waiting for local release, the industry also welcomed fellow newcomer Nonzee, whose nostalgic directorial debut *Dang Bireley and the Young Gangsters* was a huge hit with Thai audiences across generations and not surprisingly broke all-time Thai box office records. And near the year's end, yet another new director from the Thai advertising industry, Hong Kong-born Oxide Pang, entered the field with *Who Is Running?*

This is not to claim that there was suddenly a clear-cut "new Thai cinema" movement at that moment. Some notice of the new activity in production was taken by the Thai press, but this small beginning was not enough to immediately generate broad Thai interest in local production or new filmmaking styles; and, moreover, the continuing effects of the economic downturn (which were to be felt for years) meant that producers were inclined to be cautious – and that there was not much spare cash around for investment in any event.

The new energy in Thai film production did nevertheless gain momentum over the ensuing years, this development fed by a boost in Thai film culture more broadly (both mainstream and alternative, foreign and domestic) that got under way around the same time. For example, prior to 1997, there were only a few cultural institutes that provided opportunities for the public to appreciate film culture outside the mainstream. But this dearth of film activity unexpectedly and markedly began to change in 1997. In April, the first Art Film Festival was arranged by private organizations to showcase the works of Thai film and arts students who had gone to study abroad; this festival marked the first Thai showing of the work of Apichatpong Weerasethakul – now a major figure in the Thai independent film scene. In August, the first Thai Short Film and Video Festival was launched by the Thai Film Foundation, its competition open to both film students and the general public. Organized by Chalida Uabumgrungjit as a showcase for Thai shorts, the festival notably boosted the culture of short filmmaking in Thailand.

The year 1997 also saw an upswing in festivals highlighting feature films (organized variously by cultural and governmental organizations, theater chains, and other interested parties), and this has continued steadily in the years since. (Increasing numbers of non-Hollywood films, especially from Korea, Japan, and India, have been getting screened as part of the regular line-up at some Bangkok movie theaters.) The Bangkok Film Festival, begun in 1998 under the auspices of the Nation Multimedia Group (publisher of the English-language daily *The Nation*), marked an attempt to initiate a competitive international film festival with world-class standards. A still higher-profile event, the Bangkok International Film Festival, was then set up by the government through the Tourism Authority of Thailand in January of 2003. This event is intended not only to bring international film fare (and celebrities) to Bangkok but also to promote Thailand as a travel destination and, in particular with the initiation of the Bangkok Film Market as part of the Festival in 2004, to foster international film co-production in Thailand and to highlight available production services and possibilities for location shooting.

While local production has not been the central focus of these more internationally oriented festivals, the promotion of local film has nevertheless consistently been an important component of them – as evidenced in special programs set up to showcase past and contemporary Thai film production. Increased media coverage of the Thai film scene has also helped contribute to this momentum (for example in the English-language dailies, as well as in a number of new Thai-language magazines devoted to cinema).[5] All of these changes have, in the aggregate, provided a context since 1997 that has helped foster the rise of a new Thai cinema – both in helping develop an audience for that cinema and in spurring interest in potential producers – while also generating an interest in film culture in general.

Popular Thai Film Genres

One of the first noticeable generic trends in this new Thai cinema was that of crime films of various kinds – perhaps not all that surprising in light of the singular economic success of *Dang Bireley*, which focused on Bangkok-based gang rivalry in the 1950s. Most of the subsequent crime films do not follow *Dang Bireley*'s use of a period setting – but most do follow the emphasis on Bangkok life as rife with hardship, particularly for their young protagonists (not surprising, given the importance of teen audiences for the Thai film industry). Another emphasis is on lively action sequences of police pursuit and gun battles, with more than a touch of similarity to the flashy styles of the Hong Kong crime film – also not surprising, given the high popularity of Hong Kong film in Thailand in the 1980s and early 1990s. Indeed, one of the more important examples from this cycle of crime films (and one of the more widely distributed) is directed by a pair of Hong Kong-based filmmakers who split their production work between Bangkok and Hong Kong: twin brothers Oxide and Danny Pang. Their film *Bangkok Dangerous* (1999) offers up a tale of a deaf mute who has drifted toward a criminal existence (as a hit man) as a partial result of his violent and impoverished upbringing. *Fah* (1998), the debut feature by the US-trained Wych Kaosayananda (aka "Kaos"), on the other hand, pits an independently wealthy police detective against a commensurately high-living gang of jewel thieves, with a modern Bangkok backdrop of penthouse condominiums, glitzy new shopping malls, and various kinds of hi-tech urban construction in progress.

Nonzee Nimibutr's second feature film, *Nang Nak* (1999), likely deserves credit for reviving a still more substantial generic trend in recent Thai production – that of the horror film, long a staple of Thai B-film production. *Nang Nak* was much loved by local audiences for its revival of a long popular (and often filmed) tale of a devoted wife who insists upon remaining with her beloved husband even after her death in childbirth, and it set box-office records for a Thai-produced film while receiving wide exposure in the international festival circuit.[6] Significantly, the film suggested a strategy to counter the Hollywood competition on its home turf by employing higher production values than those associated with Thai horror films in decades past while simultaneously making use of indigenous story materials; what would once have been a tongue-in-cheek horror comedy became instead a moody horror-romance in authentic period settings. Some of the subsequent horror films to likewise revisit indigenous Thai horror traditions, often giving them an updated spin, include the lurid, comic, and highly successful *Body Jumper* (2001), about an ancient spirit that now possesses the bodies of a number of Bangkok college coeds, giving them an appetite for human livers, and *Krasue* (2002), a period film about a woman who dies at the behest of a sexually jealous man, only to be resurrected (in a physically grotesque and voracious form) by the spirit of a woman who has died simultaneously for like reasons. As the foregoing descriptions might suggest, the supernatural beings of Thai horror films are often the re-embodiment, in fearsome form, of women who were (in life) subject to oppression, and the films thus evince a need to make amends for past injustices that still haunt.[7]

Another ascendant broad genre preoccupied with the past – not as a site of unresolved difficulties, but as a resource for a (usually celebratory) reexamination of the roots of Thai identity – is the historical drama. Most significantly, the relatively big-budget historical epics *Bang Rajan* (2000) and *Suriyothai* (2001) celebrate key historical battles and real or legendary personages as constitutive of the Thai nation, both geopolitically and in spirit.[8] The former film, which garnered the support of Oliver Stone to gain it US distribution, concerns a group of villagers, men and women, who sacrifice themselves in bravely fighting back invading Burmese forces; while the latter film, which has gained US distribution in altered form with the assistance of Francis Ford Coppola, focuses on the heroism of a queen who selflessly supports her husband's rise to power and eventually gives her life in fighting (once more) the Burmese (see case study below).

Numerous other dramas explore more recent Thai history. For example, *Jan Dara* (2001) and *Kwan Riam* (2001) are both set primarily in the 1930s, and *Dang Bireley* in the 1950s, while *Taloompuk* (2002) dramatizes the events surrounding a major storm in the early 1960s and *The Moonhunter* (2001) approaches the politically sensitive era of the mid-1970s, a time of student uprisings that has had long-term political fallout. The musician biopic *The Overture* (2004) encompasses the period from the 1880s to the 1940s, while the time-shifting narrative *The Siam Renaissance* (2004) extends from the 1850s to the present day. *Jan Dara* is an exception among these historical films in its critical and incisive perspective on Thai culture, as these films more generally appear to evince a nostalgia for times gone past (even in their very return to old generic forms like the horror film) in an era of rapid, foreign-influenced social and economic change. The film that most lovingly and also most self-consciously evokes this sense of nostalgia is Wisit Sasanatieng's *Tears of the Black Tiger* (2000), a melancholic, color-drenched, period drama of impossible love that affectionately constructs a fictionalized image of the Thai past, inflected by overtones of spaghetti Westerns and old Thai films.[9]

One further broad generic category that deserves mention here is the comedy, long a staple of Thai cinema. One of the most successful post-1997 films was the comedy *Iron Ladies* (1999), about a volleyball team composed primarily of *kathoey* (transvestite) players; an upbeat, crowd-pleasing film with a strong narrative line (underdogs make good despite the obstacles) and well-drawn characters, it achieved the rare distinction of both performing well with popular domestic audiences and receiving wide theatrical and video distribution across Asia and in the West. Its success gave rise to a number of comedies with related themes, such as *Saving Private Tootsie* (2002), about a group of kathoeys who get caught in a Thai border dispute when their plane crashes. Another comedy achieving popularity across a broad audience, garnering positive local reviews and national film awards, was *Mekong Full Moon Party* (2002), a comedy of provincial life built around the mysterious contemporary phenomenon of the "naga fireballs" – balls of light that appear over a northern river at around the same time every year; while the film does offer its own "answer" to the mystery, its greater concern is clearly its affectionate portrayal of a changing small-town lifestyle (and in this, it is of a piece with the nostalgic films alluded to above).

Thai Film Industry: Organizations and Institutions

The majority of Thai films come from a modest-sized group of studios, some with interests in other entertainment products; RS Promotion and Grammy Entertainment in particular are larger local companies with interests in pop music, television programming, and concert promotions. RS Promotion was already starting to develop a film-production focus with a number of teen-oriented dramas in the mid-1990s; with the rise of interest in Thai film production, it has more recently reorganized its film-production arm into a number of subdivisions to develop niche markets. Grammy had likewise previously been involved in production of youth-oriented films, and, after a lull of a few years, started to return to film production again (through its GMM Pictures division), tackling a number of ambitious projects including the offbeat thriller *One Night Husband* (2003), the transsexual kickboxer biopic *Beautiful Boxer* (2003), and, in cooperation with the new production outfit Hub Ho Hin Films (itself the subsidiary of a small advertising firm), *Mekong Full Moon Party*. Most recently, in mid-2004, Grammy entered into a joint production venture with Hub Ho Hin and Tai Entertainment; the newly formed production company, under the name GTH, quickly announced close to a dozen new feature projects.

Other established operations focused more specifically on film production (and sometimes distribution) include Mongkol Film Company, Five Star Productions, and Tai Entertainment. Mongkol (the distributor for *Suriyothai*) had been since the 1970s involved in both local film production and local distribution of Western films; it too has been returning its focus to Thai production with the current upswing, emphasizing horror films, but also entering into an (albeit short-lived) production agreement with the challenging local director Apichatpong Weerasethakul. Five Star Entertainment, active since 1970, has produced a range of genre films – but is also responsible for supporting the work of Penek Ratanaruang.

Still other smaller and newer outfits that have made their mark include Film Bangkok and Cinemasia. The former, formed by Adirek Watleela (an industry veteran previously involved with Tai Entertainment and RS Promotion), has produced a limited number of high-profile films, including *Bang Rajan*, *Bangkok Dangerous*, and *Tears of the Black Tiger*.[10] The latter, founded by Nonzee Nimibutr and the late Duangkamol Limchaoren, has been primarily involved with Nonzee's work and Penek's work as directors. Cinemasia produced Nonzee's *Jan Dara* in conjunction with the Hong-Kong based Applause Pictures; Nonzee also directed the Thai-based segment of the 2002 omnibus horror film *Three* for Applause, a company formed in 2000 (with well-known Hong Kong director Peter Chan as Chief Executive) with the aim of fostering pan-Asian production and distribution.

Nonzee's distinctive significance to the new wave of Thai filmmaking, then, has been both as a director of ground-breaking films that have provided generic models and paved the way for international recognition, and as a producer who has explored modes of international financing for Thai films and has supported the work of such highly creative (if not always financially lucrative) directors as Penek, Wisit, and the Pang brothers.[11] Penek's importance to this movement has been as a director of stylistically innovative and challenging films which consistently offer a nuanced exploration of struggles over Thai identity and local culture in an age of rapid modernization. While his films have not been highly profitable in their home market (though they've managed to break even), his distinctive work has gained significant attention on the film festival circuit and he has thereby managed to substantially raise the profile of Thai film both locally and internationally.[12] Wisit has been influential both as a collaborator with both Nonzee and Penek (having written the screenplays for *Dang Birely* and *Nang Nak*) and as the director of his own aesthetically exciting film, *Tears of the Black Tiger*. All three some-time collaborators moved into filmmaking from (and still derive income from) work in the Thai advertising industry.

Other emerging figures, themselves from the Thai advertising industry, include Jira Malikhun and the aforementioned Pang brothers. Jira has shown a distinctive knack at pleasing Thai audiences both with his first film as director, the aforementioned *Mekong Full Moon Party*, and a subsequent film as producer, *Fan Chan* (*My Girl*, 2003). For *Fan Chan*, a nostalgic look at young love jointly produced by GMM Pictures, Tai Entertainment, and Hub Ho Hin Films, Jira orchestrated a collaboration among six new film directors. After his directorial debut, Oxide Pang teamed up with his twin brother Danny (who had been working as an editor) to direct *Bangkok Dangerous* and *The Eye* (2002). Noted for their flashy visual style, the brothers have alternated between solo and joint directorial ventures, as well as between Thai-based and internationally co-produced films. Another current figure of note, Prachya

Pinkaew, already had a track-record as a producer of commercial features (*Body Jumper*, for example) when he gained wide recognition as producer-director of the martial arts blockbuster *Ong Bak* (2003) – a film which did well not only across Asia but in Europe as well. Pinkaew used profits from that film to help fund his own production company (Baa-Ram-Ewe), through which he has been giving first-time directors the opportunity to make feature films.

A handful of directors have moved into Thai feature filmmaking with backgrounds in experimental film and/or video – and their works have been, not surprisingly, more formally challenging than most commercially released features. For example Pimpaka Towira gained recognition as an experimental filmmaker with her non-traditional take on the Nak legend (the 1997 short film *Mae Nak*) before going on to direct *One Night Husband* (and becoming one of the very few women to have directed a Thai feature film). Apichatpong Weerasethakul, who studied filmmaking in the United States, made several experimental shorts and an experimental documentary feature, *Mysterious Object at Noon* (2000), before achieving wide recognition with his challenging and controversial fiction features *Blissfully Yours* (2002) and *Tropical Malady* (2004), both of which won major prizes at the Cannes Film Festival.[13]

A number of more veteran Thai film directors have also plainly benefited from the new momentum in Thai filmmaking. Among these is Thailand's foremost director, MC Chatrichalerm Yukol, a member of the royal family (and a graduate of UCLA film school) who has been directing features since the early 1970s. The best of his work has explored a range of controversial issues – political unrest, drug abuse, prostitution – rarely addressed by other filmmakers (possible perhaps in part because of his own position of social privilege); his films have encompassed a wide variety of genres with fairly consistent proficiency – though the massive scale of his *Suriyothai* is exceptional. Bhandit Rittakol also started his career (as a critic and screenwriter) in the 1970s, with a regular output of films (comedies in particular) as director since the early 1980s; his post-1996 films include the historical dramas *Satang* (2000) and *The Moonhunter* – the latter dealing with student uprisings that he himself had covered as a young reporter. Manop Udomdej, too, had been directing since the 1980s, but had stopped directing features after the commercial failure of his crime film *The Dumb Die Fast, The Smart Die Slow* (1991); the hit-man drama *Beyond Forgivin'* (1999) marked his post-1996 return to feature directing, followed by the true crime story *Macabre Case of Prom Pi Ram* (2003). Lastly, Euthana Mukdasanit, who had been directing since the late 1970s – including such acclaimed works as *Namphoo* (1984) and *Butterfly and Flowers* (1985) – anticipated the 1997 upswing with his popular wartime drama *Sunset at Chaophraya*, and followed this up with the teen drama *Red Bike Story* (1997); more recently he has been involved in theater as a teacher and director.

The Direct-to-Video Phenomenon

A significant trend in contemporary Thai cinema is the sudden rise in popularity of "direct-to-video" productions – sometimes locally referred to as "tele-movies." These came to prominence as an indirect result of the increasing prevalence of the VCD format, which has for a number of years supplanted videotape as the most popular home video format in Thailand (and other Asian markets) with comparatively inexpensive VCDs and videodisc players. The industry became more aware of the profit potentials of VCD distribution following the unexpectedly high sales of a number of VCD titles (in particular, *Mekong Full Moon Party* and 2002's *Phra Aphai Manee*). Producers now noted that not only have VCD releases proven potential for large profits, a film planned for release direct-to-video could be shot in a video format, at far lower cost than a theatrical feature. As a result, 2003 saw dozens of companies, established giants and marginal outfits alike, get involved in direct-to-video film production, with a profusion of new titles surfacing on the market – some from such top filmmakers as Apichatpong and the Pang Brothers. The target audience for many of these films and their inexpensive format is the provincial one – an audience which tends to be of lower income and, in some cases, does not have ready local access to movie theaters. Prominent direct-to-video genres include thrillers, comedies, erotic films, and, following the trends of theatrically-released features, horror and transvestite-related narratives. What remains to be seen is how profound an impact the present surge in direct-to-video production will have upon indigenous filmmaking, either economically or aesthetically.[14]

Increasing Internationalization in Contemporary Thai Cinema

Thai film producers in the modern era have had a particularly strong motivation to produce films attractive to international audiences in that the overall potential for the Thai market (with its relatively low admission prices and a national population of around 63 million, many at a low standard of living) is simply not sufficient to recoup costs on any high-budgeted production. The impulse to reach out beyond Thai audiences was clear from the very start of the current new wave, with *Dang Bireley* and *Fun Bar Karaoke* being both showcased at numerous international festivals and made available in English-subtitled prints and videos. Thai film's increasing presence in international film festivals and film markets has meant increasing distribution, especially across Asia and, to a lesser extent, in Europe. Thai producers have had great difficulty, however, in procuring theatrical distribution (or even video distribution) for their films in the United States. The shortened version of

Suriyothai, with its nationwide release from Sony Classics Pictures, is the most significant exception to this; *Iron Ladies* also had a modest theatrical release, *Bangkok Dangerous* and Penek's *Last Life in the Universe* (2003) still more limited ones. On the other hand, while there had been great hope for *Tears of the Black Tiger* after it was strongly received at Cannes Film Festival and Miramax picked up the US distribution rights, Miramax insisted on altering the film and then, mysteriously, apparently opted not to release it at all.

There has also been a move toward Thai involvement in international co-production – and the internationally financed films themselves often have international casts in order to ensure a wider (especially pan-Asian) market. *Jan Dara* is an especially notable instance of this – a filmed adaptation of a Thai novel by a prominent Thai director, but starring a Hong Kong actress with pan-Asian appeal (Canadian-born, Chinese-Vietnamese Christy Chung) and with financing set up by a Hong Kong-based company, Applause Pictures, specializing in just such pan-Asian projects. While the subject matter of the film is specifically Thai history, its notoriously sexually explicit presentation also helped ensure it a wider audience. Other Thai co-productions from Applause include the horror film *The Eye* (directed by the Hong Kong-born, Hong Kong and Thailand-based Pang Brothers, starring the Malaysian-born, Taiwanese-based Lee Sin-je, and set partly in Hong Kong, partly in Thailand) and the omnibus horror film *Three* (with separate Hong Kong, South Korean, and Thai segments). Another important international co-production is Penek's *Last Life in the Universe*, which concerns a relationship between a Japanese man (played by Japanese cult star Asano Tadanobu) and a Thai woman and features cinematography by Hong Kong-based Australian cinematographer Chris Doyle.

A logical corollary of these industrial trends, as well as a reflection of an ever-growing popular preoccupation with the forces of globalization, is the rise of plotlines dealing with relationships between Thais and non-Thais, and the use of settings outside of Thailand proper. Thus, *The Siam Renaissance* straddles Thailand and France, *Last Love* (2003) features much European location shooting, the romantic comedy *Sexphone* (2003) has its concluding sequences in Australia, *February* (2003) is set in New York, and the mostly English-language *Province 77* (2003) focuses on the Thai-American community in Los Angeles.

Negotiating Nation (and National Cinema): Suriyothai's Multiple Versions

As mentioned previously in this chapter, the 2001 epic biopic *Suriyothai* is a high-profile case of a contemporary Thai film focused on the nation's heritage that garnered domestic and international attention. While *Suriyothai* might at first seem an exceptional example – having been directed by a senior director, and one with singular (i.e. royal) social status at that – it does in fact exemplify many of the trends and concerns of contemporary Thai cinema. There is the concern with revisiting Thai history as an attempt to better understand the current constitution of the nation – an interest in sketching out Thailand's historical relationship to its regional neighbors, socially, politically, and economically, as well as its negotiations with the cultural and technological influences of the West (alluded to here primarily through the presence of Portuguese mercenaries and Western firearms). And there is the narrative's overriding preoccupation with issues of gender and power which arises in numerous popular Thai narratives. There is even a nod to the ever-important teen audience – both in the devotion of an early portion of the film to a teen romance and in the casting of a number of actors popular with teens.

The story of the historical figure of Queen Suriyothai, the wife of a sixteenth century Thai king, is quite well-known in Thailand, long taught as part of the grade-school curriculum; her legendary sacrifice – her death in battle to defend Thailand against the Burmese – held up as an example of strong, patriotic womanhood. It is clear that the emphasis in Chatrichalerm's version of the story is indeed on such womanhood – and that by looking at the choices made in narrating this story, we can see what roles for women the film implicitly values or endorses. These characteristics include strength, intelligence, and initiative – though only insofar as they are put to the service of supportiveness of husband and country.

The concern with gender – and, more to the point, with the status of womanhood within Thai history and culture – is evident from the fact that many of the key historical events detailed are presented as conceived of and/or directly or indirectly spurred onward by women. For example, King Somdet Nor Putthangura does not wield adequate control over his kingdom and allows profiteering to flourish among a few insiders because of his infatuation with his consort – and the discontent that is thereby sown leads to the downfall of his intended royal lineage. The subsequent King Chai Raja also first faces a military setback because of putting too much faith in the allegiance of a queen in northern Thailand, then meets his downfall at the hands of his treacherous high consort (played by pop star Mai Charoenpura), who is responsible for spurring (or seducing) a fellow usurper into action, and who is to begin with spurred on by the high matriarch of her family line.

Suriyothai, too, wields considerable influence over the course of historical events represented in the film; it is in large measure out of love for her or her daughter that key male protagonists Prince Thienraja (her husband) and Khun Pirenthorathep take (historically) decisive action. That Suriyothai understands the importance of her own patriotic/familial obligation is made clear early on in the film. Suriyothai is introduced as a feisty teenager, happy to ignore rules of proper behavior, especially when in amorous pursuit of Pirenthorathep. When it is made clear to her, however, that marriage to a different suitor would be much more in the best interests of her family and country, she assents, setting aside her true desires in deference to what she sees as a higher responsibility. From this point on her youthful willfulness does not suddenly disappear, but it is now put purely toward ensuring the best possible future for her country, in part through support of her husband. Her marital relationship is not represented as a particularly loving one (especially in contrast to the other relationships detailed in the film), but her consistent concern for her husband is shown in scenes of her providing counsel – often forcefully, sometimes insisting he move to action, but assenting nevertheless when her husband disagrees.

The film makes clear the genuineness of this support in her faithfulness for her husband despite her possible lack of love for him; in her willingness to give up a family heirloom in order to ensure the presentability of his army; and ultimately, in her willingness to follow her husband (then King) into battle to ensure his (and thereby the country's) survival – at what turns out to be the cost of her own life – even though it is clear she disagrees with his strategic reasoning for pursuing his course of action. Indeed, the film generally shows Suriyothai to be a far wiser and more skillful strategist and coalition builder than her husband – better at divining, through both intuition and cautious research, the plans of those who would do her husband (and, from her perspective, the nation) harm.

The aforementioned issues of interaction with the West operate at both intra- and intertextual levels: *Suriyothai* is a film designed simultaneously to defend and celebrate Thai identity and to offer such identity up for circulation through the West, in part through the internalization of Western production standards (through a Western postproduction company and composer). The film's lush cinematography and period *mise-en-scène* are indeed among its strongest suits – the sweeping tracking shots of spectacular royal functions recalling the heyday of the Hollywood Technicolor epic in the 1950s and early 1960s. The access to Western standards is in turn partly a function of the director's own prior interaction with the West and connections with filmmaker Francis Ford Coppola, which facilitated distribution.

The fate of *Suriyothai* in its form for the Western gaze, under the title *The Legend of Suriyothai* (2003), however, provides an object lesson in the potential vulnerability of a culturally specific text removed from its initial context. While *Legend* does not substantially reedit individual scenes, many scenes are removed in their entirety in order to tighten up the exposition (and shorten the running time). The new version of the film concentrates on the cause-and-effect chain of events that subtend the film, in keeping with the classical Hollywood paradigm. In doing this, however, the new version loses much of the focus on Suriyothai's political and personal interactions, and ultimately, her cultural importance that is crucial to the Thai version – and distinctly Thai.

CHAPTER 5

Singapore: Developments, Challenges, and Projections

Jan Uhde and Yvonne Ng Uhde

Singapore, the tiny island city-state in Southeast Asia, reputed for its prosperity and cleanliness, is not generally known as a film-producing country. Although the city experienced vigorous filmmaking activities in the 1950s and 1960s, its studios declined in the mid-1970s, sending local film production into total eclipse for almost two decades. The 1990s saw a hesitant revival in feature production, driven by enthusiastic young filmmakers, increased government support, and private investment. Recent developments suggest that Singapore is serious about its future as a permanent member of the international film-producing community. This chapter examines developments in Singapore's cinema and society – emphasizing cultural diversity, economic incentives, state policy, and possibilities for artistic and commercial cinematic success.

Multicultural Cinema in Singapore: The Early Days

Since the first motion pictures reached Singapore more than a century ago, the medium has reflected the city's multi-ethnic society (in 2002, the 4.1 million population comprised 76.5 percent Chinese, 13.8 percent Malay, 8.1 percent Indian and 1.6 percent others). Singapore was then part of the Straits Settlements and, with the rest of Malaya, under British rule. A result of the city's political and demographic situation was that movie production in Singapore has always been a multicultural endeavor. The studios were run largely by the Chinese. Most of the filmmaking expertise – directors, cinematographers and crew – was brought from India, while the Malays made various contributions to film artistry, including acting. Hollywood and British production dominated Singapore's cinemas already before World War II, and Japanese films were shown during the Occupation. Today, Hollywood and Hong Kong movies reign in Singapore's plush multiplexes.

Throughout its history, film production in Singapore has been exposed to a variety of cultural, economic and political influences: Chinese, Indian, British,

Japanese, American, and Malay. The Malay factor was exceptionally important, as before the separation of Singapore and Malaysia most local films were
made in Malay and distributed across the Malay Peninsula. After Singapore
became an independent republic in 1965, the production split along the political boundaries and eventually gave birth to Singaporean and Malaysian
cinemas. Singapore's multiracial and multicultural blend has remained its
most durable social constant. This has left a strong imprint upon the indigenous production's thematic range, style as well as local audiences' preferences.

The first features made in Singapore appeared in the early 1930s focused on
cultural spice and spectacle. The popular *Laila Majnun*, based on an ancient
Arabian legend, was directed by the Indian filmmaker B.S. Rajhans, who
settled in Singapore and became its first prominent director. While *Laila
Majnun* is commonly believed to be Singapore's first feature, the authors'
recent research shows that another Singapore-made film, an exotic South Seas
drama called *Samarang*, directed by Ward Wing (an American) was released
in Singapore on 26 March 1934 – one day before B.S. Rajhans' *Laila Majnun*.

The 1930s also witnessed the rise of two future major players in film exhibition and production on the Malay Peninsula and beyond. The brothers Run
Run and Runme Shaw from Shanghai started the production of Malay films
in Singapore, and the Cathay Organization was set up in Singapore and Kuala
Lumpur, headed by Loke Wan Tho.

After the war, Shaw's Malay Film Productions modernized its studios and
continued their pre-war strategy of importing Indian directors and technicians.
This lent the Singapore Malay cinema of the period an unmistakable Indian
flavor rich in song and dance, a tradition that remains the hallmark of India's
"Bollywood" movies.

Singapore Golden Age of Malay Cinema

In 1953, Loke's Cathay Organization joined forces with Ho Ah Loke's Keris
Film Productions, setting up a new film company, Cathay-Keris Productions,
to compete with Shaw's Malay Film Productions (MFP). The local film
industry, which produced almost exclusively Malay-language features, hit a
high of twenty movies in 1958 when Cathay-Keris made nine films in addition
to the eleven produced by the MFP under intense competition. In the early
1960s, the combined average annual output for Malay films was about
eighteen features. The fertile period spanning the 1950s and the early 1960s
has come to be regarded as the golden age of Malay cinema in Singapore.
Surprisingly, the Chinese face of Singapore was conspicuously absent from the
local films. Singapore's productions of the 1950s and 1960s reflected mainly
the Malay community on the island and the Peninsula. Nevertheless, the
Malay movies were enjoyed by other ethnic communities in the city.

Arguably, the most important personality of the Malay cinema's golden age was the multitalented P. Ramlee (1929–73) – actor, director, writer, producer, editor, singer, composer, songwriter, and publisher in one. Born in Penang (now in Malaysia), P. Ramlee came to Singapore in 1948 to work for Shaw's MFP as a playback singer. He soon took up acting, eventually becoming a popular male lead. In 1955, Ramlee launched his own directorial debut with *The Trishaw Puller* (*Penarek Beca*). In this significant achievement, Ramlee broke with the established Indian stylistic tradition that was characteristic of Malay filmmaking of the period. Instead, he turned to contemporary social drama with a Neorealist flavor which reflected more accurately the lifestyle and everyday concerns of Malay society – a secret of Ramlee's enduring popularity. *The Trishaw Puller*, chosen as the Best Malay Film in 1956, was also a box-office success.

P. Ramlee, whose films suggest an inspiration by Japan's Akira Kurosawa and India's Satyajit Ray, acted in his lifetime in more than sixty films and directed more than thirty of them, for which he received a number of international awards. After his departure from Singapore to Kuala Lumpur in 1964, Shaw Brothers' MFP studios went into decline, finally closing down in 1967.

Another gifted Malay filmmaker, Hussein Haniff (1934–1966?), known for his innovative style, worked for Cathay-Keris in Singapore. One of the memorable titles he directed for Cathay was *Hang Jebat* (1961), inspired by a Malay legend about two friends whose relationship is tested by conflicting loyalties. Cathay's successes of the late 1950s and early 1960s also included the *pontianak* films (a vampire sub-genre), starring the Indonesian-born beauty Maria Menado. After a series of setbacks, Cathay-Keris studios closed its doors in 1972.

New Singapore Cinema

After a few isolated filmmaking attempts in the 1970s, film production in Singapore came to a complete halt and remained inactive for almost two decades. However, efforts to revive the local film industry continued into the 1980s and intensified in the 1990s. Tertiary educational institutions started to include film and media in their curricula. The Singapore Film Society expanded its programming, and a handful of enthusiasts succeeded in establishing the Singapore International Film Festival in 1987. And censorship began to weaken: in 1996 local members of the film community addressed the country's government through a White Paper which eventually led to the formation of the Singapore Film Commission two years later.

Meanwhile, Singapore rapidly rose out of poverty and achieved a high degree of economic affluence. Today, it is the richest Asian country after Japan with a per capita GDP higher than in many West European countries. These economic and social factors, including the authorities' growing recognition of the economic benefits of local film production, combined to revive feature-film production in the final decade of the last century. This began in 1991 with an unremarkable feature, *Medium Rare*, based on a macabre real-life story. However, what initially seemed like another isolated film experiment (no film was made for the next four years) turned out to be the embryo of a new Singapore cinema.

In 1995 the public interest surrounding *Bugis Street*, a film about transvestites and transsexuals, and Eric Khoo's gritty *Mee Pok Man*, the first Singapore production to receive international festival recognition, encouraged Cathay to return to feature production with the comedy *Army Daze* in 1996. The next year saw the release of three local films, including Khoo's landmark *12 Storeys*, which highlighted the problem of loneliness and alienation in an impersonal urban environment. Among the four features that followed in 1998 were Tay Teck Lock's comedy, *Money No Enough*, to this day Singapore's highest-grossing local movie, and Glen Goei's romantic musical *Forever Fever* (discussed in the introduction to this book).

For a nascent film industry, the pace of production was encouraging and film ventures became popular with investors. Local businessman Andrew Yap of YTC Corporation even made a 25 percent investment into the US/UK/Australian co-production *Paradise Road* (1997), a Singapore war story directed by the Oscar-winning director Bruce Beresford and starring Glenn Close.

Fuelled by the successes of 1998, an estimated twelve local features were planned in 1999 but only eight materialized. This unexpected slowdown heightened the atmosphere of pessimism and anxiety among producers and filmmakers triggered by a string of second-rate, money-losing local ventures such as *Lucky Number* and *Where Got Problem*. The decline of admissions was the result of a number of factors, especially the increasing thematic monotony of local movies. Only Raintree Pictures' *Liang Po Po*, directed by Teng Bee Lian, made a profit in 1999. Moreover, according to industry sources, video piracy siphoned off almost 30 percent of their profits. Still, the eight productions completed was a respectable figure for a small city-state and 1999 became the most prolific year of the decade for Singapore feature production.

In 2000 and 2001, fewer films were produced. In general, neither their artistic quality nor box-office performance inspired the confidence of critics and investors. The late 1990s euphoria had given way to a climate of uncertainty, an interval also marked by a falling admission rate. Fewer people went to the movies, as the Internet, DVD, and other means of entertainment soared, while video pirates continued to chip away at legitimate earnings. Singapore quietly slipped from its first place in world cinema attendance, held over a number of years, to fourth place in 2001.[1] Consequently, a number of theaters closed down, including some recently-built multiplexes.

Despite these setbacks, the country's filmmakers held on. Fruits of this perseverance in terms of cinema attendance and box-office profits were reaped in 2002, which was an improvement over the preceding year in terms of attendance and profits. Local movie-goers made their way to the big screen fourteen million times, averaging three-and-a-half admissions per person, a slight increase of about 3 percent from 2001. Ticket sales were also better, going up 7 percent from 2001. The success – both critical and at the box office – of Jack Neo's *I Not Stupid* and the Singaporean-Hong Kong co-production *The Eye* has brought renewed confidence in the future of Singapore film. Both films made it to the 2002 top ten box-office chart (*I Not Stupid* at number four and *The Eye* at number ten), a rare achievement for local productions. In 2003, total admissions went up by 5 percent to 14.7 million and the box office saw an improvement of about 10 percent. Jack Neo scored again with his *Homerun,* a remake of Iranian filmmaker Majid Majidi's *Children of Heaven,* the only non-English-language movie to make it to that year's top ten. On the other hand, the market share for local films in 2003 dropped to 3.25 percent from 5 percent in the preceding year.

Challenges of Developing a Local/Global Profile for Singapore Cinema

Although Singapore has maintained a relatively steady feature-film output in the last five years, fears for the continued existence of the local production have not disappeared. Singapore's film industry is still in its infancy and to survive, it needs government funding. The authorities, echoed by mainstream public opinion, used to regard the arts as a generally unproductive, if not unnecessary, activity, associated with a lower social status. The education system, too, focused on concrete, tangible, and technological pursuits rather than on the arts.

Fortunately, this perspective is now changing. The discovery of economic value in artistic activity has stimulated government interest in promoting a number of arts-oriented initiatives, such as the new Esplanade – Theatres on the Bay, a monumental, world-class performing arts center built on the Marina waterfront at the cost of S$600 million (US$350 million) which opened in October 2002.

In the area of film, the establishment of the Singapore Film Commission (SFC) by the Ministry of Information and the Arts, in 1998, was a major step forward in the development of the national film industry. On 1 January 2003, the Singapore Film Commission became part of the new Media Development Authority (MDA) which merged the Films and Publications department (censorship office), the Singapore Broadcasting Authority and the Singapore Film Commission.[2]

In July of the same year, the MDA launched its Media 21 plan which aims to develop and promote Singapore as a "global media city," to attract new investments and encourage more varied and profitable media activities. These include co-productions, animation production, multimedia content creation, content financing and ownership marketing and distribution, and research and development.[3] This new government policy does not consider film to be an isolated entity but rather as a part of a wider "media industry."

A question frequently raised is about how many features should – or could – be produced in a city of 4 million. It is a matter of simple arithmetic that a film can hardly be profitable in Singapore alone, unless its costs are kept well under S$1 million (US$580,000) – a restrictive sum for even the thriftiest filmmaker. This is why the Singapore Film Commission as well as the country's film-production companies now promote co-productions, stressing regional (Southeast Asian) co-operation. This is a useful strategy but it should be kept in mind that international co-productions are a double-edged sword and that the contribution and identity of smaller partners such as Singapore can be easily overlooked or obliterated.

Another way to profitability is to break into international markets through films with universal subjects – a task so far met with only moderate success. Out of some thirty features made between 1991–2002, only a handful have been sold outside Asia: for example, Glen Goei's *Forever Fever* (1998), *The Eye* (Danny and Oxide Pang, 2002) by Cruise-Wagner Productions, and the Singapore-Vietnamese co-production *Song of the Stork* (2002) by Jonathan Foo and Nguyen Phan Quang Binh.

The most prominent filmmaking company in Singapore is Raintree Pictures,[4] the movie-production arm of MediaCorp (the government-controlled Media Corporation of Singapore), set up in August 1998. Like the Singapore Film Commission, it follows the government policy of promoting co-productions. Raintree's film output makes it the closest thing on the island to what could be called a film studio. The remaining producers are relatively small companies with limited financial support, most of which rely on television contracts to survive.

As Singapore was without an indigenous cinema for almost a generation, a pressing problem for the fledgling film industry is the lack of local expertise in virtually every aspect of filmmaking, including competent screen acting. Moreover, there is shortage of quality post-production facilities in the city-state, forcing local productions to employ labs abroad, usually in Thailand or Australia. Furthermore, serious film preservation, necessary for the creation of a national film heritage, has only just begun in Singapore. With no national film archives, it is up to the local production companies to decide if a film should be kept and if so, how. (Recently, Cathay and Shaw have started restoring some of their older films for release on DVD, mostly from their Hong Kong productions.)

A major obstacle for the country's smaller producers appears to be the existing hegemonic distribution and exhibition system which favors large productions, especially those from major Hollywood studios. This is clearly a global problem but, without a single repertory cinema in Singapore, there is very little screen space for the local independents to show their movies. Moreover, the sale and rental of films on video, VCD, and DVD, both local and foreign, is restricted by censorship regulations, narrowing even further the communication channels between Singapore's independent filmmakers and their potential audiences. By the same token, many artistically influential films remain out of reach of Singapore's film community.

It is still too early to make conclusions about contemporary Singapore film production but some characteristics are slowly emerging. Most of the country's filmmakers are relatively young; and the features made since 1991 are mostly anchored in the present, unlike the films made in the 1950s which drew from old Malay traditions and legends.

The thematic spectrum has been rather narrow, repeating subjects and styles which have proved successful at the box-office. From the generic point of view, many of the revival movies are action-oriented comedies and farces, reflecting everyday problems (*Money No Enough, Chicken Rice War, I Not Stupid*). The focus on ordinary people and their concerns also links Singapore's modern cinema with its past, especially the P. Ramlee films.

The relatively light-hearted perspective is complemented by a parallel undercurrent of bleak, dark themes portraying the affluent society's misfits and outsiders (*Mee Pok Man, Eating Air, 15*). Eric Khoo's *12 Storeys* about urban alienation echoes a subject also found in the films of other Asian directors such as Edward Yang and Tsai Ming-liang in Taiwan. *12 Storeys* is, however, distinctively Singaporean in flavour. Though not a commercial success, it received worldwide critical attention, making Khoo one of the country's most renowned filmmakers. More recently, Royston Tan's *15* (produced by Khoo's Zhao Wei Films), the feature version of his award-winning short, presents a grim and disturbing portrayal of the country's dysfunctional teenagers, a part of reality hidden from the view of ordinary Singaporeans.

Among the international influences on contemporary Singapore filmmakers, Hollywood and Hong Kong popular cinemas figure most prominently. The local editing styles are much indebted to music video, while the acting techniques reflect television practices, perceived in film as overacting. Not surprisingly, the most convincing performances often come from nonprofessional actors. In tune with the Republic's population profile, the new generation of filmmakers now focuses on the city's Chinese community, although the minority cultures have not been excluded.

A promising creative development in Singapore is the local short-film production, driven by the younger filmmakers, often experimenting with digital technology. A number of these shorts have won international praise and prizes; several award-winning filmmakers have also been given the opportunity to direct telemovies. The continuing international success of Singapore short-filmmakers is one of the most encouraging signs for the future of the country's cinema.

The State of/and the Censor's Scissors

A parliamentary democracy, Singapore is also infamously known for its media censorship which regulates print, film, television, and home video.[5] Many features of the city's film censorship are rooted in its history. Since the colonial period, cinema on the Malay Peninsula has been under strict state control. After World War II and toward the end of the colonial era, the Board of Film Censors was established under the Cinematograph Ordinance Act in 1953. When Singapore became self-governing in 1959,[6] film censorship came under the Ministry of Home Affairs. In 1963, during the Confederation period, the censor's office was moved to the Ministry of Culture; it eventually became part of the Ministry of Information and the Arts (MITA). In 1998, the Board of Film Censors merged with the Censorship Section and the Licensing Section to become the Films and Publications Department (FPD) which in turn became part of the new Media Development Authority (MDA) in January 2003.

With the arrival of new technologies, film censorship was extended to include television, video, and the electronic information media, including the Internet. Private use of the satellite dish is banned in Singapore, and only select institutions have permission to own a satellite television receive-only dish.

A period of continued stability and increasing affluence helped to pave the way for the liberalization of censorship rules. In 1981, a Committee was set up "to review the existing censorship guidelines and laws so that they would be in tandem with the changing times."[7] Films were then passed, passed with cuts, or banned. As Singapore's film audiences became more mature, demands grew for the introduction of a rating system, such as that used in North America and Western Europe. It also became evident that if Singapore wanted to attract foreign capital and to develop a film industry, the censorship rules would have to be loosened to accommodate the potential investors' needs.

In 1991, film classification was introduced in Singapore. It comprised the following categories: "G" (General) with a "PG" (Parental Guidance) subgroup and the "R(A)" or Restricted-(Artistic). Minimum age limit for R(A) was 21. Movies of the R(A) category were banned from suburban cinemas and could be shown only in specially licensed inner-city theaters. In 1993, the "NC-16" category (No children under 16) was introduced. Films classified as NC-16 and R(A) were not to be rented or sold in video stores nor broadcast on television.

The new classification allowed films with mature themes to be shown to mature audiences, which was not possible under the old rules. It is understood today that the 1991 move toward film classification significantly contributed to the resurgence in local filmmaking activities. According to Singapore Film Society chairman, Kenneth Tan, "In essence, classification has meant liberalization. It has meant that it is possible for many films to be shown intact, hence, it is also possible for many films to be made with anticipation of being able to be shown intact ..."[8]

The censorship guidelines were reviewed in 2002/2003 and minor changes implemented in 2004. While the General (G), Parental Guidance (PG), No Children Under 16 (NC-16) categories remained, a new category, the Mature 18 (M18), was introduced. Films with the M18 rating and lower may be shown city-wide. The R(A) Restricted(Artistic) rating shed the vague "Artistic" requirement and became R21, keeping the unusually high minimum age limit and geographical restriction. Additionally, a video classification similar to that for theatrical release was introduced, allowing the sale or rental of films up to the M18 rating. (Films rated R21 will still not be allowed on video.) This restriction is particularly damaging to the country's independent and experimental filmmakers as it deprives them of a major exhibition platform and source of revenue. Even with the new classification, films may be cut, both for theatrical and video release.

Traditionally, film censors have focused on three aspects: sex, violence, and ideology (the last category includes politics, religion, and racial hatred). A unique feature of Singapore's censorship is its attention to a particular aspect of language. A quintessential multilingual and multicultural country, Singapore has four official languages: Mandarin, Malay, Tamil, and English; but it is "Singlish," the hybrid local vernacular mix of English, Malay, and Chinese dialects, that is often used by its citizens in daily communication. Since the late 1970s, the government has discouraged the use of Chinese dialects and later Singlish in the media as part of the policy to promote the use of Mandarin and proper English. As a result, Cantonese movies from Hong Kong and Taiwanese-dialect movies are still dubbed into Mandarin for theatrical release and for television.

Filmmakers who reflect the way Singaporeans speak in real life have often had to defend the use of Singlish and dialects in their films. In fact, the local vernacular plays an important role in identifying a film as Singaporean. The case of the 1998 comedy *Money No Enough* is instructive. The feature, written by Jack Neo, revolves around the financial predicament of three friends from different social backgrounds. Its exceptional local mass appeal stemmed partly from the fact that its theme was fortuitously topical, one that many viewers could identify with at a time when the entire region was facing a severe financial crisis. Also, the three lead actors, including Neo, are all popular television personalities.

However, the film's dialogues included 80 percent of Hokkien Chinese dialect, together with some Mandarin and Singlish. This bold move contributed much to the movie's slice-of-life quality and was one reason for its immense popularity. Not surprisingly, the film encountered serious problems with the censors. In what was a significant breakthrough for local filmmakers, *Money No Enough* was eventually passed intact after an appeal by the Singapore Film Society. This paved the way for other feature films such as Jack Neo's hit comedy *I Not Stupid*, which was cleared without difficulties despite its significant dialect and Singlish dialogue.

In recent years, there have been more calls from the public to relax the restrictions on the use of dialects on television and in the cinemas since most people prefer to watch movies in their original languages. Local dialects and Singlish are now becoming more prominent in Singapore movies, such as in the popular 2004 comedy *The Best Bet* by the actor-director Neo. However, in broadcast television the language rules are more strictly enforced.

Today, censorship is affected mainly by three factors: Singapore's multiracial and multireligious society, globalization, and technological advances. The latter two have brought about societal changes which the government now has to tackle. It goes without saying that it makes little sense to cut or ban films with controversial subjects when there is a virtually limitless and easy supply of erotic, pornographic, violent, and politically controversial material through other channels, such as the Internet. Moreover, strict censorship is increasingly perceived to be economically counterproductive, restricting essential information flow, creativity, and experimentation at the time when the country's economy is feeling the effects of growing regional competition, particularly from China.

The long-awaited revision of film and video censorship, implemented in the first half of 2004, proved to be less than revolutionary. To many Westerners, the city-state's tight grip on movies and videos seems almost ridiculous. Despite its modern, hi-tech surface however, Singapore remains a relatively conservative multiracial and multireligious society surrounded by even more conservative large neighbors (Malaysia, Indonesia). The Singapore government seems to be aware of this fact and its implications, both social and political. The adjustments to the existing film-classification structure, such as the already-mentioned introduction of the M18 category and the new classification for video sales and rental, may be seen as a marginal liberalization of the censorship.

On the other hand, three films were banned from the program of the 2004 Singapore International Film Festival (SIFF), and another three withdrawn by its organizers because of cuts demanded by the censors (the SIFF has a policy of showing only uncut films). Fittingly, at the same festival, the maverick director Royston Tan enjoyed great success with the premiere of *Cut*, a provocative three-minute musical spoof on local censorship. The struggle between filmmakers and censors will go on, but an eventual relaxation of Singapore's censorship laws and liberalization of its society is inevitable in the face of increased global economic integration and improved education. Considering the government's traditional cautiousness, it will likely be a very slow and gradual process.

I Not Stupid: **A Bold and Intelligent Satire**

After two lackluster years for Singapore film production, the appearance and unprecedented success in 2002 of Jack Neo's satirical comedy *I Not Stupid*, caught the film community – and indeed the much of the country – by surprise. The multitalented Neo also wrote and starred in this story about the trials and tribulations of three schoolboys. Terry Khoo (Huang Po Ju), Liu Kok Pin (Shawn Lee) and Ang Boon Hock (Joshua Ang) are classmates in the EM3 stream.[9] While the three boys struggle with school work and suffer the shame of being in a class for the less academically able, their parents find themselves worried not only about their children's school grades, but also about their own livelihoods in a period of economic uncertainty.

Terry is the pampered and sheltered son of wealthy but crude businessman Mr. Khoo (Richard Low). His efficient and authoritarian wife (Selena Tan) is the movie's tongue-in-cheek personification of the Singapore government, a mother who rules over her children "for their own good" and who demands complete obedience from them. In Terry's case, she has succeeded so thoroughly that the boy is unable to think for himself, leaving him unable to take care of himself or to speak up for his friends.

His friend Kok Pin does badly in mathematics, to the distress of his mother (Xiang Yun), who pays scant attention to his artistic ability as the latter counts for little in a school system centered on science and mathematics. Meanwhile, Kok Pin's father, Mr. Liu (Jack Neo), a Chinese-language advertising copywriter in a field where English dominates, has put his job on the line to prove that his expatriate colleague is being unjustly valued over local talent. The least well-to-do of the three friends, the hardworking and courageous Boon Hock, is obliged to help out at his family's food stall and baby-sit his brother while doing his homework.

Some of the funniest moments in the film are the confrontations between Mr. Liu and Mr. Khoo. However, these are balanced by sobering scenes, such as Kok Pin being caned by his anguished mother and his own feelings of failure and despair that lead him to contemplate suicide. In fact, the children's performances are one of the film's greatest accomplishments.

Raintree Pictures, which produced *I Not Stupid* on a modest budget of S$900,000 (US$520,000), took considerable risks. The film's satirical edge, aimed at the country's educational system and the government's authoritarianism, as well as frequent dialogues in Hokkien and Singlish, made the movie vulnerable to the censor's scissors. According to Raintree Pictures' CEO Daniel Yun, the looming danger of controversy worried the film's investors.[10] Surprisingly, instead of censuring its critical stance, the authorities praised the movie, and the director was commended by Prime Minister Goh Chok Tong for his success in applying his "creative energy" to filmmaking.[11]

The theatrical release of *I Not Stupid* saw the movie's producers on tenter-hooks. The movie was scheduled to open on February 9, 2002, during the Chinese New Year (an equivalent of the Christmas release in North America). Following a disastrous performance in the sneak-preview weekend (only S$46,000, or US$27,000 was taken), Raintree called for a dramatic change in marketing strategy which included all-out media publicity, even inviting school teachers to discuss the film and the education system. To their relief, audi-ences responded positively to this new strategy and the film became a runaway hit. After playing for about four months on some thirty screens, the movie took in S$3.8 million (US$1.7million) at the box office, becoming the second biggest local box-office success in Singapore's film production history, after *Money No Enough* (S$5.8 million, or US$3.37 million). Moreover, *I Not Stupid* was a virtually unanimous critical success.

Clearly, the subject matter of this feature had touched a nerve in the audi-ence. Beneath the surface of an innocent Singlish title in a "story about school-kids," the comedy raises questions about human dignity. For the first time, a Singaporean film reflected on the plight of children under excessive academic pressure, leading some to suicide, and the daily strife of grownups struggling to cope with parenting and problems at the workplace. More than any other local production in recent history, *I Not Stupid* produced an unexpected catharsis in Singaporean audiences, generating a stream of thoughtful and heartfelt discussions in the media about the issues brought out by the film. Schools even sent teachers and students en masse to see the movie. The success of *I Not Stupid* even spawned an eighteen-part television series on the Chinese-language Channel 8, a comic book, and children's vitamin C pills.

The film's boldness and success caught the attention of the international media. Outside Singapore, *I Not Stupid* was released in Malaysia and Hong Kong and it was warmly received at the 2002 Pusan International Film Festival in South Korea.

It is only in recent years that the government has acknowledged the need for reform in Singapore's grade-oriented, pressure-cooker school system which has bred conformism at the expense of creativity. Neo's timely film combines humor with a sharply critical stance in questioning government policies and a submissive population obsessed with school grades and material success.

It appears that, after having been flooded for years by shallow films both from abroad and at home, Singaporeans want to see on the silver screen an intelligent and honest reflection of their lives. In its combination of important issues, a believable and well-constructed narrative and good production values, *I Not Stupid* has brought more maturity to Singapore cinema allowing one to look to its future with hopeful anticipation.

CHAPTER 6

Malaysia: Melodramatic Drive, Rural Discord, Urban Heartaches

William van der Heide

As we have just seen in the previous chapter, Malaysia's cinematic history intertwines and overlaps with that of Singapore. Malaysia as we know it today is comprised of states in Peninsular Malaysia and on the island of Borneo across the South China Sea. Given the country's tangled genealogy as it emerged as a modern postcolonial nation-state, it is also marked by multiplicity – of ethnic groups, religions and languages.

The Question of Heterogeneity: Inclusion or Exclusion?

The Malaysian film industry started the 1990s, a period of societal and economic transformation, in a buoyant state, producing between twelve and fifteen films per year. However, by the end of the decade, largely as a result of the Asian economic downturn of 1997/98, the industry had slumped to crisis point, with only two or three films going into distribution. Things improved again by 2001 with the production output in 2004 matching the previous record of twenty-four films in 1962.[1] Since the mid-1990s, most Malaysian films have failed to recoup their production costs, although this period also produced the biggest box-office hits to date, directed by the two most successful filmmakers, Yusof Haslam with *Sembilu II* (1995) and Aziz M. Osman with *Lagi Lagi Senario* (2001), both working in the teen-film genre. While this genre and the demographic sector it addresses may seem a worldwide phenomenon, these films, like most Malaysian films, remain strongly influenced by both Indian and Hong Kong cinema, especially in their employment of the song routines of the former and the Cantonese and Mandarin musical melodrama characteristics of the latter. Malaysian cinema's predilection for cultural inclusivity implicitly critiques traditional ways of characterizing national cinemas, but, paradoxically, this heterogeneity is directed at a single ethnic community – the Malays. Representations of and by the other two major ethnic groups in Malaysia (Chinese and Indian) are all but invisible. Malaysian cinema has always been a commercial cinema; even the arrival of a small number of art films in the 1990s was dependent on commercial production companies, and mainstream distributors and exhibitors. However, in recent years there has arisen an independent sector that deviates from these norms: very low-budget digital video productions that reject the mainstream genres and the Malay ethnic/cultural focus (including the Malay language) of the dominant sector.[2]

Malaysian films are rarely seen outside of Malaysia, although VHS and VCD copies of popular films are watched in the Malaysian diaspora. With very few exceptions, the dialogue in these films is in the Malay language, called Bahasa Melayu.[3] While Bahasa Melayu is closely related to the Indonesian language, Malaysian films have found it extremely difficult to access the Indonesian market, due to lobbying by its film industry. Given the commercial nature of the Malaysian cinema, international film festivals, which play such an important role in drawing the world's attention to non-Hollywood films, have generally shown little interest in the country's films. This began to change with the arrival of an art cinema in the 1990s – *Kaki Bakar* (1995) was the first Malaysian film to be invited to a major film festival (Cannes). More recently, *Spinning Gasing* (2000) was distributed internationally by Columbia Tristar (no doubt due to the film's predominantly English-language soundtrack). However, Malaysian cinema is primarily a local cinema and thus an introspective cinema, further accentuated by its almost exclusive focus on audiovisual representation and discourse of Malay society and culture. It is therefore not surprising that the films are rarely subtitled in other languages.[4] All of these factors result in the near absence of references to Malaysian cinema in film books, journals, and magazines, despite an output of more than 700 films since the film industry began in 1933.[5]

Cinema Becomes "Malaysian"

It was not until after World War II that the film industry became commercially successful. It was dominated by two studios, Malay Film Productions and Cathay-Keris, both owned by Chinese entrepreneurs (the Shaw brothers and Loke Wan Tho respectively, who were also significant players in the Hong Kong film industry). The studios were located in Singapore, a predominantly Chinese city, but at the time a major centre of Malay culture. For reasons of cost, language compatibility (English), and cultural affinity (India's centuries-long impact on Southeast Asia), both studios engaged Indian film directors to make their films. It is therefore not surprising that the films resembled the song and dance melodramas of the Indian cinema of the time. The song and dance numbers in the Malay films were more arbitrarily positioned within the plots and more performance-based than those in the Indian films – in this respect, they resembled the Mandarin and Cantonese musical melodramas from Shanghai and Hong Kong. However, the films were primarily about Malay characters, despite the presence of substantial Chinese and Indian communities in what was then the British colony of Malaya. Nevertheless, these films were very popular and drew audiences from across the ethnic spectrum. During the 1950s, the studios encouraged Malays to direct films and this led to P. Ramlee, already a popular composer, singer, and actor, to become the studio era's most important and successful filmmaker. The studio era petered out in the 1970s and was gradually replaced by a Kuala Lumpur-based *Bumiputera* phase (literally "prince of the soil," more commonly translated as "sons of the soil"), in which the control of the film industry shifted to the Malays.[6]

Whereas most of the *Bumiputera* filmmakers set out to make Malaysian films (i.e. ethnically inclusive films), the vast majority of films were Malay-centered and drew predominantly Malay audiences. The influence of Indian cinema abated somewhat due to the impact of Hong Kong and Hollywood action films with their emphasis on special effects. In the early 1980s, the government demonstrated a commitment (albeit a controversial one) to the growth and administration of a national film history and local film culture by setting up the National Film Development Corporation Malaysia (FINAS), which provides financial support for script development and production. Funding is primarily derived from the entertainment tax collected by FINAS from the exhibitors; FINAS also organizes and monitors the compulsory screening of Malaysian films throughout the country. This controversial policy (disliked by exhibitors, especially when the film is not commercially successful) was based on a production output of twelve to fifteen films per year, so that the local films would not have to compete with each other in the marketplace. However, when twenty to twenty-five films are awaiting release (as in 2003 and 2004), producers are extremely concerned about their survival within a relatively small market.[7] These period-specific factors make it misleading to suggest that the production booms of 1962–63 and 2003–4 are analogous in terms of the state of the industry, which is much more fragile now than it was forty years earlier.

FINAS also administers the Malaysian Film Academy, providing skilled personnel for the film, television, and advertising industries. Nevertheless, following a diasporic pattern evident throughout Asian national cinemas, a number of the best Malaysian directors of recent times attended film schools or tertiary media courses in the US, England, India, and Australia. The subsequent influx of new ideas led to criticisms of the traditional melodramatic approach of Malaysian films and to the introduction of art-film characteristics in some of the new films. Yet all these films exist within the strongly commercial agenda of the film industry (irrespective of whether the films are successful or not); only the digital video independent films of the early 2000s operate outside the system.

There are now more non-Malay directors working in the commercial industry, e.g. Eddie Pak (*Red Haired Tumbler di Malaya*, 1994; *Syukur 21*, 2000) and Teck Tan (*Spinning Gasing*, 2001), but this (welcome) development doesn't negate the ongoing use of the *Bumiputera* label. Perhaps the 1990s did herald the arrival of a more pluralistic cinema, both in terms of film production personnel, and film plots and characters. However, this is only minimally apparent in the films themselves. Since the mid-1990s, the most popular films have been teen comedies and teen melodramas about Malays, starring Malay or Eurasian singers and models. The narrowness of the genres and the ethnic terrain is further accentuated by the fact that the most successful of these films are directed by either Aziz M. Osman or Yusof Haslam – between 1994 and 2002, one of them directed each year's biggest box-office success; surprisingly, in 2003, the less well-known A. Razak Mohaideen directed the top two hits, although the genre and ethnic aspects remain the same. This formulaic concentration is also highlighted in the serialization of these films: a box-office hit quickly leads to a further installment (or two), e.g. *Sembilu* (1994) and *Sembilu II* (1995); *Maria Mariana* (1996) and *Maria Mariana II* (1998); *Senario The Movie* (1999), *Senario Lagi* (2000) and *Lagi Lagi Senario* (2001).

Intertextual/Transtextual Dynamics in Contemporary Malaysian Films

The complex textual weave of contemporary Malaysian cinema and culture can be illustrated by an analysis of two seminal films of the early 1990s – *Perempuan, Isteri &...* (*Woman, Wife & ...*, U-Wei Haji Shaari, 1993) and *Sembilu* (*Heartache*, Yusof Haslam, 1994). Each film is then followed by a discussion of one of their directors' more recent films, *Jogho* (1999) and *Maria Mariana I* and *II* (1996 and 1998) respectively. Finally, *Spinning Gasing* (Teck Tan, 2001) will be considered in terms of its relationship to the typical *Bumiputera* film.

Perempuan, Isteri & ... is the most controversial film of the 1990s; even its original title (*Perempuan, Isteri dan Jalang*, i.e. *Woman, Wife and Whore*) was censored, as were three scenes considered too sexually explicit for local audiences. This exposé of the sexual dynamics of a Malaysian village has been labelled as an art film, but it was commercially very successful in both Malaysia and Singapore (where the uncensored version was shown). The film's director works on the borders of Malaysian cinema, literally in the case of *Jogho*, which examines a Malay community living in southern Thailand, engaged in bullfighting as an occupation and an obsession. *Sembilu* set the ground rules for the Malaysian teen movies, dealing with the lives and love traumas of young Malaysians, often employing the melodramatic mode rather than the comedic approach more typical of the Western teen genre. Yusof Haslam's *Maria Mariana I* and *II* continues this take on the genre, but sets it even more firmly within the Bollywood family genre terrain: lost-and-found plot; one sibling moving into crime, while the other joins the law enforcement agencies; the powerful moral function of the mother figure and musical numbers. *Spinning Gasing* also employs the teen melodrama form, accentuated by its "starting a band" plot, but it is probably the most ethnically diverse Malaysian film to date.

Perempuan, Isteri &... (U-Wei Haji Shaari, 1993)

Like *Spinning Gasing*, this film is important because of its contradictory relationship to the mainstream Malaysian cinema. It is a rural melodrama, focusing its attention on the Malay village, the *kampung*, which has always represented the heart of Malay culture. Except for an early scene set in southern Thailand, the film deals with Malay characters in rural Malay settings. On the other hand, apart from a remarkable and unsettling off-screen female chant in the last scene, there are no songs; and the village, far from being the sanctuary of Malay tradition, becomes the site for a devastating critique of masculine power and group solidarity. The film is U-Wei's first feature film after attending film school in New York in the 1980s, and this American film education is reflected in the film's affinities with the small-town melodramas of directors like Douglas Sirk (*All I Desire*, 1953) and Vincente Minnelli (*Some Came Running*, 1959). A "Fifth Generation" Chinese film, *Ju Dou* (directed by Zhang Yimou, 1990), is another relevant reference point, with the female protagonists of both films actively confronting patriarchy, only to eventually be destroyed by it. For a Malaysian film comparison, it is necessary to go back to a 1956 P. Ramlee film, *Semerah Padi*, in which a woman's sexual desire causes chaos (literally and morally) in her village; only her forced subjugation to the village's power elite enables the world (and the film) to return to order.

The woman and wife of the film's title is called Zaleha. The film starts with her rejecting the man chosen for her and eloping with her lover to Thailand, only to be tracked down by her intended, Amir, who sells her into prostitution, but later returns to forcefully take her back to his village. Until then, she has been nothing more than an object of exchange for the sexual and financial benefit of men. However, when she arrives in the village, she begins to assert herself through her sexuality. She displays herself to the village men, delighting in their gaze upon her, while always remaining in control of her power over them. In this respect, the film overturns the active male look/passive female object paradigm familiar from feminist film theorist Laura Mulvey's influential article on visual pleasure.[8] It soon becomes clear that such a challenge to patriarchal order, including her having sex with the "village idiot," Tapa, will not be tolerated. Amir, aided by his brother and in the presence of the whole village, kills Zaleha with the machete that Tapa had earlier used to slaughter a bull. The rather abstract final scene confirms that the destruction of such a threatening (primal) force was necessary for the revival of the patriarchal world that Zaleha had so brazenly challenged.

Perempuan, Isteri &... remains a controversial film, partly due to its art-film credentials, which tend to accentuate narrative and moral ambiguity, especially about the film's – or, typical of the art-cinema paradigm, the director/auteur's judgment – of Zaleha. The film's reception demonstrates its polysemy: some film critics and women's groups denounced the film for its degrading image of Malay womanhood, while others praised it for its fearless depiction of the plight of women.[9] Additionally, rather surprising for a Malaysian art film, it was a box-office hit – its subject matter and treatment attracting non-Malay as well as Malay audiences. It was, after all, a film "full of hot embers...!" according to a quote from the film's poster, attributed to the esteemed Malaysian novelist A. Samad Said.

Jogho (U-Wei Haji Shaari, 1999)

In contrast, *Jogho* is a realistic, almost ethnographic, depiction of a community of Patani Malays, who have lived in what is now Southern Thailand for centuries. Their allegiances are to Islam and to their fellow Malays in the northeastern Malaysian state of Kelantan and not to the Thai nation in which they now reside. The loyalties of the film's protagonists are further confined to their own extended families, irrespective of whether they live in Thailand or Malaysia. This is clearly a locale that interests U-Wei – the two main characters in *Perempuan, Isteri &...* also move back and forth between Patani and Malaysia in the first section of that film. But in *Jogho*, the border itself is irrelevant to the characters and we never see any of them passing through an official border post. In this respect, the film is unlike the 1958 Orson Welles film, *Touch of Evil*, with which it otherwise has much in common as a "border" text, such as confused and clashing cultural identities and an aura of anarchic lawlessness.

The plot reads like high melodrama. Mamat is a *jogho* (bull-trainer), who makes a living by betting money on his bull winning fights against other bulls. At the beginning of the film, his bull defeats another bull in the local arena. The losing *jogho*, Isa, and his son are so upset that they kill Mamat's bull and Mamat's brother, Lazim. This initiates a narrative of blood feuds between the two families. Despite Mamat's assertion that Patani Malays should stop killing each other (an attitude fostered by his young son, who seems to be breaking this cycle by attending a school in Kelantan), "blood keeps being paid with blood." As Mamat is taken away by the police at the end of the film, having taken the blame for Lazim's son's killing of Isa, he repeats this slogan and adds that the Patani Malays will live on forever. However, the film's treatment of this saga is anything but melodramatic. The movie doesn't identify with its characters as agents (although it does care about these people) and remains distant from their social and emotional traumas. Mamat's insistence on buying his bull the best food in the face of his family's increasing poverty is treated without condemnation of Mamat or sympathy for his wife, who is trying to make ends meet. This is achieved through a concentration on medium and long shots, often accompanied by a tracking camera observing the characters in action. In this respect, *Jogho* is the opposite to *Perempuan, Isteri &...*, where the film's perspective is that of its main character, Zaleha, even though her motivation and emotional state are as opaque as those of *Jogho*'s characters.

Such an approach to character and to the employment of the camera is quite alien to the norms of the Malaysian cinema and locates the film within the broad parameters of the European art-cinema "genre," particularly toward the end of the spectrum associated with the long-take films of Theo Angelopoulos and Bela Tarr, although U-Wei is not as formalist or rigorous as they are. However, the film's treatment of time is perhaps its most striking feature. The opening sequence is of a slow tracking shot across tree-lined fields that ends on a group of women standing in the foreground and a group of men praying around a fresh grave in the distance. After closer views of the women, some of whom are crying, and of the men, one of whom is sobbing, there is a sudden cut to a man being shot in the head, followed by a number of brief shots of men scattering and of a bull being shot, intercut with the film's credits. The film then continues with the aftermath of the killings and eventually shows Lazim's burial, with the women now in the distance and the men, led by Mamat, planting a bush on the grave. A horizontal wipe (a very self-conscious shot change) leaves Mamat at the grave by himself. The opening sequence can be interpreted as a flashforward, which is brought back into the narrative at the appropriate narrative moment. Alternatively, the killing shots represent a flashback that peters out in due course, as it catches up with the burial already shown in the opening sequence. Later on in the film there is another horizontal wipe that seems to function like the earlier one (as an ellipsis), but it becomes apparent that it triggers a long flashback that covers the events leading up to the bullfight killings and their immediate consequences (excluding the killings themselves), but now presented from a different viewpoint than in the sequence directly following the credits. Once again, the narrative is catching up with itself in a rather peculiar way and the differing functions of the wipe only add to the ambiguity of the film's rhetorical strategies. Given the attention the film demands of its viewers, it is not surprising that *Jogho* was not a box-office success, although it was critically acclaimed within Malaysia and at a number of Asian film festivals.[10]

Sembilu (Yusof Haslam, 1994)

While the two U-Wei films are important because of their departure from the mainstream Malaysian cinema, *Sembilu* is significant because it shaped the contemporary commercial cinema and instigated a series of extremely successful teen melodramas and teen comedies. However, it would be a mistake to conclude that *Sembilu* is original in content or form. In fact, the film is a very conventional Malay-focused melodrama that reaffirms traditional values in relation to gender, family authority, and morality. What is innovative about the movie is its packaging. The story of the film is derived from the love life of one of Malaysia's foremost male pop stars, Awie. (This fact is stated in the film's opening credits.) The film stars Awie himself, as well as a well-known female singer called Ziana Zain and Erra Fazira, a beauty queen and singer.[11] The first two retain their own names in the film and sing their already successful songs. This self-reflexive "package" is guaranteed to entice young Malays into the cinema. However, *Sembilu*'s innovation has to be further qualified, since all of the above elements were already present in the Malaysian cinema of the 1950s and 1960s, especially in P. Ramlee's films, some of which included his already successful songs and introduced items from his personal love life, e.g. *Penarik Beca* (1955).[12]

Nevertheless, the film is more interesting than this seemingly crass commercialism suggests. Wati, played by Erra Fazira (who is currently one of the top female stars of Malaysian cinema), is the most conventional of the three main characters. Her romantic involvement with Awie goes back to their school days and, typical of the teen melodrama genre, their relationship is tested by family disapproval, here because Awie is a musician. Awie is physically attacked by her brother and thus keeps his distance, but Wati remains resolute and eventually achieves her goal of winning Awie. On the other hand, Ziana is presented as a seductress, quickly stepping in when Wati's family rejects Awie. Unlike Wati, she is an independent and assertive woman. When Awie, reunited with Wati, predictably discards Ziana, she becomes a genuinely tragic figure, epitomized in the plaintive love song she sings in Awie's presence in a nightclub (in the most excessive scene in the film, musically and stylistically). Awie turns out to be the most intriguing character of the three. He is not really able or willing to choose between the two women. (He says that love and relationships are too difficult for him.) Therefore, he remains a passive figure in the mold of P. Ramlee characters of the 1950s and 1960s, most strikingly in *Ibu Mertua-ku* (1962).[13] Awie actually seems happiest when he is alone playing his music and singing of love (rather than living it). This character trait creates narrative open-endedness and continuity: Awie ultimately only loves (and is loved by) his fans in the audience and his romantic vacillation allows for a sequel, *Sembilu II*, which was even more successful that its predecessor.

Maria Mariana I and *II* (Yusof Haslam, 1996 and 1998)

Despite the fact that these two films were produced two years apart, they can be treated as a single entity, rather than a film and its sequel. In one respect, the *Maria Mariana* films could be categorized as a sequel to the two *Sembilu* films: the major production roles for all four are occupied by the same individuals (except for a new cinematographer for *Maria Mariana II*) and the main actors recur in them all – Awie (except for *Maria Mariana*), Erra Fazira, Ziana Zain, Noraini Hashim (the mother) and Roy Azman. It could be argued that this is just the result of Yusof Haslam maintaining a stock company, like John Ford and Rainer Werner Fassbinder, but it is also symptomatic of the rigidity of the current Malaysian film industry, with its compulsion to repeat. It also has to be admitted that actors spanning across four films can bring intertextual density to their roles. However, the links between the two *Maria Mariana* films go much further. The first film ends with the apparent death of Maria, the "good" sister, who tells her "bad" sister, Mariana, to look after their mother. This could never be the end of this teen melodrama, morally or generically. A sequel, or rather the second half of the narrative, is thus already built into the first film. This is a rather daring step for Yusof Haslam (the producer/director of all four of the above films), since he is presuming that *Maria Mariana* will do well at the box-office. He need not have worried (and perhaps did not, because the packaging is as astute as that of *Sembilu*): the film was by far the most successful of 1996, a feat repeated two years later with *Maria Mariana II*.

There is another sense in which the two films form a single unit. Even more than *Sembilu*, the *Maria Mariana* films resemble Indian popular films. First, the total length (over three hours) is not uncommon in Indian cinema. Secondly, the formal elements of the Bollywood film are also present: an emphasis on melodrama, the inclusion of songs, the introduction of the main characters as children at the beginning of the film followed by a device (e.g. a title or a matching image) that propels the characters into adulthood, a reconciliatory conclusion that reaffirms the moral order (here provided by a final title: "Man can only plan, but Allah determines everything ..."), and an emphasis on the family and the mother-child dyad. Furthermore, the *Maria Mariana* films are reminiscent of a sub-category of Indian films that deal with siblings, who through circumstance or conflict move into differing moral universes, with one of them becoming a representative of the law and the other a criminal or an outsider. Indian examples are *Mother India* (1957), *Ganga Jumna* (1962), *Deewar* (1975), *Amar Akbar Anthony* (1977) and *Ram Lakhan* (1989) – the second, fourth and last films, like *Maria Mariana*, have titles constituted of the names of the siblings. Finally, as in *Sembilu* (where it is evident in the kung fu-like fight between Awie and Wati's brother), there are also links to the Hong Kong action cinema, in particular the first two *A Better Tomorrow* films (1986 and 1987), where there are also siblings on opposite sides of the law. However, the gangster material in the *Maria Mariana* films remains tangential to the main generic concerns, functioning primarily as ways of jolting the narrative into different directions. (Much the same can be said for the gangster subplot in *Spinning Gasing*.)

The *Maria Mariana* films set up the two sisters as antagonists, although without the good-evil dichotomy of the Indian "sibling" films. Maria is an exemplary daughter and a model student, who becomes a police officer. Mariana, on the other hand, is disinterested in school and is drawn to the motorbike gangs of her neighborhood; while she is not a criminal, she moves within the criminal world. This, inevitably, causes conflict between the sisters and between Mariana and her mother. Mariana is attracted by strong and rather aggressive men – she falls in love with one of them in each of the two parts. In the first part, the man soon shifts his attention from her to Maria, who rejects his attention. Nevertheless, it results in much emotional suffering and to Maria's capture by a gang, one of whom critically wounds her at the end of the first part. Mariana continues to frequent motorbike gangs in the second part where she meets and falls in love with Sazali (Awie), who is involved with drugs and sought by the police, led by the now recovered Maria. There is a gunfight between Maria and Sazali, which results in his death. Once again, Mariana is distraught and her tearful responses to both of these shattered love affairs are expressed in the sad love ballads that recur throughout the films (bearing a strong resemblance, musically and stylistically, to the song sequences in *Sembilu*). Despite Mariana's repeated "heartaches," the sisters are both strong characters. What is remarkable about the *Maria Mariana* films is their focus on two female siblings, who operate in largely male worlds, whether professionally or socially. This is in stark contrast to the male sibling narratives of the Indian and Hong Kong films mentioned above, where women are quite perfunctory, except for the ever present mother-son dyad in the Indian films.

Spinning Gasing (Teck Tan, 2000)

Spinning Gasing has become the best-known Malaysian film internationally, largely due to its exposure at a number of international film festivals. However, it was not successful locally, where the box-office takings were just 20 percent of its production costs. The film was initially banned in Malaysia for its sexual explicitness and its insensitive treatment of religion, but was eventually released in a heavily censored version.[14] As a more covert form of censorship, there are scenes in the film where the Bahasa Melayu subtitles moderate the frankness of the English dialogue.

The film was criticized in Malaysia for its exotic representation of the country and its culture, for functioning as a tourism promotion.[15] There are certainly shots of the airport, Kuala Lumpur, the East Coast mountains, the beaches and the resort island, where the camera appears to be selling the landscape, but these are minimal digressions from the film's plot. More significantly, however, the film has cast at least one eye toward a non-Malaysian audience. This is apparent in the title that precedes the credits: "Malaysia is a multi-racial country. The main races – Malay, Chinese, and Indian – live in apparent harmony with each community having its own religions, customs and languages. As a former British colony, English is often the common language spoken between the races." Such a preamble, in English, is certainly not directed at a Malaysian viewer, except as a rationale for its predominantly English dialogue (with the rest in Bahasa Melayu and Cantonese). The information about the "races" may well be regarded as contentious, with its suggestion of cultural and linguistic separateness and isolationism, although in fact this is a view that permeates the whole film. It arises from the phrase "impossible to mix," which is first used by the Eurasian woman, Chantal, with reference to the impossibility of Harry, a Chinese Malaysian atheist, and Yati, a Malay Muslim woman, having a long-term relationship or marrying. This notion is then constantly voiced by all the main characters, including Harry and Yati themselves. More generally, it also refers to a lack of knowledge of another's culture (evidenced in the ignorance by Harry and JJ, an Indian Malaysian, of traditional Malay culture) and to the rejection (by Yati) of Harry amalgamating her traditional Malay poetry with dance music. The opening title therefore does assert what the film demonstrates: Malaysia is multiracial and not multicultural, a concept implying heterogeneity and inclusiveness. In that respect, *Spinning Gasing* resembles the vast majority of Malaysian films, even though here the ethnic focus is decidedly pluralist.

Harry returns to Malaysia, having failed numerous university courses, with the aim of setting up a dance band with Yati, JJ and Ariff, a Malay gay man. Chantal, whom they find in a nightclub, becomes their singer. Apart from the inevitable internal tensions, professional and sexual, the band is hounded by some Cantonese gangsters and manipulated by a lecherous young Malay businessman, who contracts the band to play at his island resort. The band finally breaks up, with Ariff and JJ becoming lovers, Chantal disappearing and Yati returning to Kuala Lumpur, where she sees a poster listing Harry as a disc jockey at a local event. The relationship between Harry and Yati comes to dominate the film, but their love for each other is unable to overcome religious incompatibility. Harry may well be the film's protagonist, but Yati is its main character. The film starts and ends with her and even though she is often a silent witness to the band's activities, her affirmation of her Muslim and Malay identity are at the forefront of the film's concerns: Yati's quiet insistence on going her own way in the face of her family's pressure on her to "behave like a decent Malay girl." The film repeatedly comments on her engagement with Malay history and traditional Malay poetry, but Yati's foremost cultural experience in the film is of a dance by a group of traditionally clad women on the East Coast beach to a song called *Ulek Mayang*, which, significantly, concerns an "impossible to mix" relationship between seven fishermen and the seven sea spirits who rescued them. Yati joins the women in their dance after explaining the meaning of the song to the culturally ignorant Harry. The dance is dwelt upon as a performance for quite some time (like a song and dance number in a 1950s Malaysian film). Yati looks up to where Harry is standing and notes his intense gaze upon her, as if seeing a different person to the one he had known since childhood. In response, Yati stops dancing and stares back at him. Nothing is ever said about this event or their visual communion, but its importance is underlined later in the film when Yati, seeing Harry on the floor below her in a hotel, imagines herself in costume dancing with the other women to the same song. She now looks troubled, as if the song's words confirm their incompatibility.

The *Ulek Mayang* song also occurs in Aziz M. Osman's first film, *Fenomena* (1989), where it accompanies the female protagonist taking a traditional Malay bath to cure her mysterious illness. The song here emphasizes the healing power of the seven sea spirits, but the looks exchanged between the woman and the man she comes to love are very similar to those in *Spinning Gasing*.[16] There are actually quite a few other similarities between the two films: finding one's Malay/Muslim identity, the East Coast, as the heartland of Malay/Muslim culture, cultural incompatibility (between the Westernized Eurasian woman and a Malay man in *Fenomena*) a childhood scene (only verbalized in *Spinning Gasing*) and a narrative that focuses on musicians. However, such correspondences are not confined to these two films. Quite a number of 1990s films deal with these subjects and situations e.g. *Selubung* (1992). They also frequently contain *khalwat* scenes (a term combining discourse of Islamic law and gender, literally meaning "close proximity"), where religious police check the marital status of Muslim men and women found together (also a significant event in the film *Perempuan, Isteri &...*). Its presence in *Spinning Gasing* once again stresses the difficulties facing Harry and Yati in surmounting the religious and cultural barriers to their relationship.

While *Spinning Gasing*'s teen genre credentials are obvious – young musicians trying to make a name for themselves while coping with their heartaches (virtually the plot of *Sembilu*) – its treatment of the material is most atypical. The film, even in its censored form, deals more frankly with sex, race, and religion than any previous Malaysian film. Even *Perempuan, Isteri &...* did not show the sex act, whereas here Harry and Chantal are seen to have sex in various parts of the band's house, until violently interrupted by the Cantonese gangsters. Just prior to this, Ariff is seen picking up a male client for paid sex. These characters are never punished for this behavior, with the possible exception of Chantal, whose duplicity seems to overwhelm her vulnerability. Yati is very aware of Harry's involvement with Chantal and is present when Chantal tells Harry she's pregnant by him (although later she denies he is the father). But this has nothing to do with Yati's rejection of Harry's argument that things will work out between them if they love each other enough. It is the insurmountable barrier, as she sees it, of religious and cultural difference. The film therefore tackles the teen world quite realistically, both in terms of behavior and language, and that makes it a most unusual Malaysian film. Perhaps the ethnic identities of the band members are too schematic (rather too neatly reflecting the ethnic mix in the country), but the exploration of a Malay woman's identity by a Chinese Malaysian director does indicate an interest in the "other." Stylistically, *Spinning Gasing* downplays the melodrama inherent in the genre. The camerawork has an improvisational quality to it that suits the road movie aspects of the film. The characters interact with each other within the frame rather than through incessant reverse angle cutting (typical of the television aesthetic that infects much Malaysian cinema). In these ways, the film has an international (primarily American-European) quality that extends well beyond its English dialogue to diasporic dimensions of its production.[17]

Spinning Gasing's internationalism sets it apart from the sequel-driven mainstream Malaysian cinema exemplified by *Sembilu* and the *Maria Mariana* films, with which it nevertheless intertextually has much in common in terms of themes and, to some extent, approach. Its similarity to *Perempuan, Isteri &...* and *Jogho* resides in their shared critiques of contemporary Malay/Malaysian identities and their forthright presentation of the lives of their characters, although the U-Wei films undertake this task in a more uncompromising manner.

Whether these multiple modes of production can successfully cohabit and prosper in such a small film market remains to be seen. For now, the mainstream sequel-driven teen melodramas and comedies remain the primary popular local fare.

CHAPTER 7

Indonesia: Screening a Nation in the Post-New Order

Krishna Sen[1]

The first Indonesian film was made in 1926, when the country was under Dutch colonial rule and nationalism was just beginning to stir. Since then, according to statistics collected by the Indonesian Film Archives (Pusat Perfilman Haji Usmar Ismail).[2] Indonesia has produced over 2,200 feature films. These statistics do not capture the whole gamut of filmmaking in Indonesia, but do give us a sense of the size and significance of Indonesia's "national popular" cinema. Indonesia's film industry might seem insignificant in comparison to those of the big global players: India, Hong Kong, and Hollywood. Indonesia is, however, the largest film-producing nation of Southeast Asia, even including Australia and New Zealand. This is not surprising given that Indonesia is also the most populous nation in the region, most of whose 180 million people speak the national language Bahasa Indonesia (as their first or second language). Like the other national film industries in the region, Indonesian cinema has, throughout its history, led an embattled existence, struggling for an audience against imported American, Indian, and Chinese films.

Since the production of the first film, Indonesia has experienced massive political shifts: Japanese occupation in 1942–1945, independence from the Dutch in 1949, a brief dalliance with democracy (1950–1957), left-nationalist authoritarianism (1957–1965), right-wing military rule (1965–1998), and since 1998 a new and robust engagement with political democracy.[3] At every point the political context has intersected with cinematic texts in such a way that it would be almost impossible to write about Indonesian cinema without also writing about the political context. The main focus of this chapter is to understand those intersections, to see how particular texts were created and understood within particular political regimes, not only through the simple operations of government policy, but through more complex contestations over the very notion of the Indonesian nation.

I concentrate in this chapter on the period commonly known as the New Order – General Suharto's authoritarian rule from 1965 to 1998 – and its aftermath, to explore the nature of the "national fiction"[4] created by Indonesian cinema. General Suharto came to power with overt and covert support from the US and its allies following a failed coup on 1 October 1965 and a bloodbath in which more than 500,000 people were killed under the guise of ridding the nation of communism. In the midst of mass killings, on March 11, 1966, Indonesia's first President, Sukarno, was forced to hand power over to General Suharto in order to "take all necessary steps to guarantee security and calm and stability"[5] – words that would effectively become the New Order "mantra" for the next thirty years. Suharto called his government the New Order to distinguish it from the "Old Disorder" of the previous anti-Western left-nationalist regime of President Sukarno, and through the rest of its history legitimized every restriction of collective and individual rights in the name of "restoration of Order and Security."

The film industry expanded in the 1970s as the Indonesian economy recovered rapidly. In the new political context it developed a particular social vision, and a narrative form predicated on the vision of "order" that legitimized the repressive New Order regime. Through the 1990s, while the institutions and regulations of the 1970s remained in place, new communication technologies, the ever increasing circulation of global imagery and indeed the mounting local discontent against the New Order and its mechanisms of control, transformed the way in which Indonesian film texts were constructed/encoded and received/decoded,[6] allowing after the collapse of the New Order the emergence of new national fictions in a new era of political and creative freedoms. In this chapter, I describe briefly the institutions of cinema in the New Order and its archetypal test, in order to understand the directions of change in Indonesian cinematic practices in the current process of democratic transition.

The Film Regime of the New Order

The key institutional structures through which cinema was governed and controlled in the New Order were inherited from the colonial period – the board of film censorship set up in 1925 and the state owned ANIF (Algemeen Nederlandsch-Indisch Film) which started producing features and documentaries in 1936. The Japanese period (1942–45), though brief, further strengthened the state's role in film production,[7] training native Indonesians in news and propaganda films. The national government which came to power in 1949 under President Sukarno maintained both of these institutions and the state film company (now called Perusahaan Film Negara, PFN) churned out reels of Sukarno images while the Board of Film Censorship (Badan Sensor Film, BSF) took a leading role as the ultra-nationalist gate-keeper of Indonesian culture, keeping out the political and sexual "excesses" of Hollywood cinema, until their import was banned in 1964.

Cinema was already laden with a political history by the time of the estab-lishment of the New Order. Ideals about the content of films were shaped largely by the perception of cinema as a site of political discourse in the last years of Sukarno's rule and the violent anti-communism of the early New Order period.[8] In the New Order the prime motive of censorship, and film policy more generally, shifted from the nationalist rhetoric of protecting "national culture" against foreign incursions to a concentration on policing the works of Indonesian filmmakers. In a dramatic reversal of the ban on Hollywood films, the film market was thrown open to foreign imports. In 1967 the annual number of imported films rose to about 400 and then nearly doubled in 1969.

Institutionally cinema in Indonesia was defined as a "mass medium" like radio, press, and television, and placed under the Department of Information while other cultural activities like the arts, theater and literature were under the Department of Education and Culture. This institutional demarcation between media and "art" became more marked later when, in 1978, the Department of Information was placed under the aegis of the Coordinating Minister of Politics and Security, and the Culture portfolio in the jurisdiction of the Coordinating Minister of People's Welfare. Thus the positioning of cinema within the state apparatus emphasized the ideological and propaganda aspects of films, rather than their artistic and creative dimension.

Pre-censorship[9] as a condition of production has always distinguished films from all other media. Inherited from the Dutch era, the Board of Film Censorship remained (indeed, still remains) the oldest and most persistent institution of Indonesian cinema. New layers of pre-censorship (formal and informal, sometimes operating discretely and extra-legally) were added in the first decade of the New Order, which resulted in locally produced films being more stringently censored than imported ones.[10] To all intents, administrative changes during 1978–82 (with the Information portfolio in the hands of former Intelligence Chief General Ali Murtopo) reverted film censorship to its old colonial function as an arm of the government's internal security apparatus.

While the government's public-relations pronouncements emphasized cen-sorship of sex and violence and protection of national culture, these take up a comparatively small portion of the regulatory documents produced during the New Order. The 1977 *Censorship Guideline*, for instance, has only one direct reference to sex in its list of twenty-four criteria for banning or excising films: "films which emphasize sex and violence." The "general principles" in the introduction to the *Censorship Guideline* states "As a consequence of our involvement in international communication, we cannot isolate ourselves from the influence of foreign culture entering Indonesia through film [among other means], be they foreign or national films containing foreign ingredients. This has both positive and negative elements."[11] But there is no further reference to foreign culture in the actual list of criteria, other than the banning of ideologies of "colonialism, imperialism, fascism" and all forms of communism and socialism, which in New Order political discourse were often presented as foreign.

What runs most strongly through the regulatory documents throughout the New Order period is the injunction to avoid all reference to social conflict or tension in Indonesia. Thus films are to be banned or excised if they are deemed likely to destroy the unity of religions in Indonesia, harm the development of national consciousness, or exploit feelings of ethnicity, religion or ancestry, or even arouse sentiments of ethnicity, religion and race, and engender social tension, including those between social classes. Films are forbidden too from expression of dissent against policies of the government or anything that could cause damage to persons or institutions associated with the state. The Government Regulation No. 7, 1994, states that films promoting analysis or political ideology or false accusations which might be seen as disturbing the stability of the nation will be automatically banned.

Other Regulatory documents (e.g. the *Production Codes* developed in 1981 by the National Film Council), recast the censors' proscriptions as positive prescriptions. Accordingly, Indonesian films "need to express" "the harmonious co-existence of religions" and "mutual respect for the practice of faith in accordance with the religion and belief of each person." Films are also urged to show "how Indonesian people put unity [and] unification, as well as the well-being of the nation and the state, above personal and group interests" and particularly to include episodes "which emphasize the values of ... national unity." Further, films were urged to refrain from criticizing the "upholders of law and order."[12]

Clearly the prescriptions and proscriptions were designed less to contain or curtail foreign cultural impacts than to restrict the political and cultural options of Indonesian filmmakers. The regulations and processes of censorship were designed primarily to shape the narrative of Indonesian films – to produce film texts that would speak of a state in control and of a nation united. Notably the state institutions most explicitly protected from critical scrutiny were the justice and police departments, institutions which tame the dissent of citizens. These controls seem even more odious when we recognize that since the late 1970s (after a period of import reduction in 1974–78) successive government legislation strengthened the hands of importers and permitted imported films to take a greater and greater share of the market.[13] Ironically, the assumption that national cinema had political power of persuasion worked against both the commercial viability and the artistic freedoms of Indonesian national cinema in the New Order.

Texts of Order

Censorship does not, of course, make up the entire media culture in which films are made and consumed – the channels of aesthetic judgment such as film festivals and critical acclaim, state and private funding, and the political and cultural context more generally, all impact on the formation of screen texts. Indeed any textual formation is so complex that it is impossible to isolate the precise factors that may have shaped it. We look closely here at what might be called the "archetypal" film text of the New Order to understand the way in which cinema replicated the order-restoration rhetoric of the regime.

There are examples of films where the censors intervened in ways to transform the content of the film to deliver the 'order and security' message. However, for the film discussed here, *Nopember 1828* (1978), one of the most celebrated films of the New Order era, the content and message were not in any direct sense affected by governmental intervention. The film, directed by Teguh Karya (one of Indonesia's most celebrated directors), the most expensive production of its times (costing almost twice the average film), swept up the overwhelming majority of awards at Indonesia's annual national awards in 1979. It immediately gained the status of a classic.

A film of epic proportions, *Nopember 1828* is set in the context of the Java Wars let by Prince Diponegoro. Indonesian nationalist mythology often portrays the prince as a nationalist hero, though most Western historians point to the regional and backward-looking character of this anti-Dutch resistance.[14] A story of heroism, nationalism, and betrayal told in several flashbacks, *Nopember 1828* unfolds in a village in central Java, which is an epitome of harmony, until just moments into the film, the Dutch troops occupy the village, on suspicion of its collusion with Sentot Prawirodirjo, one of the lieutenants of the Prince. Jayengwirono, a greedy opportunist, is appointed as village head and the highly respected elder, Kromoludiro, is arrested. Karto Sarjan, the respected teacher of Islam, sends his students to inform Sentot about the presence of Dutch troops. Kromoludiro dies a hero's death at the hands of the brutal Dutch commander Captain de Borst.

Inevitably, in the final part of the film, de Borst's troops are defeated by Sentot. An advance army of the Javanese commander enters the fortress disguised as a traveling dance troop. Attack is launched simultaneously by the frenzied dancers inside the fortress and masses of villagers at its gates. Just as the Dutch appear to be recovering from the unanticipated attack, Sentot rides in, resplendent in white and at the head of a well-armed battalion. De Borst is killed, the Dutch defeated. Having restored the village to the villagers, Sentot departs as well.

Director Teguh Karya has said repeatedly that he thinks of films having an important "national function" in "a country of many islands with many diverse cultural traditions" and as a "medium for expressing his feeling inspired by the call of his motherland."[15] In *Nopember 1828*, his most overtly nationalist film, the birth of the nation out of a war of independence is embedded in the idea of "restoration" rather than change. The walled village, the microcosm of the Indonesian nation, is in a state of perfect harmony until disrupted by the Dutch colonialism at the start of the film. The film ends exactly in the space where it started – the village perimeter – with the Dutch gone and therefore the pre-Dutch order and harmony restored.

As Benedict Anderson has shown in his seminal work on nationalism, all nations imagine their existence back into distant antiquity.[16] It is not surprising therefore that the Java wars, which were an attempt by the traditional rulers of Java to turn back the historical clock, should be so neatly appropriated into a nationalist film. What is more remarkable is the consistency with which every historical film made during the New Order, even when the film is set in the context of Indonesia's nationalist struggle, revolves around the idea of restoring order rather than realizing change. In the hands of a cinema brought to order by censorship and a myriad of other controls, the coming of independence is emptied of its revolutionary, transforming potential, and becomes merely the story of de-colonization and, inevitably, the restoration of order.

I have argued elsewhere that the archetypal film (indeed most films) of the New Order, whatever its genre, style, or theme, contained the same basic narrative structure which moved from order through disorder to a restoration of order. Films made before the coming of the New Order in 1965, however, contained vastly more diverse interpretations of history and society. Historical cinema of the pre-1965 period was often imbued with a sense of the socially revolutionary potential of independence and the frustration of that revolutionary potential.[17] The particular conservative rendering of nationalism-as-restoration in the films of the New Order can then be seen as the textual product of a particular kind of political regime and its specific film institutions.

For the rest this chapter, I look at the period since the collapse of the Suharto regime in May 1998, in particular to identify if and how the "ordered" text of the New Order might be being transformed by the changes in the political context.

End of Order?

After thirty-two years of authoritarian rule, faced with a severe financial crisis and mass popular uprising, President Suharto resigned from office on May 21, 1998. A period of frenzied political reforms, anarchy on the streets and three further changes to the presidency followed. With the appointment of Megawati Sukarnoputri (the daughter of the first Indonesian president,

Sukarno) as President in July 2001, the pace of reform appears to have slowed to such an extent that some commentators are suggesting that while the reign of Suharto has ended, Suharto-ism as a mode of governance perhaps has not. The lack of change in the formal institutions of Indonesian cinema does appear to confirm that sense of continuity. But the film texts themselves might well tell a different story.

Numbers of feature films had been falling throughout the decade of the 1990s – from 115 in 1990 to just 3 in 1999. Most media analysts in Indonesia have linked the fall in numbers of feature films to the spread of private television in Indonesia, legalized in 1987 and available via satellite across much of the archipelago by 1990.[18] From 2000 onward, the numbers of feature films began to increase again, though slowly: to 9 in 2001 and 15 in 2002.

These statistics do not, however, begin to capture what young Indonesian filmmakers are celebrating as the rebirth of Indonesian cinema since around 2000, represented by the enormous range of film cultural activity in the metropolitan centers, particularly those with major universities, such as Jakarta, Bandung, Yogyakarta, and Surabaya.[19] Scores of short films and documentaries, which do not get into the commercial circuit, are being produced and screened in "alternative" but technologically well-appointed theaters such as the Ruang Tengah Ardan in Bandung and Teater Utan Kayu or Sinemensa in Jakarta. Independent film and video clubs and festivals are mushrooming around university towns, with the majority of the films being shot and screened in a variety of digital formats rather than on the conventional 35mm. A small number of feature-length films shot in digital formats have had limited commercial screenings in one or two of the major Jakarta theaters which have the technological facility. Some young film activists who started in this "informal" sector of cinema are making their way into commercial screenings, with some of their works drawing more than a million spectators (e.g. *Petualang Sherina* [*Sherina's Adventure*] by Riri Riza, 2000) – a very respectable audience number in the context of Indonesian films in any period.

While new broadcast media laws have been promulgated since the fall of Suharto, the regulatory framework of cinema is yet to be formally disbanded. Since the 1970s, every member of a film crew – from the star to the studio-assistant – had been required to get approval from their respective government-appointed industry bodies prior to the start of shooting. Nor under these old regulations could shooting start until the script had been approved by the Department of Information. However, that Department, which was responsible for the implementation of the government's film policy, was itself abolished in 2000. It was replaced in 2001 by a Department of Communication, headed by a junior minister, but without the institutional capacity or indeed the political will to replicate the operations of the old and much hated Ministry of Information. As a result, the most productive of the current filmmakers are operating outside of the old, out-dated, and inoperable regulations.

The government-appointed censorship body also continues to operate without any amendments to the censorship guidelines issued in the late 1970s. As indicated earlier, every film seeking commercial release in Indonesia needs approval from this body and its local counterparts in the district capitals (which have responsibility for films screened in their local areas). While one or two films have been seriously nobbled by the censors in recent years (mainly for representation of sexuality regarded by the censors as too explicit), the clear ideological restrictions, which prevented any favorable mention of left-wing ideologies, and any mention of ethnic, religious, or class contradictions in Indonesia, seem no longer to be effective. The question then is to what extent have film texts broken out of the limits set by the New Order government for thirty-two years? Are the new political freedoms generating new content, form, and language for Indonesian cinema?

There is little doubt that many of the feature films produced since 1998 have content which, prior to then, would have been deleted by the censors. One of the most popular Indonesian films of all time, *Ada Apa Denagan Cinta* (*What's Up with Love*, 2001), contained a sub-plot dealing with a scholar being sacked from his university position because of his "1996 thesis on government corruption." But with that single reference excised or re-cast, the film would have got past the censors at any stage of the New Order. Beyond that single political statement, the teenage love story, which ends with promise of all adolescent problems being resolved with age and maturity and the prospect of young lovers meeting again, is fairly typical of the *remaja* (teenage) film genre, which had been popular through much of the 1970s and 1980s.

At the other end of the aesthetic spectrum, *Pasir Berbisik* (*Whispering Sands*, 2001), which has been promoted as an art film in Indonesia and in the international festival circuit, might not easily have passed the scrutiny of censorship during the New Order. A complex and subtly violent film, it is visually reminiscent of Chinese Fifth Generation films, particularly Chen Kaige's *Yellow Earth* (1984), depicting death and destruction in an arid countryside. The central characters, Berlian (mother) and Daya (daughter), fall from poverty to destitution as they try to escape violence, the sources of which are invisible and the causes inexplicable. For Daya, her final personal disaster comes when her father forces her into prostitution. In the final scene, the shacks in the tiny desert settlement are burning again and Berlian sends her daughter away with an old man who is leaving. We have no sense of where the young woman is headed.

Many popular feature films of the New Order depicted people living in unrelenting poverty (though I recall none that combined this with the relentless isolation and violence of this film). More importantly, written and unwritten laws of the New Order had always compelled films to end on an optimistic note, to the extent of tacking on happy endings even when this made no sense at all in the narrative logic of a particular film.[20] It is not impossible, particularly in the context of the current generation of spectators, that the violence depicted through the film, always without explanation, could be seen as the violence which the New Order visited upon many categories of Indonesians. This violence remained to many not only unjustifiable, but also erratic and illogical and therefore violence to which no one was immune. In all of this, the film invites radical political appropriation by an audience well-versed in a critique of the now discredited and failed New Order regime. But the film has no concrete historical or geographical anchoring. Indeed, it would be difficult to imagine any part of the island of Java (there are enough cultural codes to conclude that the characters are Javanese) where one can imagine the kind of isolation that the film presents in its last section – a desert with a handful of shacks. Self-consciously arty, the film appears to have been deliberately uprooted from any "real" temporal moorings.

Political and cultural critique, couched in the form of fantasy and parable, and sometimes even realist cinema couched as a moral tale (rather than social critique), were not entirely absent from Indonesian cinema in the New Order period. From time to time during the years of the New Order some of these films[21] got past the censorship process. Like these films, the reading of *Pasir Berbisik* as a radical critique (of the New Order regime) requires the application of critical analysis to unlock its immanent meaning.[22] In other words, it is not impossible to imagine *Pasir Berbisik* being made and even released prior to the demise of the New Order. While the film clearly would have stretched the limits of New Order cinema, it might not have broken its bounds altogether.

That begs the question then as to whether there is as yet a "post-New Order" in Indonesian cinema? Are we beginning to see the emergence of films which could not have been shot, let alone released commercially, at any period of the thirty-two years of the New Order?

Old History in New Cinema

The film *Ca Bau-kan* (2002) would not even have had its title (in Chinese, a language banned from all media in the New Order) approved at any time in the life of the New Order. This film is unique in a number of ways in the annals of Indonesian cinema. New Order restrictions on any public display of Chinese language and culture had effectively pushed all but the most unpleasant and stereotypical representation of the Chinese out of films. Chinese businesses were always central in funding films in Indonesia. Several prominent directors, including Teguh Karya whose work is discussed earlier in this chapter, were of Chinese descent. None ever projected their ethnicity into their films or even referred cinematically to anything but the most universal-ized forms of national identity. *Ca Bau-kan* is the first Indonesian film since 1965 that deals primarily with the Chinese community and its location in Indonesian colonial and early nationalist history. A film with a Chinese hero at the center of the story/history could not have been permitted to be made during the New Order. Such a subject was so far beyond the pale of imagina-tion in the New Order that no one, to my knowledge, ever proposed such a project in its thirty-two years.

Ca Bau-kan is also the first historical film made by a woman director in Indonesia. As in most other national film industries, women directors are few and far between in the Indonesian film industry. (The "Who's Who of Indonesian Cinema" published in 1979 did not list a single woman director.) In the 1980s, Ida Farida was the first woman to direct films. Throughout the 1990s, the rise of serialized television family drama (known in Indonesia as "Sinetron") brought a few more women into the edges of cinema. Women directors are, however, well represented among the small band of filmmakers who have risen to prominence since 1998. In particular, there are Mira Lesmana (independent producer and director), Nan T. Achnas (writer, director *Pasir Berbisik*) and Nia Dinata (director *Ca Bau-kan*), all young, articulate, trained in Western universities and in one way or another socially well connected. Lesmana and Achnas are both part of the self-aware film movement, which launched itself via the collectively produced *Kuldesak* in 1998. Nia Dinata is less central to that movement. After several years in American universities completing her tertiary education, including a degree in Mass Communication, she returned to Indonesia to work in television, mainly directing commercials and music video. *Ca Bau-kan,* her first feature film, could arguably be regarded as the first epic film in Indonesia, in terms of the scale of history it appropriates and the range and variety of voices it speaks.

The film is based on a 1999 novel by Remy Sylado[23] which won instant popularity as it dealt with the New Order taboo subject, the Chinese in Indonesian history, and was almost immediately adapted first into a somewhat esoteric stage production and then into a popular movie. The story (and the film) is set in and around the colonial capital Batavia (later Jakarta) from the early years of the nationalist movement in the 1930s to just after national inde-pendence in 1950. The film begins with a middle-aged woman, Giok Lian, with clearly Chinese facial features, returning to Indonesia from the Netherlands, where she was brought up by adoptive Dutch parents. Giok Lian wants to recover the story of her parents: her mother Tinung, a girl from a poor, rural Betawi[24] background, and her father Tan Peng Liang, a super-wealthy Chinese tobacco trader and (later) arms-smuggler.

While Tinung and Tan Peng Liang are married, most of the film deals with their separate and parallel lives. Through Tinung we see the underbelly of the colonial society: a young woman who has no capacity to survive except as a wife or courtesan (*ca bau-kan* in the film's title), sometimes protected, and at other times merely consumed by men. At times she sinks into prostitution. During the years of Japanese occupation of Indonesia (1942–45) she is gang-raped by Japanese soldiers. The film does not tell us how her life ends, as the story concludes with the murder of Tan Peng Liang, the father of her children and the love of her life, who is, however, mostly absent from her life. Though she has two children, we have no knowledge of her as a mother, other than that she is a failure as she is forced to give her firstborn up to adoption. A deeply tragic figure, she is never anything other than an object of desire of men.

Tan Peng Liang's is a story of wealth and international adventure. Through him we see the life of the Chinese businessmen, who are mostly corrupt, with little empathy with the Indonesian population and its nationalist aspirations. We see also the aristocratic Javanese, rich, sophisticated, and indolent but eventually drawn into the nationalist struggle, as are some of the young Chinese in the context of the Japanese occupation during World War II. Tan Peng Liang is himself eventually drawn into Indonesia's nationalist struggle against the Dutch, but it is never quite clear whether he is driven entirely by adventurism and money or also in part by nationalism.

The conflict between a group of Chinese merchants in Batavia and Tan Peng Liang lands the latter in jail. He escapes to mainland Southeast Asia after faking his own death. While an escapee he becomes involved in smuggling weapons for sale to the Indonesian rebels resisting the Japanese and later the Dutch. To his Javanese aristocratic friend, Tan Peng Liang claims a degree of nationalist sympathy, which he says he inherited from his Javanese mother. To his business partner in Thailand, he explains his interest in weapons smuggling as entirely driven by business opportunism.

The degree of ambiguity written into all of the key characters of the film is highly unusual in the annals of Indonesian cinema. I have shown elsewhere the degree to which Indonesian film texts depended on binaries of good versus bad, nationalist vs. pro-colonial, wife vs. whore. These binaries are particularly well-defined in historical cinema, as any detailed reading of classic New Order historical films such as *Nopember 1828* will show. The good nationalist Indonesian vs. bad pro-Colonial was underpinned by an elaborate set of restrictions and propaganda texts of the New Order. In this discourse, citizens of Chinese descent were inevitably cast as agents of foreigners, first of the colonial regime and later of Communist China.[25] In films of the New Order period, Chinese characters appear rarely, and when they do, they are crooks and buffoons. I can recall no Indonesian film, either those made in the period of the New Order or indeed films in the archives from the 1950s and 1960s, which is so centrally about the Chinese in Indonesia and their mixed role in the struggle for Indonesian independence.

The breaking of a specific ethno-political taboo of any regime is perhaps relatively easy immediately after the collapse of the regime. Politically, during the Presidency of Abdurrahman Wahid, the first democratically elected president after the resignation of Suharto, many of the restrictions on the public expression of Chinese culture and tradition were lifted. Its release timed to coincide with the first public celebration of Chinese New Year in Indonesia since 1965, *Ca Bau-kan* was marketed precisely to take advantage of the new more ethnically tolerant Indonesian politics.

What has gone unnoticed in the reviews of the film, however, is the much less overt but equally persistent demarcation between the good wife and the bad whore, which is also broken in this film. The wife-whore binary is not uncommon in many national cinemas and indeed mass cultural products more widely. In Indonesia though, this discourse has a particularly politicized history. At the moment of birth of the New Order, women associated with the Indonesian Communist Party were demonised as "murderous whores."[26] Indeed many feminist scholars have written about the construction of the ideal woman as wife and mother in the policy discourses of the New Order state.[27] It is not that there is no ambiguity about the sexualized female in Indonesian cinema – there are good prostitutes[28] and bad wives in Indonesian cinema. But in the 250 or more Indonesian films I have seen, no character so confounds the line between the whore and the wife as Tinung in *Ca Bau-kan* does.

The New Order always insisted on a clear moral message in all its audio-visual cultural texts. Even the small number of films which manipulated form and content to deliver critical political messages, on the whole had a very clear judgment on the nature of morality and an ideal moral order. Their critique of the New Order was precisely in showing its deviance from an ideal moral order, not a questioning of the ideal itself.[29] What is different about *Ca Bau-kan* is its staunch refusal of any particular moral position. Here, in the story's thirty-year span, the not-too-unwilling courtesan is a loving wife and weeping widow and then a whore and wife again. Here the Chinese hero is nationalist and a money-grabbing adventurer, a bigamist, a philanderer, and a loving husband and father. And all the while all of the central characters invite audience empathy, not their judgment.

In the context of post-New Order Indonesia, a film with a Chinese hero is, of course, at the level of its subject matter, deeply political. But it is in its refusal of political and moral judgment that this film offers a real alternative to the political and moral order of the Suharto regime. In *Ca Bau-kan* we see the possibility of a new kind of Indonesian cinema, capable of intersecting with the diverse and often contradictory moral and cultural universes which exist within the boundaries of the Indonesian nation, and thus with the potential to be a truly national-popular cinema.

CHAPTER 8

Sri Lanka: Art, Commerce, and Cultural Modernity

Wimal Dissanayake

The objective of this chapter is to explore the complex interconnections among art, commerce, and cultural modernity in Sri Lankan cinema. My focus of interest is popular cinema. However, in order to examine the nature of popular cinema, one has to relate it to art cinema, which is its constitutive other. Although three languages are spoken in Sri Lanka – Sinhalese, Tamil, and English – few Sri Lankan films have been made in the latter two languages. Hence, in this chapter my focus will be on Sinhalese cinema. (Throughout the chapter, I will be employing the two terms Sri Lankan cinema and Sinhalese cinema interchangeably.) The first Sinhalese film *Broken Promise* (*Kadauna Poronduwa*), was made in 1947, just one year prior to the island's independence from British rule. In the six decades following the birth of Sri Lankan cinema, the local film industry and film culture have been evolving steadily if somewhat unevenly, marked by moments of upheaval, triumphalism, contradiction, stagnation, and change.

The presence of India (the largest film-producing country in the world) as a close neighbor has always been a determining factor, more negative than positive, in the growth of the film industry and film culture in Sri Lanka. In addition, in more recent times, globalization has begun to inflect the art of cinema in interesting and complex ways – the influence of Hollywood, satellite television, and video cassettes. Interestingly, these forces of globalization have served to refocus attention on issues of localism, nationhood, and cultural identity.

Art Cinema and Popular Cinema in Sri Lanka

For analytical purposes, I wish to identify two main streams that constitute Sri Lankan cinema – the art cinema and the popular cinema. There is of course no waterproof separation between the two categories; the borders between them are porous and they tend to shift constantly. There is incessant cross-fertilization between the two streams resulting in hybrid and at times innovative works of cinema. However, most filmmakers as well as film critics in the island believe that art cinema has sought to define itself in opposition to the popular cinema. After all, identity is relational and the condition of its possibility is the affirmation of difference.

Hence, in the eyes of art film directors, popular cinema became the constitutive "other" of art cinema. As has been noted by film scholars such as John Hill, "art cinema has never simply been a matter of textual characteristics, but has also been allied to a particular system of production (typically, state or television subsidy) and distribution (festivals and a specialist art house circuit)."[1] The distinction between art cinema and popular cinema, though tentative and provisional, has played a crucial role in the discourse of cinema and the articulations of film culture in Sri Lanka.

One other point that needs to be made regarding the representational differences between these two forms of cinema in Sri Lanka is the centrality of the idea of realism. From the very beginning film analysis in the island centered around the notion of realism (*thathvika*). Indeed, realism came to be accepted as the hallmark of an artistic film. However, most contemporary film critics and scholars would agree that realism is a complicated concept and its privileging of a determining external reality is highly problematic. Realism is as convention-driven as any other form of cinema.[2]

The first Sinhalese film *Broken Promise* (*Kadauna Poronduwa*, 1947) marks the beginning of the popular tradition of filmmaking in Sri Lanka. It deals with a simple story that is intended to generate strong emotions. Victor Peries is wealthy and belongs to the Anglicized upper middle class. He smokes, drinks (markers of moral depravity in Sinhalese cinema), and is a philanderer. He is married and has a child. He seduces a young and innocent Ranjani who is planning to marry Samson. Once Ranjani realizes that Victor is already married, she shuns him. As with most commercial Sinhalese films, this picture ends with Ranjani and Samson uniting. It encapsulated many of the features one came to associate with popular cinema. It grew out of a highly popular stage play that was shown more than 800 times; the director and the actors were well-known stage artists. Consequently, the fact that the film was very stagy in its structure and presentation came as no surprise. It was also heavily influenced by the styles and production techniques reflective of South Indian films. *Broken Promise* was a sentimental, musical melodrama as indeed the bulk of the Sinhalese popular films continued to be.

Following *Broken Promise*, a number of interesting popular films were made. Among them, *Grisly Guardian* (*Kapati Arakshkaya*, 1948), *Defeated Aim* (*Veradunu Kurumanama*, 1948), *Mother* (*Amma*, 1949), *Changing Fate* (*Peralena Iranama*, 1949), *Hasty Decision* (*Hadisi Vnischaya*, 1950), *Ideal Woman* (*Seedevi*, 1951), *Evasive Denial* (*Sanagvunu Pilitura*, 1951), *Banda Comes to Town* (*Banda Nagarayata Peminima*, 1952), *Fanatic Faith* (*Umatu*

Vishvasaya, 1952) are significant. Sinhalese cinema was a part of the public
sphere in the sense that there was much discussion in the local newspapers and
magazines regarding the nature of significance of popular cinema. One central
criticism leveled against films made during this period was that they bore the
imprint of South Indian cinema and had very little of the flavor of indigenous
culture. As a consequence, filmmakers like Sirisena Wimalaweera who were
uneasy with the situation sought to create what he termed an indigenous
cinema foregrounding the contours and signs of local culture.

The Birth of Art Cinema

Nine years after the first Sinhalese film was made, the eminent filmmaker Lester
James Peries made *The Line of Destiny* (*Rekava*, 1956), which was to mark a
watershed in the forward march of Sri Lankan cinema. This film marked a decisive repudiation of the ruling popular genre of filmmaking in Sri Lanka. He
rejected the existing form of cinema by jettisoning the formula to which cinema
was wedded. *The Line of Destiny* was a film of the realistic mode. Instead of
shooting his film inside studios, which was the commonly accepted practice at
the time, he shot the entire film on location. He turned his back on the excessively theatrical style of acting and the declamatory style of delivery in favor of a
more controlled and realistic mode of acting. As Ashley Ratnavibhshana and I
have pointed out, "the word controlled is central to the way he looked at the art
of cinematography. He did not compel his images to glow and weep excessively.
He demonstrated a commendable grasp of the possibilities of the medium – the
purposeful and economical use of camera, editing, framing etc. – that was conspicuously absent in the Sinhalese films made until then."[3] In 1960, Peries made
The Message (*Sandeshaya*) which was not a critical success.

In 1965, Lester James Peries made *The Changing Countryside* (*Gam
Peraliya*), which constitutes the landmark in the growth of Sinhalese cinema.
Based on the well-known novel bearing the same name by the foremost novelist in the country, Martin Wickremasinghe, this film signified a turning point
in Sri Lankan cinema. It was a critical success and won the grand prix at the
International Film festival of India. The jury which consisted of Lindsey
Anderson, Andrej Wajda, Georges Sardoul, and Satyjit Ray commended it for
the "poetry and sensitivity with which it explores and illuminates personal
relationships." This film shares the collapse of the feudal social order and the
emergence of the middle class with great sympathy and discernment. Lester
James Peries's *The Changing Countryside* was generally regarded as a superior
work of cinema that drew on the poetics of neo-realism. With this film the art
cinema was well established in Sri Lanka. No new cinematic form emerges
from a cultural vacuum; all forms grow out of and in response to distinctive
social and cultural formations. The year 1956, in which *The Line of Destiny* was

made, signifies an important milestone in the evolution of Sri Lankan society. S.W.R.D. Bandaranayake was swept into power on a populist wave that was bent on getting rid of the remnants of the colonial edifice. He instituted an administration that made Sinhalese the official language of the island and of higher education. An indigenous elite securely rooted in traditional culture rose to take the place of the English-speaking, Westernized elite that had been at the helm of the Sri Lankan society. Increasing numbers from the rural areas were landing jobs in the upper echelons of administration and the centers of higher learning. What was native and indigenous was greeted with a new sense of pride. As a consequence of these social transformations Sinhalese arts and letters began to flourish with a newer sense of purpose. It is against this background that one has to examine the importance of the art cinema in Sri Lanka established by Lester James Peries. He went on to make films such as *Five Acres (Akkara Paha,* 1969), *Treasure (Nidhanaya,* 1960), *The Village in the Jungle (Baddegama,* 1981), *Age of Kali (Kaliyugaya,* 1983), *An End of An Era (Yuganthaya,* 1985). As a consequence of the newly gained recognition for Sinhalese cinema as a medium of artistic communication, a number of talented directors entered the field of cinema. Among them Siri Gunasinghe, D.B. Nihalsinghe, Piyasiri Gunaratne, G.D.L. Perera, Sugathapala Senarath Yapa, deserve special mention.

The Second Generation

In the 1970s, a newer group of filmmakers emerged who could be termed artistic filmmakers of the second generation. They all wanted to build on the achievement of Peries, while one or two among them were desirous of challenging Peries's vision and aesthetics as well. Among these filmmakers Dharmasena Pathiraja, Vasantha Obeyesekera, Sumithra Peries, and Dharmasiri Bandaranayake deserve special mention. Pathiraja is a socially committed filmmaker who wishes to expose how society confronts us with its own lives and rekindles a new urgency to speak powerfully through cinematic images. He was interested in indexing the diverse ways in which we inhabit our culture, and set in motion complex modes of seeing that would challenge the regnant forms of viewing and lay bare the ideological complicities of cinematic representation. Many of his films have not been popular because of the demands made by spectators used to easy enjoyment; his narratives were more complex than the ones that the mass of movie-goers were used to and he eschewed popular elements of filmmaking such as song and dance sequences. His film *Mr. Soldier (Soldadu Unnehe,* 1981) represents in many ways his strengths and proclivities. The film focuses on the contentious issue of cultural hegemony and the social contours of subculture. *Mr. Soldier* examines four characters who are conspicuously marginalized in society – an old soldier who is a veteran of World War II, a prostitute, an alcoholic, and a pickpocket. The story takes place within the narrow time frame of three days: Independence Day, the day preceding it and the day following it. By means of a series of flashbacks, the suffering of the four characters and how they have ended up in their present position as a consequence of inexorable and untranscendable social determinance are narrated in a way that calls attention to social oppression and inscriptions of otherness. The idea of nationhood is pivotal to the larger ambition of *Mr. Soldier*. Independence Day is commemorated with the usual pomp and pageantry and the politicians brag about the freedom and the achievements of the government. Simultaneously, the director contrapuntally brings to our field of vision the miserable lives of the four marginalized people. By portraying their degradation, he has aimed to reinforce the point that independence and freedom hold very little meaning for them.

As a filmmaker Vasantha Obeyesekera is concerned with a number of imbricated themes: the intersection of individual and social morality, the ever changing phases of human evil, the symbolic mapping of male desire, and the intrication of social power and carnal pleasure in such films as *Masquerade* (*Vesgatto*, 1970), *Grasshoppers* (*Palagetiyo*, 1979), *The Hunt* (*Dadayama*, 1984), *Reflections in a Mirror* (*Kedapothaka Chayava*, 1989), and *Death at the Door Step* (*Dorakada Marawa*, 1998). In the eyes of Obesekera the final measure of truth is both moral and social and they appear to be two sides of the same coin.

Sumithra Peries is the most significant female director in the island. Her first film *Girls* (*Gehanu Lamai*, 1978) won for her wide acclaim. Since then she has gone on to make such popular films as *By the Riverside* (*Ganga Addeara*, 1980), *Friends* (Yahalu Yehali, 1982), *The Illusion* (*Maya*, 1984), *A Letter Written in the Sand* (*Sagara Jalaya Madi Henduwa Oba Sanda*, 1980) and *Eldest Daughter* (*Loku Duwa*, 1996). As a female filmmaker Sumithra Peries has always empathized with the suffering of women. All her films are based on literary works despite the fact that many of them are not literary works of distinction. She has created for herself a style that is both elegant and visually alluring although many critics would not classify her as a feminist director because her feminist interests have not gone far enough.

Dharmasiri Bandaranayake is the author of a limited corpus of films. His first film *Swan Lake* (*Hansa Vilak*, 1980) marked the emergence of a new talent that was interested in capturing facets of a society at odds with itself. His other films like *The Third Part* (*Tunveni Yamaya*, 1983), *The Story of Suddi* (*Suddilage Kathawa*, 1984), *Worldly Suffering* (*Bavaduka Bavakarma*, 1997) display a number of common features. His desire for dealing with the conflicted lives of men and women, the transmogrification of private lives into public spectacles, unpalatable truths about marriage and society, and the exploration of the darker side of human desire. These filmmakers succeeded in strengthening the art cinema of Sri Lanka.

Third Generation

The third generation of film directors associated with the art cinema of Sri Lanka arose in the 1990s. Directors such as Prasanna Vithanage, Asoka Handgama, Somaratne Dissanayake, Linton Semage represent the trajectories of development of this new phase of art cinema in Sri Lanka. In this chapter, I wish to focus on the two most important of the newer directors – Vithanage and Handagama. Prasanna Vithanage has made films in all of which he displays a sure grasp of the media and sensitivity to local knowledge and local culture. His first film *Ice on Fire (Sisila Ginigani*, 1992) announced the arrival of a new and exciting talent. His next film *Dark Night of the Soul (Anantha Rathriya*, 1995) won for the director both local and international critical acclaim. *Walls Within (Pavuru Valalu*, 1997), Vithanage's third film, sealed his reputation as a leading Sri Lankan filmmaker. *Death on a Full Moon Day (Purahanda Kaluwara*, 1999) once again established Vithanage's ability to work through, with, and against images to construct a forceful narrative. The film deals with the ethnic conflict that has engulfed the country for the last two decades. It does not portray the conflict openly; instead it chooses to focus on the devastating impact of this conflict on the lives of a number of individuals. The story is set in an environment that is redolent of historical and cultural inscriptions giving rise to national pride. Guilt and desire are the two poles that define his art, and he has explored these concepts with a visual prescience and a probing intelligence. Another important contemporary director Asoka Handagama is perhaps the most innovative of the new filmmakers in Sri Lanka. His willingness to tackle complex themes and his desire to take risks mark his cinematic work. In his films *Nymph (Chanda Kinnari*, 1998), *Moon Hunt (Sanda Dadayama*, 1999), *This is My Moon (Me Mage Sandai*, 2000) and *Flying with One Wing (Tani Tatuwen Piyambami*, 2002), Handagama has sought to challenge the visual style of not only the popular cinema but also the art cinema of Sri Lanka in order to create a self-reflective cinema. Despite the enormous problems the local film industry has been forced to confront, filmmakers such as Vithange and Handagama inspire confidence and generate expectations for the future of art cinema in Sri Lanka.

Growth of Sri Lankan Popular Cinema

So far I have been discussing the art cinema in Sri Lanka. As the popular cinema is the constitutive other of art cinema we need to discuss the former alongside the latter. *Broken Promise* made in 1947 established the popular tradition of filmmaking, and *Sujatha* (1950) became one of the most popular Sinhalese films. The latter was based on a Hindi film and contained all the

ingredients one would associate with the Hindi commercial cinema. This
movie emblematized the essence of the Sri Lankan commercial cinema as it
began to influence more and more the sensibility of local audiences. Popular
cinema in Sri Lanka, like that of most other nations, has been powered by
commercial desire rather than artistic codes. These films, which sought to
follow Indian models, soon began to crystallize around a readily identifiable
formula: sentimental musical melodramas that opened up a celluloid fantasy.
The plot lines of these movies rarely unfold in a linear way, displaying a
passion for digression and intrusive didacticism. Song, music, dance, melodrama, and exaggerated emotions became the trademark of these films.
Judged in terms of the elitist standards of aesthetic merit, these films fall far
short of the mark as works of conscious art. However, as cultural productions
that both reflect and inflect popular consciousness they merit close study.
Popular Sinhalese films represent the commingling of diverse elements that
are regarded as being vital to mass appeal. Among them, songs, dances, melodrama, fight sequences, cabaret sequences, stunts, raw humor, glamorous
actors and actresses are perhaps the most important.

The uniqueness of Sinhalese popular cinema can be seen not only in its narrative structure, visual styles, and techniques but also in its thematics. These
films, to a very large extent bring into existence a commonly shared thought-
world given shape by the following: the glamorization of rural culture, critiques of Westernization, the upholding of traditional social norms, the
triumph of good over evil and tradition over modernity, and (perhaps the most
important) the centrality of the family. It is very clear that from the very beginning popular films in Sri Lanka imitated Indian models. For example, films
such as *Victory* (*Dinuma,*1986), *Victory is Ours* (*Jaya Apatai,*1986), *Golden
Chains* (*Ran Damvel,* 1987), *Innocence* (*Ahimsa,*1987), *My Love is for You*
(*Obatai Priye Aadare,* 1987) and *King* (*Raja,* 1987) were obviously based on
Hindi originals. The efforts of local filmmakers to imitate Hindi films can be
charted in terms of three important stages. In the first, one observed the translation and adaptation of Hindi films. In the second stage, the hallmark was the
desire to dub Hindi and to a lesser extent Tamil films. The third stage was
marked by the desire to copy blatantly Hindi originals. Moreover, some directors saw to make a composite out of a number of different Hindi films. For
example, a number of films made by Yasapalitha Nanayakkara from the 1970s
and 1980s display this trend. The blind imitation of Bombay popular films
resulted in the incorporation of several features designed to generate popular
appeal. For example, the concept of dual heroes popularized by Hindi movies
inspired many local filmmakers. Vijaya Kumaratunga and Sanath Gunatileke
were the preferred dual heroes; as in most other popular cinemas in the world,
Sri Lankan popular films also fashioned with certain prominent actors and
actresses in mind.

The producers and directors linked to the commercial cinema of Sri Lanka make the point that their aim is to offer the usual movie-goer a temporary respite from the anxieties of life and the miseries surrounding them. Rather than articulating the miseries of day-to-day life these filmmakers maintain that their intention is to offer through entertainment an escape from them. Consequently their emphasis was on entertainment and not art. Many film critics would complain that in terms of achieved art these commercial films fall far short of the mark. However, as cultural productions enunciating the consciousness of the people, the various social formations and structures of feeling, and the inscriptions of ideology, the popular films merit closer study.

Cultural Modernity in Sri Lanka

Popular cinema in Sri Lanka can be comprehended most fruitfully within the discursive parameters of cultural modernity. Modernity, according to perceptive commentators such as Marshall Berman, is a deeply complex phenomenon that bears upon diverse facets of human experience precipitating profound and far-reaching changes in society and cultural perceptions.[4] We can, for the sake of analysis, identify four significant and overlapping discourses related to modernity. The first is the socio-economic discourse that focuses on such phenomena as industrialization, urbanization, massification, technologization, commodification. The second is the cognitive discourse that aims to call attention to issues of rationality, with particular reference to the significance of instrumental rationality. The third discourse speaks to the political dimensions of modernity. Here questions of secularism, challenges to traditional norms of conduct and the nature of polity, subjectivity, and citizenship become important. Fourthly, there is the discourse of experientiality and phenomenological participation in modernity that seeks to foreground the urgency of new perspectives on society demanded by the rapidly changing contexts of living and the concomitant sensory experiences. The work of such theorists and cultural analysts as George Simmel, Siegfried Kracauer, and Walter Benjamin are central of these discussions.[5] While all four of these intersecting and interanimating discourses are crucial to an understanding of Sri Lankan popular cinema, it is the sensory and experiential dimension that is most important. It focuses on the discourse of cinema's newer perspectives and frames of intelligibility and the transformations that are taking place within the fabric of urban living.

In our explorations into the sensory and experiential aspects of modernity, we need to wrestle with the issues of tempo, fragmentation, over-stimulation, and disorder, precipitated by newer images and the various cultural displacements and dislocations ushered in by the transformations in the living environment. These are crucially linked with the appeal and the cultural meaning of the Sri Lankan popular cinema. Marshall Berman observes that what is interesting about modernity is the complex ways in which human beings become the object and subject of the modernization processes. And commercial cinema in Sri Lanka mirrors the ways in which Sri Lankan movie-goers become both the object and subject of the process of cultural modernization.

The deeper currents shaping the discourse of popular cinema in Sri Lanka, as indeed in most of the Asian countries, can best be understood in terms of the dynamics of cultural modernity. Despite the formulations of modernization theorists of the 1950s, modernity is multifaceted and is never multivalent. It is evident that modernization is a global condition that inflects our understanding of time and space, past and present, self and society in culturally specific ways. Modernity cannot be reduced solely to the imperatives of the economic, although they are very significant for the ways in which they mould our thinking. The relationship of modernity to cultural formations is significant and invites focused attention. Its engagement with tradition is not one of simple opposition; it interacts with tradition at different levels, urging revaluations and instigating relocations of traditions. Cultures are, of course, not timeless entities but products of history, geography, and ideology. They are contestatory sites in which meanings related to everyday life are constantly made, unmade, and remade. Popular cinema in Sri Lanka has to be evaluated in relation to the dynamics of modernization as they influence the cultural consciousness of the people of Sri Lanka. Ashish Nandy, commenting on the Indian scene, said that popular cinema provides the vast mass of filmgoers with the cultural categories with which to make sense of their life.[6] This observation is equally applicable to Sri Lanka.

Modernity is, of course, not confined to the popular cinema; it is equally important to a deeper understanding of the ambitions of the art cinema in Sri Lanka. However, the way in which these two traditions have sought to engage modernity differs in terms of aims, interests and preferences. The art cinema drew on modernity as a way of fashioning a cinema that placed great emphasis on individual consciousness as it battled the injunctions of social life. The aesthetics of modernism was a great source of inspiration to the art-film directors in Sri Lanka. On the contrary, the popular filmmakers drew on the ever-expanding sensorium of modernity as a means of energizing their cultural products.

Let us consider, for example, the question of foreign artistic influences. The art-film directors sought to draw on the innovations of European art-film directors and film movements ranging from Italian new wave to British social dramas and the French new wave. The popular filmmakers, on the other hand, were least interested in European art cinema. Their focus of interest was Hollywood cinema as mediated through Hindi commercial films. Popular beliefs to the contrary, Hollywood cinema is not one thing but many things.

On the one hand, there was the classic Hollywood cinema which sought to propagate a certain modern aesthetic related to the economy of narration, stylistic norms, and the psychological dispositions of the spectators. On the other hand, there were genres such as adventure films, action films, crime stories, and slapstick comedy that were considered somewhat pejoratively. It is this type of Hollywood film that struck a cord with the Hindi popular filmmakers as well as Sri Lankan popular filmmakers. Therefore in order to understand the differences between the art films and popular films in Sri Lanka we can very productively bring in the notion of cultural modernity.

Melodrama

This is, of course, not to suggest that the art cinema and popular cinema grew separately on parallel lines without any interaction between the two. Nothing could be further from the truth. Some filmmakers with an artistic disposition sought to draw on the energy associated with popular cinema. Melodrama is a case in point. Until very recent times, melodrama was considered an inferior art form given to a rhetoric of excess, sensationalism, and superficiality by film critics and film scholars in most parts of the world. However, the term has been rehabilitated and melodrama has become a site for the fruitful exploration of the nature of popular cultural production and popular cultural consciousness.

The preponderant majority of Sri Lankan popular films are melodramas. Indeed, it is their defining cinematic characteristic. However, a number of filmmakers like Vasantha Obesekera, Dharmasiri Bandaranayake, and H.D. Premaratna have drawn on the form of melodrama with encouraging results. Let us for example consider a film like *Reflections in a Mirror* (1989). The story unfolds against a backdrop marked by the disappearance of centers of moral authority and the tragic collapse of virtue. Nanda is a young girl who lives with her sister and brother-in-law Danaratne. Danaratne seduces Nanda, and later gives her in marriage to a soldier named Piyatilake with whom she has an amorous relationship. Danaratne does well in life and becomes powerful and rich. He continues to maintain his illicit relationship with Nanda even after her marriage because of her poverty; she has to depend on him for financial aid. Meanwhile, Piyatilake gets into trouble with the army for not reporting to duty. Danaratne, through his connections, obtains Piyatilake's release from the army, and sets him up in a business career. Piyatilake proves to be less than successful as a businessman, and this angers Danaratne. In the meantime, Danaratne's wife grows increasingly suspicious of her husband's behavior, and is annoyed by the financial assistance he offered to Piyatilake and Nanda. In an outburst of anger she lets out the dark truth to Piyatilake. Infuriated he confronts Danaratne. The situation worsens and, sensing the possible break-up of her marriage, Nanda visits Danaratne in hospital where he is been treated for a leg injury and kills him. She is sentenced to prison for murder. By the time Nanda is released from prison her husband has become a wealthy businessman who is unscrupulous in his dealings. Nanda's children, as well as her husband, distance themselves from her. The film ends with Nanda alone surrounded by the fragments of an empty and meaningless life. Clearly, this is a melodrama which draws attention to the plight of a woman who is a victim of brutal circumstances emanating from the patriarchal social order. While eschewing the crudities associated with melodrama as represented in popular cinema, Vasanta Obesekera has taken the form and employed it to focus attention on certain compelling social and moral issues.

Dharmasiri Bandaranayake's *Swan Lake* (1980) displays the potentiality of the melodramatic form to convey the story that holds a searching light on social misery. The director focuses attention on the institution of marriage and the torments and anxieties of desire. The film explores the complicated interaction between two families. The husband in one family has an affair with the wife in the other. The protaganist of the film, Nissanka, is guilty of having an adulterous affair and is led by force of circumstances to kill his wife. Through this tragic episode, Bandaranayake has sought to highlight such vexatious issues as the stability of the family as a social institution and the values and ideologies linked to middle-class living. Throughout the film, the trope of the prison plays a significantly symbolic role. As in Obeyesekera's film, melodrama constitutes the animating force. However, it is used in the service of deeper artistic ambitions of exploring the inner landscape of the characters and the tangled nexus of causality and responsibility.

State, Cinema, and Cultural Specificity

I wish to close this chapter on the interconnections of art, commerce, and cultural modernity in Sri Lankan cinema by focusing on two significant issues. The first is on the relationship between state and cinema. This is particularly important in relation to a small country like Sri Lanka: it needs to be said that the relationship between state and cinema in Sri Lanka is an ambivalent one marked by contradictions. On the one hand, it is obvious that a small country like Sri Lanka, facing huge economic problems, cannot sustain a vigorous and viable film industry without the assistance of the state. On the other hand, this linkage with the state can have adverse consequences in terms of censorship, political interventionism, and the slowness of the bureaucracy. Hence, one needs to strike a balance whereby the power of the state could be productively deployed for the development of the film industry in the island without yielding to the harmful consequences. The second issue is the uniqueness of popular cinema in Sri Lanka. It is indeed true that with increasing globalization a universal grammar and vocabulary of popular cinema is emerging worldwide. At the same time, these universal features get inflected by culture-specific traits. In the case of Sri Lankan popular cinema, it was Indian cinema – Hindi and Tamil – that had the greatest influence. (This is not to suggest that Hollywood films did not have an impact on the local cinematic imagination; they certainly did.) However, Sri Lankan cinema arguably lacks at present the technological sophistication and the seductive power of special effects that characterize the work of contemporary Indian filmmakers such as Mani Rathnam and Ram Gopal Varma. Much of Indian popular cinema inhabits a cultural space inflected by Hinduism, while in the Sinhalese case the cultural space is shaped largely by Buddhism. While Indian popular cinema is branching out in newer directions and opening up newer genres for exploration, Sri Lankan popular cinema still operates largely at the level of family melodrama.

CHAPTER 9

Bangladesh: Native Resistance and Nationalist Discourse

Zakir Hossain Raju

In today's globalizing mediascape of Bangladesh, the young Asian nation (independent since 1971) that shares borders with India and Myanmar, cinema is omnipresent. In the cities and towns large film posters are slapped on to spare inches of wall space. Huge-sized, glittering billboards advertising the latest films can be located in front of the major cinemas. The stars of the popular cinema are the most frequently drawn subjects of the illustrations done at the back and sidebars of rickshaws and auto rickshaws in the cities and small towns.[1] Film songs blare from horn speakers, radio sets and audio-players at all the family gatherings like weddings and puberty rites as well as religious and social festivals in both cities and villages. All the radio stations in Bangladesh play songs from the popular films around the clock. Additionally, everyday there are "sponsored" programs on radio featuring the to-be-released films. Since the 1980s, almost all the roadside tea-stalls, restaurants, barber shops, grocery stores in the urban and semi-urban areas as well as all kind of transport vehicles are equipped with radio-cum-audiotape-players.

Similar to radio, television is also an important medium that regularly enhances the presence of popular cinema within the everyday lives of ordinary people. Though satellite television channels have become accessible to the city- and town-dwellers since the mid-1990s, most of the people in rural Bangladesh until recently could watch only Bangladesh Television (BTV), the state-run public television. So the broadcast of a popular feature film at any time of the week was one of the most-loved television programs for most of the people at that time. In mid-1997 it was noted that student attendance at schools and colleges decreased on Saturdays because of the noon-time film broadcasts of Bangladesh Television.[2] Bangladesh Television and the three major satellite television channels NTV, Channel-I, and ATN Bangla broadcast popular films round the clock. On a given day, one can watch four or five feature films of Bangladeshi origin on television. The weekly programs related to cinema are also broadcast through every television channel.

Alongside the complementary relationship of electronic media with cinema, the print-medium is also busy in popularizing cinema. Numerous Bengali film magazines are published and circulated in and around the cities and small towns. All the serious dailies and weeklies also devote one or more sections for the gossip and news of the film industry. This trend started in the early 1950s in Dhaka – Bangladesh's capital city which was then in Pakistan in the post-partition, post-British colonial state of divided (East) Bengal. Alongside the newspapers and magazines, there are also postcards, notebooks, writing pads, calendars, albums – all bearing the pictures of the film stars – available at each street corner.

Cinema as Popular Entertainment

The above glimpse at the contemporary mediascape of Bangladesh makes clear that cinema has become one of the most popular modes of entertainment for a majority of the population in a globalizing Bangladesh. Seeing such popular response to cinema, noted filmmaker and film scholar Alamgir Kabir commented around twenty-five years ago that "Bangladesh will certainly be among those few countries where the cinema will probably continue to survive even when it will have moved into the museums of other countries."[3] Bangladesh popular cinema, popularly called the *Dhakai* cinema (as the film industry is centered in Dhaka) targets a very distinct market sector, a "Bangladeshi" audience. This audience is comprised of mostly Bengali Muslims in the postcolonial nation-space as well as Bangladeshis scattered around the world. Such a national market for local Bengali-language cinema exists alongside the state-level efforts of constructing a "Bangladeshi" identity amid globalizing forces. Bangladesh cinema has turned out to be the larger and stronger Bengali-language film industry in the last few decades, overtaking the other Bengali film industry located in Calcutta, India.

Despite being much older than the Dhaka film industry and the base for some renowned Indian art-cinema filmmakers like Satyajit Ray and Ritwik Ghatak, the contemporary Bengali cinema of Calcutta adopted the role of a small regional film industry serving only Bengali-speaking audiences of West Bengal in India. Indian-Bengali film historian Shomeswar Bhowmik pointed out that during the late 1960s the annual average production of the Calcutta film industry had dwindled to twenty-eight films from fifty-two films per year produced during the mid-1950s.[4] On the other hand, the Dhaka film industry came into being as a fully fledged production industry only in the mid-1960s. In its first decade (between 1966 and 1975), it produced on average twenty-eight films each year, the same number of films produced by Calcutta in the late 1960s. However, since 1976, the Dhaka industry has seen a dramatic increase in the number of films produced annually, up to on average sixty-seven films each year during the period 1984–1992.[5]

This upward tendency of film production continued in the late 1990s and beyond. The Dhaka film industry produced in total 645 feature films during the period 1996–2003, which means that during each of these eight years it produced on average eighty feature films.[6] The peak number of feature films (ninety-two) were released in 1997, and again in 2000.[7] In other words, since the mid-1970s, the annual film production in Dhaka industry has increased at a rate of 25–30 percent every five years or so while the Calcutta industry saw a sharp decline in production since the 1960s. While the Calcutta film industry produced forty-six films per year in the 1950s, this number decreased by 35 percent in the 1960s–1980s.[8] It seems clear that out of the two Bengali-language film-production industries in the world, the film industry in Bangladesh has become stronger than its Indian counterpart during the years from the 1970s to the 1990s. The industry in contemporary Bangladesh is currently producing around eighty feature films a year.

Bangladesh also saw an astounding 400 percent increase in the number of cinemas between 1971 and 1984. According to Alamgir Kabir, there were only 110–122 cinemas in operation in East Pakistan in the 1960s. He notes that during the period 1972–75, only within the first three-year period of independent Bangladesh, the number of theaters almost doubled (from 120 to 220).[9] The number of cinemas in Bangladesh doubled again in the next eight years. According to the Bangladesh Bureau of Statistics, from 220 theaters in 1975 the number had jumped to 444 by 1984.[10] In the next decade, another 300 percent increase in the number of cinemas was recorded. Quader noted the existence of 767 cinemas in 1990.[11] Film historian Anupam Hayat notes that in 1994 there were 1,400 cinemas throughout Bangladesh.[12] The web-site of the Bangladesh Film Development Corporation (BFDC) claims that there were nearly 1,800 cinemas in Bangladesh in 2001.[13] (However, this number seems a bit exaggerated. The editorial of the influential daily *Ittefaq* noted that there were 1,175 cinemas in Bangladesh in late 2000.[14]) Despite the disparities in various sources on the number of cinemas in Bangladesh, and though some cinemas in the major cities have been closed in the last few years,[15] one can still argue that at present there are more than 1,000 cinemas in Bangladesh.

Alongside the increase in film production and decrease in exhibition venues, during the late 1990s cinema attendance rose in Bangladesh especially in the rural areas. The National Media Survey 1998 notes that in 1998, 16 percent of rural people visited cinemas regularly (up from 11 percent in 1995.) The survey also records a 2 percent rise (from 20 percent in 1995 to 22 percent in the 1998 survey) in the total number of urban and rural viewers who went to the movies at least once in three months.[16] In other words, though there is only a 10 percent rise in the total national film viewership during 1995–98, there was an almost 50 percent rise in the rural viewership of popular cinema in Bangladesh in this period. This data substantiates the way that Bangladesh cinema transformed in the 1990s toward becoming an entertainment medium for the poor and less-educated population living in semi-rural and rural areas, a transformation that began in the mid-1980s. Four senior economists based in the Bangladesh Institute of Development Studies (BIDS) summarized the transformation of the Bangladesh popular cinema in 1991: "With much higher capital requirements, it became critical to reach a mass audience. The result has been the transformation of the cinema into a vehicle of mass culture which is tawdry, cheap and vulgar. More sophisticated audiences now depend on the VCR for their visual entertainment."[17]

Despite such aestheticist judgment of middle-class intellectuals, the overwhelming presence of popular cinema and the expansion of film production, exhibition, and reception in a rapidly globalizing Bangladesh cannot be overlooked. However, it needs to be noted that though Bangladesh cinema is the foremost Bengali-language film industry in the world, this is one of the least discussed Asian national cinemas. This chapter, then, can be seen as a step toward beginning a discussion around Bangladesh cinema as a national-popular cinema.

Bangladesh cinema is one of those rare species of medium-sized, vernacular-language national film industries that manages to survive, almost ignoring the Hollywood film industry, considered as a major threat to many film industries in the world. This success lies in the fact that this cinema targets a very distinct market sector: Bengali-speaking, Bengali-Muslims and some non-Muslims and non-Bengalis living within the postcolonial state called Bangladesh. In this way, this is one of the few non-Western entertainment cinemas that, in Paul Willemen's words, "have managed to prevent Hollywood from destroying their local film industry."[18] No doubt the survival of Bangladesh cinema lies in its complex, partly conflicting, and partly dialogic relationship with the nation-state in the postcolonial modernity. Exploring the institutional and textual aspects of popular cinema, my objective here is to delineate how this popular cinema functions to construct the nationalist discourse in a globalizing Bangladesh. In contemporary Bangladesh, the nationalist forces and global modernity are constantly re-defining the role of popular cinema, especially to meet the challenge of constructing and disseminating a Bangladeshi "national" identity in/of/through popular cinema.

The Industrial Context of Popular Cinema: Capitalism and the State

The contemporary industrial context of cinema in Bangladesh is very much governed by the state and works mostly in favor of the film-capitalists, especially of exhibitors. The exhibition sector plays a more important role than its production sector in determining the modus operandi of Bangladesh cinema as well as the national characteristics of this cinema. Since the mid-1970s the newly rich Bengali-Muslim trader-capitalists have taken advantage of such a pro-exhibitor film industry where they can quickly multiply their surplus money. The contemporary industrial context of the Bangladesh film industry largely depends on two key aspects: the State ban on releasing Indian and Pakistani popular films in theaters in Bangladesh and the contemporary taxation system on film exhibition. Both these state-national interventions represent the commitment of keeping a well-protected domestic market only for Bengali-language, local popular films.

The order of banning the Indian films was first issued by the Ayub government of Pakistan during the 1965 India-Pakistan war. However, even in the globalizing mediascape of 1990s and 2000s Bangladesh, both the state and the Bengali-Muslim capitalists kept the ban in effect. This, for around four decades, continuously offered the local popular film industry a protected nationalized theatrical-exhibition environment, though Indian popular films on VCDs are widely available. After the independence of Bangladesh from Pakistan in 1971, the nationalist government led by Sheikh Mujib maintained this ban against Indian films, using Bengali-nationalist rhetoric. In 1972, just after the liberation war, leading distributors and exhibitors of Bangladesh cinema expected that the newly established pro-India government of Mujib would again approve the exhibition of Indian popular films in Bangladesh. However, Sheikh Mujib and other Bengali-nationalist leaders of the new state not only kept the ban on the theatrical exhibition of Indian (Hindi and Bengali) films, but also quickly issued a complete ban on showing Pakistani (Urdu) popular films.[19] Thus the Bengali nationalist leaders of the early 1970s made sure that the local popular cinema films did not need to vie with major competitors, films made in other major film centers within the Indian sub-continent. Similar to the timing of the 1965 war, Mujib and others used a peak moment of Bengali nationalism, that is 1972 when Bangladesh had just been liberated, to order this ban against Urdu films mostly produced in Lahore and Karachi. The idea of a pure Bangladeshi-Bengali identity that can be contaminated through Indian (Hindi and Bengali) and Pakistani (Urdu) films made sure that no Indian or Pakistani film could be shown in theaters in Bangladesh since 1972. Undoubtedly, such state-national will for a "national" cinema for a national audience who can/will watch only homegrown films (and should have no access to transnational films) has determined the industrial environment of popular cinema production in Bangladesh in recent decades.

Alongside the bans, the other important aspect of the contemporary industrial framework of Bangladesh popular cinema is the changes brought about by the state-decreed taxation policy in the 1980s-1990s. These two aspects of the pro-State and pro-exhibitor framework of Bangladesh cinema ensured the maximum gain for the State and the film exhibitors in recent decades. In contemporary Bangladesh, the State makes the maximum gain from the box-office income of a popular film because of the high rate of "amusement tax" it charges on film exhibition. The official website of the Bangladesh Film Development Corporation (BFDC) claims that in recent years film exhibition in Bangladesh brought in around Taka 300 million (US$5 million) as taxes.[20]

The postcolonial state of Bangladesh inherited the "pay-per-view" method of taxation in the film exhibition sector directly from the British colonial period with some modifications. However, since 1983 the taxation on film exhibition in Bangladesh took a new turn as the government started a new rule of taxation in October 1983. The capacity-based tax, as it is called, transformed Bangladesh cinema into a larger industry, as well as encouraging it to serve the "national" public sphere at a time when Indian and Pakistani films started to be available in Bangladesh on video. This new method of collecting tax from the theaters seemed quite profitable to the exhibitors or theater-owners and also to the film producers/distributors. Under the capacity-based tax system, the entry fee to a movie theater is calculated as the summation of the basic entry fee and the air-conditioning charge, and the amusement tax is equal to (or 100 percent of) this entry fee. The theaters pay the tax as weekly installments in advance while the amount to be paid is determined by the revenue department through assessment of the capacity of a particular theater. Depending on the perceived importance of the location of a theater, the theater has to pay between 5 percent (for a rural theater) and 50 percent (for a theater in a large city) of the amount they would earn if the theater were full in all the screenings of a week.[21]

As the new tax amount (100 percent of the entry fee multiplied by 5–50 percent of the capacity) is lower and easier to manipulate than the previous pay-per-viewer system, the film theaters in contemporary Bangladesh now earn much more than before. Most of the theaters under-declare their capacity to the revenue department in order to lower the weekly tax.[22] The capacity-based tax system proved to be a very profitable step especially for the film exhibitors and, to a lesser extent, for the producer-distributors of Bangladesh popular cinema. During the years of 1983 to 1989, both the number of theaters and annual production of films saw a sharp rise. By 1989 this rise resulted in approximately 90 percent addition to the existing number of theaters (from 400 to 750) and films produced (from 40 to 78).[23] The figures of newly built theaters and the increased number of films produced post-1983 signify that the tax worked as an invigorating force for Bangladesh popular cinema, to fight the antagonistic giant of video through which the Bangladeshi state feared that the Indian and Pakistani films would flood Bangladeshis with anti-national entertainment. The Bangladesh government issued permission for importing video-players in 1979. Just after that, the chairperson of the

Bangladesh film exhibitors' association Iftekharul Alam and the renowned film director Dilip Biswas commented that from now on there will be film theaters in every household and eventually the audience in theaters will decrease in a greater number.[24] Similar to the ban of Indian and Pakistani films in theaters, capacity tax then can be seen as an incentive to keep a national film exhibition environment in Bangladesh. It represents the state-national efforts and desire to keep the national character of Bangladesh cinema intact amid the increasing availability of the banned Indian and Pakistani films on video in cities and towns of Bangladesh from the mid-1980s onward.

At the end of the 1990s, film exhibitors in Bangladesh again felt a similar anxiety, when they had to cope with the invasion of cable television. The president and secretary of Dhaka Film Exhibitors' Group complained in 1997 in an article in the *Daily Ittefaq* newspaper that film-exhibition business all over the country including Dhaka city is under serious threat of "video channels," the cable-connected local network put up by the suburban private satellite television service providers that enables people to watch films sitting in their homes paying next to nothing. The exhibitors added that the middle-class audience have stopped going to film theaters since the early 1980s as they can watch all the "Indian higher-standard films and television programs" through a number of satellite channels; only a societal slice of lower-income people had kept the industry alive. But, the exhibitors contended, now they too could now watch all the new features through the video channels. It was feared that soon the film producers would be on the streets, and film exhibitors would have to close down the theaters to avoid further losses.[25]

Nevertheless, the film business did not come to a halt by the end of 1997, as the film exhibitors forecast here; rather, that turned out to be the year when the Bangladesh film industry produced the record highest number of feature films.

Recently the government has lowered the rate of the capacity-based tax from the previous 125 percent to 50 percent of the entry price in the 2002/03 annual budget. In a call for industry reform, film journalist Manik Khondokar complained that film exhibitors had still not lowered the price of movie tickets.[26] This adjustment of the government tax in 2002 also can be seen as a new incentive provided by the State to the film producers and exhibitors to battle the new giant of satellite television that serves up anti-Bangladeshi visual entertainment.

Because of such a nationalized exhibition environment mostly secured by the State initiatives, a significantly high rate of profitability lies in the exhibition front of Bangladesh popular cinema. The reason is that there are much fewer film theaters than needed in Bangladesh. Film scholar Mirza Quader calculated that in 1991 there was 0.34 cinema seat for every 100 people in Bangladesh. This is only one-sixth of the UNESCO proposed minimum number of theater seats (two seats for 100 people).[27] Naturally because the supply of cinema screens is low, there is a high demand among the film producers to get suitable theaters for the release of the film in the big cities such as Dhaka, Chittagong, Narayanganj, Khulna, and Rajshahi. Producers want to make sure that films are released simultaneously in most of the screens of these cities, to earn a larger share of the box-office profit. Therefore, film exhibitors or theater-owners in collaboration with the intermediaries engaged in film distribution earn more money from box-office takings than the film producers.

Within such pro-state and exhibitor-dependent industrial environment in contemporary Bangladesh cinema, financing of film production also depends on state sponsorship. The state lends shooting, editing, sound-dubbing, lab, and printing facilities to almost all popular feature films at its Bangladesh Film Development Corporation (BFDC) studio, the only fully fledged 35mm film-production studio in Bangladesh. This kind of high dependency on state-run facility in the production sector of Bangladesh cinema is very different from that in neighboring India and Pakistan, where the existence of large, full-service film production-facilities under private ownership is almost commonplace. BFDC provides film producers with necessary technical support on credit. Thus the State partly finances almost all the popular films at the pre-production stage, as the State is also the main financier for BFDC. Though in its official website BFDC terms itself as a "self-financing, promotional, development-oriented organization," it has received a huge amount of state support during last few decades. From its inception in 1957 up to 2000, it received Taka 445.98 million (US$7.5 million) as a "Development Loan" and Taka 82.00 million (US$1.4 million) as "share capital" from the state.[28]

Alongside government subsidy, within the ambiguous capitalist structure of the Bangladesh film industry, film exhibitors have also become important financiers in popular-film production, in most cases allegedly investing "black" money – undeclared and untaxed capital earned dubiously. Film historian Chinmoy Mutsuddi finds that most of the major actors and technicians of Bangladesh cinema receive a substantial portion of their fees as undeclared (and thus not-to-be-taxed) money. He locates a cycle of black money here: film producers who pay the stars such money also collect similar undeclared money from the exhibitors and the exhibitors, then adjust their books showing lower sales at the box office.[29] In this cycle of utilizing and maximizing undeclared and untaxed money in the contemporary scene of Bangladesh popular cinema, the businessman who functions as the film producer collects film finances from various sources some of which might like to be kept clandestine. First he makes use of the facility of using technical services on credit from the state-run BFDC studio. Then after he has done a quarter or nearly half of the shooting, he pre-sells the film and collects advance payments from a group of distributors and/or exhibitors which controls clusters of movie houses in different regions of

Bangladesh. When the film is in post-production, the producer collects another advance sum from the exhibitors, especially those owning theaters in big cities especially to pay back the BFDC studio for the technical facilities used on credit. Imrul Shahed and Mahmuda Chowdhury, two well-known film critics for the *Weekly Bichitra* noted that in this way the film exhibitors finance around 33 percent of the budget of a film.[30] Shahed also notes that this practice gave many partner-producers the chance to become fully fledged film producers in the Bangladesh film industry during the 1990s.[31]

Film journalist Anwar Al-Deen records that in the year 2000 the film-producers would receive an advance of Taka 70,000 (approximately US$1200) from each theater in Dhaka at the post-production stage.[32] There are around 100 theaters in Dhaka, Chittagong, and Narayanganj, the three most-populated cities where new films normally get the first release.[33] If a new film can get release at half of these theaters, the producer can collect an advance of nearly half of the total production budget of a film. Journalists Shahed and Chowdhury and film director Matin Rahman point out that because of such exhibitor-based financing of a film, if a film producer in Bangladesh can somehow put together around 40 percent of the total budget of the film, he proceeds to get the film made.[34] However, pro-BFDC and pro-exhibitor financing of popular films has created a vulnerable film industry. In the absence of any formal loan facility offered by banks or other financial institutions, the producer has to organize the finance of a film first from BFDC and then from a host of exhibitors and capitalists. This complex and precarious financing process takes much longer than anticipated, and many films are never completed.[35]

The multi-source dependency model for film financing in the Bangladesh film industry means that the movie has to be completed and released very quickly as the parties investing want the quickest return. Most of the financiers come from film exhibition or another business background. Keen to get back their investment and profits quickly, they are least concerned with the difficulties, preparation, and length of time associated with producing a film that will look credible on screen. The cast and crew including the director of the film are under pressure from the financiers to complete the film and naturally all of them work in a stopgap manner. Actors and crew of popular films work in two from starting in late morning until midnight, almost seven days a week. Because of this quick-finish method, unlike their Western counterparts, the film stars in Bangladesh work simultaneously, sometimes in five to ten films. The most-loved stars of the industry may act in ten to fifteen films in a given year. Similar to the actors, a film director with a "star" profile may direct four or five films at once and around six or seven films in a given year.[36] This kind of ad hocism has become a consensual phenomenon in film production in contemporary Bangladesh.

Nationhood and the Active Texts of Bangladesh Popular Cinema

The high-risk but high-profit and quick-production orientation of the popular film industry in contemporary Bangladesh produces several kinds of film texts that directly serve the nationalist rhetoric of the State and the local film-capitalists. Social and action films, both the major genres of the recent popular films, attempt to forge a local/global Bangladeshi identity on screen.

The "social films" are actually family-drama films supposedly addressed to female viewers, especially the middle-class and working-class women living in or around towns. These films, as sentimental family dramas, began by portraying these people as simple and unproblematic iconic figures, generally within a semi-traditional social backdrop of 1960s East Pakistan. In these family-drama films, the central characters are no longer idealist rural-based male figures traumatized by the process of industrialization coupled with one or two all-sacrificing (and mostly silent) female figures frequently propagated and prevalent in the earlier popular social films. From the 1980s onward, contemporary social films struggle to represent the complexities of gender and class as their protagonists face urbanization and modernization in the context of a globalizing Bangladesh.

The transformation of conventional social films coincided with the ascent of a new genre in Bangladesh popular cinema. Action cinema as a dominant genre mainly developed in the 1980s and 1990s, especially to meet the challenges brought forward by the new viewing options such as video and satellite television. The social films transformed their narrative strategies to suit the new media scenario; however, the genre declined with the rise of the action films that have become the staple of Bangladesh popular cinema. I would argue that in the battle against Indian and other foreign films on video (and later on disc and cable television), body-focused action films became the major weapon of the Bangladesh film industry ("equipped" with state incentives such as capacity-based taxation). The exhibition of male and female bodies in different types of "action" can be located visibly in the recent action films of Bangladesh popular cinema. The film *Ammajan* (1999), a record money-spinner, underscores some of the major characteristics of popular cinema in Bangladesh today.

Ammajan (or *The Mother*) belongs to the post-cable television action genre. Kazi Hayat, a well-known director of action films in the 1990s Bangladesh film industry, scripted and directed the film, while Manna and Moushumi, two of the most sought-after actors in recent years, played the roles of the male and female protagonists (Badsha and Rina) in the film. Manna became the most reliable male star of action cinema by playing the hero in many films before and since *The Mother*. Other action films by the Hayat-Manna duo are listed among the most popular films of the last few years: *Dhar* (*Catch*, 1999), *Koshto* (*The Pain*, 2000), and *The Minister* (2003). In the case of *The Mother*, the Hayat-Manna duo became a trio incorporating Dipjol, a new actor-cum-film-producer at that time. Dipjol, who became a very popular actor from 1999 onward, was criticized for bringing extreme violence into Bangladesh popular cinema; he played the role of villain (Kalam) in *The Mother*, one of his early films as actor-producer that introduced and provided a prototype for the extreme-violence subgenre of the action film. Another addition to the film has intertextual resonance: Shabnam, a renowned female actor of social films of the 1960s and 1970s, plays the revered mother Ammajan in the film. This character actually catalyzes the narrative by permitting (and thus encouraging) her violent but very obedient son, Badsha, to fight and kill the rapists. Thus the film and Shabnam's role as Ammajan signals a diegetic reworking of the woman's role in Bangladesh action cinema.

The story of *The Mother* develops chronologically and follows a simple cause-effect chain. In the prologue, we see that Badsha's father (Lal Mia), a plumber in a government department, suddenly died in an electrical accident. While pursuing Lal's pension, his widow (Badsha's mother) gets raped by the *boroshaheb* (the department head). An adolescent Badsha while waiting outside the room understands something terrible has happened to his mother, and he stabs and kills the *boroshaheb*. We see the film's titles over a freeze frame of the murder and learn that Badsha has got a fourteen-year jail term.

Alluding to the conventions of the social film, Lal Mia and his wife are shown as idealist and nostalgic male and female characters. However, in Lal Mia's death and his wife's rape, the screen presence of such characters types is quickly minimized. They are shown only in the preamble phase of the narrative, not portrayed as glorified icons to be respected and followed, and the young Badsha loses his innocence by stabbing and killing the *boroshaheb*. This is a common narrative temporal mechanism used in action films in order to enter the "present" phase that is no longer peaceful and harmless as it was in the yesteryears. One of the main protagonists normally loses his/her innocence through a conflict or an accident related with modernization and urbanization.

In *The Mother*, after the titles on the "freeze" shot of killing the *boroshaheb*, we enter into the main narrative world of the film that is contemporary Bangladesh. Here we find that Badsha has become a very prominent gangster who now lives in a huge villa with his mother, though she stopped talking to Badsha since the day of the rape. Badsha continues killing rapists wherever and wherever he can by stabbing with a huge knife. Before each murderous mission he informs Ammajan of his intentions and takes her blessings (touching her feet, that is *salam* to elders in an Islamic fashion). He also accompanies her to the local Islamic shrine every week where she prays and hands out money and food to the poor. In the same spirit Ammajan, Badsha, and his gang give relief assistance to the flood-victims in rural areas. (As a nod to extra-diegetic national reality, there was a massive flood in Bangladesh in late 1998, presumably when *The Mother* was under production.) In the course of the relief operation, Ammajan encounters Rina, a beautiful young woman who was also engaged in providing assistance with another team and finds her suitable to be the wife of Badsha. As soon as Badsha understands Amamajan's wish he informs Rina (who happens to be the daughter of an ex-minister and engaged to a fellow university student) that he must marry her. Rina's fiancé Mijan's parents live in the US, but because Mijan loves Bangladesh so much, he stays despite his parents' repeated requests for him to move there.

In order to get rid of Badsha, Rina's father seeks help from another gangster. Kidnapping and multiple shootouts ensue, and the film ends with both mother and son dying in the same bed.

This story of *The Mother* is presented in a way that the viewers can experience the violent incidents vividly and viscerally. As a sample of the extreme-violence subgenre of Bangladesh action cinema, killing, bleeding, gunfight, rape, and chase are shown as essential ingredients (if not attractions) of the film. Stabbings are shown with close shots of the blood-drenched knife and of the dripping blood. The multiple gunfights include the prolonged final fight between Badsha that ultimately ends with the death of both the protagonists. The revenge by the killer-hero for the act of rape is the main thrust of narrative in *The Mother*.

The Mother is also notable for the apparent absence (or at least invisibility) of the nation-state. Though *The Mother* represents the contemporary social scene, almost no national institution that can be seen as an identity-marker is clearly represented. Even the state-national organs such as police and court are not present. This tendency of keeping nation-state absent or invisible on the cinema-screens signals two possibilities. First, it posits the fact that because of globalization non-Western nation-states like Bangladesh became weaker than before while other non-state institutions (such as the team of gangsters in *The Mother*) became stronger. In *The Mother* we also see strong connections of the protagonists with Western modernity (as when Rina and Mijan try to flee to the US). These indicate that the age of powerful anti-colonial Asian nation-states that mobilized people of different identities under one big umbrella against Western colonial nations is now nothing but a wistful memory.

The latter allegorical reading of the film is especially pertinent to a discussion of popular cinema and identity in Bangladesh. The apparent invisibility of the nation-state rationalizes the cultural identity of the community/group as the national identity for all Bangladeshis. In *The Mother* we see the disintegration of a Bengali Muslim family. The settings, costumes (especially of female actors), dialogues, and props used in the film clearly represent the middle-class Bengali-Muslims. We also see a number of traditional Islamic rituals such as burials, weddings, and prayers that strongly communicate that Bangladesh is a land of and for Muslims with Bengali ethnicity. The attempts of the state and middle-class Bengali Muslims to turn Bangladesh into a Bengali-Muslim nation-state, as demonstrated in the hegemonic representational politics of contemporary popular cinema, clearly undermine the cultural identities of minority groups like non-Muslims (such as Bengali Hindus, Bengali Christians) and non-Bengalis such as hill-tribes living in Bangladesh.

Thus the contemporary texts of Bangladesh popular cinema not only represent the conflict between nationalist discourse and global forces, but also reorganize nationhood by covering up the conflicts within nationalism in the age of globalization. This is happening because the Bangladesh state, film-capitalists, and nationalist middle classes associated with the global modernity in contemporary Bangladesh are constantly re-defining the role of film – especially to meet the challenge of constructing and disseminating a standard Bangladeshi national identity in/of/through Bangladesh popular cinema.

CHAPTER 10

India: Bollywood's Global Coming of Age

Jyotika Virdi and Corey K. Creekmur

In 1995, India's dominant, Bombay-based commercial film industry celebrated its centennial year in a gala that was relatively low-key in proportion to
the industry's size and penchant for glamor and hyperbole, the hallmark of its
Hindi-language film productions. The event fell in a decade when the Bombay
(now officially Mumbai) film industry as a whole witnessed notable shifts: the
rise of a new generation of directors, new technologies and modes of filmmaking, increasingly sophisticated craftsmanship, attempts to reorganize the
industry's finances and distribution, and aggressive marketing that acknowledged the changing audience by pursuing its overseas market, which in turn
revamped the film narrative that had long been considered "formulaic."

The most profound factor affecting the film industry in the early 1990s was
economic "liberalization." Making a dramatic break with four decades of commitment to Prime Minister Nehru's model of state-controlled protectionist
"mixed economy," trade liberalization coincided with the worldwide "fall of
communism" and dissipation of socialist principles. In mass-media terms, the
most immediate and palpable impact was felt on Doordarshan, the state-
owned single-channel television that, following a series of commercial and
legal challenges, had to make way for a plethora of satellite and cable television channels featuring international, national, and regional programming. As
with the entry of earlier technologies, such as audio cassettes in the 1970s and
VCRs in the 1980s, the commercial manufacture of CDs, VCDs, and DVDs
in the 1990s extended the popularity of Hindi film and its music, even as widespread piracy simultaneously hindered profits. The expansion of television in
the 1990s became the most competitive challenge facing the Hindi film
industry, replaying a scenario that has invigorated many a national cinema in
the postwar period. As in other contexts, however, cinema managed to maintain its century-old allure and retain its audience despite the challenge to its
central role in Indian popular culture.

The competition from television, along with India's leading edge in software design and the move toward media convergence enabled by digital

technologies, influenced the "look" of the Hindi film, which now relies upon the glossy visuals and rapid editing associated with Hong Kong cinema, American music videos, and global advertising. Changing technology has also been crucial for Hindi cinema's circulation and expanded consumption among its long-neglected but loyal audience throughout the South Asian diaspora. This constituency, scattered across the globe in Africa, Australia, the Caribbean, Great Britain, and North America, ranges from descendants of nineteenth-century indentured laborers to software engineers and postcolonial cultural theorists. Notwithstanding its long-standing presence overseas (for instance, in Greece, China, and the former Soviet Union, where Hindi film songs from the 1950s are still sung in local languages), popular Hindi cinema was barely acknowledged by mainstream Western audiences, or for that matter film studies, which often mistook India's art cinema – usually in the exclusive example of the Bengali Satyajit Ray's realist films of the 1950s and 1960s – as representative of Indian cinema as a whole. Although still largely invisible to Western audiences, Indian popular cinema, under the often trivializing "Bollywood" label, has gained nominal visibility with the Oscar-nominated *Lagaan* (*Land Tax*, Ashutosh Gowarikar, 2001), the London and New York theatrical production *Bombay Dreams* (produced by Andrew Lloyd Weber in 2002), and Turner Classic Movies' surprisingly successful retrospective of popular Indian cinema in June 2003. (Popular Indian film has enjoyed a more prominent recognition in the United Kingdom, assisted by the programming and groundbreaking documentaries of Nasreen Munni Kabir for Britain's Channel 4.) These events coincided with a significant and growing academic interest in mainstream Indian cinema.

Throughout the 1990s, a combination of new media forces impacted India most powerfully under the rubric of "globalization," simultaneously opening India to international markets and Indian middle-class homes to international commodities and cultural programming. Cognizant of these changes and in competition with it, the Hindi film industry was forced to systematically tap into its overseas market of NRIs ("non-resident Indians") by ingeniously reinventing itself. The 1990s, therefore, is a watershed decade marked by an economic and cultural sensibility distinct from that of the preceding era. In the decades following independence in 1947, Hindi cinema, especially in the hands of the era's outstanding directors (including Raj Kapoor, Guru Dutt, Mehboob Khan, and Bimal Roy), idealized the nation through melodramatic family-centered narratives identified generically as "socials," projecting a particularized modernity, reconciling competing interests, and (sometimes barely) containing anxieties and tensions that threatened to fracture the national polity. However, by the 1970s – deeply scarred by Prime Minister Indira Gandhi's declaration of a national "Emergency" that severely restricted civil liberties – and into the early 1980s, Hindi cinema refracted social unrest centered on the working-class hero or "angry young man" embodied by actor Amitabh Bachchan's unprecedented superstardom. This period, which saw both Indian films and film-going become more explicitly masculine and less romantic (and somewhat less musical), was followed by a lull in the late 1980s, when the massively popular serializations of the Hindu epics *Ramayana* (1986–88) and *Mahabharata* (1988–90) on Doordarshan diverted audiences from movie theaters. However, by the mid-1990s Hindi cinema began to revitalize itself by tackling globalization head on.

If films of the four decades preceding the 1990s air conflicts between familiar oppositions (industrial class vs. working class, city vs. country, landlord vs. serf, feudal vs. democratic) and often offer idealized solutions in family drama, recent Hindi cinema, especially a record-breaking strand of revived "romance" films, ingeniously resurrects the idea of the national against the global through sagas of the diasporic Indian family under cultural siege in the west, desperately seeking moorings by returning to extended families in India. The hugely successful *Dilwale Dulhania Le Jayenge* (*The Lover Wins the Bride*, Aditya Chopra, 1996) is emblematic of these films in which the conflict is staged and settled between individualistic youth choosing their romantic partners through circuits of modernity (education, travel, and tourism) and their tradition-bound parents (in this case, a stern father) bent on arranged marriage symbolizing the status quo. The family/community spirit vs. the individual becomes a trope for the traditional against the modern, the national against the international, and the local against the global, but now through the innovation of the diasporic hero who successfully balances an Indian *dil* (heart) with the pleasures of Western consumption. The films adopt multiple ways of mediating the conflict against a range of benign to authoritarian patriarchs (in some cases ironically played by former "angry young man" Amitabh Bachchan), while class conflict, prominent in many left-leaning post-Independence films, virtually disappeared except when films dramatize the subtle snobberies of a richer and richer class in films like *Dil* (*Heart*, Vinod Doshi, 1990) or *Saathiya* (*Soulmate*, Mani Ratnam, 2002).

The growing presence of transnational companies in this period coincided with a boom in middle-class wealth and consumption. A cornucopia of commodities and lifestyles replete with luxury vacation resorts and leisure pursuits dominate the *mise-en-scène* in the 1990s Hindi films as if to welcome the consumerism unavailable to the austere economy of earlier decades. In this cinema signs of globalization are quintessentially invoked through the cosmopolitan Indian, once a source of moral scorn or comic ridicule in paradigmatic films such as *Purab aur Paschim* (*East and West*, Manoj Kumar, 1970). Critics observe that the ostentatious display of wealth in films like the industry-transforming blockbuster *Hum Aapke Hain Koun!* (*Who Am I to You?*, Sooraj Barjatya, 1994) is accompanied by a strong Hindu presence on the screen, driven by neo-conservative Hindu-majority politics. A force much like liberalization, Hindu nationalism (or *Hindutva*) suddenly swept through the public sphere, only superficially appearing like a reaction against the former. Arguably Hindi cinema reconciled Hindu nationalism and "Western"-style consumerism, becoming a site where both comfortably coexisted. It also spun a sub-genre of "patriotic" films such as *Gadar* (*Mayhem*, Anil Sharma, 2001) that explicitly condemned the Muslim other collaborating with neighboring Pakistan (once invoked but discreetly unnamed in popular films) to augment separatist-terrorist politics. This is an ironic as well as disturbing development, given the earlier popularity of the genre of "Muslim socials" within Hindi cinema, as well as the prominent role of Urdu (the official language of Pakistan) in film dialogue and poetic song lyrics, not to mention the crucial and continued presence of prominent Muslim performers and creative personnel in the production of Hindi cinema.

The Indian diaspora, strongly Hindu, nationalist, and comfortable in global consumer culture, not only took center stage in the 1990s Hindi film narrative but is increasingly important to the film industry's marketing calculus as well. In an industry where 80 percent of the films are flops, there is intense pressure to succeed. After the record-breaking Rupees 2 billion (US$44 million) earning of *Hum Aapke Hain Koun!*, a family drama centered around an elaborate Indian wedding ceremony, the search for the magical combination of successful narrative, star power, and marketing resulted in glossy hits like *Dilwale Dulhania Le Jayenge*, as well as *Dil To Pagal Hai* (*This Crazy Heart*, Yash Chopra, 1997), *Hum Dil De Chuke Sanam* (*Straight From the Heart*, Sanjay Leela Bhansali, 1999), and *Kabhi Khushi Kabhie Gham* (*Happy Times, Gloomy Times*, Karan Johar, 2001). Featuring the era's biggest stars (especially boyish Shah Rukh Khan, perhaps the period's defining screen hero), luxurious homes, trendy fashions (with prominent brand logos), and MTV-influenced song sequences, such films redefined the "good Indian" as rich, cosmopolitan, and playfully youthful, an almost complete reversal of the poor, proudly regional, and somberly mature heroes of the previous generation. Although Amitabh Bachchan's lanky frame was credited with bringing a new physicality to the Indian film hero in the 1970s, a new crop of younger actors, including Salman Khan, Sanjay Dutt, and Hrithik Roshan now displayed the buff muscles of modern gym culture and American action films. Even more dramatically, the long-standing opposites of the "good Indian girl" and the Westernized "vamp" were effectively fused in the spunky and unabashedly sexy heroines played by actresses like Kajol, Aishwarya Rai, and Madhuri Dixit.

Facing relentless competition from television and video consumption, many of these films revived the form of "multi-starrers," with several stars signed onto one film ensuring a box-office draw. Star salaries, notorious for driving up film costs that in the "A picture" for instance, rose from Rupees 30 or 40 million (US$700,000–900,000) to upwards of Rupees 60 million (US$1.35 million) between 1995 and 1996. Yet stars alone do not guarantee success, as a number of star-driven flops have demonstrated. Film songs, while a staple of popular Indian cinema since the arrival of sound, have also become increasingly critical to the advance marketing (and financing) of films, and so are given their own media-covered "launches" in order to advertise films through radio and televised video clips weeks before a film opens. After a reduction of the number and significance of film songs in the action-packed films of the 1970s, it's again a common opinion that no Hindi film can succeed without hit songs, and so (as in Hollywood) the industrial links between the film and music industries have become increasingly intertwined. The industry has also expanded overseas shooting (pioneered by directors Raj Kapoor and especially Yash Chopra) driven by the logic of offering "novelty," transporting viewers beyond the television screens in middle-class homes, and potentially enticing that class back to the big screen in refurbished upscale multiplexes. Overseas location shooting costs rose from 2–3 percent in the early part of the decade to 18–20 percent by the mid-1990s. Since the 1960s Switzerland has been the most popular location, to which London, Paris, and Vancouver, or cheaper locations, were added; and collectively, in the true sense of Soviet film theorist/filmmaker Lev Kuleshov's montage experiment of "creative geography," they stand in for the countryside in New Zealand or Europe. (More recently, Hindi films have begun to use the United States for location shooting, again in recognition of an audience that plays an increasing role in a film's success.) The cost of overseas shooting was offset by taking 60 percent smaller crews, using strict time lines, and furthermore, by selling the "'A' picture" to the overseas market for upwards of Rs. 20 million (US$450,000). The visual lushness in these films is supported by other production values: excellent cinematography and editing, bolstered by greater access to state-of-the-art film equipment, digital technologies (finally providing sophisticated special effects), and expensive set designs such as "designer villages" when substituting "foreign" locales for the Indian countryside. Product placement, common in contemporary Hollywood, now also marks Hindi films. But once hefty financial investments are made in a film, to ensure good returns a growing proportion of the film budget is spent on publicity and marketing. These include special promotions with digital effects made for television and theaters that displace the old cut-and-paste scenes from films used in trailers for theatrical releases. As elsewhere, these promotional films, along with music clips and interviews, fill out more expensive "collector edition" DVD packages, as that format replaces videotape.

Revealingly, more than the film narratives became increasingly family-centered. Like its Hollywood counterpart the Indian studio system, established in the first half of the twentieth century, declined after World War II. After India's independence from British colonial rule a few powerful family businesses, such as R.K. (Raj Kapoor) Films, Yash Raj Films, and Sippy Films established themselves over two and sometimes three generations. "Newcomers" among directors have been from among the film industry's personnel (cameramen, editors, and actors) or from advertising, and they have infused mainstream commercial films with their own styles. Examples of these include successes like Santosh Sivan and Ram Gopal Varma, known for slick action films, and Karan Johar and Aditya Chopra, responsible for some of the Hindi cinema's most successful films in the romantic, middle-class family mode. Ashutosh Gowarikar and Farhan Akhtar, respectively, succeeded in experiments that strayed from the traditional formula in *Lagaan* (2001), a rare "historical" serving as a nationalist fable depicting the origin of India's obsession with cricket, and *Dil Chahta Hai (The Heart Wants*, 2002), a witty celebration of globalized youth culture (discussed in the introduction to this book).

Another successful strain of films addressed the Indian diaspora, not only as a subject but significantly as a market. Small-budget independently produced NRI films, a relatively new phenomenon, were thus successfully marketed by distributors to a niche middle-class audience interested in the cultural politics of cultural displacement. Films like *Bombay Boys* (Kaizad Gustad, 1998), *English August* (Dev Benegal, 1994), *Hyderabad Blues* (Nagesh Kukunoor, 1998), and *Split Wide Open* (Dev Benegal, 1999) have claimed 100 percent profits and have been hailed as the cinematic counterpart of the Anglo-Indian fiction (led by Salman Rushdie) that also caught the literary world's attention in the 1990s. Together these films have reconstituted art and middle cinema (discussed below) by replacing the subaltern figure's centrality with the middle-class subject's angst. They use "Hinglish," a colloquial Hindi-English hybrid popularized by cosmopolitan music television veejays. Other diasporic films from Britain, Canada, and the United States depict Indians negotiating two cultures while away from the "homeland" or when they return. Examples include *American Desi* (Piyush Dinkar Pandya, 2001), *Mitr (My Friend,* Revathi, 2001), *Chutney Popcorn* (Nisha Ganatra, 2000), and the highly successful *Bend it Like Beckham* (Gurinder Chadha, 2002). Some of these films, such as the international art-house hit *Monsoon Wedding* (Mira Nair, 2002) acknowledge, borrow, from and pay tribute to popular cinema, while others outright mock it, or do both as in *Hollywood/Bollywood* (Deepa Mehta, 2002).

Popular Hindi cinema successful in the domestic and overseas market obscures other sectors of Indian films. The industry's taxonomy of "A," "B," and "C" films accounts for different cultural/political economies of its segmented market: "A" films are popular Hindi films consumed in the Indian metropolis and overseas market; small-town circulation constitutes "B" films; and "C" films represent low-budget, semi-porn films, and old film reruns dominating working-class districts. The cinema hall has been recognized as an important site of democratization of the public sphere, itself a slow and contested process.

India's Alternative Cinemas

Outside the rubric of commercial Hindi cinema are several equally large regional cinemas, with Tamil, Malayalam, and Telugu film the most significant rivals despite their lack of Hindi cinema's international reach. Each of these cinemas, along with Bengali and Hindi cinema, has also produced art films, distinguishable from the commercial film in their mode of financial organization, narrative, aesthetics, and audience: predominantly the Indian literati and Western viewers at international film festivals. Although this cinema proliferated in the 1970s, the precursor of this practice in the 1950s and 1960s was Satyajit Ray, whose films (as pointed out previously) have too often misleadingly represented Indian cinema as a whole in the Western film canon, a perception slowly being corrected in film textbooks. (A smaller international audience was briefly attentive to the work of the other Bengali masters, Mrinal Sen and Ritwik Ghatak.)

In the 1970s, the fillip to Indian art cinema came from various institutional mechanisms created by the Indian state, such as the Film and Television Institute of India (FTII) established in 1961 and the National Film Archives of India set up in 1963, that had the effect of promoting film personnel not affiliated with the commercial industry. Additionally, the Directorate of Films under the Ministry of Information and Broadcasting promoted film festivals in India while the Film Finance Corporation (FFC) set up in 1960 helped finance and later distribute and market art films. Leading auteurs of this cinema include Shyam Benegal, Adoor Gopalakrishnan, Girish Karnad, Govind Nihalani, and Saeed Mirza, among others. This cinema even produced its own stars (including Smita Patil, Shabana Azmi, and Naseeruddin Shah) who often crossed over from theater or television, occasionally making forays into commercial cinema as well. By the mid-1970s, "middle" or "parallel" cinema had emerged as a halfway house between art and popular films by combining the aesthetic and narrative strategies used by both, although typically centered on a middle-class protagonist and setting. Films like *Ankur* (*The Seedling*, Shyam Benegal, 1974), *Chupke-Chupke* (*Silently*, Hrishikesh Mukherjee, 1975), *Gharonda* (*Home*, Bhimsain, 1977), and *Masoom* (*Innocent*, Mahesh Bhatt, 1986) are a few notable examples. By the 1980s, popular entertainment programming had begun on television, cutting into this cinema's audience, while the repetitive themes of art and middle cinema meant a loss of their initial novelty. Many of the makers of these films moved to television production before returning to filmmaking, spurred this time by a desire to reach a wider audience and a willingness to adopt aesthetic features like the song and dance sequences used in popular cinema. In 1980, the Jamia Milia Mass Communication Research Center set up a production unit to train students who would go on to work for the booming television industry, while also creating a new genre of documentary and experimental films, distinct from the propagandist documentaries produced under the aegis of the Government of India's Films Division, which exhibitors were compelled to screen along with commercial features. More recently, the once marked distinctions between the art and popular cinemas have further blurred, with formerly "alternative" figures like Shyam Bengal now working comfortably in the commercial arena with films like *Zubeidaa* (2000), featuring Bollywood stars and the voice of Lata Mangeshkar, the popular industry's legendary playback singer.

National Cinema and State Authority

If art cinema absorbed elements of popular cinema in the 1990s, it is equally true that with new entrants in the industry and competition from successful Tamil films, such as those by the controversial but unquestionably talented Mani Ratnam, popular cinema began infusing elements of art cinema by streamlining its narrative and aesthetics. Perhaps the most visible impact of realist modes on popular cinema was in the revitalized gangster genre that reveals the working of the underworld and, more boldly, its infiltration of the film industry in works like *Nayakan* (*Protagonist*, Mani Ratnam, 1987), *Parinda* (*Bird*, Vidhu Vinod Chopra, 1989), *Satya* (*Truth*, Ram Gopal Varma, 1997), and *Company* (Ram Gopal Varma, 2001). These films transformed the 1970s action tradition in commercial cinema with generic crime film elements while also drawing on middle cinema's aesthetics and realism (especially in the representation of violence and sexuality). Yet despite these mutual influences, commercial Hindi cinema still dominates the dwindling art as well as regional cinemas, along with claiming a national audience.

The Hindi film's status as India's national cinema rests on a paradoxical relation between state authority and language politics. After independence, Hindi, the language of about five northern states, was imposed as the national language despite resistance from several southern states. Yet commercial Hindi cinema and its music are embraced widely and this trans-regional, trans-lingual popularity in a country with twenty-two official languages and over four thousand dialects gives the Hindi film the status of a national cinema. The Bombay film industry's apparent endorsement and extension of the Indian state's language policy is ironic given the industry's otherwise antagonistic history toward the state on two key issues it considers punitive: state censorship and taxation. Long denied official designation as an industry (and thus denied access to banks and loans), film producers have frequently dodged severe taxation by using "black" (laundered) money to finance their business. By the 1990s the film industry's suspected links with the underworld stopped being rumors after prominent stars, distributors, and music-industry moguls made headlines when their links to underworld figures (often operating in exile) were exposed, sometimes following assassinations and extortion attempts. In the early 1990s superstar Amitabh Bachchan established Amitabh Bachchan Corporation Limited (ABCL), which took initial steps to regularize the commercial film industry's business practices and increase its rate of success. The long-delayed recognition of the film industry as a legitimate industry finally began to release filmmakers from their reliance on underworld financing, although at the same time, censorship, a legacy of the 1927 Indian Cinematographic Act, continued in the post-independence period with the Censor Board (whose official certificate appears before each approved film) using its authority to regulate the representation of sexuality (among other things) and the industry resisting and circumventing it in every possible way. Despite the conflicted relation between the film industry and the Indian state, prominent Bombay industry stars have held close links with political figures. Nargis and Raj Kapoor were closely associated with Nehru, and their widely publicized visit to the USSR in the 1950s made them quasi-cultural ambassadors of the Indian state, and Amitabh Bachchan was close to Prime Minister Rajiv Gandhi in the 1970s and 1980s and himself briefly a member of the Indian Parliament. (In south India, the elevation of film stars into prominent political positions has an even longer and often more controversial history.)

From the Heart: Pan-Indian Popular Hindi Cinema

Although Hindi cinema remains dominant, hence rendering the equally large annual production of Tamil and Telegu films "regional," a few artists have broken into the Bombay industry from outside. Most notably, the Tamil director Mani Ratnam's controversial films – including *Roja* (*Rose*, 1992), set in war-torn Kashmir, and *Bombay* (1995), set amidst the communal (Hindu-Muslim) riots that shocked the city in late 1992 and early 1993 – have attracted the national market, and his frequent music director A.R. Rahman has become even more widely prominent throughout South Asia and the diaspora: the London stage musical *Bombay Dreams* is constructed around his film songs, and his recordings have been remixed for consumption in discos worldwide.

While the large output of India's popular cinema industries has allowed India to remain one of the few nations to resist the dominance of Hollywood films, the impact of Hollywood styles and genres on Indian filmmakers is evident in the many blatant but unofficial remakes of Hollywood films; although often ridiculed by intellectuals as poor imitations, such films are often highly creative adaptations and cultural hybrids rather than simple copies, at the very least forcing Hollywood models to conform to the Indian demand for song sequences irrespective of (Western) genres. For example, the political thriller *Mission Kashmir* (directed by Vidu Vinod Chopra, 2001) borrows its special effects from *The Matrix*, while the thriller *Kaante*, shot on location in Los Angeles, fuses the Hollywood neo-noirs *The Usual Suspects* (1995) and *Reservoir Dogs* (1992). As with recent Bombay gangster films, such examples might suggest that the distinct Indian genres of the past, including "historicals," "socials," and the now-rare "mythological" are seeking redefinition even if most films adhere to the *masala* mix of drama, comedy, action, romance, and music that often confuses Western viewers. In any case, Indian cinema, for decades loved by millions but almost entirely invisible to Western audiences and critics, now seems to be genuinely global as it is finally attracting audiences beyond South Asia (and the diaspora) and simultaneously incorporating and revising international influences. A brief discussion of the 1998 film *Dil Se ... (From the Heart)* demonstrates some of the ways contemporary Indian cinema has freshened the formula.

Dil Se is the third film in director Mani Ratnam's unofficial "terror trilogy," which began with the successful but controversial films, *Roja* (1992) and *Bombay* (1995). Whereas the first two films were made in Tamil and also released in successful Hindi versions, *Dil Se* (though also released in Tamil) functions more as a Hindi film, most obviously through its casting of one of the superstars of contemporary Hindi film, Shah Rukh Khan, as its hero Amar. Although the film was only marginally successful in India, it was successful abroad, indicating the increased importance of the diasporic audience, and it generated a best-selling soundtrack of A.R. Rahman's film songs.

Playing a reporter for the state-run All-India Radio during the celebration of India's fiftieth anniversary of independence, Shah Rukh Khan again relies on the cocky persona that had endeared him to millions of fans worldwide, but the film's narrative consistently undermines him: whereas his pesky persistence inevitably charms the initially wary objects of his ardor in earlier films (such as in *Dilwale Dulhania Le Jayenge*), his pursuit of the mysterious young woman Meghna (Manisha Koirala) in *Dil Se* can only end in disaster, since she is devoted to completing a terrorist mission against the central state which he represents. When the traumatic past that has driven her political convictions is finally revealed, Amar can only assume, like a typical film hero, that love can overcome such wounds. Although many classic Hindi films end tragically (despite common claims to the contrary), the fact that this popular star's brash energy does not win the day illuminates the film's bold juxtaposition of conventional romance and contemporary political realities.

As in his earlier films, Mani Ratnam employs in *Dil Se* the popular form of commercial cinema to tackle topics usually reserved for art cinema or even documentary filmmaking. As a naive spokesman for the central government and its regulated media, Shah Rukh Khan's journalist character Amar is unprepared for the bitterness and alienation he encounters among the marginalized figures he interviews in India's peripheral northern territories for what is supposed to be a celebratory anniversary of Indian unity.

If *Dil Se* is ultimately an interrogation of the arrogance of the center from the position of the center (rather than a genuine critique from the margins), it is still a remarkable demonstration of the ability of popular cinema to engage in serious commentary without fully abandoning its formulaic elements. In fact, the film establishes its critical perspective through this form as well as its narrative content, which explicitly evokes, in its final scenes, the actual assassination of Prime Minister Rajiv Gandhi by a female suicide bomber in 1991. A song-filled political thriller with a romantic plot, *Dil Se* consistently challenges the assumption that the formula of Hindi cinema prevents serious commentary.

Unlike many Hindi films, which locate their requisite song sequences in semi-plausible locations (ranging from village festivals to urban nightclubs), all of *Dil Se*'s remarkable "picturizations" of songs seem to take place in Amar's imagination. And while the plot of the film takes its main characters through a range of actual locations, the songs move through a much greater range of geographical locations, in effect traversing the subcontinent. The songs, in other words, are not narratively integrated but in their fragmentary disruption of the storyline suggest the disintegration in "Indian" identity that is the political and historical backdrop for the love story (that itself remains largely only a male character's fantasy.) Whereas most film songs advance the narrative or seem irrelevant diversions, the song sequences in *Dil Se* tend to challenge and contradict the main plot. At times, however, the world of the narrative and the alternative, imaginary space of the songs overlaps, with the lush music audaciously accompanied by scenes of barbed wire, marching soldiers, and bomb explosions. While Western audiences are prone to see the song sequences in most Hindi films as interruptions of the narratives, many Indian films actually construct clever ways to weave songs into their overall organization. *Dil Se* instead emphasizes the disjunction between its songs and story, exploiting the most consistent convention of popular Indian cinema in order to foreground irreconcilable tensions rather than to solve them. The common cliché that Hindi films, like Hollywood, demand happy endings (a claim that any list of Hindi cinema's most popular films would challenge) is denied by the film's ambiguous and tragic conclusion, which reinvents the classic Hindi film's conflict between love and duty.

CHAPTER 11

Mainland China: Public Square to Shopping Mall and the New Entertainment Film

Augusta Lee Palmer

As contemporary urban identities in the People's Republic of China were being razed and re-formed along with the architecture of Chinese cities, what had grown up in the ruins? The resurgence of the entertainment film, which had been absent from Chinese screens for fifty years, provided a more commercial forum for imagining the transformation of Chinese society.

Perhaps the most telling metaphor for the transformation of Chinese society is the linguistic shift which transformed the public square into a shopping mall. Film and cultural critic Dai Jinhua has noted that the word *guangchang*, meaning plaza or public square (as in *Tiananmen guangchang*), was formerly used primarily to refer to public, politicized spaces; but in the latter half of the 1990s *guangchang* was appropriated for use in the names of shopping malls. In Dai's opinion, the linguistic transformation of the public space of political discourse and revolution into a space of commercialism indicates the displacement of the political and the creation of a new consumer utopia. According to Dai Jinhua, "The shopping space has become the space of reorganizing and reconstructing the social order. The image of happy consumers in the plaza has replaced the image of angry citizens at the *Tian'anmen Guangchang*. The postmodern capitalist phenomenon of obscuring the differences among classes through commercial consumption has replaced the faraway communist ideal of social equality ... Material consumption has become heaven on earth in China."[1]

Though material consumption did provide a new image of heaven, cinematic representations of shopping malls sometimes suggested their alienating qualities. Zhang Yang's *Shower* (1999), for example, features a scene in which a developmentally disabled character is lost in a Beijing shopping mall and must be "saved" by his elder brother. Some representations went even further in their diagnosis of shopping malls as symptoms of a pathological amnesia. The shopping mall built above the traditional home destroyed by the character Jiannong's bulldozer in Zhou Xiaowen's *No Regrets for Youth* (1992) not only erases the physical, architectural traces of the past, but also the characters' memory of it. When Jiannong's former lover and his widow bump into one another in the mall after his death, neither mentions or alludes to him. The violence of the past, and particularly the Tiananmen massacre, is a distinctly palpable – if unmentionable – force in art films like the underground independent production *Frozen* (1995), about a performance artist seeking freedom through creative destruction, but it seemed that commercialism and mall culture had the power to overwrite it almost completely in the new entertainment films.

The shift from politicized mass culture to a consumerist culture of individuals can be identified as the most significant aspect of Chinese society's transformation over the last decade, and the rise of the entertainment film is arguably its cinematic equivalent. The lack of profitability for art films that dominated the state-run industry of the 1980s, combined with the fact that studios had become responsible for their own bottom lines in the 1990s, made the production of profitable entertainment imperative for the Chinese film industry.[2] By the end of the decade, domestic journals like *Contemporary Cinema* (*Dangdai dianying*) emphasized the importance of the entertainment film and even stressed the duty to make profitable commercial films. Though the emphasis on making popular films could be seen as somewhat consistent with the rhetoric of the socialist past, the emphasis on profitability was a distinct change. Just as the utopian slogan "Look toward the future" (*wang qian kan*) was popularly transformed into its Chinese homonym, "Look toward the money," the larger purpose of filmmaking seemed to have shifted from political instruction to commercial enjoyment.

Hesuipian: Comedic Primers in Consumption

Shopping malls and literal consumption were mirrored and modeled in the entertainment films which rose to prominence in the 1990s. Though the development of the entertainment film industry in Mainland China is a topic worthy of its own book-length study, my aim here is merely to sketch its outlines and identify some crucial figures and films, in order to discuss the intersection of entertainment films and the documentary impulse. In the late 1990s, director Feng Xiaogang spearheaded a prominent filmmaking team which helped define Mainland entertainment filmmaking and invented the genre of *hesuipian*, or New Years' films, in particular. The formulaic *hesuipian* genre originated in 1997 with Feng's *Part A, Part B* (aka *Dream Factory*, *Jia fang yifang*). *Hesuipian* are generally urban comedies made for release during the Lunar New Year holidays, when consumers have both the time and celebratory inclination for film-going. In a sense, these films took Hong Kong comedic models like Stephen Chow (Chiau in Mandarin), whose Cantonese "cinema of nonsense" comedies were also frequently released during the Lunar New Year, and adapted them to Beijing needs by presenting Beijing-centered comedies made for release during the Chinese New Year. The popularity of *hesuipian* was so immense that even Fifth Generation auteur Zhang Yimou was inspired to make one in the year 2000, *Happy Times* (*Xingfu shiguang*).[3]

Due to the ossified nature of the studio system, private film-production companies – working in loose co-operation with state-owned studios – became the most successful producers of entertainment films. Beijing Film Studios, for example, provided access to equipment rental and a license to release the films made by Feng Xiaogang's Forbidden City Film Company.[4] Though close to the Fifth Generation directors in age, Feng was an outsider to the Chinese film industry who started as a set painter for propaganda films made by the People's Liberation Army. He became a screenwriter and then a director for immensely popular television series, such as *Beijingers in New York* (*Beijing ren zai niuyue*, 1993), in the early 1990s. (Television series were a major cultural phenomenon in Mainland China throughout the decade.) Feng worked on these television dramas, and later on his feature films, with a collaborative team that included actors like Jiang Wen and Ge You, as well as the novelist Wang Shuo, famous for his absurdist Beijing-centered fiction. Together, they created characters who spoke with a Beijing burr and encountered the transformation of Chinese urban life with a gritty sense of humor closely linked to the Northern capital.[5] *Part A, Part B*, starring Ge You, Xu Fan, and the director himself, was a comedic romp about four employees of a private company that provides the service of acting out the fantasies of its nouveau riche customers. The customers' fantasies, which range from becoming General Patton to experiencing masochistic fantasies of starvation and acquiring an elaborate decorated home, provide ample material for a slapstick comedy that fantasizes China's transition to a service-based economy. This first *hesuipian* earned a then record-breaking 30 million yuan (or US$3.57 million) at the box office. The next year's *Be There or Be Square* (*Bu jian bu san*, 1998), a comedy about Chinese immigrants in Los Angeles, was followed by *Sorry Baby* (*Mei wan mei liao*, 1999), centering on the conflict between a wily, affluent Beijing businessman and the van driver he has failed to pay for a little too long, and *A Sigh* (*Yi sheng tanqi*, 2000), which portrays an affluent TV screenwriter's extramarital affair.

As Shuyu Kong notes, the subject matter seems ripped from the human interest headlines: "... *he sui pian* are social comedies which focus on current social changes and everyday problems encountered by ordinary Chinese people. All Feng's films deal with familiar situations and human relationships, such as opening new business ventures, immigration, extramarital affairs, divisions between rich and poor ... To a certain degree, *he sui pian* has captured

Beijingers' black humor and its social function and applied it in depicting and interpreting the rapidly changing society …[6] This focus on what Kong calls "some of the most disturbing aspects of contemporary China," including the widening gap between rich and poor and the "collapse of social morality,"[7] is what I would identify as the documentary impulse in Feng Xiaogang's films. And, though I would agree with Kong's assertion that this grounding in documentary topics functions largely to reaffirm conventional values rather than to question the status quo or the repercussions of social transformation, I would still argue that Feng's films are so successful in part because of this documentary element. In other words, the appeals of their unrealistic elements – glamorous stars, absurdist comedy, and melodramatic romances – are grounded by the use of location shooting and topical stories about the struggles of contemporary urban life. It is their grounding in contemporary life that provokes the recognition and identification which, in turn, produces emotional comfort and/or catharsis when things work out well in the fictional world of Feng Xiaogang.

Imar Films' *Shower* and *Spicy Love Soup*: Family Values and Desires

Another commercial film company which has been described as focused on "new life experiences, reality, the mainstream, and commercialization"[8] is Imar Films, a private company headquartered in Beijing which made films like Shi Runjiu's *Beautiful New World*[9] and was headed by American producer Peter Loehr. Imar had its first major domestic success with its debut production, *Spicy Love Soup* (*Aiqing mala tang*, Zhang Yang, 1997). Imar had an even looser arrangement with its studio sponsor, Xian Film Studios, which merely provided the licenses for Imar films to enter the pre-exhibition censorship process and did not interfere (or contribute to) the scripting, production, or post-production process. Commercial success was certainly one of Imar's primary goals, and canny marketing strategies played a major role in the film company's success. One of Loehr's first important acts as in creating Imar was the purchase of film rights to the back catalogue of Mandarin pop from Taiwan's Rock Records, which formed the soundtrack for *Spicy Love Soup*, the first PRC film to be cross-marketed with its soundtrack album. Yet, like the films of Feng Xiaogang, *Spicy Love Soup* takes a comedic approach to contemporary social issues like divorce, the intoxicating power of accumulation, and the intersection of romance, individualism, and commerce.

Another Imar film directed by Zhang Yang, *Shower*, focuses on the collapse of a family and the demolition of their home in a Beijing *hutong*, which is topical material shared with many visual artists. It also includes a use of video footage which "documents" both the process of demolition and the mournful reaction of the developmentally disabled son[10] to the loss of his home. This use of video footage can certainly be understood as a documentary impulse in a commercial film.[11] Thus, an attention to documenting physical changes in the urban landscape and the structure of feeling associated with the sociocultural transformation of China are certainly an important aspect of these contemporary commercial films, just as they form an integral aspect of the "freedom artist" films.

In a retrospective look at the "urban generation"[12] of 1990s filmmakers, Zhang Zhen notes that the urban films of Zhang Yuan, Wang Xiaoshuai, and Wu Wenguang are "quite different" from the "commercial films that also deal with urban themes." Zhang locates this difference in the non-commercial films' experimentation with film form and their directors' positioning as individual witnesses who provide an insider's perspective on the "violent aspects of a society in transformation."[13] While I agree that formal experimentation and a pared-down observational style separate the art-cinema directors of this generation from their more commercial counterparts, I want to argue that many commercial films are just as centrally concerned with the wrenching social transformation of Mainland society. The gloss of the entertainment films and their use of a Hollywood-style omniscience rather than the self-conscious inscription of subjectivity common to most freedom artist films certainly does not give the commercial films as strong a sense of individual witness to change. Yet, they still have a sense of *xianchang*, or being on the scene provided by both location shooting and topical subject matter. Their central concern with the changing Chinese urban landscape, the shifting position of the individual in society, and their obsessive, sometimes critical portrayals of consumer culture are all strands of reflection – however facile in some cases – on contemporary Chinese urban life which betray a significant documentary impulse. That impulse, however, is intertwined with a hope for commercial, rather than artistic, success and has been geared toward a domestic, rather than an international film-festival, audience.[14] In the following paragraphs, I will trace the documentary impulse as it relates to a limited critique of commercialism contained in Zhang Yang's *Shower* and *Spicy Love Soup*.

As I noted above, the perils of consumerism are alluded to in Zhang Yang's second film, *Shower*. Not only does the youngest son, Er Ming, nearly get lost in a mall, but the older son, Da Ming, has abandoned his father and younger brother in order to pursue a lucrative business career in the South. Thus, the engine of independent business is implicated as a danger to the family system. Moreover, the shadow consumer culture and real estate speculation are the logical forces behind the bulldozing of the *hutong* and the family home within it. Thus, the transition to a market economy can be understood as destructive to both the physical and the emotional space of home. Yet, *Shower* and its director frame these events in terms of tradition versus progress, rather than tradition versus commerce. In an interview, Zhang explained his motivation for making the film in terms of the disappearance of traditional architecture: "Bit by bit the city's history and unique architectural styles are fading, becoming little more than fragments of people's memories. Traditional kinship – those intimate yet relaxed bonds that once joined people in their quadrangles – is wiped out when people move into high-rises. I am not against modernization or change. But if "progress" takes place at the expense of one's cultural heritage, then it is horrendously damaging. I made my film, *Shower*, to record this process of rapid social transition. I wanted to explore visually certain changes in human relations, particularly those between generations, that can be difficult to express verbally."[15] In the director's statement and the film itself, then, the conflict is a negotiation between "cultural heritage" and "progress" embodied by the destruction of vernacular architecture, which has the effect of setting aside questions about the role capital and consumption play in this "social transition."

This focus on "documenting" social change was a primary factor in Imar's plan to make commercial films. In a list that would become identified as the Imar formula for success, Loehr noted three requirements for an Imar film: a relatively low budget, a first- or second-time director, and topical subject matter about current social issues which a large audience could relate to. Loehr's list clearly shows not only a strong sense of the financial bottom line, but also the intertwining of commercial and social aims in Imar's production strategies. Pressing the notion of the social significance of Imar films films even further, Loehr remarked of the art cinema of Zhang Yuan and other Sixth Generation directors, "We're not going to change China through French film critics."[16] Thus, the "Imar Model" contained a clear note of social criticism as a selling point for its commercial films.

Zhang Yang's first film for Imar, *Spicy Love Soup*, places a critical view of the intersection of consumption and romantic love at the center of several of its six narratives. Like Zhang Yuan's *Beijing Bastards* (1993) a gritty docudrama about disaffected youths and the underground music scene, *Spicy Love Soup* features a multifocal narrative set against a popular music score. Unlike Zhang Yuan's film, *Spicy Love Soup*'s multifocal narratives are structured into clearly segmented vignettes, while the music of the score is more pop than rock. The six vignettes include five romantic couplings and one divorce in an attempt to portray a cross-section of contemporary romance as experienced by six generations, ranging from middle-school to retirement age. Though the characters are played by professional actors and, in some cases, acknowleged stars,[17] this portrayal of love from the point of view of characters of different ages and socio-economic strata creates a "sociological" overtone despite the alternately comic and melodramatic turns of the story.

The episodic vignettes in *Spicy Love Soup* are "held together" by the continuation, in fits and starts, of one twenty-something couple's relationship. The film opens with the introduction of the male half of the couple to the girl's parents and closes with their wedding banquet. In between each successive plot point in their trip down the aisle (or in this case, toward the banquet hall), a longer episode about each of the other five couples' romances is "sandwiched." Many of these relationships hinge on the characters' consumption of consumer goods as part of the path to romantic love. The first couple declares their relationship to her parents in an upscale Sichuan hot pot restaurant in Beijing, while the next segment of their romance features them moving in together and cuddling in front of their new TV. In the third segment of their story, they visit a department store and purchase an engagement ring. The fourth segment portrays their civil marriage, and the fifth segment of their story features the lavish and highly commercialized process of taking wedding photos.[18] The final segment depicts their elaborate wedding banquet in a luxurious banquet hall. Five out of the six segments portraying this romance, then, are linked to the new consumer culture, while only the fourth involves an encounter with governmental authority.

Since this couple's vignettes serve as the spatial-temporal points of connection between the other five stories, commerce and consumption are the major meeting point for the characters. In this sense, the mall has become the central metaphorical space for human interchange in this cinematic version of Chinese society. In the hot pot restaurant where the first couple declares their relationship to her parents, the spicy hot pot sends the male half of the couple to the bathroom, where he uses the stall next to a middle-school student listening to his walkman. The film then takes up the story of this student, whose obsession with listening to and recording cassette tapes is central to his romantic pursuit of a female middle-school student. The television set in the twenty-something couple's new apartment plays a video personal ad recorded by a 55-year-old nurse hoping to find a mate to share her retirement, prompting the narrative shift to the nurse's story. The first couple's trip to a department store is echoed by the thirty-something couple's trip to a department store to purchase a birthday gift for the wife, a purchase which ignites the obsessive collection of increasingly elaborate toys which nearly destroys their relationship. Finally, during the wedding photo session for the first couple, a chance encounter between the wedding photographer and a woman he photographs on the street starts the new story of this fifth couple's romance. In this way, consumption serves as the glue which holds both the story and this imagined society in place.

The intricate intertwining of consumption and romance not only can be remarked on in almost every one of the film's short vignettes, but also was evident in the film's Valentine's Day release and its Cadbury chocolates promotional tie-in.[19] However, the corrosive nature of overconsumption is also the central theme of one story within the film. Yu Xiaohui and Chen Jing, a thirty-something yuppie couple, develop a spiraling obsession with acquiring new toys that threatens their ability to relate to one another. Married for several years, the two seem bored with one another when their story opens. They share nearly silent meals and, after some nagging, Xiaohui accompanies Chen Jing to the department store to purchase a birthday gift for her. They wander the aisles grimly and cannot agree on what to buy. Finally, against Xiaohui's complaints that it's not an appropriate gift for an adult woman, they purchase a radio-controlled car. The purchase of this toy and their discovery of what Xiaohui calls "the joy of toys," sparks an obsessive urge to collect more and more toys. At first this seems to re-ignite their relationship, allowing them to bond by expressing their emotions and acting out their fantasies using toys as proxies. In this bourgeois consumption of progressively more elaborate toys, however, they "revert" to a solipsistic affluent childhood they've probably never experienced. Though they spend more time together than before, their interactions are always mediated by the toys, as if they cannot express their feelings or enjoy their life without constant acquisition of novel playthings. Even their decision to have a child is discussed first through the puppet proxies Xiaohui buys to celebrate their anniversary. Soon, their play turns aggressive, and the couple proceed to fight like a couple of spoiled, overgrown toddlers. It is only the arrival of what Xiaohui calls a "new toy," their baby, that brings them back to the real world they've lost touch with. The voice-over that closes this story questions whether their child was the cause or the result of their love, but viewers might wonder whether their compulsive consumption was the cause or the result of their marital conflicts.

This story contains a clear critique of a pathological over-consumption which endangers Chen Jing and Yu Xiaohui's marriage and can only be "cured" by a return to relatively conventional family values. Yet, the reception of the film provides another twist on this slick, commercial critique of consumption. Despite the fact that the couple's obsessive desire to accumulate mechanical toys exacerbates the problems in their relationship, one reaction to *Spicy Love Soup* was a desire to acquire those very same products. Zhang and Loehr noted that, after the film opened, Imar was inundated with requests for the toys featured in the film, which had been bought in Taiwan and were not readily available on the Mainland. Fairly rapidly, such toys were imported and sold quite well due to the film's popularity.[20] Thus, this cautionary tale about the dangers of consumption became a kind of inadvertent product placement that actually stimulated the consumption it half-heartedly attempted to critique.[21]

Despite the use of different media and some difference in their intended audiences, *Spicy Love Soup*, a highly commercial film which raised a moderate critique of consumerism, provoked a contradictory reception not unlike the reception of a piece of installation art, Wang Jin's *Ice: Central China* (1996).[22] The installation was commissioned by developers, who asked Wang to create a work of aesthetic beauty and conceptual content to celebrate the opening of a mall. Hoping to make a work that would serve to "cool" consumer desires, Wang embedded desirable consumer goods in a wall of ice outside the mall. Contrary to Wang's expectations, once people discovered the products within the ice wall, their desire to consume was anything but cooled. In fact, they used every available tool to break into the ice and acquire the goods for themselves. Thus, both the relatively highbrow aesthetic project of Wang Jin's installation piece and the popular cinematic art of Zhang Yang's *Spicy Love Soup* presented a critical, instructional stance on a contemporary social issue, consumerism. Though neither chose a traditional genre or presented their own position as part of the 4 May tradition of instructional reportage and social critique, both works contained a vein of this reportage on the contemporary social scene. However, in both cases, these intentions were overturned by the audience. Because of this reversal, both works not only reflected and critiqued the contemporary social scene but also played a role in altering its reality. In the case of Wang Jin's Ice: *Central China*, there was a momentary finite change in reality when the spectators were moved to break down the wall. In the case of *Spicy Love Soup*, the film provoked a desire for chocolate, Mandarin pop, and – more unexpectedly – Taiwanese toys. The additional ways in which popular cinema forms or shapes reality are more difficult to record and quantify. They may serve, Shuyu Kong suggests in her analysis of Feng Xiaogang's *hesuipian*, as a mode of disavowal, a way to acknowledge social crises in order to forget them in the romantic or comedic catharses of the films' final moments. They may also serve, as Peter Loehr and Zhang Yang hope, as a way to "change China," to bring people's attention to the destruction of traditional forms, or at least to raise awareness about the need for balance between economic demands and cultural preservation. They clearly serve as consumer primers which "teach" their audiences how and what to consume, creating the demand for goods previously unknown and, thus, undesired.

Conclusion: Consumption and the (Re)Creation of the Self

This investigation and reflection of the Consumer Revolution in the re-born Chinese commercial cinema is a document of changing social norms about romance and consumption. A mall may be a public space for consumption which in some sense could "replace" the politicized square, but the mall also exists as a source for the creation of the private sphere. Personal spaces and identities are not only expressed but also created by the music, clothes and objects purchased in the mall. There has been much debate about the emergence of a new private sphere in China following economic and political reform. While the realities of this private sphere are, naturally, variable and open to question, the fantasized creation of a private sphere constructed through consumption is quite evident in entertainment films of the 1990s. Though the accoutrements of informed consumption and connoisseurship may be available to only a privileged few, versions of this private sphere of interior decoration and designer clothes are available to a much broader base of young people through the affordable internet bars that are now a fixture in China's global cities and even its provincial towns. The now defunct weiku.com, an outgrowth of Imar Films, only cost the consumer the price of time in an internet café, but it assigned users points which were good toward virtual purchases of clothing and home accessories for an online version of themselves. In exchange, it introduced the customer to its own movies and bands and helped to guide them in their pursuit of "*weiku,*" or "way cool" lifestyles.

The power of this virtual consumption is further suggested in the opening of Feng Xiaogang's *A Sigh* (2000). A young woman brought to Hainan Island to babysit a wayward but famous writer remarks that the beach resort she is at "reminds" her of Hawaii and is "just like Europe." When asked, she admits she's been to neither place, but knows how they "feel." The implication is that these places can be found, or at least "felt" within China through the proper instruction, which is to say through the consumption of the proper images. Though viewers may laugh at the character's silliness, the scene indicates a pretension to a cosmopolitan identity that the wealthiest characters in the film actually have access to. If the freedom artist films portray characters who hope to travel through China and abroad as individuals free of government interference via their entry into the art world subculture, characters in Feng Xiaogang's films aspire to the same freedoms but assume that the way to attain them is via the more mainstream world of business and the accumulation of wealth. In both cases, the films indicate that the individual has been set adrift in the *jianghu* of art or business – both outside the realm of state subsidy and control – and must make their own way through an increasingly global world.

In an essay on the distinctions between modernist and postmodernist literature in China, Chen Maiping notes that "one of the most important ideological and cultural phenomena of the post-Cultural Revolution period in China" was "the awakening of people's consciousness about the Self." Chen reminds us that Red Guards were "... told that consciousness about the Self should be restrained, and the interests of the self should be excluded ... to have a Self meant to be selfish, to be selfish meant to be individualist, to be individualist meant to be bourgeois, and the bourgeoisie should perish."[23] Despite their differences, both independent films and the new commercial cinema are centrally concerned with the meaning of individualism and the relationship between the self and society. The freedom artist films such as *Frozen* present an alternative urban culture and the possibility that individuals can forge their own identities through the creation of art or, as in the case of *Beijing Bastards*, a new type of family produced without conventional marriage ties or civil ceremony. The commercial films discussed in this chapter suggest that identities can be forged through (controlled) consumption of consumer goods. Where films like *Beijing Bastards* and *Frozen* portray a nearly complete rejection of conventional values in favor of individual needs, popular films like *Spicy Love Soup*, *Shower*, and Feng Xiaogang's *hesuipian* require a balance between conventional norms and "progress," insisting that that the exploration of individual desires must also be balanced with societal and familial needs.

A brief use of home video footage which appears near the end of Feng Xiaogang's *A Sigh* mobilizes a documentary aesthetic to suggest that freedom for the self must be brought into balance with familial responsibility and conventional social order. In this case, video seems to have the capability to not only to record the present but also to unexpectedly give a glimpse at a past "reality." A video camera being used to record a middle-aged married man's romp with his mistress inadvertently gets switched to "play," and the two lovers find themselves watching video images of a happy moment from his earlier family life, a celebration of his wife's birthday. The first few video images we see are of the lovers, cavorting in the lavishly decorated apartment they share. The video seems to express the spontaneity and fun of their play, but this expensive accoutrement also seems linked to their self-absorption. The accidental switch from "record" to "play" contrasts the frivolity of their affair with the warmth of a celebration in the family broken apart by their affair. The notion of play is important here, because when the affair is first consummated, the man's substantially younger mistress says, "What does your wife call you?" The writer replies, "Haizi de die," or "Father of (our) child." "Here," says the mistress, "you are the child." Thus, as in *Spicy Love Soup*, the exploration of the self and emotions is implicitly infantilized by this statement and by the characters' frolic in front of the video camera. The juxtapositions of these two pieces of fictional home video suggest that there is an appropriate place for conspicuous consumption of goods like the video camera within the conventional family, while its use in the pursuit of selfish desires is a symptom of a life and, by extension a society, out of balance.

This continuing negotiation of the relationship between the self and society is the primary subject matter for many contemporary Mainland films. Yet the strain of the transformation and the inheritance of earlier forms and notions of the function of art in society are such that both of these divergent groups of filmmakers exhibit a documentary impulse, anchoring their instructional, critical, or comedic fictions with documentary aesthetics and thematic concerns. Like their art-house cousins, the commercial films of the 1990s do place emphasis on "being on the scene." In addition, though these popular comedies may have been created in imitation of the Hong Kong pop cinema competing for the same market, they created a home-grown commercial filmmaking format which portrays life in specific Mainland cities, particularly Beijing, through the use of specific accents and location shooting. They reference a documentary aesthetic with their extensive use of real urban locations and, in the case of *Shower* and *A Sigh*, the use of handheld video footage. Though commercial films rarely use non-professional actors or extremely long shots, their consistent thematic concern with polemical social issues like consumerism, demolition, and changing social morality gives them a strong documentary inflection. Yet, while they reflect and, in a limited way, critique the consumer revolution, they also serve as marketing tools to stoke the fires of commercialism, thus helping to solidify the central place of the shopping mall and popular culture, rather than the public square and mass politics, in contemporary Chinese culture. Certainly these commercial films tend to ignore the widening gap between the richest and poorest classes in China and present fairly limited critiques of rampant consumerism and mass demolition. I do not, however, agree with Dai Jinhua that this shift toward commercialism means that "a public, critical social conscience is absent in our time."[24] In fact, I would argue that an admittedly limited critique is reaching a wide audience in China through the documentary aspect of commercial cinema, while a much more scathing critique is available to a smaller audience in the films of Zhang Yuan, Jia Zhangke, and other art-cinema filmmakers.

CHAPTER 12

Taiwan: Popular Cinema's Disappearing Act

Emilie Yueh-yu Yeh

After enduring a dark decade in the 1990s, Taiwan cinema greeted the new millennium with unusual optimism. Taiwanese directors and their films were received with unprecedented exposure all over the world. First it was Edward Yang's *Yi Yi: A One and a Two*, which was awarded the best director prize at Cannes and a number of prestigious awards in the US.[1] Then Taiwan-born-and-raised director Ang Lee's *wuxia* (martial arts/swordplay) epic *Crouching Tiger, Hidden Dragon (CTHD)*. Different in conception, finance and production from Yang's intimate, realistic Taipei story, *Crouching Tiger* took four Oscars, including Best Foreign Language Film (nominated for ten). Despite conventional wisdom that Taiwan films only appeal to international film festival juries and niche audiences and remain ignored at home, *CTHD* was embraced with gusto by Taiwan audiences and remains the highest-grossing Chinese-language film in Taiwan, and in the world.[2] However while *Yi Yi* was being feted abroad, it still has not been released in Taiwan. (Its only public appearance took place at Jiaotong University, the director's *alma mater*.)

Apparently there was a stark contrast between *Yi Yi* and *CTHD*, two engaging contemporary films with radically different reception destinies. *Yi Yi*'s domestic no-show testifies to a long-standing sickness of Taiwan's film culture: generally there is no Taiwanese audience for Taiwan film. In this regard, *CTHD*'s mainstream commercial success in Taiwan should be treated as an anomaly, a pleasant but not completely unexpected surprise since it carries a Hollywood brand name. Moreover, juxtaposing *Yi Yi* and *CTHD* suggests that all along, critics and audiences may have categorically treated locally made films as art films because that's the only rubric under which Taiwan cinema is releasable. Art film is the reputation Taiwan cinema has built for itself in the past two decades. This makes it almost impossible to conceive of a Taiwan-made popular film since the category of popularity has been forfeited entirely to imports. Both *Yi Yi* and *CTHD* salvage a disappearing popular tradition, the *wenyi* (art and literature) narrative style, a dominant genre in the heyday of Taiwan popular cinema. *Yi Yi* is a male *wenyi* picture while *CTHD* is a martial arts *wenyi*. Thus *Yi Yi* and *CTHD* bring up questions central to the cinema of Taiwan: what is Taiwan popular cinema after all? Is there, or can there be such a thing as a home-grown, popular film? What are the constraints and prospects, if any, for Taiwan popular cinema?

To me, *Yi Yi* and *CTHD* are both popular films with a potentially broad mainstream appeal in their story and style. *Yi Yi* is a bittersweet melodrama touching on urban pathos of puberty and neurosis. It deals with masculine crises of all sorts – sexual, paternal, career, and existential. Watching *Yi Yi* is like enjoying a sophisticated three-hour Japanese soap neatly organized into a life-cycle narrative ready-to-view by a large, mainstream audience.[3] Resonant with its melodramatic but sophisticated storyline, the film's *mise-en-scène* looks like quality television, with glittering cosmopolitan settings (five-star hotels, upscale apartments, piano recitals, chic cafés, Tokyo trains, Japanese temples, multilingual, high-tech environments), lit by high-key illumination that emphasizes a brighter, breezier version of Taipei (and East Asian) modernity. Most important, there is Beethoven's *Moonlight* sonata, lending a noticeable acoustic aura of a tasteful lifestyle. In many ways, *Yi Yi* relies heavily on transnational/transcultural borrowing of ingredients from Japanese "trendy drama" (*dorama*) known for its mastery of a global consumer culture and skillful manipulation of the melodramatic form in its packaging of a high-end, advertiser-friendly television product. In short, *Yi Yi* is a popular film mistaken for (or crouching as) art cinema.

It was speculated that Edward Yang refused to release *Yi Yi* in Taiwan as a protest against Taiwan's film establishment, dominated by a handful of distributors and exhibitors who had long abandoned Taiwan films, including Yang's prior work, in favor of Hollywood blockbusters. For nearly two decades now, the traditional distribution outlets for domestic film has collapsed, and Chinese films have been replaced by Hollywood and a small number of European art films. Edward Yang's superb black comedy *Mahjong* (1997), a film he made before *Yi Yi*, was first shown in Taipei for only two days, selling 207 tickets. Because of an initial slow build-up, theater operators couldn't wait to pull the film out to reduce their loss. But when the film was nominated for the Golden Horse Film Awards (Taiwan's Academy Awards), opportunistic distributors screened it right away, hoping to extract some surplus value. This time it stayed up for twenty days, accumulating a box office of less than US$20,000.[4]

Yang's difficulty with local distribution and exhibition machinery is not atypical. In the past ten years, even films that are backed by Central Motion Picture Corporation (CMPC, Taiwan's longest-running studio) are all too often lowest priority for exhibition at movie theater. For the same reason that a Taiwan film would not be distributed and marketed properly, a Hollywood picture, or at least a hybrid such as *CHTD*,[5] will be showered with favors, priorities, and privileges because to the film establishment, only Hollywood films make money. The state of film distribution, marketing, and exhibition in Taiwan has fallen into a total surrender to Hollywood. Critics in Taiwan, Hong Kong, and China unanimously attribute the phenomenal success of *CTHD* to its kinship with a Hollywood major (Columbia Tristar) and a canny strategic campaign based on Hollywood protocols. (Riding the horseback of Hollywood is apparently very problematic to many critics. In a number of articles, in English as well as in Chinese, most have chosen to focus on the identity politics of *CTHD* and query the "Chineseness" of this film.[6])

Current State of Distribution and Exhibition

It is now commonplace to assume that Taiwan cinema has been in a deep sleep, like the grandmother in *Yi Yi* who goes into a coma right after the opening of the film. And like grandma's miraculous recovery shortly before her death, any attempt to awaken her is doomed to be wishful thinking by her grandchildren. Taiwan popular cinema appears to have entered a long dormancy, considering the following statistics. The number of non-Taiwan films, including Hollywood, Hong Kong, and other foreign pictures, shown on Taiwan's screens in 2002 was 250 while the number for Taiwan-made films was 16, just over 6 percent. In 2001, it was 212 non-Taiwan versus 10 Taiwan; in 2000, 273 versus 19; in 1999, 306 versus 12; in 1998, 309 versus 15; in 1997, 304 versus 17; in 1996, 230 versus 23; in 1995: 454 versus 18.[7]

In line with the prevailing film policy specific to the nation-state, administrations in Taiwan imposed restrictions on foreign films since the end of the nineteenth century, for political censorship and economic protection. The Japanese colonial administration restricted screenings of mainland Chinese films during the Pacific War (1937–45) for fear of encouraging Chinese identity among local Taiwanese. Later when the mainland Chinese-led Nationalist Party, or Kuomingtang (KMT) moved to Taiwan, it banned all films from China and leftist Hong Kong films; during the period between 1972 and 1994, the KMT government either banned (1972–83) or restricted (1984–94) the import of Japanese films. In addition, foreign films (excluding Hong Kong films) were regulated under a quota system and high tariffs and taxes on foreign imports were imposed to ensure domestic production was protected. Through these policies, from the early 1960s Taiwan-made films prospered for almost two decades. But when the country began to become more entrenched in the global economy, especially its substantial trade surplus with the US, Taiwan was pushed to open her markets. Beginning from 1994, all foreign films could be imported with low tariffs and no restrictions on the number of prints. Since then, Taiwan film production has dropped sharply.

As discussed elsewhere in this book, despite Hollywood's strength, some countries/regions in Asia such as South Korea, India, Hong Kong, and Japan still maintain a healthy share of production, distribution, and exhibition, which hardly exists in Taiwan today. For more than a decade, Taiwan's film capital has either turned to producing Hong Kong films (with higher production quality and efficiency, as well as bankable stars) for local and overseas markets, or poured money into distributing Hollywood and other foreign films. For instance, Taiwan-made films were 6 percent of all the films shown in local screens in 2002, but in revenue, Taiwan films generated less than one (0.7) percent of the total box office. Hollywood films, on the other hand, took more than 90 percent.[8]

In fact, since the late 1980s Hollywood majors have been making a very handsome return in the Taiwan market. Usually their distribution takes up less than 30 percent of all the films shown in Taiwan, but their revenues have continuously remained above 70 percent.[9] What this reveals is that while there is plenty of investment in distributing foreign films, there is little money available for local film production.

An Overview of Taiwan Cinema: Stateless or National? Taiwanese or Chinese?

Before a more detailed description of Taiwan's film industry, it is necessary to briefly delineate the political and sociocultural history of Taiwan. A small island off the east coast of China, Taiwan is politically and culturally unique. With a current population of 23 million, it is ethnically diverse: aboriginal tribes of the interior; Fukienese-speaking Chinese from the coast of Fujian province; the Hakka (literally guest people), migrants from Canton since the sixteenth century; and the most recent arrivals, Chinese from all provinces who fled the civil war with the Communists in 1949. These four groups all speak different languages. This diversity, combined with a long colonial occupation by the Japanese (1895–1945) and prior to that, Portuguese, Spanish, and Dutch traders/missions, has resulted in a polyglot, pluralistic society only recently enjoying full democratic institutions.

In 1949 when the Nationalist Party fled to Taiwan, it moved its entire mainland administration to Taiwan and called the island the base for repatriation. Since then, Taiwan changed from a colony to the Republic of China (ROC), which was recognized by the world as a state and a member of the United Nations. This recognition, however, was reversed in 1972 when mainland China (People's Republic of China, PRC) was permitted to become a UN member. Under the One-China policy undersigned by the US government, Taiwan became a country without a state. On the other hand, Taiwan's democracy began to grow strongly and in 1996 Lee Teng-hui became the first directly elected president in this stateless island.[10]

Meanwhile, Taiwan opened up, allowing for rigorous (sometimes rancorous) political debates and oppositional cultures. Economically, Taiwan was one of the so-called mini-dragons in East Asia – referring to her rapid economic growth based on robust export manufacturing and high technology. Paradoxically, Taiwan's popular cinema declined sharply in this period of openness and prosperity. This was due to the forced opening of Taiwan's movie screens to the world. The ambiguous statelessness of Taiwan ironically cultivated a steady output of internationally acclaimed art films. Since the mid-1980s, Taiwan's leading studio CMPC recognized the need for an expanded audience served by updated film expression. It sponsored a movement known as Taiwan New Cinema (1982–1987), which forever changed the reputation of Taiwan film and culture.[11] From this time on, and especially with Hou Hsiao-hsien's 1989 historical epic *City of Sadness* (awarded the Golden Lion at the Venice International Film Festival), the country without a state came to be internationally recognized at major film festivals. It seemed, however, that the recognition was purchased at the cost of a viable popular cinema.

Like many other countries, Taiwan once had a vibrant commercial film industry. In the symposium on the twentieth anniversary of Taiwan New Cinema, producer Xiao Ye remarked that "there was so much money being made in the 1970s that investors used rice bags to store their hot cash from the distributors."[12] Even though Taiwan popular cinema was produced by a cottage industry for quick returns, as long as cash flow was good, money kept pouring into production, keeping open a viable distribution system. This pipeline remained open from the late 1950s for about forty years, reliant on a large appetite for popular films in the region, especially in Southeast Asia. Throughout this period Taiwan was under martial law (1947–89), which suspended freedom of speech, public assembly, and a critical media.

In the 1950s the film industry was mainly supported by a large number of low-budget dialect films called *taiyu pian* (the Taiwanese-language film). Between 1956 and 1959, over 170 Taiwanese-language films were produced, whereas only eighty Mandarin films were made.[13] This period is considered the first golden age of *taiyu pian*. Between 1962 and 1969, more than 1,000 such films were made and watched by Fukienese-speaking audiences in Taiwan and Southeast Asia. In 1962 alone, 120 *taiyu* films came out, whereas there were only seven Mandarin films.[14]

Political, economic and cultural conditions in the postwar period provided an accidentally nourishing climate for dialect films to prosper. Right after CMPC was established in 1954, the studio made only two or three films annually for the following ten years.[15] This production vacuum allowed for utilization of CMPC's facilities and staff by the dialect independents. The burgeoning *taiyu pian* found a great opportunity to access a government-owned infrastructure for their fast-running film production. A special film stock allowance for Hong Kong producers also helped to push local film production. Many *taiyu pian* producers collaborated with Hong Kong companies to import film stock with lower tax and tariffs.[16]

Though foreign films and lavish Mandarin genre pictures from Hong Kong took the lead in local box offices continuously during this period,[17] low-budget Taiwanese films used the language, familiar opera, and folk repertoires to attract Taiwanese-speaking audiences (80 percent of the population) until 1969, when they began to show signs of decline. In 1969 numbers of Mandarin films for the first time exceeded those of Taiwanese films (89 versus 84).[18] The decline was sparked by a changing mediascape: a full-fledged Mandarin film production led by CMPC's new management (see below) and strategic alliance between distributors and directors between Hong Kong and Taiwan, combined to lead Taiwan cinema with large-scale production, genres, and stars; the rise of television and *taiyu pian*'s inability to convert to color; more important still was the language policy that favored a dominant use of Mandarin, the national language, in all mass media.

Taiwan popular cinema of the 1950s and 1960s can therefore be characterized as parallel cinemas: Mandarin and Taiwanese film production ran alongside each other. Within Mandarin-language production, there is another parallel system: commercial cinema transplanted from Hong Kong versus the state-operated, propaganda-driven, nation-building cinema.[19] But the industry as a whole was led by CMPC, owned and operated by the ruling Nationalist Party. In its early days in the 1950s CMPC's film production moved slowly, with a total of fourteen films made in the period 1954–59.[20] Not until ten years later when the political situation and economy became stabilized, did CMPC begin to seriously consider the role of cinema in propagating policy, promoting national culture and constructing a new national image. In addition, CMPC found cinema useful for pushing greater use of the Mandarin language among Taiwanese subjects.

Under the able management of Henry Gong Hong, in 1963 CMPC launched a series of films called "healthy realism" to undertake an aggressive production orientation. Healthy realism was a type of melodrama with a strong civic message of conscientiousness, charity, hygiene, and environmentalism. These films were directed primarily at provincial audiences in need of tutelage, while also reinforcing Nationalist authority. CMPC's production output number immediately jumped to twenty-two, leading a healthy boom in local Mandarin film production. Gong stayed in office until 1972 and produced ten healthy realist pictures.[21] Besides the imperatives of policy, the success of healthy realism was a combination of production values (color, widescreen), authentic locations/situations, and clever use of genre elements and stars. In healthy realist classics *Oyster Girl* (1964) and *Ducklings* (1965), one can see that the appealing style and pastoral subject matter were keys to its sustainability. Although Henry Gong Hong claimed Italian neo-realism as inspiration, the similarity is almost nil, other than the poor, working-class and peasant settings. Since healthy realism is meant to be counter-revolutionary (opposing socialist realist pictures from the PRC), valuing the traditional Confucian virtues, its aim was to create a healthy, sound, harmonious Chinese polity in which social and class conflicts would be peacefully resolved. Apart from being implicitly propagandistic, healthy realism is virtually no different from romantic melodrama. *Wenyi* (literature and arts) is the term used in Taiwan to refer to melodrama of all kinds, family-ethical, romance, sing-song, and comedy.

Despite CMPC leading the industry, Hong Kong's two studios Cathay and Shaw Brothers remained the major players in Mandarin-film exhibition in Taiwan.[22] Cathay's Hollywood-style melodrama and musicals and the Shaws's lavish costume and opera dramas were very popular in Taiwan. With Taiwan as its main overseas market, soon Hong Kong filmmakers and producers set up shop there to seek better opportunities and lower production costs. Prominent examples are Grand Pictures, led by the Shaws's leading director Li Hanxiang and martial arts auteur King Hu with his Taiwan backer Union Film. Grand Pictures played an important role in the development of Taiwan's cinema in the 1960s. Based on a studio model, Grand Pictures owned its own sound stage, actors, writers, directors, and technical staff. It also published a film monthly promoting its products. Although Grand was short-lived (1962–67) due to Li Hanxiang's financial disputes with distributors, it produced many quality genre pictures (costume, sing-song, comedy, romantic melodrama, and ghost thrillers) which helped expand Taiwan cinema's repertoire and substance.[23] Many of Grand's personnel later became main players within the Taiwan film industry.

Union Film lured the Beijing-born King Hu, a meticulous prodigy who made a smashing martial arts hit *Come Drink with Me* (Shaw Brothers, 1965), from Shaw Brothers. With the promise of creative independence Hu made his two martial arts masterpieces with Union, the 1967 *Dragon Gate Inn* (aka *Dragon Inn*) and his action epic *A Touch of Zen* (1970). These two made-in-Taiwan films are often considered milestones of Chinese-language cinema for creating benchmarks for the martial arts genre.

With these companies operating parallel to CMPC's healthy realism, Taiwan cinema began to build up a strong foundation, later developing into a robust industry in the1970s. Annual average production remained above 300 films throughout the decade.[24] Kung fu, martial arts, action, war pictures, healthy realist, romantic melodrama, thrillers, comedy, opera sing-song, and pornography were all regular formulas for the industry to churn out expensive quality films as well as quickies. But three genres appeared to dominate the assembly line of production and hence represented Taiwan's high visibility in the regional market: Qiong Yao romantic melodrama, martial arts/kung fu, and war pictures.

Qiong Yao romantic melodrama or Qiong Yao film (*qiong yao dianying*) refers to literary adaptations based on Taiwan's most famous romance fiction writer Qiong Yao (a pen name for a woman writer Chen Ping), arguably the best-known Taiwan popular genre. Beginning with *My Cousin* (1965) to the last adaptation *Light of Yesterday* in 1983, a total of fifty films were based on her work. The longevity of the genre can be attributed to the continuous reproduction of the ethos of Chinese melodrama (*wenyi*), established in the 1920s: the conundrum of family order in conflict with personal love. Most of these films deal with individual negotiation with traditional culture and ethics. They are not romance stories centering on sexuality or libido. On the contrary, sexuality is generally missing but family order, filial piety, and emotional overkill dominate the melodramatic sentiment of these films. The second important attribute of Qiong Yao film is the centrality of women. Although it would be an overstatement to call Qiong Yao romantic melodrama "women's film," the genre as a whole does exhibit a strong female-centered narrative often accompanied by weak masculine characters. This is pronounced in the later films of woman director Liu Lili for Super Star, Qiong Yao's own production company, to ensure an exclusive franchise of her literary work. The third attribute is the thoroughly "modern" look of Qiong Yao movies. Interior design, costume, urban setting, architecture, and audio design exemplify a desirable model of modernity for the consumer audience.

The second leading genre is martial arts/kung fu pictures. In terms of sheer numbers, this was the dominant genre in Taiwan's popular film production in the 1970s, around 50 percent.[25] The kung fu craze was sparked by Jimmy Wang Yu, the star of the Shaws's *One-Armed Swordsman* (1967, directed by Zhang Che). After a record-breaking success and a failed negotiation for a higher billing with Shaws, Jimmy Wang Yu moved to Taiwan to make his own kung fu pictures. Wang's relocation to Taiwan led a major injection of capital to Taiwan's kung fu productions. With the star's name as a guarantee, producers were able to finance many kung fu pictures through presales to overseas distributors. During this period, the prolific Jimmy Wang Yu was making three films at a time on three different sets.[26]

Shaw Brothers branched into Taiwan in the 1970s in order to expand its kung fu repertoire and exploit low tax benefits provided by the KMT government. In addition, Taiwan's opera schools supplied young martial arts talent. Taiwan's locations and its armies, logistics, equipment, and large-scale combat also allowed Shaws to boost production values for elaborate historical set pieces for kung fu pictures set in the Republican period (1911–49). Action actors, stuntmen, and choreographers were recruited and trained to support the rapid proliferation of action movies.

The third major genre is policy and propaganda films, mainly produced by official studios such as CMPC or by Central Production Studio, owned by the

Ministry of Defense, and Taiwan Film Studio, owned by now-defunct Taiwan Provincial Government. There are nine sub-categories of policy films: resistance against the Japanese, anti-Communism, nationalism, military education, moral education, agricultural reform, economic development, ethnic harmony, and Republican revolution against the Manchu Qing court in the early twentieth century.[27] With official support from the military, Taiwan's war pictures (including famous anti-Japanese war epics) boasted high production values of spectacular scenes: air raids, naval fleets, massive explosions, marching, personnel assembly on a mass scale, all of which were difficult for Hong Kong productions to replicate. In the late 1970s war films were "downgraded" to military comedies, to be closer to the daily experience of the Taiwan audience. Since it is required by the constitution that all adult Taiwanese men must serve in the army for at least two years, a series of military comedies were produced to depict training life on army bases.

As elsewhere in Asia and around the world, a vibrant movie industry depends on stars, which constituted the backbone for low-budget Taiwan films to prevail in overseas markets, especially Thailand, Malaysia, Vietnam, and Singapore, as in the case of Jimmy Wang Yu. In the 1960s Taiwan began to cultivate stars, borrowing the factory model set up by Hong Kong movie giants Cathay and Shaws. By the 1970s, Taiwan stars had already become the main drawing power to distributors in the region. Stardom, genre, and economic achievement explain why the 1970s were regarded as the golden age of commercial cinema. But the same things that created the good old days brought Taiwan cinema down. By the late 1970s, capital would be spent mostly on start-ups rather than updating and upgrading production facilities. Generic formulas and low budgets proved to be losing audiences faster than the film establishment had anticipated.

Although the 1980s saw declines in local production, Taiwan film producers/distributors did not withdraw from the business. Instead, they switched their business focus to Hong Kong and allocated large amounts of capital to producing and distributing Hong Kong popular films. Two major players in this new game were Long Shiong and Scholar. In the early 1990s, both companies supported directors like Wong Kar-wai, Tsui Hark, Wong Jing, and Andrew Lau with highly bankable stars like Andy Lau, Jet Li, Joey Wang, Stephen Chow, Chow Yun Fat, and Maggie Cheung. By the time the Asian financial crisis hit the regional economy in 1997, Hong Kong films' loss of creativity and commercial credibility was apparent. Taiwan investors, alarmed at the degradation and rampant gangsterism in the industry, pulled their money completely out of production.

Taiwan Popular Cinema and Problem(s) of Hegemony

There was a popular Taiwan cinema until 1994, when the entertainment "barbarians" (the Hollywood hordes) swept onto Taiwan screens. Before this, popular Chinese-language cinema still largely reigned, with mainly Hong Kong actioners and comedies claiming the lucrative Taiwan market. Many of these pictures were bankrolled with Taiwan funding, since local Taiwan production had slowed due to a number of factors: depletion of generic and star resources, centering mainly on melodrama (*wenyi*) and kung fu; decline of the Southeast Asian overseas market because of rising national assertion against Chinese business hegemony; lifting of martial law within Taiwan, along with associated liberalization of media and entertainment and, finally, a gradual recognition of Taiwan art cinema's triumphant achievements on the international festival circuit. Thus, a certain trade-off eventuated: Taiwan independent producers aimed for international exposure and prizes, while Taiwan audiences were served by Hollywood imports, happily distributed by local companies with no particular interest in maintaining indigenous production.[28]

All these contribute to the dearth of Taiwan popular cinema. There is now a sharp division between commercial cinema, completely dominated by Hollywood, and art cinema, represented by renowned New Cinema auteurs such as Hou Hsiao-hsien, Tsai Ming-liang, and Edward Yang. Cinema in Taiwan has split into two institutions: one represents the symbolic presence of an aesthetic cinema as Taiwan's national treasure, like other internationally known artistic bodies such as Cloud Gate Modern Dance Theatre. This aesthetic claim for Taiwan cinema is an "invented tradition," given popular film's former vitality. The other side is occupied by Hollywood majors and their Asian subsidiaries, busy producing as well as distributing Hollywood pictures for Asian audiences. One continues to draw on the cultural capital of Taiwan nativism, emphasizing aesthetic refinement and historical uniqueness. The other, a commercial path, has extended from distribution/exhibition and evolved into a synthetic glocal (global/local) commodity made for local consumption with multinational resources and production values. An example of this is the trial run that unexpectedly hit the box office jackpot of NT 80 million (US$2.6 million), *Double Vision* (2002), directed by Chen Kuo-fu, a longtime veteran of the highly artistic Taiwan New Cinema.

It was not an easy transition for Taiwan filmmakers to kowtow to Hollywood. Filmmakers in Taiwan in the past two decades have been accustomed to making art films, since it has been the only tangible payoff they know. Having forgotten how to make popular cinema, they see little call for it because it is unlikely Taiwan filmmakers could rival the blockbuster power of Steven Spielberg, Ron Howard, Peter Jackson, and so forth. But Taiwan directors are aware of the risk of overspecialization, as flagged by domestic audiences' automatic rejection of Taiwan-made product as a marginal "brand." Since 1994 Taiwan has always been among the global top ten earners for Hollywood pictures.

Some directors, inspired by Ang Lee, might want to make popular movies but they dare not take the plunge, especially when it is next to impossible to raise funds for a popular genre picture made locally. It appears very risky compared to making art films, with their high-profile record, that have no difficulty attracting money from international or government resources. A telling example comes from the New Cinema director Wan Ren, who was once criticized by Edward Yang in the 1980s for attempting to make popular films for it might risk upsetting the momentum achieved by the Taiwan New Cinema movement.[29]

A Case of *Double Vision*

Given this seeming impasse, a veteran of the Taiwan New Cinema, Chen Kuo-fu seems an unlikely revivalist of Taiwan's popular film. Though Chen never worked the mainstream commercial sector, unlike Taiwan auteur Hou Hsiao-hsien, he always wanted to make interesting thrillers *à la* Hitchcock. Before becoming a director, Chen was a critic, highly familiar with Hollywood and European classics. His earlier films like *Treasure Island* (1993) and *The Personals* (1998) are stylish fusions of genre elements and personal flourishes.

Chen's *Double Vision* was produced by Columbia Pictures-Asia in order to further capitalize on Taiwan's lucrative box office. As the same company that handled Ang Lee's *CTHD*, Columbia wanted to follow up on its success and reap the benefits of production as well as those of distribution. It did this by creating a new hybrid, shrewdly combining local Taiwanese and Hollywood ingredients: the pitch for *Double Vision* was an ingeniously simple "Taoist Se7en," referring to the 1995 David Fincher thriller. *Double Vision* contains a Taiwan-America cultural theme, with American character actor David Morse appearing in Taipei as an FBI agent investigating a series of bizarre murders. The Morse character is like the film itself: a Taiwan story unfolding through a Hollywood generic and narrative formula. *Double Vision* addresses contemporary Taiwanese social problems like the spiritual degradation underneath the rise of high technological materialism, as well as the anguish experienced by the whistle-blowing hero. Hong Kong star Tony Leung Ka-fai plays a policeman in charge of international affairs who is about to lose his family as well as his job because of his intolerance to corruption, leading to the suicide of his cousin. Consequently Leung's character is wracked by debilitating guilt. This is noticed by the American, who proceeds to first annoy (as only Yanks can) then provoke, befriend, and unfailingly support his Taiwan counterpart. So in addition to its other affiliations, the film is also a familiar interracial buddy film.

The title *Double Vision* uncannily epitomizes a parallel between the narrative and the making of the film. A "double vision" sees things in two parts: between a spiritual and economic outlook; between reason (FBI's scientific investigation) and superstition (Taoist deciphering of the mysterious crime); between local (on-location shooting) and Hollywood investment (the presence of foreign crew) and management (Columbia's production schedule, accounting methods, etc). Funds from Hollywood also allowed the Taiwan production company Nan Fan (Southern, headed by Chen himself) to design a web-based marketing campaign that turned the enigmatic narrative of the film into a game to generate interest before the film's release.[30] Chen and his company saw that in order to lure an audience back to locally made films, one vision is insufficient. You need to have another eye on marketing to inform and to propagate. Chen's marketing campaign, capitalizing on its Hollywood connection, paid off handsomely. It was the key to the success of *Double Vision*, whose NT39 million (in the capital city Taipei alone)[31] surpassed Universal's thriller *Red Dragon*'s 27 million and prompted Columbia's CEO to fly from Los Angeles to congratulate Chen on his success. Chen had turned water into wine, miraculously transforming a B-grade noir-thriller into a local blockbuster.[32]

The key to *Double Vision*'s victory, similar to that of *CTHD*, is its Hollywood backing, through resources and experience as well as money. It clearly shows that collaboration with Hollywood is possibly the only way to revive local commercial cinema, and to change the public perception of Taiwan film. *Double Vision* proves that Taiwan can and will make popular films. The irony is that Taiwan filmmakers now rely on Hollywood, the main culprit for the disappearance of local popular cinema, in order to claw back a share of the local market. In 2002 *Double Vision* ranked in the foreign-movie chart, alongside *Lord of the Rings: The Twin Towers* and the second *Harry Potter* film.

Double Vision is possibly a one-off, just like *CTHD*, which can hardly be treated as a formula or pattern. For instance, Taiwan-born actress/director/producer Sylvia Chang's 2004 romantic comedy *20:30:40*, a typical woman's story about love, career, and aging, was also backed by Columbia Asia, with Chen Kuo-fu as the executive producer. The film was in competition at the Berlin International Film Festival. But its box-office record in Taiwan was modest. Most local producers believe that cases like *Double Vision* and *CTHD* are like migrating birds for whom Taiwan is a place of temporary rest and transfer. Only by making films with Taiwan characteristics can local popular films have a chance to survive. Many local companies continue to develop new strategies in order to attract investment and to cultivate audiences, operating on small but carefully planned projects. Script doctoring, talent scouting, marketing gimmicks, and regional alliances have already saturated local production. The films of Zoom Hunt and Arc Light represent this new direction.

Zoom Hunt is headed by Xu Ligong, former manager of CMPC and co-producer for *CTHD*. Since its establishment in the mid-1990s, the company is known for its star appeal (Rene Liu, currently the leading Taiwan actress) and literary features (*CTHD* writer Wang Huiling). Arc Light was formed by Taiwan's eminent critic/producer Peggy Chiao. With financial backing from France and talent scouting in Taiwan, Hong Kong, and the Chinese mainland, Arc Light aims to make artful films with a popular lure and international sales potential. Arc Light's films are especially attractive to certain niche audiences: gay, urban youth, and film-festival followers. One of its early endeavors was Tsai Ming-liang's queer musical *The Hole* (1999), co-produced with the French company Pyramid. Then Arc Light launched its "Tales of Three Cities" series with Wang Xiaoshuai's *Beijing Bicycle* (2000), Chin-yen Yee's *Blue Gate Crossing* (2002) and Hsu Hsiao-ming's *Love of May* (2004). *Blue Gate Crossing* is a youth romance packaged as a clever Euro-friendly trifle, and proved successful in Taiwan, Hong Kong, and Japan. Its comely lead Chen Bolin broke into the mainstream Hong Kong industry, bound for stardom. These sporadic, small-scale efforts to court niche markets also include such productions as the gay-themed independent *Formula 17* (2004) and the pornography spoof *Better than Sex* (CMPC, 2002).

A force, still quite feeble, is alive in the film industry, trying to re-grow the market for Taiwan pictures. It has become clear that film producers are reaching out to audiences who wish to be entertained by storytellers who dwell among them, not just by blockbusters from afar.

CHAPTER 13

Hong Kong: Cinematic Cycles of Grief and Glory

Anne T. Ciecko

Flashing backward and forward in time, the culminating film in the epic trilogy, *Infernal Affairs III* (*Wu jian dao III*, 2003), rationalizes its folded temporality with geopolitics and transgressive gangster logic. As a mainland arms smuggler explains to his underworld partner, a Hong Kong triad (organized crime syndicate) boss, it's "one country two systems – as long as money breeds money, we'll let you run the show." The third installment is also a Hong Kong and mainland co-production between the Hong Kong company Media Asia and mainland's Tianjin Film Studio, and this arrangement had a representational impact on the ultimate anti-crime message of the film. (The first *Infernal Affairs* actually had an alternate, less ambiguous ending for mainland audiences. As the online Hong Kong media and advertising magazine *Danwei* notes, it has also become "one country, two versions."[1]) Hong Kong, the most dominant film producer in East Asia for nearly half a century, has recognized the need for regional co-productions, and favorable governmental and cultural policy relations with the mainland, for the film industry to remain viable.

Hong Kong film's developmental narrative is situated historically within a triangulated saga of British colonial rule (Hong Kong becoming a British colony in 1842 after the Anglo-Chinese or "Opium" Wars); the emergence of Hong Kong as a cosmopolitan city under *laissez-faire* colonial policy; and an ongoing, constantly negotiated relationship with China. With the signing of the Sino-British Joint Declaration in 1984 that led to the 1997 Handover of Hong Kong to China after 157 years of British colonial governance, Hong Kong became a Special Administrative Region (SAR) of the People's Republic of China under the "one country two systems" principle espoused by Deng Xiaoping. The imagination of Handover as an impending transition or crisis has been widely discussed and debated by film scholars and cultural critics as a galvanizing moment and thematic motif in 1980s and 1990s Hong Kong cinema. Into the new millennium, Hong Kong cultural productions (including popular films) continue to grapple with the past, present, and the unknown future – and obsess over the "vanishing" city in displays of postmodern nostalgia.[2]

Writing in anticipation of the Handover, cultural critic Ackbar Abbas noted that "1997 will not simply be the moment of liberation from colonial rule [or colonialism for that matter]; it will also mark a moment of transition to a form of governance that has no clear precedents."[3] Handover has caused ruptures in temporality and development as Hong Kong was upon its "return" situated in an atypical paradigmatic relationship – more advanced than its colonizer, China. Therefore, Abbas underscores the importance of reduplicated and doubled narrative frameworks in Hong Kong cinema as they navigate time and space. Hong Kong will never be a nation, but it has been and is an anomalous "postculture" subject to the "disjunctures of colonialism and globalism."[4]

Flashback to 1986: Heroism and its Cyclical Sequels

One wistful cinematic scene of recognition of culture at the verge of disappearance occurs in an exemplar of the "New" Hong Kong cinema of the 1980s, John Woo's *A Better Tomorrow* (the Cantonese title translates more literally as *Essence of a Hero* or *True Colors of Valor*). The charismatic star Chow Yun-Fat's anti-heroic counterfeiter character Mark Gor looks out over the city at night musing that its beauty won't last. This scene prompted a number of film critics and scholars (including this one) to ruminate over its allegorical portent: then-impending Handover and the likely exodus of some of Hong Kong's leading talent to Hollywood.[5]

A Better Tomorrow launched a series of urban films about blurred boundaries between criminals and law enforcers, and codes of brotherhood – *yingxiong pian* (hero movie).[6] The film also consolidated a particular authorial style associated with director John Woo and transformed Chow Yun-Fat into a superstar. Writer Bey Logan has described such films as "heroic bloodshed;" film historian Stephen Teo asserts that *A Better Tomorrow* "struck a nerve in the development of genres in Hong Kong action cinema."[7] The movie (also featuring Cantopop's Leslie Cheung) was a huge commercial success – breaking local and regional box-office records in East and Southeast Asia. It also helped introduce Woo's signature directorial style and Chow's persona to international crossover audiences in and beyond diasporic cultural locations (e.g. "Chinatowns") around the globe. In the early 1990s, Woo became the first Hong Kong director to sign a contract with a major Hollywood studio, and later that decade Chow also made his Hollywood debut.

Produced by Woo and Vietnam-born Tsui Hark for his company Film Workshop, known for its ability to creatively reinvent popular genres, *A Better Tomorrow* was a remake of a Hong Kong film from the 1960s, itself an adaptation of a French New Wave film (an American co-production).[8] Chinese folktales illustrating feats of heroism and chivalry predate cinema by centuries, and contemporary action films have antecedents in a variety of pan-Asian cultural forms.[9]

A Better Tomorrow owes a debt to the sentimental themes of many *wuxia* (martial arts/swordplay) stories serialized in popular Chinese literature, and represents the legacy of Hong Kong's popular Cantonese and Mandarin swordplay movies. It is also linked dialogically to Japanese *chambara* films, swordplay films set during feudal times with cultural antecedents in combat styles used in Kabuki theater. Additionally, the film employs a pastiche of techniques that reference visual cinematic techniques used by Hollywood and French New Wave filmmakers.

As a testimony to its extraordinary commercial success, the film inspired countless imitators at home and abroad and spawned sequels, with the third installment directed by Tsui Hark instead of John Woo. While *A Better Tomorrow II* allows superstar Chow to return after the demise of his character Mark as his identical brother Ken, *A Better Tomorrow III* is a prequel set in Vietnam. As a touchstone contemporary Hong Kong film, *A Better Tomorrow* continues to spark and provoke, as in the apparent title-play of the Asian American high school crime drama *Better Luck Tomorrow* (2002). After *A Better Tomorrow*, producer and cinematic multi-talent Hark (frequently called the Stephen Spielberg of Asia) went on to direct his own trilogy of tales of legendary folk hero Wong Fei Hung (the subject of many earlier Hong Kong martial arts films) with the long-running *Once Upon a Time in China* series initiated with films starring Beijing-born Jet Li. In 1986, the same year as *A Better Tomorrow*, a colorfully hybrid period film Hark directed called *Peking Opera Blues*, with a trio of three strong female characters, also appeared to critical and popular acclaim.

During the mid-1980s, Hong Kong was becoming the "Hollywood of the East,"[10] one of the largest film producers and exporters in the world. Hong Kong was also struggling with both the Chinese and British governments over the shape of its political structure.[11] Later in the decade, the state force used to squelch 1989's student democracy movement in Beijing generated fearful views in Hong Kong for the territory's future. *A Better Tomorrow* taps into cultural uncertainty, and discourse of the triads (the "brand" name for the local/global crime syndicates) – and of a porous and gray pirate economy. Throughout the past several decades, the close connections between the triads and Hong Kong and transnational Chinese culture have been recognized cinematically with pervasive movie imagery and gangster motifs, high-profile scandals including crimes involving film-industry personnel, protection money, nepotism, and public protests.

During the period between *A Better Tomorrow* and the first installment of the *Infernal Affairs* trilogy, the economic infrastructure of the Hong Kong film industry was challenged by criminal property theft, first by video piracy and later via illegal DVDs and VCDs. Attempts to regulate and "combat" piracy have included the establishment by the Motion Picture Association of an Asia Pacific antipiracy headquarters in Hong Kong; regulations on manufacturing and customs; crackdowns on criminal offenses with rewards, raids, arrests and sentences; and educational campaigns. By the new millennium, Hong Kong's economic, political, and cultural vicissitudes – including severe pan-Asian recession and lost investments – had taken their toll on the volume and quality of, and local receptiveness to, domestic film production. Theatrical movie attendance had declined (although people were watching films at home), and the influx of Hollywood movies cut the Hong Kong market share from a high of approximately 80 percent to about 50 percent.[12]

Flashforward to 2002: Blockbuster Box-office and Anti-hero Redux

With the first installment of the ultra-stylish *Infernal Affairs*, a thriller about moral breakdown and duplicity released in December 2002, Hong Kong rediscovered itself at the domestic box office with a narrative about the doubled relationship between Yan, a cop, embedded in the mob as an informer for the police, and Ming, a police officer, who's actually a mole for the triad boss working for Hong Kong's Organized Crime and Triad Bureau (OCTB). While not as viscerally violent as the "heroic bloodshed" films, *Infernal Affairs* is genealogically related, and gave birth to its own franchise in the form of a sequel and prequel (both released in 2003). Each of the *Infernal Affairs* films employ epigraphs and references to Buddhist conceptions of circles of hell, as characters' violations of codes of ethical behavior result in perpetual suffering and repetition. Film critic Tony Rayns notes that the film's smash opening in December 2002 was "at the end of the industry's worst year in decades;"[13] and he points out that the narrative is a remake of previous Hong Kong films from the 1980s and 1990s, including one made by one of *Infernal Affairs'* co-directors.

The first *Infernal Affairs* introduces some of the trilogy's central dramatis personae in the form of the characters of Yan (Tony Leung) and Ming (Andy Lau), as well as the mob boss Sam (celebrated character actor Eric Tsang), minor love interests in the form of a female psychiatrist for Yan and a fiancée for Ming (Kelly Chen and Sammi Cheng, both also Hong Kong pop singers), Police Superintendent Wong (Anthony Wong) and Yan and Ming's younger selves (Shawn Yue and Edison Chen). To apply a term from Bollywood parlance, *Infernal Affairs* is a "multistarrer" with Leung and Lau particularly appealing box-office draws. (Each has played cop and gangster characters in myriad films.) Lau is also a major Cantopop star, and his profile as screen hero and multimedia multitasker gives the casting an added *frisson* of intertextuality. Due to the presence of megastars, the film's state of the art production values, its grandiose score, and its astronomical budget (for a Hong Kong film), the first *Infernal Affairs* film had a scale suggesting the Hollywood model of blockbuster filmmaking.[14] The film also references Hong Kong cinema's creation of its own history and mythology.

Infernal Affairs reflexively reengages with the time periods that so many Hong Kong films of the 1980s and 1990s anticipated and encountered, as its story flashes from the present back to the pre-Handover period when Yan and Ming were both cadets at the police academy together. A particularly poignant parallel between *Infernal Affairs* and *A Better Tomorrow* is the use of image of the Hong Kong skyline. A rooftop location is the rendezvous point for Yan and Ming in one of the final scenes where Yan demands to be restored his identity. The elevated perspective affords a spectacular view of the city that still exists but is not the same, one that cannot be enjoyed by the characters engaged in life-and-death, gun-to-the-head crisis. For one of the characters, it is quite literally his last sight of the city. The Hong Kong skyline is refracted and distorted in the mirrored windows of a glittering steel-and-glass sky-rise, and the images deceive and overwhelm Ming when Yan points at his back with a loaded gun; Yan visually emerges from behind Ming in a manner that suggests a doubling of identity as he takes Ming's gun and removes the bullets and locks him up with his own handcuffs. The shots are framed with a compositional balance that reminds the viewer of the dynamics of powerplay between the two characters, also underscored by the music. An aerial shot dwarfs and situates the two figures in an omniscient establishing point of view, and Yan raises his gun to Ming's forehead, creating a tableau that recalls the choreography of Woo's heroic Hong Kong gangsters. The situation becomes a visual triad as another police officer with a gun appears. The final showdown in an elevator is elliptically edited with a blackout and intercut with flashbacks to the characters' days in cadet school, Ming's initiation into the triad gang, and the third cop's ambiguous positioning. A fatal shooting is edited in backwards time, and the dialogue of the flashbacks carries over in a soundbridge into the present. The image of one man on his identity tag is matched with the photograph of another on his gravestone; and in a final flashback, the characters' older selves are sutured into a flashback of their conjoined pasts. Temporal disjunctures are marked by juxtaposition of the more mature/younger actors and color/black-and-white cinematography, and, in another display of folded time, a reenacting of a critical line of dialogue: The sergeant at the cadet school asks, "Who wants to be like him?"

What does Hong Kong cinema want to be like? *Infernal Affairs* offers one model of contemporary Hong Kong cinema that aims to please audiences at home and internationally. The film was made by the production and distribution company Media Asia (established in 1994) that has been active in pursuing regional partnerships and co-production arrangements with Taiwan, Japan, Singapore, and Mainland China. Media Asia distributes Chinese-language films including pre-1993 films by Golden Harvest (a company started in 1970 by Raymond Chow that launched the careers of Bruce Lee, Jackie Chan, and John Woo). Other companies such as Applause Pictures led by Hong Kong-based Bangkok-born director/producer Peter Chan have also successfully created interregional collaborations; Applause's self-described mission is to "expand the regional and global distribution possibilities for the new pan-Asian films."[15] In the realm of production, star power is parleyed into green-light clout. The year of *Infernal Affairs*' domestic release, Hong Kong's top action actress, Malaysia-born (ethnic Hokkien Chinese) Michelle Yeoh – famous for doing her own risky stunts (like Jackie Chan) – made her debut as a producer via her company Mythical Films. Regularly described in Western media as one of Asia's highest-paid actresses, Yeoh had already displayed her considerable crossover currency by appearing as an actress in Hollywood as an atypically independent "Bond girl" in *Tomorrow Never Dies* (1997), and also starred in the Chinese/Hollywood/global neo-*wuxia* film *Crouching Tiger Hidden Dragon* (2000) partnered with Chow Yun-Fat (each speaking Mandarin, a dialect of Chinese in which they were not fluent at the time of filming.) In contemporary popular Hong Kong cinema, dialogue has become increasingly multilingual. The *Infernal Affairs* films are mainly in Cantonese – although, like many contemporary Hong Kong films, also sprinkled with English. The expanded use of English and adoption of English words by Hong Kong Cantonese speakers into the ever-hybridizing dialect speaks to both postcolonialism and globalization. Some characters in the *Infernal Affairs* films speak and/or understand Mandarin and Thai as well.

Flashback to 1973: Martial Arts Mania and Hong Kong Cinema's Global Kick

The cultural politics of language has impacted Hong Kong film production throughout its history. As chronicled in the chapters on Singaporean and Malaysian cinema in this book, the mainland-born brothers Shaw formed a truly transnational company involved in making Malay films in Singapore. In its earliest incarnations, the company made the first Chinese film with a sound-track and the first Cantonese-language sound film (in Shanghai). Once established in Hong Kong in the 1950s, Shaw Brothers produced films in both Mandarin and Cantonese dialects. According to film scholar David Desser in his analysis of the US reception of kung fu movies, films produced in Cantonese, the main dialect spoken in Hong Kong, dwindled from 35 releases out of 118 films produced in 1970, to 1 in 1971, to none in 1972. The Shaw Brothers' production *Five Fingers of Death* (1973), which launched the international kung fu craze, was produced in Mandarin, which by the early 1970s had become (until the end of the decade) the *lingua franca* of Hong Kong film.[16]

The movies that began the world's fascination with popular Hong Kong cinema, and its genres and stars, date back to kung fu films of the 1970s, especially those starring Bruce Lee (although martial arts films were made in China as early as the 1920s). In May 1973, according to Desser, three Hong Kong-produced films of the genre (*Five Fingers of Death*, a Golden Harvest film *Deep Thrust – The Hand of Death*, and a Bruce Lee starrer for Golden Harvest titled *Fists of Fury* for American audiences) topped *Variety*'s box-office list, a phenomenon made all the more extraordinary given the fact that no Hong Kong film had previously been shown in mainstream movie theaters. All three films were dubbed into English (or whatever the language of the distributor); the poor sound dubbing quality and manhandling of those imported films by distributors colored many Westerners' initial perceptions of popular Hong Kong cinema as campy, cultish, cheaply produced "chop-socky." Further, kung fu films in America were also treated as "exploitation" genres, cross-matched generically with blaxploitation films, and with urban African American audiences.[17] The polysemy of kung fu movies was enhanced by their frequent and triumphant displays of anti-colonial, anti-imperial sentiments. *Deep Thrust – The Hand of Death*'s English title played off of the frenzy caused another genre, specifically the porno hit *Deep Throat*.

Deep Thrust starred Angela Mao as a vengeful female kung fu fighter; the woman warrior was an image in Hong Kong films from its earliest days. Also in 1973, another accomplished precursor to contemporary Hong Kong action screen heroines, Shanghai-born Cheng Pei-Pei, appeared in the Shaw Brothers film *Kung Fu Girl*. Making a transition from "double-fisted" swordplay to "open-handed" kung fu, she would soon temporarily retire until later screen comebacks (including her appearance as the villainous Jade Fox in 2000's *Crouching Tiger*). Back in 1973, while still in her twenties, Cheng Pei-Pei had already made some twenty films as Shaw Studios' top action heroine.

The Shaw Brothers' *Five Fingers of Death* and its director also demonstrate the transnational Asian dimensions of popular action cinema, and, specifically, martial arts films. *Five Fingers* was directed by Jeong Chang-hwa, a Korean-born filmmaker considered a pioneer of action-movie genres (including thrillers and martial arts, although he also made melodramas and historical films). After directing some of the earliest Hong Kong/Korean co-productions and Hong Kong films in Korea beginning in 1958, Jeong was recruited to make films in Hong Kong for Shaw Brothers, and later Golden Harvest from 1969 to 1977. According to Hong Kong film curator and critic Law Kar, Jeong (credited as Chung Chang-wha, Cheng Chang-ho, and Chung Chang-hwa) created filmic characters who display a restless transnationalism – traveler figures and mercenaries. Jeong's films at Shaw included costume swordplay, contemporary kung fu, spy films, and thrillers; and his less studio-bound (location-wise) Golden Harvest films focused on contemporary action with frequent use of Southeast Asian settings. Law Kar emphasizes Jeong's contributions to more realistic and violent depiction of action in Hong Kong films.[18]

Although he had been approached to make films for Shaw Brothers, Bruce Lee, another transnational figure, signed a more lucrative contract with Golden Harvest. Already a former child star in Hong Kong and a television actor in Hollywood (although a white actor was cast in the "Kung Fu" TV series instead of him), Lee emerged as Hong Kong's biggest star with three triumphant films – *The Big Boss*, *Fist of Fury*, and *Way of the Dragon* – the latter of which he wrote, directed, and choreographed. (All three films had multiple English titles.) Born in San Francisco's Chinatown to parents from Hong Kong, Lee was an American citizen who grew up in Hong Kong and studied philosophy in the United States. As Stephen Teo has asserted, "No other figure in Hong Kong cinema has done as much to bring East and West together in a common sharing of culture as Bruce Lee..."[19] His film roles engage with issues of nationalism (especially cultural aspects of Chineseness or "*tianxia*") and assert strong images of masculinity that counter racist stereotypes. In July 1973, Bruce Lee died unexpectedly at age thirty-two, his young death fueling fan culture and his star mythology. Posthumously released that year, *Enter the Dragon* was Lee's first and only film made in Hollywood.

The first Hong Kong kung fu films distributed in North America were handled by companies such as Warner Brothers, which also recognized the potent mainstream commercial possibilities of the martial arts film in 1973 with the first Hollywood-Hong Kong co-production *Enter the Dragon*. This arrangement included the collaboration of Bruce Lee, Raymond Chow of the legendary Hong Kong production company Golden Harvest, and Warner Brothers studio, which promised international distribution. The film did indeed become a global hit, and Hollywood adapted aspects of martial arts movies into its own formulas through the 1970s.[20]

As Abbas notes, the decade progressed from the middle to late 1970s into a time of optimism in Hong Kong local culture. This was evidenced by the international reception of kung fu films and the commercial vernacular phenomena of Cantopop music and film comedies, such as those of TV comedian-turned-movie actor Michael Hui (of the Hui Brothers Show for TVB, Hong Kong's dominant television station).[21] Television proved to be an important training ground for film talent, and grooming for the big screen led to the collaborative writing of Jackie Chan's first commercial hit, *Snake in the Eagle's Shadow* (1978), a prototype of the melded formula of kung fu and comedy that would enrich and extend each of the genres, attract mass audiences, and make Jackie Chan a star.[22] Reportedly the "first action comedy dubbed in Cantonese," the film was directed by Yuen Woo-ping, who would later become Hollywood's most in-demand martial arts choreographer. Building upon *Snake in Eagle's Shadow*'s success, *Drunken Master*, starring Jackie Chan as a young Wong Fei-Hung, was released the same year.

The man who would later become the biggest box-office draw in Asia and one of the most popular stars in the world (also director, producer, and stunt choreographer) is actually one of the uncredited extras in 1973's *Enter the Dragon*. The Peking-opera-trained Chan defined himself in contradistinction to Bruce Lee's iconic image in the 1970s. He developed his trademark blend of comedy and kung fu in an (ultimately) internationally successful fusion of generic elements.

Flashforward to 2001: Global/Local Genreplay and Neo-Auteurism

By 2001, the Hong Kong film industry was feeling its way past the Handover and the dawn of the new millennium. The year saw the appearance of several Jackie Chan vehicles, a Hollywood sequel *Rush Hour II* and the Hong Kong-produced *The Accidental Spy*, a Chinese New Year release set mostly in Turkey. After unsuccessful attempts to break into Hollywood and the US market in the 1980s, Chan had finally succeeded with the 1996 release by North American distributor New Line Cinema of his forty-third film, *Rumble in the Bronx*. The Hong Kong-financed production was dubbed into English, edited, and repackaged with a new soundtrack for its US release. The same year, Miramax released *Supercop* (actually the third installment of the *Police Story* trilogy previously released in Hong Kong), which also underwent a radical postproduction makeover; and New Line put out *First Strike* (aka *Police Story IV*) set in the Ukraine and Australia. While Chan continued to make Hong Kong films, he worked within multiple production paradigms of "global entertainment."[23] Chan's acceptance into the Hollywood star pantheon was sealed with the lucrative Hollywood buddy films, *Rush Hour* (1998) and *Shanghai Noon* (2000).

In addition to Chan's physical comedy, Hong Kong director/producer/writer/actor Stephen Chow's Cantonese wordplay and sight-gag driven "nonsense" humor took some time to find crossover success in the West.[24] Chow's *Shaolin Soccer* proved to be the biggest local hit in 2001 but was not released by the US distributor that bought the rights until several years later and after considerable controversy and fan outrage at the planned dubbing/cutting/soundtrack changes. The challenges of "translation" of Hong Kong Cantonese comedy also factors into the relative unknown (outside Hong Kong) status of one of contemporary Hong Kong cinema's most prolific filmmakers, Wong Jing. His critically denigrated but locally popular low-budget quickies tend to be topical, parodic, screwball-silly, titillating, and focused on body humor. In 2001, three films directed by Wong appeared in the theaters (as well as several other movies he produced and acted in). Wong is also associated with action movies and sex films, especially the subgenre of the gambling film (the *God of Gamblers* series), and the infamous Category III films (restricted to viewers age 18 or above) he wrote or directed featuring nearly naked avenging femme fatales.

In the economy of Hong Kong in the post-Handover era, it is clear that the underestimated genre of Cantonese comedy and its infinite and generically flexible variations still has significant popular cultural value. Milkyway Image production company is a banner created in 1996 by filmmaker Johnny To and a team of collaborators. In the summer of 2000 when the multiplex screens were filled by the work of Hong Kong auteurs and stars gone Hollywood such as Woo and Chan, the biggest local box-office hit was a Milkyway comedy called *Needing You* starring Andy Lau and Sammi Cheng. In 2001, the belovedly bantering stars were reteamed, wearing padding and prosthetics in another Milkyway comedy, *Love on a Diet*. As Andrew Grossman has noted in an article on To's work (calling him a "belated auteur"[25]), the filmmaker has worked through myriad genres including comedy, martial arts fantasies (co-directed with Ching Siu-tung), and melodrama. The Milkyway-produced movies have continued to engage local audiences with generic conventions and successful formulas, especially slick thrillers and romantic comedies that To has co-directed with Wai Ka-Fai.

The auteur status of Shanghai-born Hong Kong director Wong Kar-Wai was firmly solidified in the international arthouse with his internationally critically acclaimed film *In the Mood for Love* (made when Wong had to abandon another project because he could not get permission to shoot in Tiananmen Square). Awarded best director prize at Cannes in 1997 for his diasporic melodrama *Happy Together* starring Tony Leung and Leslie Cheung as gay lovers, Wong Kai Wei returned to the big screen with his sixth screen collaboration with cinematographer Christopher Doyle. *In the Mood for Love* continues Wong's cinematic meditations on the poetry of time, memory, and loss with scenes shot primarily in Bangkok to recreate 1960s Hong Kong. The surrounding discourse of the vanishing Hong Kong cityscape has been related to use of locations in contemporary Hong Kong films more generally, and also to the appearance of strong Asian cinema players on the Hong Kong mediascape. In 2001, South Korea released a record number of films in Hong Kong, more than any country other than the United States and local productions.[26] This signaled the possibility of another sort of disappearance or diminished presence, with the growing impact of Korean and Thai films in Asia watched carefully by the Hong Kong film industry.

Esther Yau has noted that Hong Kong cinema has had a "hegemonic practice" in Southeast Asian countries "without attending to their cultures."[27] Arguably this is beginning to change with pan-Asian production and distribution initiatives. In 2001, Peter Chan (together with the company he co-founded, Applause Pictures) was executive producer for the Thai period drama *Jan Dara*, based on the popular Thai erotic novel and directed by Thai filmmaker Nonzee Nimibutr. Chan had previously directed the gender-bending comedy *He's a Woman, She's a Man* (1994) and its sequel, as well as the touching 1997 romance *Comrades* about mainland young people in Hong

Kong. He then left Hong Kong temporarily for the United States (where he made a Hollywood film *The Love Letter* in 1999). As a cultural figure, Chan has become associated with models of filmmaking that bridge "independent" and industrial modes (he also co-founded a Hong Kong studio called UFO in the early 1990s), and art house and commercial cinema.

Other filmmakers who have ridden the generational waves of internationally recognized Hong Kong art cinema and made forays into more commercial film-making, include three of Hong Kong's most important contemporary women filmmakers, Clara Law, Mabel Cheung, and Ann Hui. Macao-born Law emi-grated to Australia in 1995, and in 2001, she made the Australian-funded *Goddess of 1967*. Her Hong Kong features frequently address issues of diaspora and displacements, and intercultural relationships – China and Hong Kong, Japan and Hong Kong. 1996's *The Floating Life* is a particularly poignant tale of a family of Hong Kong immigrants in Australia, the first non-English film to be financed by Australia as part of multicultural policy initiatives. Law also made a segment for the international omnibus *Erotica* (1994) with short films by female directors. (Omnibus filmmaking – also called "portmanteau" and "anthology" – is particularly conducive to contemporary international collabo-ration, as in the example of recent horror-anthology films featuring work by Hong Kong, Japanese, South Korean, and Thai filmmakers.)

Mainland-born Mabel Cheung studied filmmaking in the US, and her ear-liest films like 1987's *An Autumn's Tale* (Chow Yun-Fat as a Hong Kong immigrant in New York) directly address questions of diaspora. Cheung's 2001 film *Beijing Rocks* uses the backdrop of the rock music scene in Beijing to explore the identity confusion of a Hong Kong-born character, and also the ways piracy is equated with popularity.

In 2001, one of the most celebrated and versatile Hong Kong New Wave directors, Manchuria-born Ann Hui, made her nineteenth film, a ghost story called *Visible Secrets*. Having started her career with such films as the murder mystery *The Secret* (1979), *The Spooky Bunch* (1980, a Cantonese opera comedy), and *Boat People* (1982, a drama in Hui's "Vietnam trilogy"), the ghosts of the past figure quite literally in Hui's *Visible Secrets*. Her return to decidedly commercial moviemaking taps into the pan-Asian (and global) trend of supernatural horror; in Hui's film, Taiwanese actress Shu Qi plays a young woman whose left eye sees ghosts. The ongoing hybridization and currency of the contemporary horror film in Hong Kong is connected to influential films from Japan and Korea that have made an impact on the domestic market, as well as Hollywood films such as *The Sixth Sense* (1999), written/directed by Asian American filmmaker M. Night Shyamalan. The trope of the eye as an organ of ghostly perception would find one of its most popular and imitated incarnations in the Hong Kong, UK, Thai, and Singaporean co-production called (of course) *The Eye* (2002).

Flashback to 1987: Seeing Ghosts and Seeing Stars

Ackbar Abbas has made the historical assertion that that the ghost in Hong Kong films has been present ever since the Kwomintang government banned ghost movies and martial arts films in its 1935 campaign against superstition and moral decadence.[28] To this day in Hong Kong, supernatural films (domestic or imported) rarely make their debut during the Chinese New Year period, because of an industry belief that audiences would rather not begin the year on a superstitious note. However, contemporary Hong Kong audiences have been incredibly receptive to ghosts, with previous Hong Kong films (both Cantonese and Mandarin) dating back to the 1940s, and other classical and popular cultural forms of much earlier origin. The Chinese ghost stories that have had their strongest impact on Hong Kong cinema are arguably the film versions told in the Cantonese dialect. 1987's *Chinese Ghost Story* is considered a classic that set a new standard in its blending of horror, supernatural action, and fantastic special effects, swordplay and martial arts, period/costume drama, and romance. Its success resulted in two sequels and even a 1997 animated version. *Chinese Ghost Story* taps into centuries of Chinese and pan-Asian folk traditions as Leslie Cheung plays an itinerant tax collector who falls in love with a seductive ghost after finding shelter in an abandoned monastery. *Chinese Ghost Story* also builds upon the popularity and East/West melding of another subgenre, *jiangshi dianying*, films that featured the distinctive stiffly animated cadavers and the Daoist *fat-si* or priest with spiritual powers to control them.[29]

Within a year after the release of *Chinese Ghost Story*, in the parallel universes of art cinema and category III films, Leslie Cheung also appeared in *Rouge*, an acclaimed film by New Wave master Stanley Kwan, in which Anita Mui plays a reincarnated ghostly courtesan;[30] and Amy Yip, the queen of Hong Kong softcore, haunted *Erotic Ghost Story*, which spawned its own two sequels.

Flashforward to 2003 and Beyond

Having proven its gift for creatively reviving popular genres, the Hong Kong film industry suffered a year marked by tragedy and hope in 2003. The *annus horribilis* began with the SARS epidemic's devastating impact on film attendance, production schedules in Hong Kong and throughout the region, film-festival and promotions travel, etc. – and general economic and social malaise. It seemed as if a horror film curse had become a reality. And on 1 April 2003, the beloved star of film and popular music Leslie Cheung committed suicide, falling to his death from the top of the Hong Kong Mandarin Hotel. Eerily, in his very last role in *Inner Senses* (2002) he had played a psychiatrist who assists a haunted girl who is nearly driven to suicide by ghostly apparitions. Cheung's character is himself tempted to leap from a tall building by the ghost of a former lover. During his lifetime, Cheung's body of films and his vibrant live concert performances offered meta-texts to the complex narrative of his private and public identities. And tragically, the end of the year, Anita Mui (Cheung's co-star in *Rouge*, and another of Cantopop and Hong Kong cinema's biggest stars), succumbed to cancer.

In political and economic arenas, Hong Kong engaged in debates with Mainland China on democratic reform issues, and in summer of 2003 the Closer Economic Partnership Agreement (CEPA) was signed, going into effect January 1, 2004. Some of the main challenges in negotiating Hong Kong cinema's relationship with the mainland Chinese market have included import quotas, limited access to investment opportunities, censorship, co-production restrictions, distribution monopoly, and a lack of structured profit-sharing.[31]

As the year 2003 drew to a close, there was a glimmer of box-office hope as the prequel and the sequel to the local blockbuster *Infernal Affairs* were released in Hong Kong in October and December. Both films were co-financed by mainland China and the prequel was funded by Singapore as well. Although neither *Infernal Affairs II* nor *III* matched the local box-office take of the original, the last installment was the biggest box-office draw of the year in Hong Kong, opening on a record number of screens. The film also broke opening records in Malaysia, Singapore, and Taiwan; and in mainland China, it was the biggest opener of the year.[32] However, as film critic Li Cheuk-to has pointed out, audiences were not quite prepared for the relentlessly pessimistic depths of *Infernal Affairs III*'s vision of relived memories.[33] Nevertheless, the franchise promised to be reincarnated yet again, as Hollywood studio Warner Brothers bought the remake rights to the original film.[34]

Film scholar Rey Chow has queried, in relation to the experience of Hong Kong cinema and culture, whether nostalgia needs to be linear, a recovery of the lost past: "Could the movement of nostalgia be a loop, a throw, a network of chance, rather than a straight line?"[35] *Infernal Affairs II* and *III* flash backward and forward, allowing the characters to continually remember (as indicated by the epigraphs: "Uninterrupted time," "Unlimited Space," "Boundless Suffering"). In *Infernal Affairs II* ("The Forgotten Period"), the narrative returns to 1991 and shifts forward to 1995, and again finally to 1997. At the close of *Infernal Affairs II*, the reasons for celebrating are conflated as Sam becomes the triad kingpin precisely at the moment Hong Kong is turned over to Mainland China. In *Infernal Affairs III*, the narrative shifts constantly and frenetically between past and present, and the traumatic dis-order even allows the living to identify with the dead.

No matter what direction the future may take, contemporary popular Hong Kong cinema is eternally bound to its memories of economic prosperity, extraordinary achievement, regional dominance, and global impact.

CHAPTER 14

South Korea: Film on the Global Stage

Hyangjin Lee[1]

As with other popular Asian cinemas, the success of South Korean cinema offers a new perspective on the homogenizing trends of globalization led by Western cultural commodities. Until recent years, Korea was a Hollywood-dominated market, but it is now the world third-largest film exporter, after the US and France. When the government lifted its sanctions on the direct importation and distribution by foreign film companies in the mid-1980s, the Korean film industry seemed to be on the point of extinction owing to its vulnerability to the hostile marketing strategies of Hollywood. Despite the relentless protests of South Korean filmmakers, the UIP (United International Pictures) began oper-ations in 1987. The domestic market share of Korean films sharply declined from 38.5 percent in 1984 to 15.9 percent in 1993.[2] Faced with the threat of its disappearance, the national cinema needed a decisive strategy to revitalize its industry. In response to the efforts of the filmmakers, the public expressed strong support for a national cinema. As a reaction against the Americanization of its national film culture, the Screen Quota Civil Society was established in 1985. Responding to popular demand, the government increased the mandate number of showing days for Korean films from 121 days to 146 days per year. Korean filmmakers highlighted the exceptional provision for the cultural commodities to preserve and realize the collective identity of the people, opposing the indis-criminate operation of free and fair market principles. The "sense of crisis" con-cerning the loss of cultural identity resulted in the revival of the film industry.[3] Accordingly, the thriving film culture in contemporary Korea is due to a cultural resistance to the power of Western-led globalization.

New Identity Politics of Contemporary Korean Cinema

The rise of South Korea films in world markets, especially in East and Southeast Asia, can attest the role of a national film industry in enriching the diversity and multiplicity of contemporary film practices. During the last two decades, Korean film has undergone tremendous changes in its industrial structures, thematic features, generic experiments, and aesthetic attributes. Through these radical developments, Korean national cinema has seen a dramatic reversal in its fortune since the late 1990s. In 2003, Korean films were exported to fifty-six countries including Japan, Hong Kong, China, and those of Europe and the Americas.[4] The domestic market share of Korean film also has significantly increased since the late 1990s. In 2003, Korean cinema saw record-breaking ticket sales in the domestic market.[5] On the other hand, the national cinema has constantly sought to establish an international reputation for its artistic achievements, having won awards at the various international film festivals since the mid-1980s. The new sensibility and the creative imagination in representing the local history and cultural tradition are the new challenges for global audiences who are familiar with Hollywood films. Furthermore, the film industry is the leading force in spreading the *Hanryu* (i.e. the fever of Korea, or Korean wave) in Asia. At the same time, the Korean film practitioners have contributed to the creation of pan-Asian film culture. Among the various international film events staged in Korea, the Pusan International Film Festival which started in 1996 is the largest and most successful offering a range of new conceptual approaches to global film culture.

The remarkable growth of the Korean film industry was possible due to the democratic transition of its society. South Korea used to be known for its rapid economic development led by the authoritarian military regimes (1962–1987). During this period, a strong but politically uncompromising state achieved an economic miracle at the cost of suppressing democratic freedom. As a consequence, civil society suffered from social injustice, economic instability, and political corruption. The deepening economic gap between rich and poor became the prime concerns of the filmmakers. However, their cinematic renditions tended merely to expose political passivity encouraged by commercialist populism. Any scenes which could provoke popular criticism of the government, or discourage the foreign investment, were strictly censored by film authorities. Under such a repressive political climate, the filmmakers had to accept the enforced patronage of the state, producing numerous national-policy films or apolitical commercial films. To a greater extent, national cinema was used to promote the current political ideology. However, when the mid-1980s democratization of South Korea ended the rule of military dictatorship, Korea slowly developed its democratic political system. Society finally allowed freedom to the filmmakers who were craving for the realization of their creative imagination in exploring colonial/post-colonial history, and the harsh experiences of the "compressed" modernization process.[6]

The new identity politics of Korean national cinema emerged during this revolutionary period.[7] The film industry has been no longer subject to the abuse of state power. Thus contemporary Korean filmmakers enjoy an unprecedented freedom of expression. However, the national cinema urgently needs a new identity reflecting the dynamics of social and democratic change. Audiences reject films that reiterate political apathy or cultural conservatism. In order to meet these new preferences and tastes, new identity politics aims to change the old image of the national cinema into a more progressive paradigm. By blending familiarity and novelty, the new identity politics expresses the transitional identity of contemporary Koreans.

The hybridism of commercialism and artistic experimentalism is a significant factor in contemporary Korean cinema as it has successfully created its new identity politics in Asia. The creative adaptation of Hollywood dramatic conventions flavored by the locality is essential to capture the audiences. The filmmakers exploit history and cultural tradition to make national melodramas. The audience appears to experience the escapist pleasure in the new imaginary space, exposing the resentment to the hegemonic ideologies of global powers. Also, the physical and cultural similarities strike a cord with audiences. They can easily associate with the fictional stories set in familiar landscapes. In a sense, the historical and cultural intimacy presented by Korean films tends to appeal to audiences through emotional identification of being victimized by Western hegemonic powers – offering nostalgic romanticism, but with a local flavor.

The Rise of the South Korean Blockbuster

When *Shiri* (Kang Je-gyu, 1999) renewed the biggest box office record made by *Sopyonje* (Im Kwon-taek, 1993), many of the Korean film practitioners saw a hope in making a Korean-style blockbuster. The unprecedented success of *Shiri* led the creation of new jargon, "*Shiri* Syndrome," leading the nationalistic mass psychology with such catchphrases as: "If you want to recover the national economy, see Korean films as much as you spend the local products" and "To overcome the dominance of America, help *Shiri* beat *Titanic*."[8] The spy thriller won the patriotic sentiments of the audience who had suffered from the IMF financial crisis in 1997. Newspapers and broadcasting media reported the daily box-office records. This phenomenon, the so-called myth of Korean blockbuster, was the most significant cultural development during the financial crisis, transferring the revival of the film industry into popular civil movements. In a sense, the Korean film industry transformed the economic crisis of the country into a springboard for success.

Contemporary South Korean film has been enjoying widespread popularity with its home audience, reaching the highest world record of domestic market share since 2000. Since the success of *Shiri*, record-breaking box-office sales of big-budget historical dramas clearly marked this new development. The constant success of the big-budget films, such as *Joint Security Area* (Park Chan-wook, 2000) and *Friend* (Kwak Kyung-taek, 2001) created the business-oriented filmmaking culture. *Taegukgi* (Kang Je-gyu, 2004) and *Silmido* (Kang Woo-suk, 2003) ranked first and second in the list of top box-office hits in 2004, by recording over 11.5 million and 11.1 million ticket sales, respectively. (Each of these figures is about 25 percent of the whole population of South Korea.) Also, romantic comedies fusing traditional Confucian family values and gender relations with Hollywood-style gangster films or screwball dramas, such as *My Sassy Girl* (Kwak Jae-yong, 2001) and *My Wife is a Gangster* (Jo Jin-Gyu, 2001), generated the synthesis of different genres for the international best sellers. These films and others are slated to be remade by Hollywood studios.[9] Selling the rights to re-make is one of the ways for Korean filmmakers to access the American film market. Regarding this phenomenon, imitation of Hollywood tends to be suggested as the most effective way to challenge Hollywood's dominance in Asia and lead the successful "internationalization" of Korean national cinema. The popularity of *My Sassy Girl* in Hong Kong, Taiwan, and Vietnam, and *Shiri*, *JSA*, and *Taegukgi* in Japan seems to support this argument.[10] In addition, the fusion of horror or crime thriller with the conventional family melodramas and slapstick comedies is a newly emerging genre to lead the further adventure of Korean cinema in other regions in Asia, as seen by the surprising success of such films as *Tell Me Something* (1999) and *The Quiet Family* (1998) in Japan and Hong Kong, *Whispering Corridors* (1998) in Taiwan and Singapore, and *A Tale of Two Sisters* (2003) in Malaysia.

As noted above, the revival of Korean film-industry cinema is due to the success of its commercial films. However, this remarkable industrial expansion cannot overshadow the accumulated achievements of the filmmakers in improving the quality of national cinema. The artistic pursuit of the "unique" national cinematic form has engendered the vitality and maturity of national cinema. Significantly, as with the successful commercial films, these so-called "international film festival awarded" films show a wide spectrum of genres, themes, and film styles. Also, the frequent box-office successes in art-house-oriented films blur the distinction between commercial and non-commercial films. Starting with Im Kwon-taek's *Chunhyang* in 2002, the commercial theatrical releases of *Shiri*, *Taegukgi*, and *Spring, Summer, Fall, Winter … and Spring* in America and Europe, suggested that this hybrid tendency, blending commercialism with artistic experiments, serves to expand the international market for Korean films beyond Asia.[11]

The various generic experiments and film styles pursued by contemporary Korean filmmakers are promising signs for Korean film, indicating the presence of an alternative film culture for a global audience. However, the future of Korean film industry is still uncertain. Increased production costs and the theatrical monopoly of a small number of "well-made" films cast the serious doubts on the long-term stability and maturity of the film industry. For example, Bong Joon-ho's *Memories of Murder*, Kim Kyung-hyung's *My Tutor Friend*, E J-yong's *Untold Scandal*, Park Chan-wook's *Old Boy*, and Kim Ji-woon's *A Tale of Two Sisters* are the most representative works that reclaimed national pride from the market dominance of Hollywood in 2003. Shown to over 3.3 million people respectively, the five films helped the film industry overcome the huge losses created by a series of big-budget films. However, the whole industry still suffers from the serious deficits, highlighting its perennial financial problem. The competition between *Silmido* and *Taegukgi* increased audience numbers in national film history, involving the most expensive budget and marketing cost to date. However, the success of the two films can stimulate more speculative investment, threatening the diversity of a national film culture. The spread of the uncompromising commercialism pursued by the overconfident investors resulted in many films unable to attract a buyer for their release and distribution.

Despite the success of Korean film in recent years, the fact remains that the world film market is still dominated by America; maintaining 85 percent of the international marketplace and 97 percent of its own domestic marketplace. From this perspective, South Korea needs to protect its domestic film industry and national cinema. Film is a cultural practice of people and needs to be treated differently from other consumer products. The indiscriminate application of the rationales of a free market economy can restrict freedom of expression and free speech. There are many countries maintaining similar film policies and raising serious concerns on the issue, including France, Spain, and Canada. Also, there are countries which sustain a stricter protectionist policy, such as India, China, Egypt, and Russia.[12] The international support for the South Korean movement of the anti-abolishment of screen quota systems clearly reflects the significance of the preservation of cultural diversity in the age of globalization.

A Short History of Korean National Cinema

The rise of South Korea was driven by a nationalistic response to the transnational trends of contemporary film practices. However, when we examine the earlier history, it can be discerned that a protectionist Korean film culture has deep-rooted historical origins. Since Japanese colonial rule (1910–45), political, economic, and military dependence constantly undermined the national identity of Koreans, resulting in an influx of foreign films. When General Park Chung Hee took over power from the civilian government in 1961, the policy-makers conceived film as a relatively insignificant social sector to set the extravagance with the foreign capital and public fund. The government reduced the film importation quota as part of the economic policy of the developmental state, using this move to control the film industry. The importation sharply decreased from 203 films in 1959 to 72 films in 1962. The economic protectionism sought to realize the developmental state ideology and to control the film industry. Consequently, the nationalistic film policy was continuously challenged by another form of nationalism stressing cultural protectionism for the national cinema. Furthermore, whenever critical diastrophism occurred in the political landscape of the country, filmmakers tended to perceive this as an opportunity to protect cultural autonomy and boost the film industry. Throughout, the concomitant rise and decline of film industry relative to the social upheavals of the country clearly demonstrate that, as a popular medium for culture and art, film has always caught been in the power struggles of society, with alternating retrogression and revival.

Between 1897 and 1903, film was introduced in Korea as a tactic to advertise Western commodities. The first public screening of a motion picture in Korea is known to be in 1897 at a storehouse located at Jongro in Seoul, to promote streetcar sales. During the Japanese colonial rule, around 160 Korean films were produced by about 60 film-production companies. However, most of the films in the theaters were foreign films and the majority of theaters were also owned by the Japanese.

The first Korean "kino-drama" *The Righteous Revenge* was produced by Park Seung-pil and directed by Kim Do-san in 1919, which was part of the backdrop of stage drama. The first Korean feature film *The Plighted Love under the Moon* appeared in 1923, directed by Yun Baek-nam and produced by Japanese colonial government. In the same year, Japanese filmmaker Hayakawa Sōtarō made *The Tale of Chunhyang*, based on the most representative traditional tale of Korea. Alarmed by the Japanese film production of this film, Park Seung-pil produced *The Tale of Janghwa and Hongryeon* in the following year. Produced by only Korean staff and based on another traditional tale, this film was the first Korean commercial film. In 1926, Na Un-gyu made *Arirang*, the biggest box-office hit film made during the colonial period. Dealing with an oppressive colonial power coupled with the wretched living conditions of poor Korean farmers, *Arirang* set a model for a series of nationalistic resistance films made in later years, and stimulated the first socialist film movement in Korea. The KAFP (Korean Proletariat Art Federation) filmmakers made five films. However, the first Korean sound film *The Tale of Chunhyang*, made by a Korean director, was financed by the Japanese in 1935. Between 1926 and 1935, Korean film finally began to develop its own national identity and cinematic form, but most Korean-owned film companies failed to finance the production cost of color films. Coupled with the harsh censorship of the colonial government, the first rise of the national cinema was doomed to fail with the introduction of sound films. As the result, foreign films overwhelmingly outnumbered Korean films, so the profits went to the Japanese.

When the first Korean sound film appeared in 1935, the government actually prohibited a film recorded in the Korean language or even using Korean names for credits. When Japan invaded China and World War II began in 1937, the colonial government forced the Koreans to make propaganda war films. In 1941, the colonial government organized the Joseon Film Distribution League to ban film importation and distribution except of films from Japan and its allies. Therefore, under the newly introduced film law, Koreans were only allowed to make pro-Japanese national-policy films or war films, otherwise they had to choose the so-called "pure literary films." This extreme politicization of film practices deepened the enmity between the film-makers and tended to justify the total denial of the past history by the next generations.

When Korea was liberated from Japanese rule in 1945, it was divided into two by the Allies: the North and the South. Koreans had maintained a polity for more than 1,300 years, but the 3-year military administration by the US and the USSR created two antagonistic regimes in 1948 which resulted in a civil war between the two Koreas. The Korean War (1950–53) was the first major conflict caused by Cold War power politics. In the South, the Americans gave priority to the establishment of an anti-communist regime with a capitalist market system.[13] Due to the fear of communist expansionism in the region led by the USSR and China, the Americans strictly controlled the cultural discourse of the post-liberated country. The film industry was no exception. The administrative government introduced film laws to institutionally assist American film distributors to take up the dominant position in Korea. For the purpose of political control, the Americans also maintained a system of film censorship very similar to that of the Japanese; the filmmakers had to choose whether to be anti-communist or to remain apolitical. The ironic conversion of a group of filmmakers from pro-Japanese into nationalist or anti-communist reveals the tragic reality of the postcolonial country. This kind of confusion and contradiction in the ideological stance of Korean filmmakers has often been repeated. Despite the arrival of the new generation of film-makers, the Korean film industry was soon engulfed by the trauma of the civil war. During the war, most filmmakers were again forced to choose between the North and the South and consequently mobilized for war propaganda films.

After the war, Korean film industry slowly recovered when Syng Man Rhee, the first president of South Korea, introduced tax-exemptions. The number of films made each year rapidly increased from 8 in 1954 to 108 in 1959, with the most popular genres being historical drama and melodramas. The 1960s witnessed the renaissance of Korean national cinema. The most significant changes occurred after the April 19th Student Revolution in 1960, which resulted in a shift in film censorship from the government to civil organizations. The filmmakers quickly participated in the democratic transition of society, producing masterpieces of social critique.

However, the May 16th Military Coup led by Park in 1961 gradually sup-pressed the vitality of the national cinema within a decade. First, the military government introduced a series of reforms in the film industry in 1962, such as the Korean Motion Picture Act, a registration system for filmmaking, and the Grand Bell Award, a form of film recognition system.[14] Under this law, small production companies were forced to close because they could not meet government prerequisites such as the number of films made each year, studio size, employed staff number, or even the possession of film equipment. Only sixteen of the original sixty-three film companies survived this period. The import quota system and screen quota system were also enacted in 1965. According to the new film law, a company which made four films could import one foreign film, and total number of imported film could not exceed twenty. The films made annually increased dramatically. The filmmakers made numerous anti-communist, national-policy films or literary films, to secure the allocation of the foreign-film import quota, and melodramas still remained the most successful genre. However, the government control over the film industry eventually led to the decline of the national cinema. The Korean Motion Picture Promotion Corporation was established in 1973, but the erosion of the national cinema could not be avoided. The total number of features produced between 1969 and 1977 decreased by more than 50 percent. Also, beginning in the late 1960s, the film industry began to lose its audience to television.

The 1980s were very violent years in South Korea's political history. Park's assassination in 1979 led the people to hope for restored democratic social orders, which is succinctly expressed in the term "1980, Spring of Seoul." However, the second military intervention by another general, Chon Doo-hwan, brutally suppressed the popular democratic movements. The 1980 Kwangju massacre claimed more than 200 citizens' lives. During the democ-ratization movement period, Korean filmmakers were influenced by the social radicalism supporting the struggle against the state. The political passivity of the existing commercial film culture was criticized by the revolutionary forces, but the film industry gradually began to take part in the democratic transition of society. The national film movement (*Minjok Yeonghwa Undong*) and inde-pendent film movements, led by university students, emerged in this period.

Transition and Reform

The changing features of Korean national cinema since the 1980s can be dis-cussed by dividing events into two time frames: the democratic transitional period and its aftermath. During the democratic transition period, some film-makers contributed to the materialization of the new film movements within the existing film industry; others made their directing debut by reflecting the new social climate, making crucial contributions to the current direction of

New Korean Cinema. Regardless of the differences in directing experiences, ideological inclinations, film styles, and thematic concerns, there was a common underlying belief that film should reflect the democratic transition of society and contest the deep-seated prejudice of local audience to "poor quality" Korean films. Since the mid-1980s, Korean national cinema has received international recognition for its artistic achievements.

Since the 1990s, The Korean film industry has been actively engaged in far-reaching structural reforms. First, the increasing commercial values of film led to investment by large co-operations Samsung and Daewoo. A group of venture-capital firms also joined the film industry. Secondly, the major film-distribution companies, such as CJ Entertainment, Cinema Service, Korea Pictures, Cineclick, Mirovision, Ilshin Pictures, and Showbox Inc., emerged to lead the rationalization of management systems and the more business-oriented filmmaking practices. Starting in 1992, box-office receipts suggest the growing popularity of local film to its home audience and the rapid expansion of the market size for the industry. The growth of the multiplex phenomenon reached 1,271 screens in 2003 at the national level.[15] The accumulated experiences and confidence of the producers/distributors, gave an opportunity for new talented, art-house-oriented filmmakers as well.

The Korean New Wave and International Recognition

Indeed, there is no national cinema quite like the Korean industry, which has successfully challenged the stronghold of Hollywood in its own territory, and rapidly gained an excellent reputation in international film markets. Although the ongoing disputes between Korea and the US on the screen quota system still remain as the most serious concern, the astonishing achievements of Korean cinema since the late 1990s capitalize the vibrant response of a small national cinema. Along with the commercial success demonstrated by the works of Kang Je-gyu, Kang Woo-suk, E J-yong and Bong Joon-ho, the daring experimental works of a group of new talented filmmakers, such as Hong Sang-soo, Park Chan-wook, and Kim Ki-duk all refute the ideological passivity and aesthetic conventionality in depicting the reality of their own society. Im Kwon-taek, the most famous and experienced filmmaker in Korea, is credited with launching the New Korean Wave in international film circuits.[16] Awarded many times at international film festivals, Im's works have thematically tended to address gender issues, emphasizing repressive social norms and political oppression in ordinary people's lives.[17]

Im's *Chihwaseon* was the first South Korean film to win a prize in competition at Cannes, and many Koreans believed that this recognition at Cannes was symbolic as it initiated the appearance of their national cinema on a global stage.[18] By competing at Cannes, Im lived up to the expectations of the people who nicknamed him '*Gukmin Gamdok*' (i.e., the national director). A biopic of Jang Seung-eop, one of the great painters of the Joseon Dynasty (played by charismatic actor Choi Min-sik), the film reenacts Jang's anarchic life and paintings, recreating the turbulent history of Korea – and thus the evolution of its national film. Jang is a self-reflective figure of film-director Im, as he suffered political upheavals and the restrictive ideological hegemony of the state, but he persistently sought to create a new form of national cinema.[19] Im's interpretation of colonial history exposes the perspective of "Orientalism imported from the West."[20]

The constant challenges of the new generation of filmmakers contributed to raise the overall quality of Korean national cinema. This trend emphasizes their confidence in protecting their small national cinema in the age of globalization. Park Chan-wook's stylish *Old Boy* (2003, starring Choi Min-sik once again) set an ideal for contemporary Korean cinema with the successful combination between commercialism and artistic experiment.

Director Lee Chang-dong has asserted that "Hollywood seems to take the audience away from the reality and make them forget reality."[21] Lee's social criticism departs from attitudes of earlier Korean directors who relied on melodramatic conventions, predictable narrative deployments, stereotyped characterizations, and clichéd relationships.[22]

Kim Ki-duk's work to date has had only limited success at the box-office, but he is one of the most internationally acclaimed Korean filmmakers of recent years. Possessing no formal training in film art or filmmaking, he exhibits an unconventional and anti-mainstream sense of aesthetic taste. His 2002 film *Address Unknown* has a rich political text revealing the post colonial identity of contemporary Koreans. Based on Kim's own memories, it deals with the story of people who have no means of livelihood except being parasitic on the derivative economy of an American military camp town. Korean society allows the presence of foreign troops on its soil but rejects the consequences of the people living at the borderline between the two groupings. There are prostitutes and mixed-race children, and even their neighbors are not allowed to speak about their presence. They do not have a homeland. Although the notion of nation can be seen as the "imaginary community,"[23] a demarcation between the insider and the outsider in reality is unmistakably clear for them. The main character, Chang-guk is a teenager of mixed race, living with his ex-prostitute mother. His father, a black American GI father, never keeps his promise to invite his family to their other homeland, the US. His "shameful birth" also made him to be rejected, wandering around the village in "unhomeliness."[24] It is a depressing tale of rape, violence, death, and social rejection. Through the tragic death of Chang-guk and his mother, Kim raises his own voice: "The 'Subaltern' *speak*,"[25] but their voices are silenced by society. Questioning the meaning of "purity of blood" and national homogeneity with violent images of the youth and their American dreams, *Address Unknown* expresses the undeniable presence of cultural hybridity and ambivalence, as well as the social dislocation of the postcolonial Korea.

In a more commercial arena, box-office record-breaker *Taegukgi* (Kang Je-gyu, 2004) demonstrates the ways South Korean cinema is revisiting national history and memory.

Taegukgi: The Brotherhood of War

In Kang Je-gyu's 2004 film, the Korean War is a site of exploration of brotherhood and national identity. Jin-tae and Jin-seok are drafted into the military. In order to return the younger brother Jin-seok to his widowed mother, Jin-tae tries to win a medal which, he believes, can help Jin-seok escape from the war. However, the precarious development of the war never allows Jin-seok's discharge and results in Jin-tae becoming a brutal, psychopathic killer. The war claims Jin-tae's life but his madness cannot be justified by the cause of the war or even the brotherhood of war.

Before making *Taegukgi* (which takes its name from the flag of Korea), Kang Je-gyu made *Ginko Bed* (1996) and *Shiri*. In a sense, the success of *Taegukgi* was predicted by Kang's previous films, box-office hits. Many commentators compared *Taegukgi* with *Saving Private Ryan* (1998). The Korean referencing of Hollywood war film reiterates the themes of brotherhood, and it also echoes themes from the 1960s and 1970s, such as *A Stray Bullet* or *Horseman*.[26] *Taegukgi* deals with the psychological complex of a man in relation to his family, the eldest son (older brother as well); the film deftly communicates the inhumanity and brutality of war, but never politicizes the conflict in the appropriate historical contexts. Kang rejects the sentimental humanitarian universalism expressed by Spielberg. The brothers' agony and emotion may not be able to be shared by the audience unaware of the cultural norms of a post-Confucian society or the political implications of the war. However, the nostalgic images of the prewar time and idyllic family life are incredibly powerful cultural symbols to Asian audiences. The Confucian familial morality grants the eldest son's unbounded authority and responsibility to look after his siblings and old mother in the absence of father. The madness of war in *Taegukgi* is the agony of the nation who lost its father figure. The film does employ some crude stereotypes and gendered allegory, representing woman as the symbolic victim of the national conflict: the division of Korea (just as in Kang's previous film *Shiri*). Nevertheless, the commercial success of *Taegukgi* and the blockbuster trend adds a new chapter to the history of Korean film industry – creating the future while reflecting on the nation's past.

CHAPTER 15

Japan: Cause for (Cautious) Optimism

Darrell William Davis

Japanese film is a category encompassing activity outside the mainstream industry's focus on box-office returns, from independents to avant-garde to amateur films. While the following touches on box-office and industry trends, my approach combines themes connected to audiences, genres, directors, and historical issues. These themes reflect on the concept of popularity, its historical contingency, and especially how mass popularity took its leave of the cinema years ago. Only now, tentatively, is it approaching Japanese film again – but in new, diversified forms.

Audiences and Markets

Japan's movie-going public is the second-largest market in the world. But Japanese film-goers have not lately been in the habit of watching Japanese-made films; they flock to Hollywood movies. The Japanese public abandoned theaters in the 1960s for television and in the 1980s for home video. The contemporary audience for Japanese films has been characterized as an "hourglass" demographic, dominated at the top by those over age forty and at the bottom by kids who require distraction during school holidays.[1] The mainstream audience has been woefully under-served, indeed ignored, by major Japanese film producers.

The reasons for this abandonment of core audiences begin with poor-quality exhibition and monopolies on distribution. Vertical integration in the film industry has ensured that the three big studios (Toho, Shochiku, Toei) tightly control exhibition and distribution. Until recently theaters remained in congested urban areas, badly maintained with poor amenities and high prices. Though prices remain high, the late 1990s saw development of suburban multiplexes, which recently surpassed urban cinemas in revenues; in 2000 multiplexes made up 44 percent of all theaters.[2] Still, despite the dereliction of the old city cinemas, real estate values propped up their nominal worth. The bottom line, whether it comes from films, real estate, theme parks, or baseball teams, is and always will be the major studios' focus.

Historically, studios stood on solid genre classifications, with swordfight-laden period films (*jidaigeki*), gangster pictures (*yakuza*), melodramas, and comedies (*kigeki*). Toho was known for its period films, Toei for gangster pictures, which appealed to students, and competed with Nikkatsu in the 1950s and 1960s for the rebellious youth market (known in Japan as the *après guerre* generation). Since the 1930s, Shochiku has specialized in modern-day comedies, romances, and women's pictures. One of Japan's most revered filmmakers, Ozu, was a home drama specialist for Shochiku. By the 1970s these distinct categories were in disarray because the studios, as small cogs within entertainment and transport conglomerates, cut back on production in favor of other activities.[3]

Subsequently studios were not all that concerned with the decline of theatrical venues anyway because it didn't matter whether people came. This was due to pre-sales schemes (where studios would dump thousands of tickets on subsidiaries and associated companies) meaning that in Japan, box-office sales did not count real popularity. The arrival of foreign exhibitors like Warner-Mycal and Virgin showed the power of amenities (flexible pricing, comfortable lobbies and seats, digital sound, and parking) and marketing a new leisure "experience" in spatial terms. The multiplex was offered as a phenomenal spatial experience, like a theme park, with theatrical space merging and symbiotic with the "feature" presentation as the major attraction. An enhanced "experience" that could generate true box-office returns was devised, eliminating the need for dummy accounting. Once the profitability of these practices was established, the majors moved in and followed suit. Now Toho is the biggest exhibitor of all, though it was the last to invest in multiplexes. Consequently it has recently boasted nine out of the top ten films.[4]

Majors like Toho and Shochiku are sufficiently diversified to "farm out" production to independents and still make handsome profits from distribution. So-called independent production has made up the majority of popular film production for some time: 234 out of 287 total films released in 2003 were technically independents. Japanese films made by major studios count for less than a fifth of the whole. In 2003, 53 major releases out of 287; 45 out of 293, and 57 out of 281 for 2002 and 2001, respectively. For 2000 the proportion is identical to that of 2001 but, in 1998 and 1999, the studios produced ten films more than in the new millennium.[5] This points to a greater role for independent producers. But independent does not always mean marginal, or oppositional. Blockbusters like the animated features of Studio Ghibli are independents, distributed by Toho, which enjoys enormous profits without interfering in Miyazaki Hayao's painstaking but highly profitable aesthetic. Ghibli, though, is owned by Tokuma Shoten, a leading publishing firm. Ghibli even boasts its own theme park in western Tokyo.

When a company controls distribution, it hardly matters what comes down the pipeline. The studio lock on distribution entailed a conservative program of low-budget serials, such as the *Otoko wa tsuraiyo* Tora-san movies, Shochiku's old-fashioned peddler series, and *Tsuribaka nisshi* (*Free and Easy*, co-scripted by Yamada Yoji), another comedy serial about a fishing-mad company president. Other venerable studio lines include monster films, initiated by Toho's Godzilla franchise, est. 1954, and animal pictures, the last big hit being *Hachiko Story* (1987), a blockbuster about a dog with filial loyalty. A recent film about a seeing-eye dog (*Quill*, Sai Yoichi, 2004) has done well by retrieving this long-neglected recipe, combining adorable canine *kawai'i* ("cute") with the pathos of blindness.

It would be a mistake to overestimate the market for popular Japanese cinema, relative to that of other media. The film market is dwarfed by the so-called Big Four: television, newspapers, magazines, and radio. Here are some statistics: in 2000, the Big Four together brought in Y3,971 billion. The smallest is radio, at Y207 billion (3.4 percent of total media revenue). That year movies earned just Y171 billion, including imports.[6] In 2001 there was a boost, bringing the total to over Y200 billion, the highest return in over twenty years.[7] This was due to Miyazaki Hayao's *Spirited Away*, which alone grossed a record-breaking Y30 billion. There were just over 163 million admissions for the year 2001. This was the highest number of admissions since 1983, at nearly 175 million, a descending figure until it touched bottom in 1996, at 120 million. Miyazaki's film, which stayed in the top ten for nearly a year, outstripped the American behemoth *Titanic*, which earned Y26 billion in 1998.

But these numbers do not compare with the 2000 income for television, at Y2,079 billion; little wonder that film gets short shrift by media power brokers and policy-makers. This suggests perhaps the most pertinent definition of popular cinema: proximity to TV. If a Japanese film resembles or remakes a television series with the same premise and stars, then this is the golden calf of popularity, more than celebrity, box-office, or genre pedigree. Television, not film, is the great multiplier: it is fertile ground for moving images and narratives to sprout, and possibly fly to enticing markets like the internet, games, mobile phones, and cinema. The popularity of Japanese cinema is highly dependent on synergies with television and other moving-image media. The outstanding performance of theatrical event pictures like Studio Ghibli's is quite extraordinary.

In live-action film it was *Bayside Shakedown* and its sequel *BS2* (1998, 2003) that warrant attention here. These theatrical blockbusters were made on the back of a prime-time series from Fuji TV. Unlike American TV spinoffs, they did not camp up their sources, nor did they rely on in-depth knowledge of the television series. Absorbing, surprisingly humorous, yet suspenseful detective stories were delivered by director Motohiro Katsuyuki, based on carefully wrought scripts by Kimizuka Ryoichi. The producer, Fuji TV's

Kameyama Chihiro, has said the *BS2* plot was based on *Toy Story*, with a clean, three-act structure derived from *Star Wars*.[8]

In the mid to late 1990s, Japanese films became more attractive to ordinary audiences, but not because of multiplexes or any help from the majors. The independent sector, working with television producers and other corporate partners, reached a critical mass. Television was behind the efforts of super-producer Sento Takenori. Japanese cinema has been tardy in finding joint ventures with television, whether free-to-air or subscription. This has markedly changed. Sento assisted in this shift, developing material for pay channel Wowow (JSB, Japan Satellite Broadcasting). Known for his strict control of budgets, organizational acumen, and excellent taste, Sento has been responsible for a large number of foreign festival prizes for his projects. "The Japanese film industry is lagging behind that of Europe and the US," he says. "I would like to introduce Western production methods into that industry as soon as possible."[9] Sento's activities included establishing J-Movie Wars, a low-budget series begun in 1992 to make art-house films. The series helped launch the careers of directors Nakata Hideo (*Joyurei/Actress Ghost*, 1996 and *Ringu*, 1998) and Kawase Naomi (*Moe no Suzaku*, 1997). While her films are unlikely to reach a mass audience, Kawase won the 1997 *Caméra d'Or* prize at Cannes. Another Sento initiative, Suncent Cinema Works, was a broader slate of pictures organized by Sento in late 1998. This was aiming at a wider audience of cable subscribers.

With Project J-Cine-X, set up in 1999, Sento moved to theatrical pictures, "a major project that will assemble directors who have gained strong reputations at foreign film festivals and make films with them aimed at the overseas market."[10] These directors include Kawase, Kore-eda Hirokazu, Shinozaki Makoto, Riju Go, and Aoyama Shinji. All are associated with Sento Takenori's package-unit system, a method of spreading resources and risk in order to boost production. With sufficient efficiency of scale and international exposure, Sento is wagering that his stable of talent will find success within Japan.

Another key person is Kitano "Beat" Takeshi, who made yakuza pictures hip, minimalist, and occasionally absurd.[11] Kitano is another crossover from television, first stand-up comedy and then wacky variety shows. As a top celebrity in each of the Big Four media, Kitano is now all but inescapable. Though he claims to keep his roles scrupulously separate, many Japanese attend his films out of curiosity toward the comic iconoclast. Kitano is a genre opportunist, taking advantage of his own celebrity, but also helping himself to once vibrant traditions of *yakuza* (gangster films *Boiling Point*, *Sonatine*, *Hana-Bi*, *Brother*, etc.), samurai pictures (*Zatoichi*) and even the ultra-traditional *bunraku* doll theater (*Dolls*).

Both yakuza and *jidaigeki* genres (period drama, referring to feudal-era stories before 1868) used to be mainstays of Japanese domestic production.

Their recalibration for younger audiences may be revivifying Japanese popular film and genre traditions. But this is a potential to be carefully handled. There must be innovation in recycling or renovating the genre standards, because a cinema of nostalgia or neoclassicism can easily backfire. Reinventing, repackaging or repopularizing Japanese cinema for younger viewers must be integrated with other forms of software, like comics, games, internet, and mobile phones. In turn, this implies reinvention of popular cinema itself within a Japanese context.

Reconsidering the (Japanese) Popular

Popularity gets its validity from a specific confluence of production and consumption. Between official Culture on the one hand (traditional Japanese aesthetics, the arts, crafts, and skills promoted by the government) and everyday life on the other (the commercialization of skills and performance in objects or events), popular culture straddles both. Ideas of tradition usually align with the authority of musical, painterly, or literary traditions. Popular cultures draw on these, as well as developing internal formations of tradition over shorter time spans. High turnover means popular cultural material is compressed into tighter, fast-flowing cycles. The enormous "productivity" of popular cultures, their disposability and recyclable seriality, accelerates generic, stylistic, and thematic currents that make up tradition. The best image of contemporary Japanese pop culture may not be film or even television, but *manga*, comic books that dominate any Japanese bookstore: endless shelves of identically packaged volumes. These point to intricacies of plot, variation, and longevity that dwarf even the longest-running film serial, Shochiku's *Otoko wa tsuraiyo* series (*It's Tough to be a Man*, 1969–96), at forty-eight installments.

If we turn back to Japanese film history, period films used to be the dominant mega-genre for sheer numbers. *Jidaigeki* (period drama) declined sharply in the 1970s, after being devoured by the thousands – potboilers and prestige alike – since the 1920s. Eclipsed by yakuza films, samurai stories then rested in *chinpira* peace on television, especially on the public broadcaster, NHK. There may be a small revival of interest in the *jidaigeki*, promising an almost endless library of story ideas. Likewise yakuza traditions, which, according to Kurosawa Kiyoshi, are now the dominant in Japanese film, and acts as a kind of "default" for young directors.[12]

The *jidaigeki*, a popular action-suspense tradition that long predates its incarnation in cinema, is such a rich lode of narrative material that its reappearance is not limited to Japan, as in the American-made *The Last Samurai* (Ed Zwick, 2003). Because of its runaway success we are bound to see many more variations and spin-offs. In Japan *The Last Samurai* outdid its American benchmark, making over US$130 million in 2003. In the 1960s the samurai films of internationally acclaimed director Akira Kurosawa and others were imitated and recycled – not only in America but in Italy, Hong Kong, and elsewhere. Ironically, genre fertility is activated by its disappearance from *Japanese* movie screens and mindscreens, providing opportunities for a powerful novelty-effect via temporary forgetting. As producers and marketing executives find ways of amalgamating global audiences and building synergies, the distinctions marking erstwhile Japanese genres like *jidaigeki* or yakuza pictures start to fall away.

Samurai Resurrection?

This is not only the name of a wild CG-based fantasy (*Makai tensho*, 2003) by horror director Hirayama Hideyuki. Samurai resurrection is also a version of pop cultural reincarnation. Hirayama's film is itself a remake of a 1981 film of the same title, directed by yakuza master Fukasaku Kinji. Bringing back dead samurai assumes the expiry of a generic statute of limitations: a portion of Japan's youth sufficiently unfamiliar with the trappings of *jidaigeki*, memories expunged of the period film. Evidently the *jidaigeki* field has lain fallow long enough. Hirayama's film boasts spectacular swordfights but losers do not bleed, they "electronically deliquesce," like vanquished videogame gladiators.[13] The plots are just as exotic to a 15-year-old Japanese fan as they would be to one from Baltimore. Conventions like *katana* longsword, *chonmage* topknot, ninja, and seppuku are the stuff of international advertising and video games, rather than a Japanese cinematic tradition, still less an actual historical period with flesh-and-blood figures.

Another samurai resurrection is *Owl's Castle* (*Fukuro no shiro*, Shinoda Masahiro, 1999), a spectacular return to form by one of Japan's top New Wave directors of the 1960s. With its garish visual effects and hyperbolic camerawork, this is more typical of contemporary revivals of samurai pictures, given its director. Costume drama as dazzling special effects and the novelty of high-tech archaism sums up the overall affectations of *Owl's Castle*, *Samurai Resurrection*, and the occult *Yin-Yang Master* (*Onmyoji*, Takita Yojiro, 2001, part two released 2003). *Yin-Yang Master*, a Heian-era fairy tale, was the only *jidaigeki* in the top five box-office of the year (Y3 billion) along with *Battle Royale*, *Twixt Calm and Passion*, and the Korea-themed *The Firefly*, with Takakura Ken. *Azumi* (directed by Kitamura Ryuhei) is a Koyama Yu manga-derived high-tech *chambara* (swordplay) film by the director of *Versus*, a popular high-tech yakuza update accused of hollow affectation.[14] The flashy, technology-laden samurai resurrection also has forerunners like *Zipang* (Hayashi Kaizo, 1990) and a 1997 film *Misty* by TV director Saegusa Kenki, a slick remake of Kurosawa's classic *Rashomon* (1950) – both of which were premature efforts to rejuvenate the genre for young viewers. *Misty* was also designed to reach the large East Asian following of Japanese-Chinese star Takeshi Kaneshiro (*House of Flying Daggers*).

A new comic-book aesthetic of samurai (and yakuza) has engulfed any plausible substance filmed samurai may have had; yet the genre survives on the big screen. This is what makes old-fashioned pictures like *Twilight Samurai* (Yamada Yoji, 2002), so intriguing. The film's critical and box-office success (hitting Y12 billion or US$10.8 million, and nominated for a Best Foreign Film Oscar) was not unique. Two other *jidaigeki* paved the way, and were made from Akira Kurosawa scripts: *The Sea is Watching* (Kei Kumai, 2002) and *When the Rain Lifts* (*Ame agaru*, Koizumi Takashi, 1999). Like Yamada's these are gentle, elegiac stories of human yearnings within warlike communities. Home dramas with topknots? This formulation, though not completely wrong, trivializes the matter, especially when we remember some of the most celebrated films ever made were hauntingly human *jidaigeki*, like Kurosawa's *Seven Samurai* and Mizoguchi Kenji's *Sansho the Bailiff,* both made in 1954. Yamanaka Sadao's deeply moving prewar films such as *Humanity and Paper Balloons* (1937) were also *jidaigeki*.

Between the feverish vehicles of exoticism and the unpretentious, sentimental humanism of Yamada there appears the delightful *Zatoichi* (2003), Kitano's musical remake of the venerable blind swordsman serial (25 films from 1963–73). Kitano's film, his first *jidaigeki*, updates the genre through fine characterization but does not neglect pacing and comic spectacle. It did solid business in Japan (US$6.8 million). The bottom line in contemporary samurai pictures is an ample opportunity for intrigue, combat, and violence. This is something *jidaigeki* has in common with the revival of yakuza pictures.

Yakuza Reinvented

The main appeal of yakuza to younger people has to be in their ever-intensifying spirals of violence and outlaw behavior. Compare the ferocious killings of Fukasaku Kinji's *Battles Without Honor* series from the 1970s with Miike Takashi's admired *Dead or Alive* (1999) or *Ichi the Killer* (2001). In the latter, the gore quantum suggests detachment from all human passion, fueled by a giddy outlandishness. The toughness of classic yakuza, flowing from the hardship and sacrifice of organized crime, is missing from most contemporary versions of the genre. This may be due to the difference in rank between genuine big-screen yakuza and the small-time hoods and lackeys known as *chinpira*, whose misadventures are just as likely to play the central roles now. *Chinpira* (2000) is the title of a film by Mochizuki Rokuro, a porn-trained yakuza director who nevertheless finds room for human emotions within the mayhem. Art director Aoyama Shinji made a film with the same name in 1996, usually translated as *Yakuza Trainee*. If *chinpira* appeared in orthodox yakuza films of the 1970s, it was for comic relief. Now, in Japanese films one may encounter challenges not only from underlings, but from foreign gangs, like Chinese, Korean, or Southeast Asians. Miike's *Rainy Dog* (1998), a Taiwan co-production about a Japanese hit man in Taipei, signals the global dimensions of crime, organized or otherwise. A breakdown in traditional hierarchies and stock situations corresponds to a more inclusive yakuza mythology, reaching the lower rungs of the organization as well as complete outsiders. This mirrors the globalization or "equal opportunity" extended within yakuza stories.

Yakuza as a "rationalized," formula product is therefore compromised, making yakuza pictures less predictable, except in their ultra-violence. They are apt to swerve into farce, melodrama, or horror. Unlike classic gangster pictures, there is little that is redemptive or cathartic about contemporary yakuza violence. The delirium of the Miike yakuza vehicles, including *Gozu* (2003), described as yakuza horror, points toward a keen sense of low black humor and absurdity. Directors Ishii Takashi (*Gonin*, 1995, starring Kitano), Ishii Katsuhito (*Shark Skin Man and Peach Hip Girl*, 1999), Miike, and their imitators assume an informed audience, keenly aware of intertextual references that trade on generic fine points. These always involve disemboweling genre conventions whether yakuza, horror (*Audition*, Miike, 1999) or even the musical (*Happiness of the Katakuris*, Miike, 2000).

Does this archness rob violence of its power to shock? In fact the horrific carnage, often fascinating in its elaboration, takes on its own momentum, overwhelming narrative or theme. There is admittedly something liberating, but also melancholic about this effect, consistent with Miike's belief that "movie viewers really want to see some sort of breakdown, whether it be huge failure or absurdly reckless thinking."[15] Miike appears as a true anarchist, espousing violence without meaning. As a consequence the viciousness and malignant behavior of villains in conventional crime or horror pictures is unnecessary and goes missing. Punishment and crime are superfluous. Most younger directors know that there is always a market for hyperbolic violence. Older directors also realize this but in their case violence is built on a paroxysm of transgression and sociopathic collapse.

For Miike, the violence and gore seems removed from social problems of crime and punishment, referencing cinematic and *manga* forms of representation. Unlike his elders Kitano and the late Fukasaku, Miike is very prolific and fast; he works largely outside the established entertainment media, though his fame at Western festivals generates much interest; and his pictures tend to mix generic forms, with copious ejaculations of gore. If Kitano comes from network television and Fukasaku studio production, Miike cut his teeth on straight-to-video releases in the early 1990s (known as OV in Japan) giving him great versatility with low-budget sensationalism.

Consider a true veteran of yakuza filmmaking, Fukasaku Kinji. His *Battles Without Honor and Humanity* (*Jingi naki tatakai*, 1973) initiated a series that ferociously indicted postwar Japan. Its abject corruption and poverty is squarely blamed on American occupation. The chronic disloyalty of the hero (Sugawara Buntaro) is associated with betrayals inherent in victors' justice. Just as the Japanese people were sold out during the war by their own leaders, so Japanese movie audiences were hoodwinked by trappings of righteousness in yakuza ideology, built on semi-feudal bonds of clan and shared resentment. Fukasaku's pictures ruthlessly twisted the knife in the phony heart of yakuza mythology, which had reinforced wider social norms of conservative, capitalist, masculine values (embodied by actor Takakura Ken as the perennial good-hearted gangster). Fukasaku had a strong social conscience derived from his firsthand experience of the war and its devastating conclusion. Consequently his films were known as *jitsuroku rosen* (line of realism) yakuza films. Fukasaku claimed to use the form for social comment: "My contribution to the development of Japanese cinema was to abolish the star system. The traditional yakuza film depicted a clear-cut struggle between good and evil. Casting was entirely predictable. The odd thing was the good yakuza in these films were portrayed as being much better than your average law-abiding citizen. I was always puzzled by this ... I bucked the convention by playing up the negative aspects of yakuza life."[16]

The yakuza genre and its samurai antecedents were codified, with certain invariable events, encounters, and postures. Like westerns, yakuza pictures are "rationalized," with their standard moments of "return," "identification," and naturally, "revenge."[17] Rationalization lowers per-unit production cost by automating narrative patterns. Peter B. High describes this in relation to *chambara* swordplay programmers, whose structures were inherited by the modern setting of yakuza pictures.[18] Narrative formulae in both film types centered on personal revenge despite the presence of an ethical code: *bushido*-warrior for samurai and *ninkyo*-chivalry for the yakuza. Climactic vendettas would be carried out after a series of escalating humiliations. Late installments in a yakuza series inevitably bring sclerosis and creative exhaustion, a kind of life cycle of popular genre. The whole tottering thing is ripe for iconoclasm, as Fukasaku says. Of course this process is not unique to yakuza or any other Japanese genre but a feature of capitalist seriality and Fordist economies of scale. Sooner or later the popular form will detach from people's everyday life, becoming insular and irrelevant. Repetition promotes standardization but this breeds ever-greater refinements in variation. Eventually ordinary consumers cannot follow the intricacies and a once-popular form arguably speaks only to snobs or die-hard fans like trekkies or *otaku* (trivia junkies). Fukasaku's *Battles Without Honor* detonated the yakuza genre but half a dozen pictures later this series became the new format and he begged Toei studio for different projects.

Fukasaku continued his prolific career in other genres, replacing Akira Kurosawa in the famous Pearl Harbor co-production *Tora Tora Tora* (1970). Another Fukasaku screen battle was *Battle Royale* (2000), his sixtieth and last completed film.

Youth Films, Horror, Love, and Export

Battle Royale was one of the most notorious in recent Japanese cinema, sparking a national debate over violence, censorship, and youth. Here too violence is a tool to blast complacent audiences. But this dystopic youth picture is not set in a subcultural ward, quarantined from reality. It's an allegory of society eating its young and a black comedy about forcing delinquent teenagers to kill each other as media event. Swiftean in its smooth blend of science fiction, game shows, and hunter-prey thrillers, the film bears comparison with *The Most Dangerous Game*, *A Clockwork Orange*, or *Lord of the Flies*. Yet it is not so pretentious, thanks to Beat Takeshi's appearance as the malevolent, charismatic MC/referee. He watches as schoolchildren turn themselves into icy killers – or rapidly die off. It is the zero-sum game of survival, the price at which we want to continue living, that *Battle Royale* targets. Fukasaku was scheduled to direct the sequel, then succumbed to cancer at age seventy-two. His son, who scripted both films, completed the picture but it was marred by post-9/11 hectoring on global terrorism and American culpability. Exploiting the original's notoriety, part two also performed well at the box-office (US$16.8 million vs. 28 million for the original). Like the first film, the sequel caused a national outcry when an eleven-year-old girl who fatally stabbed her classmate claimed to have seen it. As a result Toei video delayed releasing the DVD. As mentioned below, youth seem to be a lightning rod for public anxiety about Japanese society's degeneration.

The main genre with which Japanese cinema recovered its footing is horror. Nakata Hideo's clever *Ringu* (*The Ring*, 1998) was a phenomenon in Japan, debuting on a double bill with another film *Spiral* (*Rasen*, Iida Joji). Both films were based on bestsellers by Suzuki Koji. For a horror picture, *Ringu* has a low-key, quotidian atmosphere with its premise of a killer videotape. The title refers to the startling ring of the telephone that initiates the killing, as well as the view upward from the bottom of a well. Yet it too has surprising social resonance. Nakata said the film is structured on an "anxiety curve," just like the tension and climax built into porn films, on which he assisted for many years at Nikkatsu.[19] The anxiety is linked, however, to a sense of unease, uselessness, unfulfilled emotions, and futility, unemployment – for Nakata himself had just quit Nikkatsu to go freelance. The vulnerability, threat of superfluity, of panic at being forgotten at the bottom of a well, connects with one's place in a competitive, heartless system. Isolation, despair, and failure can be overcome only if they are understood and embraced. The monster of conventional horror is revealed as an abused, abandoned child. When the heroine embraces it and takes it in, then the curse lifts and the vengeful spirit mollified. Nakata is repeatedly drawn to women as both monster and heroine because of his interest in broken families, and the difficulty of socialization through separation and divorce.

Kurosawa Kiyoshi, another horror director, aims higher in terms of thematic and conceptual ambition. *Cure* (1997) was an international festival hit. This film, along with *Pulse* (*Kairo*, 2001), *Charisma* (*Karisuma*, 2000), *Doppleganger*, and *Bright Future* (both 2003), has a more clinical feel, though like *Ringu* Kurosawa's films explore technology as pestilence. Like the films of Tsukamoto Shinya, who made the cyberpunk *Tetsuo* series, they also have a strange "retro" quality that might be called post-digital. Kurosawa deliberately suppresses special effects and optical processing. This enhances Kurosawa's evocations of contamination and dread, especially depopulation in post-apocalyptic landscapes. The end of *Pulse*, for instance, has a strange pop-up book effect, at once artificial, expressive, and quaint. The dead prevail by quietly infesting the internet. Technology creeps in as an insidious usurper, as virus or rot, rather than the explosive destruction of bombs, robots, or irradiated latex monsters.

This unusual approach to horror has proved surprisingly popular, not only in Japan but worldwide. Nakata's *Ringu* not only brought in US$7.24 million on a tiny initial investment (thanks to producer Sento), it also spawned a US remake from Dreamworks that doubled that amount, taking US$14.5 million in Japan and much more abroad. A trend ensued for US producers to cherry-pick remake rights to a whole spate of Asian films, especially Japanese horror. Other examples include: Nakata's *Chaos* (1999), *Dark Water* (2002), and *Don't Look Up* aka *Actress Ghost* (*Joyurei*, 1996), Shimizu Takashi's two-part *The Grudge* (*Juon*, 2003), which Shimizu himself remade as an American production shot in Tokyo, and many others. A Dreamworks producer says "There is more access to Asian cinema now than probably at any other time in film history ... For the last ten years, a generation of American kids has been growing up on *Pokemon*, Japanese anime, and manga, which may be causing certain sensibilities to evolve."[20]

Regional Flows and Generic Association

There is a new alignment of genre with East Asian regional cinemas, within their respective potential for global export or remake. Contemporary Japanese films are linked with horror, now the most visible Japanese genre worldwide besides anime, Korean films with comedies, and Hong Kong with thrillers.

This ongoing development, along with Hollywood launch of Asian production subsidiaries, may further integrate global markets and audiences. Could this be a reduction in the distance between Asian pictures and Western audiences? Or is it a more insidious Trojan Horse for preempting Japanese production plans by Western conglomerates? Many Asian producers are now packaging projects expressly for remake option rights in the US. They are indifferent to whether their films ever get made, so long as their idea is optioned by a lucrative foreign acquisition.

Other foreign acquisitions include melodramas and romantic comedies. These, like horror films, aim primarily at a youth audience. But they are a specific kind known as "trendy drama," prime time television series based on beautiful dwellings and their inhabitants, enduring unrequited love. These started broadcasting in the early 1990s with series like *Tokyo Love Story* (1991), *Under One Roof* (1993), *Love Generation,* and *Long Vacation* (both 1996).[21] Trendy dramas impacted Japanese film production a few years after their television release.

In the trendy drama vein we find Iwai Shunji's *Love Letter* (1995), a romantic quest for identity across the divide of mortality. In Hong Kong, *Love Letter* was the top-grossing Japanese film ever and drove a huge appetite for trendy drama series circulated on illegal VCDs. The film remains one of the most profitable Japanese films in the entire region. Iwai, originally a director of commercials, lards his work with striking, exotic imagery that makes characters and settings appear quite removed from everyday Japanese life. Iwai calls himself *eizo sakka* (image composer) rather than *kantoku* (director), going for compositional flourish over narrative coherence. Perhaps this has given his films currency throughout the East Asian region.

Iwai's subsequent pictures push further at this hybrid, yet televisual aspect, combining *kawaii*-adorable and *mukokuseki*-cosmopolitan.[22] This culminated in *Swallowtail Butterfly* (1996), a relentlessly postmodern fantasy of Yentown, a squatters' village of international nomads, and fashionably post-national in its patois of Chinese, English, and Japanese. Drawn to orphans and refugees from the pressures of Japanese society, Iwai indulges in vivid daydreams of bohemian community. This is something the trendy drama films have in common with horror and dystopic-youth pictures: a brave new world whose fetters of nationality are conspicuously absent. In Iwai's *All About Lily Chou-Chou* (2001), he addresses typical youth problems like bullying and *enjo kosai* (date-for-hire, pairing young girls with middle-aged men) but also shows their typical escape hatch, through internet fan sites and devotion to pop music idols.

One of the biggest hits of 2001, *Twixt Calm and Passion* (*Reisei to jonetsu no aida,* Nakae Isamu) exemplifies best the trendy drama aesthetic of cosmopolitan consumerism. Produced by Fuji TV, much of the film is set in Florence and Milan, featuring Japanese-speaking Hong Kong star Kelly Chen and music by Enya. Chen was first introduced to Japanese audiences on a trendy drama television series. What's appealing about this film is its breezy incorporation of European art history, architecture, languages, and cuisine, not as tourist attractions but as alternative lifestyles of the young Asian protagonists. This has nothing to do with internationalization, the producer says, but with brand names: "we went to Italy on location [and it was] the same device we use in making trendy dramas. Japanese women love Italy because of fashion, you know, Gucci, Ferragamo ... tons of brand names, exquisite food, a lot of beautiful historical buildings. I think Italy tops the list of places Japanese women yearn to visit. The film thus had the three important elements of a trendy drama: fashion, beautiful landscape and romance."[23] As for production, the film was a pre-packaged project utilizing a number of top people – original romance novelist, producer (*Under One Roof*), director (*Tokyo Love Story*), and art director (*Love Letter*) – from trendy drama on television and film.

Another blockbuster from a few years back is Morita Yoshimitsu's *Lost Paradise (Shitsurakuen,* 1997), which garnered US$80 million that year, second only to Miyazaki's animation *Princess Mononoke.*[24] *Paradise* too has a strong connection with adjacent industries, based on a bestseller by Watanabe Junichi, serialized in an economic daily, then turned into a television series. This was part of an overall trend exemplified by a fiction-comic-anime series called *Ai no kusabi (The Wedge Between)* about adulterous, romantic liaisons. The film *Lost Paradise* was produced by Kadokawa, a production company started by a giant publishing firm. This sultry story was aimed squarely at women viewers but unlike the trendy drama, the demographic was raised above age twenty-five, explaining the successful crossover from print to large and small screens. Both versions offered liberal doses of bare flesh but the love scenes were tasteful, due to the presence of big stars, Yakusho Koji and Kuroki Hitomi. (Donald Richie unaccountably says this film reanimates Mizoguchi Kenji, the acclaimed director of melancholy women's stories, but it is too maudlin to hit its intended tragic target.[25] However, Morita's film has little in common with Mizoguchi save its length, slow pace, and that it is a women's picture.)

Rebounding ...

Lost Paradise romanticized a lost Japanese fashion, ritual love suicide (*shinju*). This alludes to popular theater of the eighteenth century, but proved highly attractive in the mid-1990s as well. The Heisei era, beginning 1989, immediately brought a decade of severe economic and social dislocation. The stock market plunged. Prosperity did not bring security or higher living standards to the majority of citizens. The bubble economy also failed the film industry, with the 1980s proving a nadir in both quality and quantity. In 1986 there were just twenty-four studio-made Japanese films,[26] this from an industry that for decades was one of the top three film producing countries in the world.

On the other hand, production has bounced back in the late 1990s. Cause for cautious optimism, for several reasons: First, Japanese producers and their corporate fiefs understand that films can generate major returns in their own right, but may also perform as engines of ancillary and adjacent product lines (publishing, shopping, tourism, etc.) This ensures a more secure place for films, filmmakers, and even critics in the media food chain. Second, audiences have begun to take note of their own film culture, especially since Japanese films have been making waves abroad since the mid-1990s. Admittedly festival favorites are not the ones general audiences wish to see, but nearly every Japanese has an insatiable curiosity about how things at home are received abroad. Now, if foreign exposure of Japanese films is the channel by which curious youth discover the cinema, that is fine. All the better if a whole generation of pop culture connoisseurs decide that Japanese cinema, its former magnificence as well as a recent turn to the quotidian, is worthy of further pursuit. If so, then Japanese films have a long life to run.

Notes by Chapter

INTRODUCTION

1. My information on the distribution and reception of the film was acquired from a range of Asian and North American sources including trade papers and newspapers. For example, *The Straits Times* (Singapore) covered the movie from its preproduction days to its DVD release, as well as the subsequent careers of its director and stars. See the following articles in *The Straits Times*: Kelvin Tong, "Goei Visits Disco Dancing Days" (November 23, 1997) and "Temperature Rising for Fever Movie" (May 19, 1998); Renee Wu, "Forever Fever Forever" (May 22, 2000).

    The film reportedly had a 70-day domestic run and earned a disappointing S$840,000 at the box-office. The production team had an international composition with an Australian camera crew. (Post-production was also completed in Australia.) Director Glen Goei signed a multi-picture deal with Miramax, but these projects were never realized due to a variety of challenges.

2. See Anthony Milner and Deborah Johnson's essay "The Idea of Asia" on the Australian National University website www.anu.edu.au/asianstudies/idea.html

3. See Edward Said's classic book *Orientalism: Western Conceptions of the Orient* (London: Penguin, 1991 [1978]. Ella Shohat and Robert Stam in their book *Unthinking Eurocentrism: Multiculturalism and the Media* (London and New York: Routledge, 1994) remind us that "If Edward Said in *Orientalism* points to the Eurocentric construction of the East within Western writing, others, such as Martin Bernal in *Black Athena* [1987], point to the complementary Eurocentric construction of the West via the 'writing out' of the East (and Africa)," p. 15.

4. I examine this construction of racial identities ("Black," "Asian", and "British") in terms of cinema in my article "Representing the Spaces of Diaspora in Contemporary British Films by Women Directors," in *Cinema Journal* 38, (3) (Spring 1999): 67–90.

5. Michael Hardt and Antonio Negri, *Empire* (Cambridge, MA: Harvard University Press, 2000), p. 154.

6. See Shehkar Kapur's commentary in *The Guardian* (August 23, 2002), available at his website, http://www.shekharkapur.com/next.htm

7. By Asian diasporas I am referring to dispersions of people and culture – multiple trajectories and narratives of Asian experience. See *Theorizing Diaspora*, ed. Jana Evans Braziel and Anita Mannur (Malden, MA: Blackwell, 2003) and Aihwa Ong, *Flexible Citizenship: The Cultural Politics of Transnationality* (Durham, NC: Duke University Press, 1999).

8. See Shirley Geok-lin Lim and Wimal Dissanayake, "Introduction," *Transnational Asia Pacific: Gender, Culture, and the Public Sphere*, ed. Shirley Geok-Lin Lim et al. (Urbana and Chicago: University of Illinois Press, 1999), p. 1.

9. Ibid. p. 3.

10. See for instance, *Trajectories: Inter-Asia Cultural Studies*, ed. Kuan-Hsing Chen (London and New York: Routledge, 1998) and *Mobile Cultures: New Media in Queer Asia* ed. Chris Berry et al. (Durham: Duke University Press, 2003).

11. Scholars in the growing field of Asian American (or Asian Pacific American) cinema studies have done very important work in this regard that needs to be acknowledged here – e.g. Gina Marchetti's *Romance and the "Yellow Peril": Race, Sex, and Discursive Strategies in Hollywood Fiction* (Berkeley: University of California Press, 1993); Peter Feng's *Identities in Motion: Asian American Film and Video* (Durham NC: Duke University Press, 2002) and his edited collection, *Screening Asian Americans* (New Brunswick NJ: Rutgers University Press, 2002); Sheng-Mei Ma's *The Deathly Embrace: Orientalism and Asian American Identity* (2000) [which discusses Asian American literature as well as film]; Darrell Y. Hamamoto and Sandra Liu's edited anthology *Countervisions: Asian American Film Criticism* (Philadelphia: Temple University Press, 2000); and the Roger Garcia-edited catalogue, *Out of the Shadows: Asians in American Cinema* (Locarno, Switzerland: Festival Internazionale del Film di Locarno, 2001). From many other vantage points (besides North America), exciting scholarship has also looked, for example, at "Asian Australia," – e.g. *Floating Lives: The Media and Asian Diasporas*, ed. Stuart Cunningham and John Sinclair (St Lucia: University of Queensland Press, 2000) and Tseen Khoo et al., *Diaspora: Negotiating Asia-Australia* (University of Queensland Press, 2000).
12. See Minh-Ha T. Pham, "The Asian Invasion in Hollywood," *Journal of Popular Film and Television*, 32(3) (Fall 2004): 122.
13. See Ella Shohat and Robert Stam, "De-Eurocentrizing Cultural Studies: Some Proposals," in *Internationalizing Cultural Studies: An Anthology*, ed. Ackbar Abbas and John Nguyet Erni (Malden, MA: Blackwell, 2005), p. 496.
14. Richie is one of the most prolific writers in English about Japanese cinema, and *Rashomon* is perhaps Japanese cinema's most widely analyzed text. For a useful resource on critical and scholarly appraisals of the film, see his edited volume on the film *Rashomon* (New Brunswick, NJ: Rutgers University Press, 1987), and his "Introduction," pp.1–28.
15. See Gina Marchetti, "Chinese Feminist Film Criticism," *Jump Cut* 46 (Summer 2003), http://www.ejumpcut.org/archive/jc46.2003/marchetti.dai/index.html
16. I discuss such issues in my essay "Ways to Sink the *Titanic*: Contemporary Box-Office Successes in the Philippines, Thailand, and South Korea." *Tamkang Review* 3(2) (Winter 2002): 1–29.
17. Julian Stringer, "*Boat People*: Second Thoughts on Texts and Contexts", in Chris Berry (ed.), *Chinese Films in Focus: 25 New Takes* (Berkeley: University of California Press, 2004), pp. 15–22. The author creatively applies the "interzone" concept developed by anthropologists George E. Marcus and Fred R. Mayers to the cultural phenomenon of the international film festival.
18. G. Allen Johnson, "Worldwide, Asian films are grossing millions. Here they're either remade, held hostage or released with little fanfare." sfgate.com (Thursday, February 3, 2005), http://www.sfgate.com

CHAPTER 1 THEORIZING ASIAN CINEMA(S)

1. See Robert Stam, *Film Theory: An Introduction* (Malden, MA: Blackwell, 2000).
2. One of the contributors to this anthology, William van der Heide, discusses the shadow puppet theater tradition in his book *Malaysian Cinema, Asian Film: Border Crossings and National Cultures* (Amsterdam: Amsterdam University Press, 2002).
3. K.M. Gokulsing and Wimal Dissanayake, *Indian Popular Cinema: Narrative of Cultural Change*, 2nd edn (Stoke-on-Trent: Trentham Books, 2004), pp. 19–24.

4. Wimal Dissanayake, "Issues in World Cinema," in *The Oxford Guide to Film Studies*, ed. John Hill and Pamela Church Gibson (New York: Oxford University Press, 1998), p. 532.

5. Christian Metz, *Film Language: A Semiotics of the Cinema*, trans. Michael Taylor (New York: Oxford University Press, 1974).

6. See Sergei Eisenstein, "The Cinematographic Principle and the Ideogram," in *Film Theory and Criticism*, ed. Leo Braudy et al. (New York: Oxford University Press, 1992), pp. 127–38.

7. See Hu Ke, "Contemporary Film Theory in China," in the online journal *Screening the Past* (25 March 1998), http://www.latrobe.edu.au/screeningthepast/reruns/hkrr2b.html Also see Chris Berry's introduction " Hu, Where and When: Locating 'Contemporary Film Theory in China'," *Screening the Past* (25 March 1998), http://www.latrobe.edu.au/www/screeningthepast/reruns/hkrrintro.html Berry brings up the important point that much film theory and criticism in Asian languages has not been made widely available or translated into English.

8. See Brian Larkin, "Indian Films and Nigerian Lovers: Media and the Creation of Parallel Modernities," in *The Anthropology of Globalization: A Reader*, ed. Jonathan Xavier Inda and Renato Rosaldo (Malden, MA: Blackwell, 2002).

9. Examples include David Bordwell and Kristen Thompson's widely used textbook, *Film Art: An Introduction*, now in its 7th edn (Boston: McGraw-Hill, 2004), as well as Bordwell's *Planet Hong Kong: Popular Cinema and the Art of Entertainment* (Cambridge, MA: Harvard University Press, 2002).

10. For a discussion of the ideal of the "suture," see the essays in *Narrative, Apparatus, Ideology: A Film Theory Reader*, ed. Philip Rosen (New York: Columbia University Press, 1986), especially Jean-Louis Baudry, "Ideological Effects of the Basic Cinematographic Apparatus," pp. 286–98.

11. See Stanley Fish, *Is There a Text in this Class?: The Author of Interpretive Communities* (Cambridge, MA: Harvard University Press, 1980) and Janice Radway, *Reading the Romance: Women, Patriarchy, and Popular Literature* (Chapel Hill, NC: University of North Carolina Press, 1980).

12. A key text on the cinematic uses of Bakhtin's work is Stam's *Subversive Pleasures: Bahktin, Cultural Criticism, and Film* (Baltimore: Johns Hopkins University Press, 1989). See also Mikhail Bakhtin, "Discourse in the Novel," in *The Dialogic Imagination: Four Essays by M.M. Bakhtin*, ed. Michael Holquist (Austin: University of Texas Press, 1981), pp. 259–422.

13. See Raymond Williams, *Keywords: A Vocabulary of Culture and Society* (New York: Oxford University Press, 1983), pp. 236–8.

14. See Michel Foucault, "The Order of Discourse," trans. Ian McLeod, in *Untying the Text: A Post-Structuralist Reader*, ed. Robert Young (Boston and London: Routledge, Kegan Paul, 1981), pp. 51–78.

15. Ciecko, "Ways to Sink the *Titanic.*"

16. See Fiske's entry on "context" in Tim O'Sullivan, et al. eds, *Key Concepts in Communication and Cultural Studies*, 2nd edn (London/New York: Routledge, 1994).

17. See Albert Moran "Terms for a Reader: Film, Hollywood, National Cinema, Cultural Identity, and Film Policy," in his edited book *Film Policy: International, National, and Regional Perspectives* (London and New York: Routledge, 1996), p. 10.

18. Hamid Naficy explores these tropes in his book *Accented Cinema: Exilic and Diasporic Filmmaking* (Princeton: Princeton University Press, 2001).

19. Benedict Anderson, *Imagined Communities: Reflections on the Origins and Spread of Nationalism*, London and New York: Verso, 1983.

20. Andrew Higson, "The Limiting Imagination of National Cinema," in *Cinema and*

Nation, ed. Mette Hjort and Scott Mackenzie (London and New York: Routledge, 2000), p. 67.

21. Ibid., p. 69.
22. See Andrew Lam (Pacific New Service), "Thai Cinema Ready to Roll," at http://www.imdiversity.com/villages/asian/arts_culture_media/lam_thai_cinema_0 604.asp
23. Michel Foucault, "What is an Author?" in *Language, Counter-memory, Practice,* ed. Donald Bouchard (Ithaca: Cornell University Press, 1977), pp. 113–38.
24. Dissnayake, "Issues in World Cinema," pp. 528–9.
25. See Marcia Landy, *Film, Politics and Gramsci* (Minneapolis: University of Minnesota Press, 1994).
26. Higson, p. 73.
27. See Lau's discussion in her introduction to *Multiple Modernities: Cinemas and Popular Media in Transcultural East Asia* (Philadelphia: Temple University Press, 2003), pp. 1–10.
28. See Tu Weiming "Cultural China: The Periphery as the Center," in *Daedalus* 120(2) (Spring, 1991), reprinted in *The Living Tree: The Changing Meaning of Being Chinese Today,* ed. Tu Weiming (Palo Alto CA: Stanford University Press, 1994), pp. 1–34.
29. Ackbar Abbas and John Nguyet Erni address the challenges of a developing a critical international cultural studies in the introduction to their ground-breaking edited volume *Internationalizing Cultural Studies: An Anthology* (Malden, MA: Blackwell, 2005), pp. 1–12.
30. See Derek Elley, "CineAsia: Asia Accents Collaboration," Variety "CineAsia: Asia Accents Collaboration," *Variety* 6–18, December 2004: 18.
31. See Stephen Crofts, "Concepts of National Cinema," in John Hill and Pamela Church Gibson, *The Oxford Guide to Film Studies,* Oxford: Oxford University Press, 1998), pp. 385–94.
32. See Fernando Solanas and Octavio Getino, "Towards a Third Cinema: Notes and Experiences for the Development of a Cinema of Liberation in the Third World," in *Twenty-Five Years of the New Latin American Cinema,* ed. Michael Chanan (London: British Film Institute, 1983), pp. 17–28.
33. The book *Questions of Third Cinema,* ed. Jim Pines and Paul Willemen (London: British Film Institute, 1989) is a collection of many important essays on the Third Cinema question, including Teshome H. Gabriel's "Towards a Critical Theory of Third World Films," pp. 53–64. More recently, the debate is taken up in the collection *Rethinking Third Cinema,* ed. Anthony Guneratne and Wimal Dissanayake (London and New York: Routledge, 2003).
34. Dissanayake, "Issues in World Cinema," p. 528.
35. See Susan Hayward, *Key Concepts in Cinema Studies* (London and New York: Routledge, 1996), p. 385.
36. For an overview of postmodernism see John Storey, *An Introductory Guide to Cultural Theory and Popular Culture* (Athens, GA: University of Georgia Press, 1993), pp. 154–80.
37. See Fredric Jameson, "Third World Literature in the Era of Multinational Capitalism," *Social Text* 15 (Fall 1986): 65–88, and Aijaz Ahmad's *In Theory: Classes, Nations, Literatures* (London: Verso, 1992). For a brief discussion of the implications of allegory for cultural studies, see the entry in the critical glossary, *Key Concepts in Post-Colonial Studies* by Bill Ashcroft et al., pp. 9–11.
38. Robert J.C. Young, *Postcolonialism: A Historical Introduction* (Oxford: Blackwell, 2001), p. 170.
39. Arjun Appadurai, *Modernity at Large: Cultural Dimensions of Globalization*

(Minneapolis: University of Minnesota Press, 1996), p. 148.

40. John Tomlinson, *Globalization and Culture* (Chicago: University of Chicago Press, 1999), p. 118.

41. For a discussion of "global/local" and "glocal" and related terms see Rob Wilson and Wimal Dissanayake, eds., *Global/local: Cultural Production and the Transnational Imaginary* (Durham NC: Duke University Press, 1996) and Roland Robertson, *Globalization: Social Theory and Global Culture* (Newbury Park, CA and London: Sage, 1992).

42. For an interesting overview of the local and the global in MTV Asia programming, see Kenny Santana, "MTV Goes to Asia," *YaleGlobal* (12 August 2003), http://yaleglobal.yale.edu/display.article?id=2211

43. See Jurgen Habermas, *The Structural Transformation of the Public Sphere*, (Cambridge, MA: MIT Press, 1991); also Carol Breckenridge (ed.), *Consuming Modernity: Public Culture in a South Asian World* (Minneapolis: University of Minnesota Press, 1995).

44. See Toby Miller et al., *Global Hollywood* (London: British Film Institute, 2001), especially Chapter Five, "Distribution, Marketing and Exhibition" and the section called "Textual Gatekeepers: Positioning, Playability, Marketability," pp. 152–60.

45. Ibid., p. 9.

46. Ibid., p. 87.

47. Ibid., p. 133.

48. See David Harvey, *The New Imperialism*, Oxford: Oxford University Press, 2003. See also the "Conversations with History" series interview with David Harvey at the University of California, Berkeley: "A Geographer's Perspective on the New American Imperialism: "Conversation with David Harvey" by Harvey Kreisler (March 2, 2004), Part V: "Scenarios for the Future," http://globetrotter. berkeley.edu/people4/Harvey/harvey-con0.html

49. See Peter J. Williamson, *Winning in Asia: Strategies for Competing in the New Millennium* (Cambridge, MA: Harvard Business School Press, 2004).

50. See W. Dissanayake (ed.), *Melodrama and Asian Cinema* (Cambridge: Cambridge University Press, 1993).

51. For more on melodrama, affect, and gender constructions in Asian cinema see Ravi S. Vasudevan, "The Politics of Cultural Address in a 'Transitional' Cinema: A Case Study of Indian Popular Cinema," in *Reinventing Film Studies*, ed. Christine Gledhill and Linda Williams (New York: Oxford University Press, 2000), pp. 130–64; *South Korean Golden Age Melodrama: Gender, Genre, and National Cinema*, ed. Kathleen McHugh and Nancy Abelmann (Detroit: Wayne State University Press, 2005); Laleen Jayamanne, "Sri Lankan Family Melodrama: A Cinema of Primal Attractions," *Screen* 33(3) (1992): 145–53. See also Kyung Hyun Kim's discussion of what he calls "genres of post-trauma" in his book, *The Remasculinization of Korean Cinema* (Durham NC: Duke University Press, 2004).

52. John Lent, *The Asian Film Industry* (Austin: University of Texas Press, 1990), p. 51.

53. See Shuyu Kong, "Big Shot from Beijing: Feng Xiaogang's *He Sui Pian* and Contemporary Chinese Commercial Film," *Asian Cinema* (Spring/Summer 2003): 175–87. For another perspective see Shujen Wang, "Big Shot's Funeral: China, Sony, and the WTO," *Asian Cinema* (Fall/Winter 2003): 145–54.

54. See the essays collected in John Caughie, *Theories of Authorship: A Reader* (London and Boston: Kegan Paul/British Film Institute, 1981.

55. See Henry Jenkins' classic study, *Textual Poachers: Television Fans and Participatory Culture* (New York: Routledge, 1992).

56. I address these issues in my essay "Muscles, Market Value, Telegenesis, Cyberpresence: The New Asian Movie Star in the Global Economy of Masculine Images," in *Global Currents: Media and Technology Now*, ed. Patrice Petro and Tasha Oren (New Brunswick NJ: Rutgers University Press, 2004), pp. 186–99.

57. For theoretical and critical perspectives on cross-cultural or intercultural cinematic engagement, see Laleen Jayamanne, *Towards Cinema and its Double: Cross-Cultural Mimesis* (Bloomington: Indiana University Press, 2001) and Laura Marks, *The Skin of the Film: Intercultural Cinema, Embodiment, and the Senses* (Durham NC: Duke University Press, 2000).

58. Roland Barthes, "Leaving the Movie Theater," in *The Rustle of Language*, Berkeley and Los Angeles: University of California Press, 1986, pp. 345–9.

59. Jacques Lacan, "The Mirror Stage as Formative of the I," *Ecrits: A Selection*, trans. Alan Sheridan (New York: Norton, 1977).

60. For an overview of feminist film theories, see the anthology *Feminist Film Theory: A Reader*, ed. Sue Thornham (New York: New York University Press, 1999).

61. Laura Mulvey, "Visual Pleasure and Narrative Cinema," *Screen* 16(3) (1975): 6–18.

62. For some perspectives on transnational feminism see Caren Kaplin et al. (eds.), *Nationalism, Transnational Feminisms, and the State*, Durham, NC: Duke University Press, 1999.

63. See Gayatri Spivak, "Can the Subaltern Speak?," in *Colonial Discourse and Post-Colonial Theory*, eds. Patrick Williams and Laura Chrisman (Hemel Hempstead: Harvester Wheatsheaf, 1993.

64. See Homi Bhabha, *The Location of Culture* (London: Routledge, 1994).

CHAPTER 2 PHILIPPINES

1. Tom O' Regan discusses the "relational" dimension of Hollywood cinema's presence within national cinemas in his monograph, *Australian National Cinema* (London and New York: Routledge, 1996).

2. Andrew Higson mentions but does not elaborate upon the concept of hybridity in national cinema in "The Limiting Imagination of National Cinema," in *Cinema and Nation*, ed. Mette Hjort and Scott Mackenzie (New York: Routledge, 2000), pp. 63–74.

3. For an authoritative discussion of hybridity and its usage in both racial discourse and literary/cultural criticism, see Robert J.C. Young, *Colonial Desire: Hybridity in Theory, Culture, Race* (London: Routledge, 1995), pp. 1–28.

4. For a critique of Philippine cinema's escapism and imperialism along the lines of the Frankfurt School of critical theory, see Bienvenido Lumbera's "Ang Kasaysayan at Tunguhin ng Pelikulang Pilipino" ["The History and Prospects of the Filipino Film"] in *The Urian Anthology*, ed. Nicanor G. Tiongson (Manila: Manuel L. Morato, 1983), pp. 22–47.

5. The popularity of local action, drama, and sex films over that of many other genres and, at times, over foreign releases, has been a trend since at least the late 1970s as *Variety* reports in 1979: "While foreign features corner 60% of the outlets, their local counterparts enjoy bigger and more regular following. One reason may be the general appeal of homespun stories of sex, love, action and intrigue." See "79 percent of Manila Goes for Tagalog," *Variety*, 9 May 1979: 250. For a related discussion of generic configurations in 1990s cinema, see Jerry Respeto's "Tradisyon

at Supling: Mga Anyo ng Pelikulang Pilipino ng Dekada Nubenta," in *Sampung Taong Sine: Philippine Cinema, 1990–1999* (Manila, NCCA: 2002), pp. 60–3.

6. See Leah Salterio, "Assunta, husband clears Bong of 'rape'," *Philippine Daily Inquirer*, 22 May 2002.

7. See "Of Mimicry and Man: The Ambivalence of Colonial Discourse," in Homi K. Bhabha, *The Location of Culture*, pp. 85–92.

8. See Nicanor Tiongson's useful discussion of Hollywood imitation and influence in "The 'Gaya-Gaya' Syndrome in Philippine Movies," *The Urian Anthology 1980–1989* (Manila: Antonio Tuviera, 2001), pp. 28–33.

9. At least five *Dyesebel* remakes and one spin-off were produced in 1953, 1964, 1973, 1978, 1989, 1996. See *CCP Encyclopedia of Philippine Art*, Vol. VIII, p. 154.

10. See "Mega Mother Lily: Superstar for all Seasons," Jo-Ann Maglipon's profile of film mogul Lily Yu-Monteverde in *Primed: Collected Stories, 1972–1992* (Pasig City: Anvil Publishing, 1993), pp. 186–97.

11. For a lucid discussion of the relationship between popular (and art) cinemas in the context of national cinema studies, see Natas̆a Ďurovičová, "Some Thoughts at an Intersection of the Popular and the National," *The Velvet Light Trap* 34 (Fall 1994), pp. 3–9. See also Stephen Neale's "Art Cinema as Institution" in *Screen* 22(1) (1981): 11–39 and Andrew Higson, "British Film Culture and the Idea of National Cinema," in *Waving the Flag: Constructing a National Cinema in Britain* (Oxford: Clarendon, 1995), pp. 4–25.

12. Rey Chow, *Primitive Passions* (New York: Columbia University Press, 1995), p. 180.

13. See Fernando Solanas and Octavio Getino, "Towards a Third Cinema: Notes and Experiences for the Development of a Cinema of Liberation in the Third World," in *Twenty-Five Years of the New Latin American Cinema*, ed. Michael Chanan (London: British Film Institute, 1983), pp. 17–28.

14. An article in a Philippine daily newspaper reports the story of *Sibak*'s development: "Last year, David Overby of the Toronto Film Festival committee contacted Brocka's friends to come up with a movie of a similar theme [to that of *Macho Dancer*]." See "'Sibak,' a film with an international calibre," *Manila Bulletin*, 14 July 1995, AT1–2.

15. Filipinos abroad reportedly protested the grim representation of post-EDSA conditions in Lino Brocka's *Orapronobis* (*Fight for Us*), especially a scene depicting cannibalism, which was excised from the film's American version. See "Pro and Contra *Orapronobis*," *Manila Chronicle*, 11 November 1989: 17.

16. In "Form in the Filipino Film," Emmanuel Reyes argues unconvincingly that Philippine films differ from Classical Hollywood Cinema because they "have thinner plots ... are weak on logic and motivation ... Their narrative structure is loose and prone to digressions. They are also very escapist in concerns." For him, Philippine film form is characterized by "a scene-oriented narrative, a tendency for overt representation, circumlocutory dialogue and a narrative that emphasizes the centrality of the star." See *Notes on Philippine Cinema* (Manila: De La Salle University Press, 1988). Suggestions that Philippine film aesthetics draws from native theatrical and literary traditions are legion. See, for example, Agustin Sotto's monograph *Pelikula: An Essay on the Philippine Film: 1897–1960* (Manila: Cultural Center of the Philippines, 1992) or Bienvenido Lumbera's "Flashbacks on Film and Theatre as Interlocked Forms," in *The Urian Anthology 1980–1989*, ed. Nicanor Tiongson (Manila: Antonio Tuviera, 2001), pp. 80–7.

17. The figures for the 1970s and 1980s are based on a report of films reviewed by censors, as quoted in an unpublished report by the Philippine Institute for Development Studies. See Leonardo R. Garcia, Jr. and Carmelita B. Masigan,

"An In-depth study on the Film Industry in the Philippines," 15; available from
http://serp-p.pids.gov.ph Internet. The figures from 2001 are from Clodualdo Del
Mundo, Jr.,"The Film Industry is Dead! Long Live Philippine Cinema!" in
Sanghaya 2002: Philippine Arts and Culture Yearbook, ed. Bienvenido Lumbera
(Manila: National Commission for Culture and the Arts, 2003), pp. 42–9.

CHAPTER 3 VIETNAM

1. This data is drawn from the French Embassy's fascinating study on Vietnamese
   cinema, "Action Audiovisuelle" (August 2002) [Ambassade de France en
   République Socialist du Vietnam].
2. Since the 1950s, Vietnamese studios have produced feature films, documentaries,
   and animated features. In the 1980s Vietnam produced around thirty feature-
   length 35mm films a year, and only ten, in the 1990s. In 1999, VND 10 billion
   was spent on ten Vietnamese productions. In 2000, the entire film budget was
   VND 9 billion ($715,000). In 2001, it increased to (VND 15 billion $1.8 million).
   Between 1998 and 2000, only around twenty-five films were shot. But films shot
   in video increased to 150 films in two years [statistics from "Action
   Audiovisuelle"].
3. See my "'La Trace lumière': Early Cinema and Colonial Propaganda in French
   Indochina," in *Le Cinématographe, nouvelle technologie du XXe siècle*, eds. André
   Gaudreault, Catherine Russell and Pierre Véronneau (Lausanne: Editions Payot,
   2004), pp. 329–39.
4. According to a 1998 a US Department of Commerce report, "The bulk of films
   imported – about 80 percent – come from Hong Kong. Vietnam last year imported
   about 120 productions from Hong Kong, most of which were mini-series produced by the ATV and TVB Television companies. FaFilm in 1998 closed an
   agreement with Media Asia Films, which has one of the largest catalogues in Hong
   Kong, including films featuring action stars Chow Yun-fat and Jackie Chan. Media
   Asia plans to supply largely 35 mm stock. FaFilm last year (legitimately) imported
   26 films, some of them American-made, through the Hong Kong-based distributor
   Golden Harvest. A smaller number of films are imported from Thailand, the
   Philippines, Malaysia, Germany and Singapore. Again, the bulk of these have been
   for video release" (US Department of Commerce).
5. *The Bangkok Post* of February 26, 2000 reported that "A young seller of roasted
   corn on Hong Bai road, for example, whose daily income never exceeds 7,000
   VND (19 bath) says she has never stepped inside a movie theater and probably
   never will because of the high price of a ticket." See Wanphen Sreshthaputra, "A
   Brand-New Day for the Vietnamese Film Industry."
      My friend and colleague Nora Taylor reports that in September 2004, the price
   of a ticket can vary widely: the most expensive is 25,000 Dongs or US$1.50. But
   it can cost as little as 10,000 Dongs. Moreover, she adds, the price changes not
   only from one theater to the other, but also within the same theater. Tickets can
   be more expensive for the seats in the middle of the screening room.
6. Dao Duy Phuc, a 2001 graduate of the Hanoi Cinematography College, and the
   director of such television series as *Dua Con* (*The Child*) and *Nghi He Ra Pho*
   (*Going on a Summer Holiday*), and touted as an "up-and-coming director" by the
   Vietnamese press, even claims that "Films that do not cater to the interests of
   young audiences become obstacles to the industry's progress." See the article titled
   "Young auteur sets box office jangling" in *VNS* [*Viet Nam News*] Tuesday, July 27,

2004, http://vietnamnews.vnagency.com.vn/2004–07/26/Stories/20.htm

7. See n. 5.
8. See article cited in n. 6.
9. For a discussion of *Three Seasons*, see my "Aestheticizing Urban Space: Modernity in Postcolonial Hanoi and Saigon." *L'Esprit Créateur* XLI (Fall 2001): 73–87.
10. See n. 6.
11. See Greg Lockhart's informative introduction of his edited book *The Light of the Capital* (Kuala Lumpur: Oxford University Press, 1996), "Introduction: First Person Narratives from the 1930s," p. 3.
12. Ibid., p. 3.

CHAPTER 4 THAILAND

1. Another complexity which needs to be noted at the outset is that there have been in effect two popular markets: an urban (Bangkok) and generally better educated, more middle- and upper-class market, and a provincial market. While the urban audiences overwhelmingly prefer Hollywood fare, which dominates in local Thai exhibition, quite a few of the more innovative new Thai films have made inroads into that market as well; these same Thai films do not have any draw in the upcountry market – but, on the other hand, Thai genre films have perennially performed well with audiences in the rural provinces. The contemporary Thai films discussed in this chapter fall into both of these (not mutually exclusive) filmmaking categories.
2. For more background on the history of Thai filmmaking prior to the mid-1990s, see Boonrak Boonyaketmala, "The Rise and Fall of the Film Industry in Thailand, 1897–1992," *East-West Film Journal* 6(2) (1992), esp. 71–90; Scot Barmé, "Early Thai Cinema and Filmmaking: 1897–1922," *Film History* 11(3) (1999): 308–18; Chalida Uabumgrungjit, "Cinema in Thailand before 1970," in *Film in South East Asia: Views from the Region*, ed. David Hanan (SEAPAVAA, Vietnam Film Institute, and ScreenSound Australia, 2001), pp. 90–105; and Anchalee Chaiworaporn, "Thailand: Endearing Afterglow," in *Being and Becoming: The Cinemas of Asia*, ed. Aruna Vasudev et al. (Delhi: Macmillan, 2002), pp. 441–61. Another English-language overview, featuring reproductions of numerous posters and other artifacts related to Thai cinema, is Dome Sukwong and Sawasdi Suwannapak, *A Century of Thai Cinema*, trans. and ed. D. Smyth (London: Thames & Hudson, 2001).
3. Production figures reported in *Starpics Magazine* 15 (January 2000): 72.
4. In keeping with Thai convention, subsequent references to individuals are by first (given) name, rather than second (family) name – hence, here, "Penek."
5. Whether or not editorial willingness to highlight such coverage can be seen as part of a global "infotainment" trend in the news media, the Bangkok papers have in recent years provided not only more and more reviews of Thai films and features about Thai directors and filmmaking trends, but also coverage of how Thai films have done on the international festival circuit as well as coverage of the increased film festival activity in Bangkok – and even reviews of DVDs of various Asian and Western film releases as they become available in Thailand.
6. Posters from numerous filmed versions of the Nak narrative can be found in Dome Sukwong and Sawasdi Suwannapak, 52–5.
7. Adam Knee, "Thailand Haunted: The Power of the Past in the Contemporary Thai Horror Film," in *Horror International*, ed. Steven Jay Schneider (Detroit: Wayne State University Press, forthcoming).

8. For a related discussion of these films, see Glen Lewis, "The Thai Movie Revival and Thai National Identity," *Continuum: Journal of Media & Cultural Studies* 17(1) (2003): 69–78.
9. See Chuck Stephens, "Tears of the Black Tiger," *Film Comment* 37(3) (2001): 16–17.
10. Following a reorganization, Film Bangkok's production work is now handled by Chalerm Thai Studio.
11. A case is also made for Nonzee's importance in Kong Rithdee, "Kong Rithdee on Cinematic Renewal in Thailand," *Film Comment* 38(5) (2002): 12–13.
12. On Penek, See Adam Knee, "Gendering the Thai Economic Crisis: The Films of Pen-ek Ratanaruang," *Asian Cinema* 14(2) (2003): 102–22; and Chuck Stephens, "Jewels in the Lotus," *Film Comment* 38(6) (2002): 36–41.
13. For more on the work of Apichatpong, see Chuck Stephens, "Jewels in the Lotus."
14. For further discussion of the direct-to-video phenomenon, see Kong Rithdee, "VCD Killed the Movie Star," *Bangkok Post*, 11 July 2003, "Realtime" section: 1+.

CHAPTER 5 SINGAPORE

1. See "Australia and the World: International Comparisons" on the Australia Film Commission website: http://www.afc.gov.au/GTP/acompadmitper.html
2. See the Singapore Film Commission website, http://www.sfc.org.sg/
3. More information on Singapore Film Commission funding programs is available at http://www.sfc.org.sg/funding/funding.shtm
4. For more information about Raintree see the following sites: http://raintree.mediacorpstudios.com/ http://www.mediacorpraintree.com/
5. More on the subject in: Hoo Hui Teng, "Film Censorship in Singapore", *Journal of the History Society 1992/1993*, National University of Singapore: 15–19.
6. Singapore became an independent republic on 9 August 1965.
7. This data was provided by the Films and Publications Department (FPD) to the authors upon request [Zaitun Ali, compiler: "Materials on Films and Publications Department," January 1999].
8. Kenneth Tan, in an interview with Jasmine Alimin and Angelia Seetoh, 7 September 1998. Special project *FMS Online: Film In Singapore*, Department of Film and Media Studies, Ngee Ann Polytechnic.
9. At the end of primary four, students are channeled into one of three streams based on their ability to learn English, Mother Tongue (Chinese, Malay or Tamil), and mathematics. Unlike those in EM1 (for students who do very well) and EM2 (for the majority), those in EM3 study these three subjects at a basic level and are not required to do science.
10. Interview with the authors, February 2003.
11. Jack Neo received the prestigious International Management Action Award (IMAA) "for his ability in managing artistes and partners to create box-office hits." (Lorna Tan, "Jack Neo, Manager Exemplary," *Straits Times*, 14 November 2002.)

CHAPTER 6 MALAYSIA

1. The statistical information in this paragraph is taken from the Filem Malaysia website, http://www.filemkita.com

2. Discussion of the independent sector lies outside of the concerns of this chapter. For further information about this movement's most regarded filmmaker, James Lee, see Nazir Keshvani, "The James Lee Story," *Cinemaya* 56/57 (2002): 13–15 and Khoo Gaik Cheng, "Contesting Diasporic Subjectivity: James Lee, Malaysian Independent Filmmaker," *Asian Cinema* 15(1) (2004): 169–86.

3. The politics of language is intimately connected to the politics of ethnicity in Malaysia. From the early 1970s to the mid-1990s, the Malay language was renamed *Bahasa Malaysia* to accentuate inclusivity, but it has now reverted to its original name, *Bahasa Melayu*. See van der Heide, *Malaysian Cinema, Asian Film: Border Crossings and National Cultures*, 92–3, 98–100.

4. A number of the films made in the 1950s and the 1960s do have English subtitles, due to the British colonial legacy and the multicultural/multilingual character of the film industry of that time.

5. The annual *Variety International Film Guide* and two Asian film journals, *Cinemaya* and *Asian Cinema*, do regularly mention Malaysian cinema.

6. The political and cultural forces that led to demise of one industry structure and the rise of another are discussed in van der Heide, 87–100, 145–50.

7. See Meor Shariman, "Box Office Battles," *Malay Mail*, 9 December 2003, posted on the National Film Development Corporation Malaysia (FINAS) website, http://www.finas.gov.my/media/media_battlebox.shtml

8. Laura Mulvey, "Visual Pleasure and Narrative Cinema," *Screen* 16(3) (1975): 6–18.

9. van der Heide, 225–6.

10. See the Filem Malaysia website entry on *Jogho*, http://www.filemkita.com/filem/j/jogho_01.html U-Wei continues to incorporate international material in his work; his 2004 film *Buai Laju-Laju* (Swing My Swing High, My Darling) is a reworking of the 1946 American film *The Postman Always Rings Twice*, http://www.filemkita.com/filem/b/buai_laju-laju_01.html

11. Fuziah Kartini Hassan Basri and Raja Ahmad Alauddin, "The Search for a Malaysian Cinema: Between U-Wei, Shuhaimi, Yusof and LPFM," *Asian Cinema* 7(2) (1995): 69.

12. These 1950s and 1960s Malaysian films were themselves influenced by Indian melodramas and Chinese films, especially the so-called "exploitation musicals." See van der Heide, p. 143.

13. Passive male protagonists also recur in the Indian cinema of the 1950s (e.g. Dilip Kumar in *Devdas*, 1955) and in Cantonese films of the same period (e.g. *Love in Penang*, 1954).

14. See the Filem Malaysia website entry on *Spinning Gasing*, http://www.filemkita.com/filem/s/spinning_gasing_01.html

15. See Ashok Soman, "Spinning Gasing," *Cinemaya* 50 (2000): 29.

16. van der Heide, 215–16.

17. Teck Tan studied at the Australian Film, Television and Radio School in the 1980s and made a number of short films in Australia, before returning to Malaysia in 1996. Especially interesting is his 1991 film, *My Tiger's Eyes*, which sardonically examines the relationship between a Chinese Australian family and its European Australian neighbors in the 1950s through the eyes of the former family's young son.

CHAPTER 7 INDONESIA

1. Many thanks to Wendy Sahanaya who has contributed to this chapter in many ways. All errors and flaws are, of course, entirely my responsibility.

2. Pusat Perfilman Haji Usmar Ismail was established as a film archive, library and film-training support in 1975. It is named after Usmar Ismail, the most prominent of Indonesia's post-independence film makers. The archive and library are located in the central district of Indonesia's capital Jakarta and are the best source of information for anyone wishing to study Indonesian cinema.

3. For a twentieth century history of Indonesia see M.C. Ricklefs, *A History of Modern Indonesia* (London: Macmillan, 1981), chapters 4, 5, and 6. For a detailed history since 1965 see Adam Schwarz *A Nation in Waiting* (NSW: Allen & Unwin, 1999).

4. The idea of 'national fiction' derives from Ben Anderson's seminal work *Imagined Communities* (London and New York: Verso, 1983), extended by textual theorists to look at the way any narrative fiction is constantly implicated in constructing and contesting the way any nation is pictured, imaged, imagined. See also Homi Bhabha (ed.), *Nation and Narration* (London and New York: Routledge, 1990).

5. Full text of Presidential Decree in O.G. Roeder, *The Smiling General: President Suharto of Indonesia*, (Jakarta: Guning Agung, 1969), pp. 217–18.

6. For a clarification of the terminology "encoding/decoding" see Stuart Hall, "Coding and Decoding in the Television Discourse," in Hall et al. (eds.), *Culture, Media, Language* (London: Hutchinson, 1980), pp. 197–208.

7. Aiko Kurasawa, "Propaganda Media on Java under the Japanese 1942–1945," *Indonesia* 44 (October 1987): 59–116.

8. See Krishna Sen, "Hidden from History: Aspects of Indonesian Cinema 1955–65," *Review of Indonesian and Malaysian Affairs*, 19(2) (1985): 1–50.

9. During the New Order in Indonesia, censorship of one sort or another affected all media, but in the case of print media or the radio, all texts did not have to be checked by censors before release. This is not unusual as in many countries film is singled out in this way for categorization or denial of release permit. But in Indonesia censorship of a film started even prior to the completion of the film; that is, the script and the rushes had to be cleared by government bodies before the film was completed and submitted to the Board of Censorship for final permission to release.

10. See Krishna Sen, *Indonesian Cinema: Framing the New Order* (London and New York: Zed Books, 1994), pp. 55–69.

11. See Badan Sensor Film, *Kriterium Penyensoran Film*, published by the Department of Information, Jakarta, 1978.

12. See Dewan Film, *Kode Etik Produksi Film Nasional*, published by the Department of Information, Government of Indonesia, 1980.

13. Sen, *Indonesian Cinema: Framing the New Order*, pp. 56–66.

14. Ricklefs, M.C., *History of Modern Indonesia*, pp. 111–13.

15. See Teguh Karya, "In Search of Ways and Means for Making the Film an Instrument of Expression," in K. Sen (ed.), *Histories and Stories: Cinema in New Order Indonesia* (Clayton: Centre of Southeast Asian Studies, Monash University, 1988), p. 7.

16. Anderson, *Imagined Communities*, p. 19.

17. Sen, *Indonesian Cinema: Framing the New Order*, chapter 2.

18. See Krishna Sen and David T. Hill, ed., *Media, Culture and Politics in Indonesia* (Melbourne: Oxford University Press, 2000), p. 4.

19. C.Q. van Heeren is working on the topic of alternative cinema in the post-Suharto period for her doctoral research, which will no doubt produce a vastly more

detailed and significant (and possibly very different) analysis of this period than I can possibly hope to achieve.

20. Sen, *Indonesian Cinema: Framing the New Order*, chapter 5.

21. For instance *Si Mamad* in 1973 [see K. Sen, *Indonesian Cinema: Framing the New Order*, pp. 109–12] and several of Garin Nugroho's films such as *Surat Untuk Bidadari* (*Letter for an Angel*) in 1996 [See Sen, 'What's "Oppositional" in Indonesian Cinema?' in A.R. Guneratne and N. Dissanayake (eds.), *Rethinking Third Cinema* (New York and London: Routledge, 2003), pp. 146–65)] and *Daun Diatas Bantal* (*A Leaf on the Pillow*) in 1997.

22. It is worth thinking here of Teshome Gabriel's foundational work on third-world cinema where he argues that Western Film theory is quite useless in analyzing third-cinema texts, as Western theory is geared to "find immanent meaning in works whose deeper meaning is concealed" whereas third-cinema films "do not try to hide their true meaning." See Gabriel, *Third Cinema in the Third World* (Ann Arbor: UMI Research Press, 1982), pp. 1–5. Clearly this does not take into account films made in the context of repressive regimes in the third world where these films can only be made if the textual "surface" conceals some of its possible "meanings."

23. Remy Sylado, *Ca Bau Kan: Hanya Sebuah Dosa* (Jakarta: Gramedia, 1999).

24. Betawi are the indigenous farming population of the area which became the Dutch colonial capital in Indonesia. The ethnic Betawi population was marginalized from the wealth and metropolitan culture of the colonial and later national capital. In the 1990s there was quite a lot of interest in recovering the stories of Betawi people in various forms of media texts, including some very popular television drama and comedy.

25. For a detailed account of the Chinese in Indonesia see Charles Coppel, *Indonesian Chinese in Crisis* (Kuala Lumpur: Oxford University Press, 1983).

26. See Saskia Weiringa, "Ibu or the Beast: Gender Interests in Two Indonesian Women's Organisations," *Feminist Review* 41 (1992): 98–113.

27. See Valerie Hull, *Women in Java's Rural Middle Class: Progress or Regress?*, (Jogjakarta: Population Institute Gajah Mada University, 1976) and Julie Suryakusuma "The State and Sexuality in New Order Indonesia," in *Fantasizing the Feminine in Indonesia*, ed. Laurie Sears (Durham NC: Duke University Press, 1996), pp. 92–119.

28. See for instance the film *Suci Sang Primadona* [*Purity/Suci, the Divine Primadonna*] directed by Arifin C. Noer, 1977 and *Rembulan Dan Matahari* [*The Moon and the Sun*] Slamet Raharjo, 1979, both discussed in K. Sen, "Repression and Resistance: Interpretations of the Feminine in Indonesian Cinema," in ed. *Culture and Society in New Order Indonesia*, Virginia Hooker (Kuala Lumpur: OUP, 1993), pp. 116–33.

29. K. Sen, *Indonesian Cinema: Framing the New Order*, pp. 159–61.

CHAPTER 8 SRI LANKA

1. John Hill, *Sex, Class and Realism: British Cinema 1958–1963* (London: British Film Institute, 1986).

2. For an example of classical realist film theory see Siegfried Kracauer, *Theory of Film: The Redemption of Physical Reality* (New York: Oxford University Press, 1968).

3. Wimal Dissanayake and Ashley Rathnavibhushana, *Profiling Sri Lankan Cinema* (Colombo: Asian Film Center, 2000).

4. See Marshall Berman, *All That Is Solid Melts Into The Air* (London: New Left Books, 1983).

5. See in particular Walter Benjamin, *Illuminations* (London: Verso, 1970); Kracauer, *Theory of Film*; and Georg Simmel et al., *Simmel on Culture: Selected Writings* (London and Thousand Oaks, CA.: Sage, 1997).

6. See Ashish Nandy, *The Secret Politics of Our Desires* (Delhi: Oxford University Press, 1998).

CHAPTER 9 BANGLADESH

1. See Jinat Zahan, "Star-Faces on Rickshaws," *Anandabhuban* 2(17) (16 January 1998): 15–18.

2. In Bangladesh the weekly holiday in the educational institutions and the state offices is only Friday, the holy day of Islamic tradition. See, "Film Broadcast on Saturdays: Attendance Decreases in Schools and Colleges," *Daily Janakantha* (31 July 1997): 4.

3. Alamgir Kabir, *Film in Bangladesh* (Dhaka: Bangla Academy, 1979), p. 92.

4. Someswar Bhowmik, *Indian Cinema: An Economic Report* (Calcutta: Papyrus, 1996), pp. 120–1.

5. Figures here are calculated from the table in Mirja T. Quader, *Film Industry of Bangladesh* (Dhaka: Bangla Academy, 1993), p. 211.

6. Calculated from the data presented in the annual reviews on the Bangladesh film industry published in various Bangladeshi magazines and newspapers of this period. See *Jai Jai Din* 20(12) (30 December 2003): 27, 19(12) (31 December 2002): 35, 14(13) (30 December 1997): 29 and 13(13) (31 December 1996): 39, *Weekly 2000* 4(33) (4 January 2002): 78, *Daily Banglabazar* (30 December 1999): 16 and *Anandabhuban* 3(16) (1 January 1999): 17.

7. See Manik Zaman, "Now We Are All Waiters in the Film World," *Jai Jai Din* 14(13) (30 December 1997): 29; Juton Chowdhury, "Bengali Cinema: Annual Review 2001," *Weekly 2000* 4(33) (4 January 2002): 78.

8. Calculated from the table in Erik Barnouw and S. Krishnaswamy, *Indian Film* (New York: Oxford University Press, 1980), pp. 294–5.

9. Alamgir Kabir "The Cinema in Bangladesh," *Sequence* 2(2) (Spring 1975): 17.

10. Bangladesh Bureau of Statistics (BBS), *Statistical Year Book 1984*, cited in Quader, p. 397.

11. Ibid.

12. Anupam Hayat, "The History of Bangladesh Cinema: The Trends," *6th International Dhaka Film Festival Bulletin* 1 (20 January 2000): 4.

13. "Financial Position and Benefits (of FDC)" on the Bangladesh Film Development Corporation website http://www.fdcbd.com/business_industry.html [link active when viewed in 2002].

14. See "On the Lame Condition of Bangla(deshi) Cinema," editorial, *Daily Ittefaq* (27 September 2000): 4.

15. For example, five cinemas in Dhaka were closed or transformed to shopping centers during 1999/2000. See "On the Lame Condition," 4.

16. Khalid Hasan (ed.), *National Media Survey 1998* (OMQ: Dhaka, 1999), p. 51.

17. Abu Abdullah et al., *Modernisation at Bay: Structure and Change in Bangladesh* (Dhaka: University Press, 1991), p. 136.

18. Paul Willemen, "The Third Cinema Question," *Framework* 34 (1987): 25. A version of this essay also appears in his co-edited book with Jim Pines, *Questions of*

Third Cinema (London: British Film Institute, 1989), pp. 1–29.

19. Quader, *Bangladesh Film Industry*, pp. 432 and 441.

20. These figures are from "Financial Position and Benefits (of FDC)" available (in 2002) from the Bangladesh Film Development Corporation website cited in n. 13. Please note that for transforming Taka, the local currency, into US $ I used the 2004 exchange rate, that is, US$1 = Taka 60.00.

21. The importance of a theater means mainly the level of urbanization and the density of population of the particular locality. See the following: Quader, *Bangladesh Film Industry*, pp. 412–13; Chinmoy Mutsuddi, *Social Commitment in Bangladesh Cinema* (Dhaka: Bangladesh Arts Academy, 1987), p. 179.

22. Such falsification happens mostly in collaboration with the revenue department officials who are regularly bribed by the theater-owners. During my field visit to some theaters in cities such as Dhaka and Faridpur and country such as Rajbari, Narayanganj, Madhukhali, and Savar in Bangladesh in 1997/98, the theater management seemed hesitant in quoting their actual capacity.

23. Quader, *Bangladesh Film Industry*, pp. 211 and 397.

24. "Filmmakers Afraid for VCR and TV," *Weekly Bichitra* 8(7) (29 June 1979): 74.

25. "Stop Illegal Film Exhibition through Video Channels," *Daily Ittefaq* (23 October 1997): 20.

26. Manik Khondokar, "We need *Operation Clean Heart* in Film Industry," *Jai Jai Din* 19(12) (31 December 2002): 37.

27. Quader, *Bangladesh Film Industry*, 396 and 401.

28. "Financial Position," from the official website of BFDC.

29. Mutsuddi, *Social Commitment in Bangladesh Cinema*, p. 126.

30. Imrul Shahed and Mahmuda Chowdhury, "Cinema 1993: The Year of Business Development," *Weekly Bichitra* 22(33) (7 January 1994): 141.

31. Imrul Shahed, "Cinema: Annual Review 1994," *Weekly Bichitra* 23(28) (2 December 1994): 60.

32. Anwar Al-Deen, "The Exhibitors of Dhaka Put 300 Film Prints on Hold," *Daily Ittefaq* (21 September 2000): 14. Al-Deen reveals that because these films flopped and the box-office could not even get the amount paid as advance to the producer, the theaters kept hold of the film print.

33. In late 2000, though five cinemas closed down, still there were forty-six cinemas in Dhaka. See 'On the Lame Condition,' 4.

34. Imrul Shahed and Mahmuda Chowdhury, "Cinema 1993," p. 141; Matin Rahman, "Film Production and Marketing" (Dhaka, unpublished typescript, 1995), p. 17.

35. It is revealed that there are around fifty incomplete or postponed feature films which started production in Bangladesh between 1973 and 1995. See Omar Faruk, "Half-a-century Film Postponed in FDC," *Daily Manavjamin* (22 November 2001): 12.

36. Numerous names of actors and directors engaged in multi-tasking can be forwarded here. However, two examples will suffice. Dipjol, an actor renowned for villain roles in action films acted in 24 films in 2000. See Juton Chowdury, "Cinema: Still the Old Stars," *Anandadhara* 3(60) (January 2001): 19. Delwar Jahan Jhantu, a well-known film director of Bangladesh, directed 50 films alongside writing 150 film scripts and 700 film songs in 19 years of his career. See Ahmed Azad, "One Jhantu: 50 Films in 19 Years," *Fortnightly Tarakalok* (15 November 1998): 14.

37. The wedding ceremony is seen as a major life-event in middle-class families in Bangladesh as in the whole of South Asia. Such ceremonies have been depicted in numerous South Asian (including Bollywood) films in the last few decades. More

importantly, among the Bangladeshi middle classes, the ability to offer a huge ceremony on a daughter's marriage is seen as essential on the part of the bride's father.

CHAPTER 11 MAINLAND CHINA

1. See Dai Jinhua. "Invisible Writing: The Politics of Chinese Mass Culture in the 1990s," in *Cinema and Desire: Feminist Marxism and Cultural Politics in the Work of Dai Jinhua*, ed. J. Wang and T.E. Barlow (London: Verso, 2002), p. 43.
2. Chinese cinema was said to be experiencing an "economic crisis" as early as the late 1980s, and film studios fully entered the market economy in the early 1990s. See Chris Berry, "Market Forces: China's 'Fifth Generation' Faces the Bottom Line," Continuum 2(1) (1988/89), pp. 106–27.
3. Though *hesuipian* are a new development on the Mainland, Hong Kong and Taiwan distributors have long viewed the season as the optimal time for the release of local blockbusters. See the following scholarly discussions of the genre: Shuyu Kong's *"Big Shot From Beijing"* (see this volume, ch. 1 n. 53); Xu Ying and Xu Zhongquan, "A 'New' Phenomenon of Chinese Cinema: Happy-New-Year Comic Movie," *Asian Cinema* (Spring/Summer 2002): 112–27; and Yingjin Zhang's discussion of new year's films in *Screening China: Critical Interventions, Cinematic Reconfigurations, and the Transnational Imaginary in Contemporary Chinese Cinema* (Ann Arbor: University of Michigan Press, 2002), pp. 317–20. (Interestingly, none of these articles mentions the longer history of scheduling big-budget Hong Kong and Taiwan entertainment films, and specifically comedies, for release during the Chinese Lunar New Year.)
4. By the late 1990s, directors and producers might own and/or have working relationships with several private production companies. Feng Xiaogang, for example, has co-founded several private production companies: Seahorse Film and TV Production Company, Feng Xiaogang Film Studio, and Forbidden City Films.
5. At least initially, the use of Beijing humor and Beijing-accented speech meant that Feng's *hesuipian* were not as popular in Shanghai or other southern cities. See Xu Ying and Xu Zhongquan's "A 'New' Phenomenon of Chinese Cinema": 117.
6. See Shuyu Kong, *"Big Shot From Beijing,"* 179–80.
7. Kong, *"Big Shot,"* p. 180.
8. Xu Ying, "Impact of Globalization on the Cinema in China," *Asian Cinema* (Spring/Summer 2002): 41. Imar is also discussed at some length in Yingjin Zhang's *Screening China*, pp. 325–7.
9. In 2001, Imar Films was re-formed into the more transnational Ming Productions, which has offices in Los Angeles as well as Beijing.
10. There is another, unrealized, documentary aspect of *Shower*. Unlike Zhang Yuan's *Mama*, *Shower* casts a non-disabled actor in a disabled role. However, the director originally intended to cast a disabled man in the role. Zhang and the actor Jiang Wu, who was campaigning for the role, visited many institutions searching for someone to cast in the role and doing research on the developmentally disabled. See Augusta Palmer, "After *Spicy Love Soup*, Zhang Takes a *Shower*: An Interview with Zhang Yang and Peter Loehr," in the online publication, *indiewire*: http://www.indiewire.com/people/int_Zhang_Loehr_000707.html
11. The anthology *Zhongguo dianying meixue: 1999 (Aesthetics of Chinese film: 1999)*, edited by Xu Ke et al., which contains six essays and one interview about *Shower*, most of which debate the film's realism or lack thereof.
12. "Urban generation" is a term coined by Zhang Zhen and Jia Zhijie due to their dis-

satisfaction with terms such as "Sixth Generation" or "underground cinema." The group this term includes are directors who emerged in the 1990s but cannot be confined to the strict definition of "Sixth Generation" because some, like Ning Ying, belonged officially to the Fifth Generation, while others, like Zhang Yang, do not fit into any "generation" because they are not graduates of the Beijing Film Academy. See Zhang Zhen, "Building on the Ruins: The Exploration of New Urban Cinema of the 1990s," in *Reinterpretation: A Decade of Experimental Chinese Art: 1990–2000*, ed. Wu Hung et al. (Guangzhou: Guangdong Museum of Art, 2002), p. 119, note 1.

13. Zhang Zhen, "Building on the Ruins," p. 113.

14. Some commercial films, notably *Shower*, were successful both at international film festivals and in the domestic marketplace. *Hesuipian*, on the whole, have remained a local product.

15. See Zhang Huaxun and Zhang Yang, "Zhang Yang and His Father Talk About Their Generations," *Time Asia* 156(16) (October 23, 2000). The trope of changes in human emotions and generational divide are further expressed in this pair of statements written by Zhang and his father (Zhang Huaxun), who pioneered the return of martial arts films to the Mainland in the 1970s. The article is available at the following link on the website of "Asian Film Connections" (an inter-institutional initiative for the promotion of Asian cinema). http://www.asianfilms.org/china/zhangyang/fuzi.html

16. Interview with the author, March 2000.

17. Xu Fan, star of several Feng Xiaogang films (as well as Feng's wife) had been an established star for some time.

18. Taking wedding photos is now a ritualized part of weddings in many cultures. In urban China, the process can be quite elaborate as well as quite expensive. Day-long wedding photo sessions often require multiple costume changes, including at minimum a Western-style wedding dress and a Chinese *qipao*, and shifts of backdrop ranging from seasonal changes to a variety of images of European capitals. One essay which includes accounts of 1990s wedding fashions for both Han and Hui brides is Maris Gillette's "What's in a Dress: Brides in the Hui Quarter of Xi'an," in *The Consumer Revolution in Urban China* ed. Deborah S. Davis, (Berkeley: University of California Press, 1999), pp. 80–106.

19. See Yingjin Zhang, *Screening China*, p. 326.

20. Interview with the author, May 2000.

21. Only a few years later, the practice of product placement had become so common that a Feng Xiaogang film produced with funding from the Sony-owned Columbia Pictures Asia, *Big Shot's Funeral* (*Da wan'r*, 2002), satirized the process by portraying a funeral in which ad space was sold even on the side of the coffin. Alongside its satirical take on advertising and product placement, the film featured ample genuine product placements of its own.

22. Two accounts of the reception of this installation can be found in the essay by Gao Minglu, "From Elite to Small Man: The Many Faces of a Transitional Avant-Garde in Mainland China," in his catalogue for the exhibition *Inside Out: New Chinese Art* (Berkeley: University of California Press, 1998), p. 164; and in Wu Hung's *Transience: Chinese Experimental Art at the End of the Twentieth Century* (Chicago: David and Alfred Smart Museum of Art, University of Chicago, 1999), p. 159.

23. Chen Maiping, "On the Absence of the Self: From Modernism to Postmodernism," in *Inside Out: Modernism and Postmodernism in Chinese Literary Culture*, ed. Wendy Larson and Anne Wedell-Wedellsborg (Aarhus C., Denmark: Aarhus University Press, 1993), pp. 78–90.

24. Dai Jinhua, "Invisible Writing," p. 55.

CHAPTER 12 TAIWAN

1. These awards include best foreign film, Los Angeles Film Critics Association Awards; best film, National Society of Film Critics Awards; best foreign-language film, New York Film Critics Circle Awards. *Yi yi* also tied with *Once Upon a Time in America* (1983) at the number ten spot in *Sight and Sound*'s 2000 "greatest films of the past 25 years.

2. In 2000, *Crouching Tiger* grossed New Taiwan $101 million in Taiwan (US$3.3 million). Its box office leads the second-highest-grossing film, an animated puppet epic *Legend of the Sacred Stone* (41 million); and the third highest in Taiwan, a gay period picture *Fleeing by Night* (5 million). Source: *Cinema in the Republic of China 2001 Yearbook* (Taipei: ROC Film Development Foundation, 2001), p. 117.

3. These prime-time television programs have a special name, "trendy drama." See Darrell William Davis and Emilie Yueh-yu Yeh, "VCD as Programmatic Technology: Japanese Television Drama in Hong Kong" in *Feeling Asian Modernities*, ed. Koichi Iwabuchi (Hong Kong: Hong Kong University Press, 2004), pp. 227–47.

4. See *Cinema in the Republic of China 1997 Yearbook* (Taipei: ROC Film Development Foundation, 1997), p. 38.

5. It is worth noting here that *CTHD* was not distributed by Columbia but by Buena Vista, Disney's distribution company in Taipei.

6. Chia-chi Wu provides a useful summary of both cultural and critical reception of *CTHD* in Los Angles and Taiwan. See her "*Crouching Tiger Hidden Dragon* is not a Chinese Film," *Spectator: USC Journal of Film and Television Criticism* 22(1) (Spring 2002): 67–79. See also Ken-fang Lee's "Far Away, So Close: Cultural Translation in Ang Lee's *Crouching Tiger, Hidden Dragon*," *Inter-Asia Cultural Studies* 4(2) (2003): 281–95. Ang Lee's Chinese autobiography also discusses cultural political debates spawned by the international success of *CTHD*. See Zhang Jingpei and Ang Lee, *My Ten-year Dream as a Filmmaker* [*Zhinian yi jao dianying meng*] (Taipei: China Times, 2003), pp. 432–4.

7. The sources here are as follows: *Cinema in the Republic of China 2003 Yearbook* (Taipei: ROC Film Development Foundation, 2003), p. 56. *Cinema in the Republic of China 2002 Yearbook* (Taipei: ROC Film Development Foundation, 2002), p. 47. *Cinema in the Republic of China 2001 Yearbook* (Taipei: ROC Film Development Foundation, 2001), p. 111; *Cinema in the Republic of China 2000 Yearbook* (Taipei: ROC Film Development Foundation, 2000), pp. 64–8; *Cinema in the Republic of China 1999 Yearbook* (Taipei: ROC Film Development Foundation, 1999), pp. 65–84; *Cinema in the Republic of China 1998 Yearbook* (Taipei: ROC Film Development Foundation, 1998), pp. 86–100; *Cinema in the Republic of China 1997 Yearbook* (Taipei: ROC Film Development Foundation, 1997), pp. 35–40; and *Cinema in the Republic of China 1996 Yearbook* (Taipei: ROC Film Development Foundation, 1996), pp. 69–75.

8. *Cinema in the Republic of China 2002 Yearbook*, p. 38.

9. Ibid.

10. For a concise historical review of Taiwan's political development, see Perry Anderson's "Stand-Off in Taiwan," *London Review of Books* 26(11) (3 June 2004). See also John F. Copper, *Taiwan: Nation-State or Province?* 4th edn (Boulder, CO: Westview, 2003).

11. See Emilie Yeh and Darrell William Davis, "Challenges and Controversies of Taiwan New Cinema," *Taiwan Film Directors: A Treasure Island* (New York: Columbia University Press, 2005).

12. Xiao Ye, The Symposium on the 20th Anniversary of Taiwan New Cinema. Taipei Golden Horse Film Festival, Westin Hotel, Taipei, October 18, 2002.
13. Lu Feiyi, *Taiwan Cinema: Politics, Economy and Aesthetics (Taiwan dianying: zhengzhi, jingji, meixue)* (Taipei: Yuan-liou, 1998), table 11a.
14. Ibid.
15. Liang Liang, *A Complete Record of Films Shown in the Republic of China* (1949–1982), Vol. 1 (Taipei: National Film Library, 1984): 62–163.
16. Lu, *Taiwan Cinema*, p. 56.
17. Huang Ren, "The Rise and Influence of Healthy Realist Pictures," *Film Appreciation* 12(6) (November/December, 1994): 29–30.
18. Lu, *Taiwan Cinema*, p. 80.
19. Yeh and Davis, "Parallel Cinemas: Postwar History and Major Directors," in *Taiwan Film Directors*.
20. Liang, *Complete Record*, pp. 62–102.
21. Huang Ren, "The rise and influence of healthy realist pictures," p. 35.
22. Yeh Yueh-yu, "Taiwan: the Transnational Battlefield of Cathay and Shaw Brothers," in *The Cathay Story* ed. Wong Ain-ling and Sam Ho (Hong Kong: Hong Kong Film Archive, 2002), pp. 142–9.
23. Jiao Xiongping (Peggy Chiao), *Grand Pictures: The Five Years that Changed History (Guolian dianying: gaibian lishi de wunian)* (Taipei: Variety, 1994).
24. Huang Zhuohan, *My Life in Film Production: A Memoir by Huang Zhuohan (Dianying rensheng: huang zhuohan weiyi lu)* (Taipei: Variety, 1994), p. 188.
25. *Cinema in the Republic of China 1980 Yearbook*, p. 22.
26. Huang Zhuohan, p. 187.
27. Huang Ren, *Film and Political Propaganda (Dianying yu zhengzhi xuanchuan)* (Taipei: Variety, 1994), pp. 57–366.
28. See Yeh and Davis, *Taiwan Film Directors*.
29. Interview with Wan Ren, Taipei, October 2002.
30. Interview with Zhang Fengmei, Executive Assistant, Nan Fan Film Productions, May 2003.
31. *Cinema in the Republic of China 2002 Yearbook*, p. 38. Different sources have indicated *Double Vision* grossed NT80 million in Taiwan. See next note.
32. Liang Liang, "*Double Vision* Creating Taiwan Box Office Miracle: Interview with Chen Kuo-fu," *City Entertainment* 616 (21 November 2002): 48–9.

CHAPTER 13 HONG KONG

1. *Danwei: Media and Advertising in China*, "One Country, Two Versions" (February 3, 2005) www.danwei.org/archives/001293.html
2. See Ackbar Abbas, *Hong Kong: Culture and the Politics of Disappearance* (Minneapolis: University of Minnesota Press, 1997).
3. Ibid., p. 2.
4. Ibid., pp. 142–5.
5. I analyze John Woo's Hong Kong gangster films in "Transnational Action: John Woo, Hong Kong, Hollywood," in *Transnational Chinese Cinemas*, ed. Sheldon Lu (Honolulu: University of Hawaii Press, 1997), 221–37.
6. For an extended discussion of Woo's catalytic film and the genre, see Karen Fang's monograph on the film *A Better Tomorrow* (Hong Kong University Press, 2002). Fang discusses how Woo's film, its sequels, and imitations by other directors became known by a genre term that drew directly from the Cantonese title of *A*

Better Tomorrow. For analysis of the discursive creation of the genre and the Hong Kong reception of the film, see her pp. 50–63.

7. Stephen Teo, *Hong Kong Cinema: The Extra Dimensions* (London: British Film Institute, 1999), p. 175. Teo's work has been ground-breaking for English-language scholarship on Hong Kong cinema, For further discussion of action films see chapter 11, "The New Wave's Action Auteurs" in his book. See also Bey Logan, *Hong Kong Action Cinema* (London: Titan Books, 1997), chapter 7 ("Heroic Bloodshed: the Ballistic Ballet of John Woo), pp. 115–39.

8. See Fang's discussion of the influence of the French film (and others) in her monograph (see n. 6 above), Chapter 2, pp. 7–35.

9. In his *Planet Hong Kong*, (see this volume Chapter 1 n. 9) David Bordwell describes the cultural background and genealogy of contemporary Hong Kong "hero" films in his Chapter 2, pp. 26–48.

10. This phrase has been widely used in Western journalistic media and fan discussion of Hong Kong cinema. See for example, Fredric Dannen and Barry Long's *Hong Kong: An Insider's Guide to the Hollywood of the East* (New York: Hyperion/Miramax, 1997) and Stefan Hammond's *Hollywood East: Hong Kong Movies and the People Who Make Them* (Chicago: Contemporary Books, 2000). The latter also includes an endorsement by Hong Kong superstar Michelle Yeoh. (Asian film-star endorsements also appear in more scholarly studies, such as Rachel Dwyer's about contemporary Indian popular culture—including Hindi cinema—*All You Want is Money, All You Need is Love: Sex and Romance in Modern India* (London and New York: Cassell, 2000) with a forward by Bollywood star Amitabh Bachchan.)

11. See Yingchu Chu, *Hong Kong Cinema: Coloniser, Motherland and Self* (London/New York: Routledge, 2003) on the development of Hong Kong cinema as "part of Chinese national cinema (1913–56)" and as "Chinese diasporic cinema (1956–79)." See also Poshek Fu's historical analysis of the intersections between mainland and Hong Kong in *Between Shanghai and Hong Kong: The Politics of Chinese Cinemas* (Palo Alto: Stanford University Press, 2003).

12. For information on Hong Kong cinema's dwindling market share see Simon Jones, "The Hong Kong Film Industry," www.kamera.co.uk/features/the_hong_kong_film_industry.php See also Stephen Teo, "Post '97 Hong Kong Cinema: Crisis and Its After Effects," published on the Council on Foreign Relations website www.cfr.org/pdf/correspondence/xTeo.php Information on Hong Kong film industry and economic trends (sites, screens, and box-office earnings) are also available at www.screendigest.com and from the Hong Kong Trade Development Council www.tdctrade.com

13. See Tony Rayns' article "Deep Cover" in *Sight and Sound* 14(1) (January 2004): 26–9.

14. See Charles Leary, "*Infernal Affairs*: High Concept in Hong Kong," in *Senses of Cinema*, where the author applies to Hong Kong cinema the concept of the blockbuster developed in Justin Wyatt's book, *High Concept: Movies and Marketing in Hollywood* (University of Texas Press, 1994), http://www.sensesofcinema.com/contents/03/26/internal_affairs.html

15. See Applause Pictures' website, www.applausepictures.com

16. See Desser's analysis, "The Kung Fu Craze: Hong Kong Cinema's First American Reception," in the book he co-edited with Poshek Fu, *The Cinema of Hong Kong: History, Arts, Identity* (Cambridge: Cambridge University Press, 2000), pp. 32–3.

17. Desser addresses this phenomenon in his essay "The Kung Fu Craze." See also Gina Marchetti's "Jackie Chan and the Black Connection," in *Keyframes: Popular Cinema and Cultural Studies*, ed. Matthew Tinkum and Amy Villarejo (London and New York: Routledge, 2001), pp. 137–58.

18. See Law Kar's essay, "Chung Chang-wha: Can Direct, Will Travel" and other interesting articles and interviews in the dossier "Chung Chang-Wha: Man of Action!" prepared for the 8th Pusan International Film Festival, www.asian-films.org/korea

19. See Teo's chapter, "Bruce Lee: Narcissus and the Little Dragon" in *Hong Kong Cinema: The Extra Dimensions* (see n. 7 above), where he analyzes aspects of cultural nationalism in Bruce Lee's persona and performances, pp. 110–21.

20. Desser (see n. 16 above) discusses how the Hong Kong kung fu fad began to shift into an appropriative phase. See "The Kung Fu Craze," pp. 35–6. For an overview of Hong Kong martial arts films see "A Brief Historical Tour of the Hong Kong Martial Arts Film" by Sei Kei et al. in *Bright Lights Film Journal*, www.bright-lightsfilm.com/31/hk_brief1.html

21. See Abbas, *Hong Kong: Culture and the Politics of Disappearance*, 30–1.

22. See the report on the seminar "Time and Tide: Changes in Hong Kong Cinema of the 1970s" in issue 30 of the Newsletter (November 2004) on the Hong Kong Film Archive website www.lcsd.gov.hk/CE/CulturalService/HKFA

23. I am referring here to the trope used by Steve Fore in his article "Jackie Chan and the Cultural Politics of Global Entertainment," in *Transnational Chinese Cinemas* (Honolulu: University of Hawaii Press, 1997), pp. 239–62. See also Fore's essay "Life Imitates Entertainment: Home and Dislocation in the Films of Jackie Chan," in *At Full Speed: Hong Kong Cinema in a Borderless World*, ed. Esther C.M. Lau (Minneapolis: University of Minnesota Press, 2001).

24. For more on Cantonese comedy, see Jenny Lau, "Besides Fists and Blood: Michael Hui and Cantonese Comedy," in Fu and Desser (eds.), *The Cinema of Hong Kong* (see n. 16 above), pp. 158–75.

25. See Andrew Grossman, "The Belated Auteurism of Johnny To," in *Senses of Cinema*, www.sensesofcinema.com/contents/01/12/to.html

26. See Darcy Paquet's 2003 Pusan International Film Festival Report at his website http://koreanfilm.org/piff03.html

27. See Esther Yau's introduction to her book *At Full Speed: Hong Kong Cinema in a Borderless World* (Minneapolis: University of Minnesota Press, 2001), in particular her key points about the local and the global in Hong Kong cinema, p. 5.

28. See Abbas, *Hong Kong: Culture and the Politics of Disappearance*, p. 40.

29. In his *Hong Kong Cinema: The Extra Dimensions* (see n. 7 above), Teo offers a particularly informative archaeology of the myths and images of Hong Kong ghost movies and the ways they are in dialogue with Hollywood and international horror films, but also with cultural themes such as reincarnation and anxious allegorical issues of the impending apocalyptic "China Syndrome" of 1997.

30. For another eloquent perspective on nostalgia in Hong Kong film and culture focusing on the film *Rouge*, see Rey Chow's essay "A Souvenir of Love," in Yau, *At Full Speed*, pp. 209–29.

31. These perspectives on the Closer Economic Partnership Agreement (CEPA) are culled from reports in international film industry trade papers over the past year.

32. This information is reported by Chau Nguyen in "Box Office Abroad 2003," on the UCLA Asian Institute website http://www.asiaarts.ucla.edu. See the article at http://www.International.ucla.edu/articleasp?parentid=9956.

33. See Li Cheuk-to's remarks in "Journal: Hong Kong," in *Film Comment* 40(5) (September/October 2004): 10–12.

34. The remake-in-progress is *The Departed* to be directed by Martin Scorcese and made for Warner Brothers by Plan B (Brad Pitt's production company), starring Leonardo diCaprio and Matt Damon.

35. Chow, "A Souvenir of Love," p. 211.

CHAPTER 14 SOUTH KOREA

1. Research for this chapter was supported by Korea Foundation.
2. Korean Motion Picture Promotion Corporation (ed.), *Korean Film Year Book* (Seoul: Dongmyeong, 1997).
3. Eungjun Min et al., *Korean Film: History, Resistance, and Democratic Imagination* (Westport CT: Praeger, 2003), p. 181; Sang-min Shim, "Success Factors of the Korean Film Industry," *Korean Herald* (5 October 2001).
4. Hee-seong Park, "Current Status of Korean Film Exports to Overseas' Markets," *Korean Film Observatory* 11 (2004): 12, available at http://kn.koreaherald.co.kr/SITE/data/html_dir/2001/11/19/200111190038.asp.
5. Mee-hyun Kim and Hyun-chang Jung, "A Review of the 2003 Korean Film Industry," *Korean Film Observatory* 11 (2004): 4.
6. For further study on the state-led modernization process and social changes in Korea, see Hagen Koo, "The State, *Minjung*, and the Working Class in South Korea," in *State and Society in Contemporary Korea*, ed. Hagen Koo (Ithaca: Cornell University Press, 1993), pp. 51–94.
7. For further study on the changing identity politics of Korean national cinema, see Hyangjin Lee, *Contemporary Korean Cinema: Identity, Culture and Politics* (Manchester: Manchester University Press, 2000).
8. Kyeong-ok Kim, *Blockbuster-ui hwansang, Hanguk Yeonghwa-ui Narcissism* (*Fantasy of Blockbuster, Narcissism of Korean Film*) (Seoul: Chaeksesang, 2002), pp. 13–21.
9. Yong-shik Choe, "Cinema Reborn," *Korea Now* (9 March 2002): 40.
10. Anthony C.Y. Leong, *Korean Cinema: The New Hong Kong* (Victoria: Trafford, 2003), pp. 1–2.
11. Mark Russell and George Wehrfritz, "Blockbuster Nation," *Newsweek*, international edn (3 May 2004), available at http://www.msnbc.msn.com/id/4825402/
12. Joongi Kim, "The Viability of Screen Quota in Korea: The Cultural Exception under the International Trade Regime," *Korean Journal of International and Comparative Law* 26 (1998): 215.
13. Jang Jip Choi, "Political Cleavages in South Korea," in *State and Society in Contemporary Korea*, ed. Hagen Koo (Ithaca, NY: Cornell University Press, 1993), pp. 13–50.
14. For details, see Young-il Lee and Young-chol Cheo, *The History of Korean Cinema: Main Current of Korean Cinema*, trans. by Richard Lynn Greever (Seoul: Motion Picture Promotion Corporation/Jimoondang International, 1998), pp. 143–8.
15. Kim and Jung, "Review," 2.
16. See Rob Wilson, "Melodrama of Korean National Identity: From *Mandala* to *Black Republic*," in *Colonialism and Nationalism in Asian Cinema*, ed. Wimal Dissanayake (Bloomington: Indiana University Press, 1994), p. 91; Tony Rains, *Seoul Stirring: 5 Korean Directors* (London: Institute of Contemporary Art, 1994), p. 7.
17. David E. James, "Im Kwon-Taek: Korean National Cinema and Buddhism," in *Im Kwon-Taek: The Making of a Korean National Cinema*, ed. David E. James and Kyung Hyun Kim (Detroit: Wayne State University Press, 2002), p. 69.
18. *Choson Ilbo*, "Recognition at Cannes," translated by and reprinted in *Korea Now* (1 June 2002): 50.
19. Interview, "Im Kwon-taek and Hwang Sok-yeong, Sesang-eul Malhada" (Im Kwon-taek and Hwang Sok-kyong Talk about the World), *Choson Ilbo* (16 August 2004): A5.
20. Said, *Orientalism*, see "Introduction" of present volume, n. 3.

21. "Interview, Best Director Reveals All: Crafting the Most Believable Fantasy Ever", *Korea Now* (September 21, 2002): 41.
22. Isolde Standish, "Korean Cinema and the New Realism: Text and Context," *Colonialism and Nationalism in Asian Cinema*, ed. Wimal Dissanayake (Bloomington: Indiana University Press, 1994), pp. 65–89.
23. Anderson, *Imagined Communities*, p. 17 (see this volume Chapter 1, n. 19).
24. See Homi K. Bhabha, *The Location of Culture* (London: Routledge, 1994), p. 9. He explains that 'unhomeliness' is the estranging sense of the relocation of home and the world ... that is the condition of extra-territorial and cross-cultural initiations."
25. See G.C. Spivak, "Can the Subaltern Speak?," in *Colonial Discourse and Post-Colonial Theory*, eds. Patrick Williams and Laura Chrisman (Hemel Hempstead: Harvester Wheatsheaf, 1993), p. 83. She addresses the problem of representation and unrepresentatibility of the subaltern's voice.
26. For further discussion of these two key films see Lee, *Contemporary Korean Cinema* (see n. 7 above), pp. 118–25; Nancy Abelman, *The Melodrama of Mobility: Women, Talk, and Class in Contemporary South Korea* (Honolulu: University of Hawaii, 2003), pp. 193–201.

CHAPTER 15 JAPAN

1. See Mark Schilling, *Contemporary Japanese Film* (New York: Weatherhill, 1999), p. 15.
2. The source of this data is *Uni Japan* Vol. 28 (Tokyo: Association for the Diffusion of Japanese Film Abroad, 2001): 64.
3. Further reading on Japanese film genres should include: Mark Schilling, cited above; Donald Richie's article "Japanese Film" in P. Duus et al. *Cambridge History of Japan*, Vol. 6, *The Twentieth Century* (New York: Cambridge University Press, 1989) and Alain Silver, *The Samurai Film*, expanded and rev. edn (New York: Overlook Press, 2004). For more specialized studies on Kurosawa, see M. Yoshimoto, *Kurosawa: Film Studies and Japanese Cinema* (Durham NC: Duke University Press, 2000) and S. Prince, *Kurosawa: The Warrior's Camera*, rev. and expanded edn (Princeton: Princeton University Press, 1999); on Ozu, D. Bordwell, *Ozu and the Poetics of Cinema* (Princeton: Princeton University Press/British Film Institute, 1998); on the whole sweep of Japanese film from a semiotics-of-culture perspective, N. Burch, *To the Distant Observer: Form and Meaning in Japanese Cinema* (Berkeley: University of California Press, 1980); and on the period film, D.W. Davis, *Picturing Japaneseness: Monumental Style, National Identity, Japanese Film* (New York: Columbia University Press, 1996).
4. Mark Schilling, "Toho Lords it Over Japan," *Screen International* (April 25, 2003): 15.
5. Source: *Kinema Jumpo* (Film Record, Tokyo) annual yearbooks. Thanks to HC Li of Hong Kong Polytechnic for help with these figures.
6. All these figures come from Watanabe Takesato, "Japan: Status of the Media," in *International Media Communications*, Vol. 2 (Elsevier Science, 2003), pp. 649–50.
7. Uni Japan Vols 28, 29 (2001, 2002): 64.
8. Patrick Frater, "The Japanese Bruckheimer," *Screen International* (April 30, 2004): 9.
9. Schilling, *Contemporary Japanese Film*, p. 32.
10. Ibid.
11. For more on Kitano see my "Re-igniting Japanese Tradition with *Hana-Bi*," *Cinema Journal* 40(4) (Summer 2001): 55–80.

12. Donald Richie, *One Hundred Years of Japanese Cinema* (New York: Kodansha International, 2001), p. 215.

13. "Japanese Fantasy Plays with Afterlife," *Screen International* (April 18, 2003): 18.

14. Regarding *Versus*: "Far from Asian-looking [and] depressingly derivative of the Asian-influenced action aesthetic as recently assimilated by Hollywood [with] endless shots of prancing and preening yakuza in shades striking poses. *Versus* may be a technical tour-de-force, but you have a feeling its director may be better suited to a career in advertisements than feature fiction. *Versus* is just too silly to prove effective." Japanese film website www.Midnighteye.com Kitamura was given the helm to direct what Toho insists is the absolutely final installment of the Godzilla series.

15. "Return of the Japanese Film," *Pacific Friend* 29(11) (March 2002): 21.

16. Keiko Iwai McDonald, "The Yakuza Film, an Introduction," in *Reframing Japanese Cinema: Authorship, Genre, History*, ed. A. Nolletti (Bloomington: Indiana University Press, 1992), pp. 165–92.

17. Richie, *One Hundred Years*, p. 209.

18. Peter B. High, *The Imperial Screen* (Madison: University of Wisconsin Press, 2002), p. 427.

19. Interview with Muzushi Kunio (in Japanese). *Koukoku* review, special issue on Japanese cinema and interviews with seven filmmakers. *Koukoku-hihyo* No. 261 (June-July 2002): 125–33 (on Nakata; for Morita): 134–44.

20. Patrick Frater quoting Walter Parkes in "Remaking the Remake," *Screen International* (June 6, 2003): 9–10.

21. The number of television "doramas" is staggering, as seen in Jonathan Clement and Motoko Tamamuro's reference book *The Dorama Encyclopedia* (Berkeley CA: Stone Bridge Press, 2003, 448 pp. More than 1,000 entries). Again, this rather than cinema signals "pops'" true home.

22. *Mukokuseki*, literally no-citizenship, often translated "statelessness," arises in discussions of manga and anime because of the distinctly un-Japanese appearance of most characters. See Susan Napier, *Anime: from Akira to Princess Mononoke* (New York: Palgrave, 2000) and Antonia Levi, *Samurai from Outer Space: Understanding Japanese Animation* (Chicago: Open Court, 1996). Japanese animation is a huge field, necessitating its own methods and scholarly production.

23. Ota Toru, "Producing (Post-)Trendy Japanese TV Dramas," *Feeling Asian Modernities*, ed. Koichi Iwabuchi (Hong Kong University Press, 2004), p. 78. For more on Japanese trendy drama circulation, see in the same volume Darrell William Davis and Emilie Y.Y. Yeh, "VCD as Programmatic Technology: Japanese Television Drama in Hong Kong," pp. 227–47.

24. See Thomas Weisser and Yuko Miharra Weisser, *Japanese Cinema Essential Handbook*, rev. and updated, 4th ed. (Miami: Vital Books, 1998), p. 199.

25. Richie, *One Hundred Years*, p. 221.

26. "Return of the Japanese Film," *Pacific Friend*: 19.

Bibliography

Abbas, A. and J.N. Erni (eds), *Internationalizing Cultural Studies: An Anthology*, Malden, MA: Blackwell, 2005.

Abbas, A., *Hong Kong: Culture and the Politics of Disappearance*, Minneapolis: University of Minnesota Press, 1997.

Abdullah, A., et al., *Modernisation at Bay: Structure and Change in Bangladesh*, Dhaka: University Press, 1991.

Abelmann, N., *The Melodrama of Mobility: Women, Talk, and Class in Contemporary South Korea*, Honolulu: University of Hawai'i, 2003.

—— and K. McHugh (eds.), *South Korean Golden Age Melodrama: Gender, Genre, and National Cinema*, Detroit: Wayne State University Press, 2005.

Ahmed, A. *In Theory: Classes, Nations, Literatures*, London: Verso, 1992.

Al-Deen, A. (??), 'The Exhibitors of Dhaka Put 300 Film Prints on Hold', *Daily Ittefaq*, 21 September, pp. 4–5.

Ambassade de France en République Socialiste du Vietnam, 'Action Audiovisuelle,' August 2002.

Anderson, B., *Imagined Communities: Reflections on the Origins and Spread of Nationalism*, London and New York: Verso, 1983.

Anderson, P., 'Stand-Off in Taiwan', *London Review of Books*, 26(11), 3 June 2004.

Appadurai, A., *Modernity at Large: Cultural Dimensions of Globalization*, Minneapolis: University of Minnesota Press, 1996.

Ashcroft, B., G. Griffiths, and H. Tiffin, *Key Concepts in Post-Colonial* Studies, London and New York: Routledge, 1998.

Australia Film Commission website, www.afc.gov.au

Azad, A., "One Jhantu: 50 Films in 19 Years," *Fortnightly Tarakalok*, 15 November 1998: 14–5.

Badan Sensor Film, *Kriterium Penyensoran Film*, Ministry of Information, Jakarta, 1978.

Bae, C.' "Seoul in Korean Cinema: A Brief Survey," *East-West Film Journal*, 3, December 1988: 97–104.

Bakhtin, M., "Discourse in the Novel," in M. Holquist (ed.) *The Dialogic Imagination: Four Essays by M.M. Bakhtin*, Austin: University of Texas Press, 1981: 259–422.

Bangladesh Bureau of Statistics (BBS), *Statistical Year Book 1984*, Dhaka: BBS, 1984.

Barmé, S, "Early Thai Cinema and Filmmaking: 1897–1922," *Film History* 11 (3), 1999: 308–18.

Barnouw, E. and S. Krishnaswamy, *Indian Film*, New York: Oxford University Press, 1980.

Barthes, R., "Leaving the Movie Theater," in *The Rustle of Language*, Berkeley and LosAngeles: University of California Press, 1986: 345–9.

Basri, F.K.H. and R.A. Alauddin, "The Search for a Malaysian Cinema: Between U-Wei, Shuhaimi, Yusof and LPFM," *Asian Cinema* 7:2, 1995: 58–73.

Baudry, J., "Ideological Effects of the Basic Cinematographic Apparatus," in P. Rosen (ed.), *Narrative, Apparatus, Ideology: A Film Theory Reader*, New York: Columbia University Press, 1986: 286–98.

Benjamin, W., *Illuminations*, London: Verso, 1970.

Berman, M., *All That Is Solid Melts Into The Air*, London: New Left Books, 1983.

Bernal, M., *Black Athena*, New Brunswick: Rutgers University Press, Vols. I and II.

Berry, C., "Market Forces: China's 'Fifth Generation' Faces the Bottom Line," *Continuum* 2(1) 1988–89: 106–27.

——, "Hu, Where and When: Locating 'Contemporary Film Theory in China'." [introduction to Hu Ke, "Contemporary Film Theory in China"] *Screening the Past*, 25 March 1998, http://www.latrobe.edu.au/www/screeningthepast/reruns/hkrrintro.html

——, "What's Big about the Big Film?: 'De-Westernizing' the Blockbuster in Korea and China," in J. Stringer (ed.), *Movie Blockbusters*, London: Routledge, 2003.

——, et al. (eds), *Mobile Cultures: New Media in Queer Asia*, Durham, NC: Duke University Press, 2003.

Bhabha, H., *Nation and Narration*, London and New York: Routledge, 1990.

—— *The Location of Culture*, London: Routledge, 1994.

Bhowmik, S., *Indian Cinema: An Economic Report*, Calcutta: Papyrus, 1996.

Boonrak B., "The Rise and Fall of the Film Industry in Thailand, 1897–1992," *East-West Film Journal* 6(2), 1992: 62–98.

Bordwell, D., *Ozu and the Poetics of Cinema*, Princeton: Princeton University Press/British Film Institute,1988.

—— *Planet Hong Kong: Popular Cinema and the Art of Entertainment*, Cambridge, MA: Harvard University Press, 2002.

—— and Kristen Thompson, *Film Art: An Introduction*, 7th edn, Boston: McGraw-Hill, 2004.

Bowyer, J. (ed.), *The Cinema of Japan and Korea*, London: Wallflower Press, 2004.

Braziel, J.E. and A. Mannur (eds.), *Theorizing Diaspora*, Malden, MA: Blackwell, 2003.

Breckenridge, C. (ed.), *Consuming Modernity: Public Culture in a South Asian World*, Minneapolis: University of Minnesota Press, 1995.

Burch, N., *To the Distant Observer: Form and Meaning in Japanese Cinema*, Berkeley: University of California Press, 1980.

Caughie, J., *Theories of Authorship: A Reader* (London and Boston: Kegan Paul/British Film Institute, 1981.

CCP Encyclopedia of Philippine Art, Vol. VIII.

Chaiworaporn, A., "Thailand: Endearing Afterglow," in A. Vasudev (ed.), *Being and Becoming: The Cinemas of Asia*, Delhi: Macmillan India, 2002: 441–61.

Cheah, P. "Can Singapore Build a Film Industry?" *Singapore Monitor*, 2 July 1984.

——, "Life in the Lion City," *Cinemaya* 17/18, Autumn/Winter 1992–93: 32–33.

——, "Singapore Rediscovered," 10th Singapore International Film Festival 1997 catalogue.

——, "Film in Singapore from 1972: The Reconstruction of a Film Industry," in D. Hannan (ed.), *South East Asia: Views from the Region*, Vietnam: SEAPAVAA and Vietnam Film Institute, 2001.

Chen, K., *Trajectories: Inter-Asia Cultural Studies*, London and New York: Routledge, 1998.

Chen, M., "On the Absence of Self: From Modernism to Postmodernism," in W. Larson and A. Wedell-Wedellsborg (eds.), *Inside Out: Modernism and Postmodernism in Chinese Literary Culture*, Aarhus C., Denmark: Aarhus University Press, 1993: 78–90.

Cheng, K.G., "Contesting Diasporic Subjectivity: James Lee, Malaysian Independent Filmmaker," *Asian Cinema* 15(1), 2004: 169–86.

Cho, F., "The Art of Presence: Buddhism and Korean Films," in S.B. Plate (ed.), *Representing Religion in World Cinema: Filmmaking, Mythmaking, Culture Making*, New York: Palgrave Macmillan, 2003, 107–19.

Cho, H. "Is the Screen Quota Really Relevant?," *Korea Focus*, 11(4), December 2003.

Choe, Y., "Cinema Reborn," *Korea Now*, 9 March 2002: 40.

Choi, J., "Political Cleavages in South Korea," in H. Koo (ed.), *State and Society in Contemporary Korea*, Ithaca, NY: Cornell University Press, 1993: 13–50.

Chow, R., *Primitive Passions: Visibility, Ethnography, and Contemporary Chinese Cinema*, New York: Columbia University Press, 1995.

——, "A Souvenir of Love," in E. Yau (ed.), *At Full Speed: Hong Kong Cinema in a Borderless World*, Minneapolis: University of Minnesota Press, 2001.

Chowdhury, J., "Cinema: Still the Old Stars," *Anandadhara* 3(60), January 2001: 18–19.

——, 'Bengali Cinema: Annual Review 2001," *Weekly 2000* 4(33), 4 January 2002: 77–9.

Chu, Y., *Hong Kong Cinema: Coloniser, Motherland and Self*, London and New York: Routledge, 2003.

Chung, H.S., "From Saviors to Rapists: G.I.s, Women, and Children in Korean War Films," *Asian Cinema* 12(1), 2001: 103–16.

Ciecko, A.T., "Transnational Action: John Woo, Hong Kong, Hollywood,' in S. Lu (ed.), *Transnational Chinese Cinemas*, Honolulu: University of Hawaii Press, 1997, pp. 221–37.

——, 'Representing the Spaces of Diaspora in Contemporary British Films by Women Directors," *Cinema Journal* 38(3), Spring 1999: 67–90.

——, 'Ways to Sink the *Titanic*: Contemporary Box-office Successes in the Philippines, Thailand, and South Korea,' *Tamkang Review* 3(2), Winter 2002: 1–29.

——, 'Muscles, Market Value, Telegenesis, Cyberpresence: The New Asian Movie Star in the Global Economy of Masculine Images,' in P. Petro and T. Oren (eds.), *Global Currents: Media and Technology Now*, New Brunswick, NJ: Rutgers University Press, 2004, pp. 186–99.

Cinema in the Republic of China 2003 Yearbook, Taipei: ROC Film Development Foundation, Years 1980, 1996–2003.

Clement, J. and M. Tamamuro, *The Dorama Encyclopedia*, Berkeley, CA: Stone Bridge Press, 2003.

Coppel, C., *Indonesian Chinese in Crisis*, Kuala Lumpur: Oxford University Press, 1983.

Copper, J.F., *Taiwan: Nation-State or Province?* 4th edn, Boulder, CO: Westview, 2003.

Crofts, S., "Concepts of National Cinema," in J. Hill and P.C. Gibson, *The Oxford Guide to Film Studies*, Oxford: Oxford University Press, 1998, pp. 385–94.

Cunningham, S. and J. Sinclair (eds.), *Floating Lives: The Media and Asian Diasporas*, St Lucia: University of Queensland Press, 2000.

Dai, J., *Cinema and Desire: Feminist Marxism and Cultural Politics in the Work of Dai Jinhua*, eds J. Wang and T.E. Barlow, London: Verso, 2002.

Dannen, F. and B. Long, *Hong Kong: An Insider's Guide to the Hollywood of the East*, New York: Hyperion/Miramax, 1997.

Davis, D.W., *Picturing Japaneseness: Monumental Style, National Identity, Japanese Film*, New York: Columbia University Press, 1996.

——, "Re-igniting Japanese Tradition with *Hana-Bi*," *Cinema Journal* 40(4), Summer 2001: 55–80.

—— and E.Y.Y. Yeh, "VCD as Programmatic Technology: Japanese Television Drama in Hong Kong," in K. Iwabuchi (ed.), *Feeling Asian Modernities: Transnational Consumption of Japanese TV Drama*, Hong Kong University Press, 2004, pp. 227–47.

Del Mundo, C., "The Film Industry is Dead! Long Live Philippine Cinema!" in B. Lumbera (ed.), *Sanghaya 2002: Philippine Arts and Culture Yearbook*, Manila: National Commission for Culture and the Arts, 2003, pp. 42–9.

Desser, D., "The Kung Fu Craze: Hong Kong Cinema's First American Reception," in D. Desser and P. Fu (eds.), *The Cinema of Hong Kong: History, Arts, Identity*, Cambridge: Cambridge University Press, 2000.

Dewan Film Nasional (National Film Committee), *Kode Etik Produksi Film Nasional,* Department of Information, Government of Indonesia, 1980.

Dissanayake, W. (ed.), *Melodrama and Asian Cinema,* Cambridge: Cambridge University Press, 1993.

——, "Issues in World Cinema," in J. Hill and P.C. Gibson, *The Oxford Guide to Film Studies,* Oxford: Oxford University Press, 1998, pp. 527–34.

——, and A. Rathnavibhushana, *Profiling Sri Lankan Cinema,* Colombo: Asian Film Center, 2000.

Ďurovičová, N., "Some Thoughts at an Intersection of the Popular and the National," *The Velvet Light Trap* 34, Fall 1994: 3–9.

Dwyer, R., *All You Want is Money, All You Need is Love: Sex and Romance in Modern India,* London and New York: Cassell, 2000.

Eisenstein, S., "The Cinematographic Principle and the Ideogram," in L. Braudy, M. Cohen, and G. Mast (eds.), *Film Theory and Criticism,* New York: Oxford University Press, 1992, pp. 127–38.

Elley, D., "12 Storeys," *Variety* 9–15, June 1997.

——, "Forever Fever," *Variety* 3–9, August 1998.

——, "Money No Enough," *Variety* 10–16, August 1998.

——, "CineAsia: Asia Accents Collaboration," *Variety* 6–18, December 2004.

Erni, J.N. and A. Abbas, "General Introduction," in J.N. Erni and A. Abbas (eds.), *Internationalizing Cultural Studies: An Anthology,* Malden, MA: Blackwell, 2005, pp.1–12.

Fang, K., *A Better Tomorrow,* Hong Kong: Hong Kong University Press, 2002.

Faruk, O., "Half-a-century Film Postponed in FDC," *Daily Manavjamin,* 22 November 2001, pp. 12–13.

Feng, P., *Identities in Motion: Asian American Film and Video,* Durham, NC: Duke University Press, 2002.

——, *Screening Asian Americans,* New Brunswick, NJ: Rutgers University Press, 2002.

Filem Malaysia website, http://www.filemkita.com

Filem Malaysia 1975–1999, Hulu Kelang: FINAS.

"Film Broadcast on Saturdays: Attendance Decreases in Schools and Colleges," *Daily Janakantha,* 31 July 1997, p. 4.

"Filmmakers Afraid for VCR and TV," *Weekly Bichitra* 8(7), 29 June 1979: 74–5.

Fish, S. *Is There a Text in this Class?: The Author of Interpretive Communities,* Cambridge, MA: Harvard University Press, 1980.

Fore, S., "Jackie Chan and the Cultural Politics of Global Entertainment," in S. Lu (ed.), *Transnational Chinese Cinemas,* Honolulu: University of Hawaii Press, 1997, pp. 239–62.

——, "Life Imitates Entertainment: Home and Dislocation in the Films of Jackie Chan," in E. Yau (ed.), *At Full Speed: Hong Kong Cinema in a Borderless World,* Minneapolis: University of Minnesota Press, 2001.

Foucault, M., " What is an Author?," in D. Bouchard (ed.), *Language, Counter-memory, Practice,* Ithaca: Cornell University Press, 1977, pp. 113–38.

——, "The Order of Discourse," trans. I. McLeod, in R. Young (ed.), *Untying the Text: A Post-Structuralist Reader,* Boston and London: Routledge, Kegan Paul, 1981. pp. 51–78.

Frater, P., "Remaking the Remake," *Screen International,* June 6, 2003: 9–10.

——, "The Japanese Bruckheimer," *Screen International,* April 30, 2004: 9.

Fu, P., *Between Shanghai and Hong Kong: The Politics of Chinese Cinemas,* Palo Alto, CA: Stanford University Press, 2003.

——, and D. Desser (eds.), *The Cinema of Hong Kong: History, Arts, Identity,* Cambridge: Cambridge University Press, 2000.

Gabriel, T.H., *Third Cinema in the Third World,* Ann Arbor, UMI Research Press, 1982.
——, "Towards a Critical Theory of Third World Films," in J. Pine and P. Willemen (eds.), *Questions of Third Cinema,* London: British Film Institute,1989.
Gao, M., "From Elite to Small Man: The Many Faces of A Transitional Avant-Garde in Mainland China," in G. Minglu (ed.), *Inside Out: New Chinese Art,* Berkeley: University of California Press, 1998.
Garcia, R., (ed.), *Out of the Shadows: Asians in American Cinema,* Locarno, Switzerland: Festival Internazionale del Film di Locarno, 2001.
Garcia, L.R. and C. Masigan, "An In-depth Study on the Film Industry in the Philippines," available from the Philippine Institute for Development Studies, SocioEconomic Research Portal for the Philippines, http://serp-p.pids.gov.ph./details.php3?tid=1284
Gateward, F., "Youth in Crisis: National and Cultural Identity in New South Korean Cinema," in Lau, J.K.W. (ed.), *Multiple Modernities: Cinemas and Popular Media in Transcultural East Asia,* Philadelphia, Temple University Press, 2003, pp. 114–27.
Gilette, M., "What's in a Dress: Brides in the Hui Quarter of Xi'an," in D.S. Davis (ed.), *The Consumer Revolution in Urban China,* Berkeley: University of California Press, 1999, pp. 80–106.
Gokulsing, K.M. and W. Dissanayake, *Indian Popular Cinema: A Narrative of Cultural Change,* 2nd edn, Stoke-on-Trent: Trentham Books, 2004.
Grossman, A., "The Belated Auteurism of Johnny To," *Senses of Cinema,* www.sensesofcinema.com/contents/01/12/to.html
Guneratne, A. and W. Dissanayake (eds.), *Rethinking Third Cinema,* London and New York: Routledge, 2003.
Habermas, J., *The Structural Transformation of the Public Sphere,* Cambridge, MA: MIT Press, 1991.
Hall, S., "Coding and Decoding in the Television Discourse," in Hall, et. al. (eds.), *Culture, Media, Language,* London, Hutchinson, 1980, pp. 197–208.
Hamamoto D.Y. and S. Liu (eds.), *Countervisions: Asian American Film Criticism,* Philadelphia: Temple University Press, 2000.
Hammond, S., *Hollywood East: Hong Kong Movies and the People Who Make Them,* Chicago: Contemporary Books, 2000.
Hanguk Yeonghwa Yeongam [Korean Film Year Book], Korean Motion Picture Promotion Corporation, Seoul: Dongmyeong, 1997.
Hardt, M. and A. Negri, *Empire,* Cambridge, MA: Harvard University Press, 2000.
Harvey, D., *The New Imperialism,* Oxford: Oxford University Press, 2003.
Hasan, K. (ed.), *National Media Survey 1998,* OMQ: Dhaka, 1999.
Hayat, A., "The History of Bangladesh Cinema: The Trends," *6th International Dhaka Film Festival Bulletin* 1, 20 January 2000, pp. 3–5.
Hayward, S., *Key Concepts in Cinema Studies,* London and New York: Routledge, 1996.
High, P.B., *The Imperial Screen,* Madison: University of Wisconsin Press, 2002.
Higson, A., "British Film Culture and the Idea of National Cinema," in *Waving the Flag: Constructing a National Cinema in Britain,* Oxford: Clarendon, 1995, pp. 4–25.
——, "The Limiting Imagination of National Cinema," in M. Hjort and S. Mackenzie (eds.), *Cinema and Nation,* London: Routledge, 2000, pp. 63–74.
Hill, J., *Sex, Class and Realism: British Cinema 1958–1963,* London: British Film Institute, 1986.
Hjort, M. and S. Mackenzie (eds.), *Cinema & Nation,* London: Routledge, 2000.
Hooker, V. (ed.), *Culture and Society in New Order Indonesia,* Kuala Lumpur: Oxford University Press, 1993.
Hu, Ke., "Contemporary Film Theory in China," *Screening the Past,* 25 March 1998, http://www.latrobe.edu.au/screeningthepast/reruns/hkrr2b.html

Huang, R., *Film and Political Propaganda* [Dianying yu zhengzhi xuanchuan], Taipei: Variety, 1994.

——, "The Rise and Influence of Healthy Realist Pictures," *Film Appreciation* 12(6) November/December 1994: 25–37

Huang, Z., *My Life in Film Production: A Memoir by Huang Zhuohan* [*Dianying rensheng: huang zhuohan weiyi lu*], Taipei: Variety, 1994.

Hull, V., *Women in Java's Rural Middle Class: Progress or Regress?*, Jogjakarta: Population Institute Gajah Mada University, 1976.

Im K. and S. Hwang, "Im Kwon-taek, Hwang Seok-kyeong, Sesang-eul Malhada" [*"Im Kwon-taek and Hwang Seok-yeong Talk about the World"*], *Choson Ilbo*, 16 August 2004, p. A5.

James, D.E., "Im Kwon-Taek: Korean National Cinema and Buddhism," in D.E. James and K.H. Kim (eds.), *Im Kwon-Taek: The Making of a Korean National Cinema*, Detroit: Wayne State University Press, 2002, pp. 47–83.

Jameson, F., "Third World Literature in the Era of Multinational Capitalism," *Social Text* 15, Fall 1986: 65–88.

'Japanese Fantasy Plays with Afterlife," *Screen International*, (April 18, 2003), p. 18.

Jayamanne, L., "Sri Lankan Family Melodrama: A Cinema of Primal Attractions," *Screen* 33(3), 1992: 145–53.

——, *Towards Cinema and its Double: Cross-Cultural Mimesis*, Bloomington: Indiana University Press, 2001.

Jenkins, H. *Textual Poachers: Television Fans and Participatory Culture*, New York: Routledge, 1992.

Jiao, X. (Chiao, P.), *Grand Pictures: The Five Years that Changed History* [*Guolian dianying: gaibian lishi de wunian*], Taipei: Variety, 1994.

Johnson, G.A., "Worldwide, Asian films are grossing millions. Here they're either remade, held hostage or released with little fanfare," sfgate.com, Thursday, February 3, 2005, http://www.sfgate.com

Jones, S., "The Hong Kong Film Industry," kamera.co.uk,www.kamera.co.uk/features/the_hong_kong_film_industry.php

Kabir, A., "The Cinema in Bangladesh," *Sequence* 2(2) Spring 1975: 16–19.

——, *Film in Bangladesh*, Dhaka: Bangla Academy, 1979.

Kaplin, C. et.al. (eds.), *Nationalism, Transnational Feminisms, and the State*, Durham, NC: Duke University Press, 1999.

Kapur, S., "The Asians Are Coming," *The Guardian*, August 23, 2002, http://www.shekharkapur.com/next.htm

Kar, Law. "Chung Chang-wha: Can Direct, Will Travel," in the dossier "Chung Chang-Wha: Man of Action!" prepared for the 8th annual Pusan International Film Festival, http://www.asianfilms.org/korea/

Karya, T., "In Search of Ways and Means for Making the Film an Instrument of Expression," in K. Sen (ed.), *Histories and Stories: Cinema in New Order Indonesia*, Clayton, Victoria: Centre of Southeast Asian Studies, Monash University, 1988.

Kei, S., R. Chu, and G. Foerster, "A Brief Historical Tour of the Hong Kong Martial Arts Film," *Bright Lights Film Journal*, www.brightlightsfilm.com/31/hk_brief1.html

Keshvani, N., "The James Lee Story," *Cinemaya* 56/57, 2002: 13–15.

Khondokar, M., "We need *Operation Clean Heart* in Film Industry," *Jai Jai Din* 19(12) 31 December 2002: 36–9.

Khoo, E. and J. Toh. *The Singapore Film Commission: A White Paper* (manuscript), 10 June 1996.

Kim, J., "The Viability of Screen Quota in Korea: The Cultural Exception under the International Trade Regime," *Korean Journal of International and Comparative Law* 26, 1998: 199–242.

Kim, K., *Blockbuster-ui hwansang, Hanguk Yeonghwa-ui Narcissism* [*Fantasy of Blockbuster, Narcissism of Korean Film*], Seoul: Chaeksesang, 2002.

Kim, K.H., "Post-Trauma and Historical Remembrance in the Recent South Korean Cinema: Reading Park Kwang-su's *A Single Spark* and Chang Son-u's *A Petal*," *Cinema Journal* 41(4) 2002: 95–115.

——, *The Remasculinization of Korean Cinema*, Durham, NC: Duke University Press, 2004.

Kim, M., and H. Jung, "A Review of the 2003 Korean Film Industry," *Korean Film Observatory* 11, 2004: 4.

Kim, S. and C. Berry, "'Suri suri masuri': The Magic of the Korean Horror Film: a Conversation," *Postcolonial Studies* 3(1) 2000: 53–60.

Kinema Jumpo (Film Record, Tokyo) annual yearbooks.

Kitley, P., *Television, Nation and Culture in Indonesia*, Athens, OH: Ohio University Research in International Studies, 2002.

Knee, A., "Gendering the Thai Economic Crisis: The Films of Pen-ek Ratanaruang," *Asian Cinema* 14(2) 2003: 102–22.

——, "Thailand Haunted: The Power of the Past in the Contemporary Thai Horror Film," in S.J. Schneider (ed.), *Horror International*, Detroit: Wayne State University Press, forthcoming.

Kong, S., "Big Shot from Beijing: Feng Xiaogang's *He Sui Pian* and Contemporary Chinese Commercial Film," *Asian Cinema*, Spring/Summer 2003: 175–87.

Koo, H., "The State, *Minjung*, and the Working Class in South Korea," in H. Koo (ed.), *State and Society in Contemporary Korea*, Ithaca: Cornell University Press, 1993, pp. 51–94.

Korean Motion Picture Promotion Corporation (ed.), *Korean Film Year Book*, Seoul: Dongmyeong, 1997.

Koukoku-hihyo [*Koukoku review*] 261, special issue on Japanese cinema and interviews with seven filmmakers, June/July 2002.

Khoo, T. et al. (eds.), *Diaspora: Negotiating Asian-Australia*, St Lucia: U of Queensland Press, 2000.

Kracauer, S., *Theory of Film: The Redemption of Physical Reality*, New York: Oxford University Press, 1968.

Kreister, H., "A Geographer's Perspective on the New American Imperialism: Conversation with David Harvey," March 2, 2004, Part V: "Scenarios for the Future," http://globetrotter.berkeley.edu/people4/Harvey/harvey-con0.html

Kurasawa, A., "Propaganda Media on Java under the Japanese 1942–1945," *Indonesia* 44, October 1987: 59–116.

Lacan, "The Mirror Stage as Formative of the I," *Ecrits: A Selection*, translated by Alan Sheridan, New York: Norton, 1977.

Lam, A., "Thai Cinema Ready to Roll' (Pacific News Service) http://www.imdiversity.com/villages/asian/arts_culture_media/lam_thai_cinema_0604.asp

Landy, M., *Film, Politics and Gramsci*, Minneapolis: University of Minnesota Press, 1994.

Larkin, B. "Indian Films and Nigerian Lovers: Media and the Creation of Parallel Modernities," in J. X. Inda and R. Rosaldo (eds.), *The Anthropology of Globalization: A Reader*, Malden, MA: Blackwell, 2002.

Latif, B., "Malaysia," in P. Cowie (ed.), *International Film Guide*, London: Faber & Faber, 1972.

——, "A Brief History of Malaysian Film," in D. Hanan (ed.), *Film in South East Asia: Views from the Region*, SEAPAVAA, Vietnam Film Institute, and ScreenSound Australia, 2001.

Lau, J.K.W., "Besides Fists and Blood: Michael Hui and Cantonese Comedy," in P. Fu and D. Desser (eds.), *The Cinema of Hong Kong: History, Arts, Identity*, Cambridge: Cambridge University Press, 2000.

——, (ed.), *Multiple Modernities: Cinemas and Popular Media in Transcultural East Asia*, Philadelphia, PA: Temple University Press, 2003.

Leary, C., "Infernal Affairs: High Concept in Hong Kong," *Senses of Cinema*, http://www.sensesofcinema.com/contents/03/26/internal_affairs.html

Lee, C. "Interview, Best Director Reveals All: Crafting the Most Believable Fantasy Ever," *Korea Now*, 21 September 2002): 40–1.

Lee, H., *Contemporary Korean Cinema: Identity, Culture and Politics*, Manchester: Manchester University Press, 2000.

Lee, K., "Far Away, So Close: Cultural Translation in Ang Lee's *Crouching Tiger, Hidden Dragon*," *Inter-Asia Cultural Studies* 4(2), 2003: 281–95.

Lee, Y., "Mapping the Korean Film Industry," *Cinemaya* 37, 1997, http://www.asianfilms.org/korea/mapping.html

Lee, Y., and Y. Choe, *The History of Korean Cinema*, trans. R.L.Greever, Seoul: Motion Picture

Promotion Corporation/Jimoondang International, 1998.

Lent, J. A. *The Asian Film Industry*, Austin: University of Texas Press, 1990.

Leong, A.C.Y., *Korean Cinema: The New Hong Kong*, Victoria: Trafford, 2003.

Levi, A., *Samurai from Outer Space: Understanding Japanese Animation*, Chicago: Open Court, 1996.

Lewis, G., "The Thai Movie Revival and Thai National Identity," *Continuum: Journal of Media & Cultural Studies* 17(1), 2003: 69–78.

Li, C., "Journal: Hong Kong," *Film Comment* 40(5) September/October 2004: 10–12.

Liang, L., *A Complete Record of Films Shown in the Republic of China* (1949–1982), 2 vols., Taipei: National Film Library, 1984.

—— 'Double Vision Creating Taiwan Box Office Miracle: Interview with Chen Kuo-fu," *City Entertainment* 616, 21 November 2002: 48–9.

Lim, K.T., *Cathay: 55 Years of Cinema*, Singapore: Landmark Books, 1991.

Lim, S.G. and W. Dissanayake, "Introduction," in S.G. Lim, (eds.), *Transnational Asia Pacific: Gender, Culture, and the Public Sphere*, Urbana and Chicago: University of Illinois Press, 1999, pp. 1–9.

Lockhart, G., "Introduction: First Person Narratives from the 1930s," in G. Lockhart (ed.), *The Light of the Capital*, Kuala Lumpur: Oxford University Press, 1996, pp. 1–49.

Logan, B., *Hong Kong Action Cinema*, London: Titan Books, 1995.

Lu, F., *Taiwan Cinema: Politics, Economy and Aesthetics* [*Taiwan dianying: zhengzhi, jingji, meixue*], Taipei: Yuan-liou, 1998.

Lumbera, B. "Ang Kasaysayan at Tunguhin ng Pelikulang Pilipino," in N.G. Tiongson (ed.), *The Urian Anthology*, Manila: Manuel L. Morato, 1983, pp. 22–47.

——, "Flashbacks on Film and Theatre as Interlocked Forms," in N.G. Tiongson (ed.), *The Urian Anthology 1980–1989*, Manila: Antonio Tuviera, 2001, pp. 80–7.

Ma, S., *The Deathly Embrace: Orientalism and Asian American Identity*, 2000.

Maglipon, J. "Mega Mother Lily: Superstar for all Seasons," in *Primed: Collected Stories, 1972–1992*, Pasig City: Anvil Publishing, 1993, pp. 186–97.

Marchetti, G. "Excess and Understatement: War, Romance, and the Melodrama in Contemporary Vietnamese Cinema," *Genders* 10, Spring 1991: 47–74.

——, *Romance and the "Yellow Peril": Race, Sex, and Discursive Strategies in Hollywood Fiction*, Berkeley: University of California Press, 1993.

——, "Jackie Chan and the Black Connection," in M. Tinkum and A. Villarejo (eds.), *Keyframes: Popular Cinema and Cultural Studies*, London and New York: Routledge, 2001, pp. 137–58.

——, "Chinese Feminist Film Criticism," *JumpCut* 46 (Summer 2003), http://www.ejumpcut.org/archive/jc46.2003/morchetti.dai/index.html

Marks, L., *The Skin of the Film: Intercultural Cinema, Embodiment, and the Senses*, Durham NC: Duke University Press, 2000.

Marshall, F., "Singapore," in P. Cowrie (eds.), *International Film Guide 1991–1993*. London: Tantivy, 1990–1992.

Martinson, J. "One Country, Two Versions," *Danwei: Media and Advertising in China*, February 3, 2005, www.danwei.org/archives/001293.html

McDonald, K.I., "The Yakuza Film: an Introduction," in A. Nolletti (ed.), *Reframing Japanese Cinema: Authorship, Genre, History*, Bloomington: Indiana University Press, 1992, pp. 165–92.

Mes, T. and J. Sharp, *The Midnight Eye Guide to New Japanese Film*, Consortium, 2004.

Metz, C., *Film Language: A Semiotics of the Cinema*, trans. Michael Taylor, New York: Oxford University Press, 1974.

Miller, T., N. Goval, J. McMurria, and R. Maxwell, *Global Hollywood*, London: British Film Institute, 2001.

Millet, R., *Le cinéma de Singapour: Paradis perdu, doute existentiel, crise identitaire et mélancolie contemporaine*, Paris: L'Harmattan, 2003.

Milner, A. and D. Johnson, "The Idea of Asia," Australian National University website www.anu.edu.au/asianstudies/idea.html

Min, E., J. Joo, and H.J Kwak, *Korean Film: History, Resistance, and Democratic Imagination*. Westport, CT: Praeger, 2003.

Moran, A., "Terms for a Reader: Film, Hollywood, National Cinema, Cultural Identity and Film Policy," in A. Moran (ed.), *Film Policy: International, National, and Regional Perspectives*, London and New York: Routledge, 1996.

Mulvey, L. "Visual Pleasure and Narrative Cinema," *Screen* 16(3) Autumn 1975: 6–18.

Mutsuddi, C. *Social Commitment in Bangladesh Cinema*, Dhaka: Bangladesh Arts Academy, 1987.

Naficy, H., *Accented Cinema: Exilic and Diasporic Filmmaking*, Princeton, NJ: Princeton University Press, 2001.

Nandy, A., *The Secret Politics of Our Desires*, Delhi: Oxford University Press, 1998.

Napier, S., *Anime: From Akira to Princess Mononoke*, New York: Palgrave, 2000.

Neale, S., "Art Cinema as Institution," *Screen* 22(1) 1981: 11–39.

Ng, Y., "Singapore," in P.Cowie (ed.), *International Film Guide 1998–2004*, London: Variety, 1997–2003.

Nguyen, C., "Box Office Abroad 2003' [UCLA Asian Institute website], http://www.international.ucla.edu/article.asp?parentid=9956

Norindr, P., "Aestheticizing Urban Space: Modernity in Postcolonial Hanoi and Saigon," *L'Esprit Créateur* 41, Fall 2001: 73–87.

——, "'La Trace lumière': Early Cinema and Colonial Propaganda in French Indochina," in A. Gaudreault, C. Russell, and P. Véronneau (eds.), *Le Cinématographe, nouvelle technologie du XXe siècle*. Lausanne: Payot, 2004, pp. 329–39.

"On the Lame Condition of Bangla(deshi) Cinema" [editorial], *Daily Ittefaq*, 27 September 2000, p. 4.

"One Country Two Versions," *Danwei: Media and Advertising in China*, February 3, 2005, www.danwei.org/archives/001293.html

Ong, A. *Flexible Citizenship: The Cultural Politics of Transnationality*, Durham, NC: Duke University Press, 1999.

O' Regan, T., *Australian National Cinema*, London and New York: Routledge, 1996.

O'Sullivan, T., *Key Concepts in Communication and Cultural Studies*, 2nd edn, London and New York: Routledge, 1994.

Otu, T., "Producing (Post-)Trendy Japanese TV Dramas," in K. Iwabuchi (ed.), *Feeling Asian Modernities*, Hong Kong: Hong Kong University Press, 2004.

"Drama in Hong Kong," in K. Iwabuchi (ed.), *Feeling Asian Modernities*, Hong Kong University Press, 2004, pp. 227–47.

Palmer, A., "After *Spicy Love Soup*, Zhang takes a *Shower*: An Interview with Zhang Yang and Peter Loehr," http://www.indiewire.com/people/int_Zhang_Loehr_000707.html

Paquet, D., "Korean Film' [website], www.koreanfilm.org

Park, H., "Current Status of Korean Film Exports to Overseas' Markets," *Korean Film Observatory* 11, 2004: 12–22. Available at http://kn.koreaherald.co.kr/SITE/data/html_dir/2001/11/19/200111190038.asp

Pham, M.T., "The Asian Invasion in Hollywood," *Journal of Popular Film and Television* 32(3), Fall 2004: 121–131.

Phillips, R., "An Interview with Viet Linh, Director of *Collective Flat*," Singapore Film Festival, April 21, 2000, http://www.wsws.org/articles/2000/apr2000/sff2-a21.shtml

Pines, J. and P. Willemen (eds.), *Questions of Third Cinema*, London: British Film Institute, 1989.

Prince, S. *Kurosawa: The Warrior's Camera*, revised and expanded edn, Princeton: Princeton University Press, 1999.

'Pro and Contra *Orapronobis*," *Manila Chronicle*, 11 November 1989.

Quader, M.T., *Film Industry of Bangladesh*, Dhaka: Bangla Academy, 1993.

Radway, J., *Reading the Romance: Women, Patriarchy, and Popular Literature*, Chapel Hill, NC: University of North Carolina Press, 1980.

Rahman, M., "Film Production and Marketing," Dhaka, unpublished typescript, 1995.

Rayns, T., *Seoul Stirring: 5 Korean Directors*, London: Institute of Contemporary Art, 1994.

——, "Deep Cover," *Sight and Sound* 14(1) January 2004: 26–9.

'Recognition at Cannes," translated and reprinted from *Chosun Ilbo* (*Chosun Daily News*) in *Korea Now*, 1 June 2002: 50.

Respeto, J., "Tradisyon at Supling: Mga Anyo ng Pelikulang Pilipino ng Dekada Nubenta," Film Desk, Young Critics Circle (ed.), *Sampung Taong Sine: Philippine Cinema, 1990–1999*, Manila: NCCA, 2002, pp. 60–3.

'Return of the Japanese Film," *Pacific Friend* 29(11), March 2002.

Reyes, E., *Notes on Philippine Cinema*, Manila: De La Salle University Press, 1988.

Richie, D., "Introduction," in D. Richie (ed.), *Rashomon*. New Brunswick, NJ: Rutgers University Press, 1987, pp. 1–28.

——, "Japanese Film," in P. Duus, et al., *The Cambridge History of Japan*, Vol. 6, *The Twentieth Century*. New York: Cambridge University Press, 1989.

——, *One Hundred Years of Japanese Cinema*, New York: Kodansha International, 2001.

Ricklefs, M.C., *A History of Modern Indonesia*, London: Macmillan, 1981.

Rithdee, K., "Kong Rithdee on Cinematic Renewal in Thailand," *Film Comment* 38(5), 2002: 12–13.

——, "VCD Killed the Movie Star," *Bangkok Post*, 11 July 2003, "Realtime' section, 1+.

Robertson, R., *Globalization: Social Theory and Global Culture*, London: Sage, 1992.

Roeder, O.G., *The Smiling General: President Suharto of Indonesia*, Jakarta: Guning Agung, 1969.

Rosen, P. (ed.), *Narrative, Apparatus, Ideology: A Film Theory Reader*, New York: Columbia University Press, 1986.

Russell, M., and G. Wehrfritz, "Blockbuster Nation," *Newsweek*, internatl edn, 3 May 2004. Available at http://www.msnbc.msn.com/id/4825402/

Said, E. *Orientalism: Western Conceptions of the Orient*, London: Penguin, 1991 [1978].

Salterio, L., "Assunta, husband clears Bong of 'rape'," *Philippine Daily Inquirer*, 22 May 2002.

Santana, K., "MTV Goes to Asia," *YaleGlobal*, 12 August 2003, http://yaleglobal. yale.edu/display.article?id=2211

Schilling, M., *Contemporary Japanese Film*, New York: Weatherhill, 1999.

——, "Toho Lords it Over Japan," *Screen International*, April 25, 2003: 15.

Schwarz, A., *A Nation in Waiting: Indonesia's Search for Stability*, 2nd edn, St Leonards, NSW: Allen & Unwin, 1999.

Sen, K., "Hidden from History: Aspects of Indonesian Cinema 1955–65," *Review of Indonesian and Malaysian Affairs* 19(2), 1985: 1–50.

——, "Repression and Resistance: Interpretations of the Feminine in Indonesian Cinema," in Virginia Hooker (ed.), *Culture and Society in New Order Indonesia*, Kuala Lumpur: Oxford University Press, 1993, pp. 116–33.

——, *Indonesian Cinema: Framing the New Order*, London and New York: Zed Books, 1994.

——, "What's "Oppositional" in Indonesian Cinema?' in A.R. Guneratne and N. Dissanayake (eds.), *Rethinking Third Cinema*, New York and London: Routledge, 2003, pp. 146–65.

—— and Hill, D., *Media, Culture and Politics in Indonesia*, Melbourne: Oxford University Press, 2000.

Shahed, I. "Cinema: Annual Review 1994," *Weekly Bichitra* 23(28), 2 December 1994: 60–1.

—— and M. Chowdhury, "Cinema 1993: The Year of Business Development," *Weekly Bichitra* 22(33), 7 January 1994: 140–3.

"79 percent of Manila Goes for Tagalog," *Variety*, 9 May 1979.

Shariman, M., "Box Office Battles," *Malay Mail*, 9 December 2003, available on the National Film Development Corporation Malaysia (FINAS) website, http://www.finas.gov.my/media/media_battlebox.shtml

Shim, S., "Success Factors of the Korean Film Industry," *Korean Herald*, 5 October 2001.

Shohat, E. and R. Stam, *Unthinking Eurocentrism: Multiculturalism and the Media*, London and New York: Routledge, 1994.

——, "De-Eurocentralizing Cultural Studies: Some Proposals," in A. Abbas and J.N. Erni (eds), *International Cultural Studies: An Anthology*, Malden, MA: Blackwell, 2005.

"*Sibak*, a film with an international caliber," *Manila Bulletin*, 14 July 1995, AT1–2.

Silado, R., *Ca Bau Kan: Hanya Sebuah Dosa*, Jakarta: Gramedia, 1999.

Silver, A., *The Samurai Film*, expanded and rev. edn, New York: Overlook Press, 2004.

Simmel, G., D. Frisby, and M. Featherstone, *Simmel on Culture: Selected Writings*, London and Thousand Oaks, CA: Sage Publications, 1997.

Singapore Film Commission Annual Report 2001, Singapore Film Commission, 2002.

Singapore Film Commission website Singapore Film Commission website, http://www.sfc.org.sg/

Singapore International Film Festival catalogues, 1987–2003.

Solanas, F. and O. Getino, "Towards a Third Cinema: Notes and Experiences for the Development of a Cinema of Liberation in the Third World," in M. Chanan (ed.), *Twenty-Five Years of the New Latin American Cinema*, London: British Film Institute, 1983, pp. 17–28.

Soman, A., "Spinning Gasing," *Cinemaya* 50, 2000: 29.

Sotto, A., *Pelikula: An Essay on the Philippine Film: 1897–1960*, Manila: Cultural Center of the Philippines, 1992.

Spivak, G., "Can the Subaltern Speak?," in P. Williams and L. Chrisman (eds.),

Colonial Discourse and Post-Colonial Theory, Hemel Hempstead: Harvester Wheatsheaf, 1993.

Sreshthaputra, W., "A Brand-New Day for the Vietnamese Film Industry," *The Bangkok Post*, February 26, 2000.

Stam, R., *Subversive Pleasures: Bakhtin, Cultural Criticism, and Film*, Baltimore: Johns Hopkins University Press, 1989.

——, *Film Theory: An Introduction*, Malden, MA: Blackwell, 2000.

——, and E. Shohat, "De-Eurocentrizing Cultural Studies: Some Proposals," in A. Abbas and J.N. Erni (eds.) *Internationalizing Cultural Studies: An Anthology*, Malden, MA: Blackwell, 2005: p. 481–98.

Standish, I., "Korean Cinema and the New Realism: Text and Context," in W. Dissanayake (ed.), *Colonialism and Nationalism in Asian Cinema*, Bloomington: Indiana University Press, 1994, pp. 65–89.

Starpics Magazine 15, January 2000: 72.

Stephens, C., "Tears of the Black Tiger," *Film Comment* 37(3) 2001: 16–17.

——, "Tears of the Black Tiger," *Film Comment* 37(3) 2001: 16–17.

——, "Jewels in the Lotus," *Film Comment* 38(6) 2002): 36–41.

'Stop Illegal Film Exhibition through Video Channels," *Daily Ittefaq*, 23 October 1997: 20–1.

Storey, J., *An Introductory Guide to Cultural Theory and Popular Culture*, Athens, GA: University of Georgia Press, 1993.

Stringer, J., "*Boat People*: Second Thoughts on Texts and Contexts," in Chris Berry (ed.), *Chinese Films in Focus: 25 New Takes*, Berkeley: University of California Press, 2004, pp. 15–22.

Sukwong, D. and S. Suwannapak, *A Century of Thai Cinema*, trans. and ed. D. Smyth, London: Thames & Hudson, 2001.

Suryakusuma, J. "The State and Sexuality in New Order Indonesia," in L.J. Sears (ed.), *Fantasizing the Feminine in Indonesia*, Durham, NC: Duke University Press, 1996, 92–119.

Takesato, W., "Japan: Status of the Media," in *International Media Communications*, Vol. 2, Elsevier Science, 2003, pp. 649–50.

Tan, K.C.S., *Cinema Management in Singapore*, Singapore: Singapore Film Society, 1988.

Tan, L., "Jack Neo, Manager Exemplary," *Straits Times*, 14 November 2002.

Tan, Y.S. and S.Y. Peng, *The Development of Singapore's Modern Media Industry*, Singapore: Times Academic Press, 1994.

Teng, H.H., "Film Censorship in Singapore," *Journal of the History Society 1992/1993*, National University of Singapore, pp. 15–19.

Teo, S., *Hong Kong Cinema: The Extra Dimensions*, London: British Film Institute, 1999.

——, "Post '97 Hong Kong Cinema: Crisis and Its After Effects," Council of Foreign Relations website www.cfr.org/pdf/correspondence/xTeo.php

Thornham, S. (ed.), *Feminist Film Theory: A Reader*, New York: New York University Press, 1999.

"Time and Tide: Changes in Hong Kong Cinema of the 1970s" [report of Hong Kong Film Archive seminar] http://www.lcsd.gov.hk/CE/CulturalService/HKFA/english/newsletter02/nl30_9.html

Tiongson, N., "The 'Gaya-Gaya' Syndrome in Philippine Movies," in N. Tiongson (ed.), *The Urian Anthology 1980–1989*, Manila: Antonio Tuviera, 2001, pp. 28–33.

Tomlinson, J., *Globalization and Culture*, Chicago: University of Chicago Press, 1999.

Tong, K., "Goei Visits Disco Dancing Days," *Straits Times* (Singapore), November 23, 1997.

——, "Temperature Rising for Fever Movie," *Straits Times* (Singapore), May 19, 1998.

Tu, W. (ed.), *The Living Tree: The Changing Meaning of Being Chinese Today*, Palo Alto, CA: Stanford University Press, 1994.

Uabumgrungjit, C., "Cinema in Thailand before 1970," in D. Hanan (ed.), *Film in South East Asia: Views from the Region*, SEAPAVAA, Vietnam Film Institute, and ScreenSound Australia, 2001, pp. 90–105.

Uhde, J. and Y.N. Uhde, *Latent Images: Film in Singapore*, Singapore: Oxford University Press, 2000.

Uni Japan Vol. 28, Tokyo: Association for the Diffusion of Japanese Film Abroad, 2001.

Uni Japan Vol. 29, Tokyo: Association for the Diffusion of Japanese Film Abroad 2002.

U.S. Department of Commerce, Report on Competitive Situation Domestic Production, 1998, pp. 12–16.

van der Heide, W., *Malaysian Cinema, Asian Film: Border Crossings and National Cultures*, Amsterdam: Amsterdam University Press, 2002.

Vasudevan, R. "The Politics of Cultural Address in a 'Transitional' Cinema: A Case Study of Indian Popular Cinema," in C. Gledhill and L. Williams (eds.), *Reinventing Film Studies*, New York: Oxford University Press, 2000, pp. 130–64.

VNS [*Viet Nam News*], Tuesday, July 27, 2004, http://vietnamnews.vnagency. com.vn/2004–07/26/Stories/20.htm

"Vietnamese HCM City to Unveil New Cinema Complex," *Vietnam Forum*, March 13, 2003.

Wang, G. "Gengnian, 'Jiu jiushi niandai zhongguo dianying fazhan taishi da dang dai dianying jizhe wen'" ("Chinese Cinema in the 1990s: General Trends of Development – an interview with Wang Gengnian").

Wang, S., "Big Shot's Funeral: China, Sony, and the WTO," *Asian Cinema*, Fall/Winter 2003: 145–54.

Weiringa, S., "Ibu or the Beast: Gender Interests in Two Indonesian Women's Organisations," *Feminist Review* 41, 1992: 98–113.

Weisser, T. and Y.M. Weisser, *Japanese Cinema Essential Handbook*, revised and updated, 4th edn, Miami: Vital Books, 1998.

Willemen, P., "The Third Cinema Question: Notes and Reflection," *Framework* 34, 1987: 4–38.

——, *Questions of Third Cinema*, London: British Film Institute, 1989.

Williams, R., *Keywords: A Vocabulary of Culture and Society*, rev. edn, New York: Oxford University Press, 1983.

Williamson, P., *Winning in Asia: Strategies for Competing in the New Millennium*, Cambridge, MA: Harvard Business School Press, 204.

Wilson, R., "Filming 'New Seoul': Melodramatic Constructions of the Subject in *Spinning Wheel* and *First Son*," *East-West Film Journal* 5(1), 1991: 107–17.

——, "Melodrama of Korean National Identity: From *Mandala* to *Black Republic*," in W. Dissanayake (ed.), *Colonialism and Nationalism in Asian Cinema*, Bloomington: Indiana University Press, 1994, pp. 90–105.

—— and W. Dissanayake (eds.), *Global/Local: Cultural Production and the Transnational Imaginary*, Durham, NC: Duke University Press, 1996.

Wu, C., "*Crouching Tiger Hidden Dragon* is Not a Chinese Film," *Spectator: USC Journal of Film and Television Criticism* 22(1), Spring 2002: 67–79.

Wu, H. *Transcience: Chinese Experimental Art at the End of the Twentieth Century*, Chicago: David and Alfred Smart Museum of Art, University of Chicago, 1999.

——, et.al. (eds.) *Reinterpretation: A Decade of Experimental Chinese Art: 1990–2000*, Guangdong Museum of Art, Guangzhou, 2002.

Wu, R. "Forever Fever Forever," *Straits Times*, Singapore, May 22, 2000.

Xu, Ke, Zhang Jianyong, and Chen Mo (eds.), *Zhangguo diangying meixue: 1999* [*Aesthetics of Chinese Film: 1999*].

Xu, Y., "Impact of Globalization on the Cinema in China," *Asian Cinema*, Spring/Summer 2002: 39–43.

——, and Z. Xu, "A 'New' Phenomenon of Chinese Cinema: Happy-New-Year Comic Movie," *Asian Cinema*, Spring/Summer 2002: 112–27.

Yau, E.C.M. (ed.), *At Full Speed: Hong Kong Cinema in a Borderless World*, Minneapolis: University of Minnesota Press, 2001.

Yeh, E.Y.Y., "Taiwan: the Transnational Battlefield of Cathay and Shaw Brothers," in A. Wong and S. Ho (eds.), *The Cathay Story*, Hong Kong: Hong Kong Film Archive, 2002, pp. 142–49.

——, Interview with Wan Ren, Taipei, October 2002.

——, Interview with Zhang Fengmei, Executive Assistant, Nan Fan Film Productions, May 2003.

——, and D.W. Davis, *Taiwan Film Directors: A Treasure Island*, New York: Columbia University Press, 2005.

Yoshimoto, M., *Kurosawa: Film Studies and Japanese Cinema*, Durham, NC: Duke University Press, 2000.

Young, R.J.C., *Postcolonialism: A Historical Introduction*, Malden, MA: Blackwell, 2001.

——, *Colonial Desire: Hybridity in Theory, Culture, Race*, London: Routledge, 1995.

"Young autur sets box office jangling," *VNS* [*Viet Nam News*], Tuesday, July 27, 2004, *VNS* [*Viet Nam News*] Tuesday, July 27, 2004, http://vietnamnews.vnagency.com.vn/2004–07/26/Stories/20.htm

Zahan, J., "Star-Faces on Rickshaws," *Anandabhuban* 2(17) 16 January 1998: 15–18.

Zaman, M., "Now We Are All Waiters in the Film World," *Jai Jai Din* 14(13), December 30, 1997: 28–32.

Zhang, H., "Zhang Yang and His Father Talk About Their Generations," *Time Asia* 156(16), October 23, 2003. http://www.asianfilms.org/china/zhangyang/fuzi.html

Zhang, J. and A. Lee, *My Ten-year Dream as a Filmmaker* [*Zhinian yi jao dianying meng*], Taipei: China Times, 2003.

Zhang, Y., *Screening China: Critical Interventions, Cinematic Reconfigurations, and the Transnational Imaginary in Contemporary Chinese Cinema*, Ann Arbor: University of Michigan Press, 2002.

Zhang, Z., "Building on the Ruins: The Exploration of New Urban Cinema of the 1990s," in H. Wu, et.al, (eds.) *Reinterpretation: A Decade of Experimental Chinese Art: 1990–2000*, Guangzhou: Guangdong Museum of Art, 2002.

——, *The Urban Generation*, Durham, NC: Duke University Press, forthcoming.

Index